Colombian Peasants in the Neoliberal Age

Colombian Peasants in the Neoliberal Age

Between War Rentierism and Subsistence

NAZIH F. RICHANI

SUNY
PRESS

Cover Credit: Nazih Richani, Peasant Reserve Cimitarra

Published by State University of New York Press, Albany

For information, contact State University of New York Press, Albany, NY
www.sunypress.edu

Library of Congress Cataloging-in-Publication Data

Name: Richani, Nazih, author.
Title: Colombian peasants in the neoliberal age : between war rentierism
    and subsistence / Nazih F. Richani.
Description: Albany, NY : State University of New York Press, [2023] |
    Includes bibliographical references and index.
Identifiers: LCCN 2022049712 | ISBN 9781438494128 (hardcover : alk. paper) |
    ISBN 9781438494135 (ebook) | ISBN 9781438494111 (pbk. : alk. paper)
Subjects: LCSH: Peasants—Colombia—History—21st century. | Subsistence
    farming—Colombia. | Rentier state—Colombia. | Colombia—Economic
    conditions—1970– | Colombia—Politics and government—1974–
Classification: LCC HD1339.C7 R53 2023 | DDC 305.5/63309861—dc23/eng/20221017
LC record available at https://lccn.loc.gov/2022049712

10 9 8 7 6 5 4 3 2 1

To those struggling for social and environmental justice

Colombia

Contents

Illustrations

Figures

Maps

Tables

Foreword

Dario Fajardo Montaña

*Vice Minister for Rural Development and
professor, Externado University, Bogotá, Colombia*

From Subsumption to Re-peasantization

Colombia's social and armed conflicts are expressions of profound problems and disequilibrium in its political, economic, and social order that emerge whenever the country changes its development model. Moreover, these conflicts are manifested most profoundly in the country's rural social relations. Therefore, it is essential to understand the unique characteristics of the Colombian rural communities and their political organization orienting their relationships with the broader sociopolitical context. Nazih Richani's book provides an in-depth look into these dynamics and their linkages to historical antecedents, legal frameworks, and policy decisions of the Colombian state since its independence. But most importantly, this narrative presents the Colombian peasants' views of their struggle, resilience, resistance, and formidable agency in preserving their communities and way of life and shaping their future trajectory.

In analyzing the sociopolitical and economic contexts of the communities under study, Nazih Richani argues that social conflicts are deeply embedded in the power relationships that have determined land access and use. He provides a diagnosis of the conditions of the peasants in Colombia most affected by the neoliberal economic policies, the increasing food insecurity, and environmental degradation. In this context, he underlines the importance of the UN declarations recognizing peasants' rights and the significance of family-based farming in satisfying global food demand.

The author undertakes a critical review of the most relevant literature on peasants' economies, assessing their contribution to global food production, their relationship with capitalism, and zeroing on their importance to Colombia. Next, Richani analyzes the salient aspects of the central debates within the literature on peasants. Finally, he assesses the theses that peasants are a "vanishing class" as well as those that consider peasants a vibrant sociohistorical adaptive configuration capable of offering distinct modes of resistance in the face of the forces encroaching on them.

The key components of Richani's theoretical framework are *subsumption, rentierism,* and *war rentierism,* around which the communities built their adaptability and devised defensive strategies based on their cumulative historical and cultural experiences. As articulated by the Marxist tradition, subsumption focuses on the peasant economies and their dialectical relationship with capital; it is an interdependent relationship in which the peasant economy depends on capital while capital cannot accumulate without it. Rosa Luxemburg underscored the pivotal role of noncapitalist relations and their centrality in subsumption. One can argue that this subsumption process occurred after the Spanish Conquest of Colombia. From that point onward, the historical socioeconomic process extended and developed into mercantilism, subjugation, and slavery as forms of labor exploitation, reaching the current phase of war rentierism. David Ricardo, the political economist, defined the economic rent(rentier) as a reward of "unearned revenue" that flows from land ownership, which also includes mining.

In the Colombian case, Richani proposed *war rentierism,* which he defined as the use of violence to promote and accelerate the transformation of land use from food production to other ends, including agroindustry, mining, oil, and gold extraction, cattle ranching, services, and speculation. War rentierism became the tool to dispossess the peasants, appropriating their lands while exploiting their labor power, enhancing their extractions of surplus value, and accumulating capital. Consequently, war rentierism formed the linchpin to consolidate an economic model that served best the dominant classes and groups, which included the conglomerates, cattle ranchers, narcobourgeoisie, and multinational corporations.

The author's approach to the peasants as a historical, cultural construction problematizes the notion of a vanishing group that some attributed to Marx's interpretations. Richani, building upon Marx's theory, framed the relationship between capitalism and the peasant economies within the process of subsumption. At the same time, he highlights their capacities for resistance and adaptability. One relevant area is the perspective of the peasant's struggle of Chayanov and Luxemburg. While the first highlighted the resilience and survival capacities of the peasants, the second underscored the process of subsumption of the noncapitalist modes of production within the capitalist expansion logic that is essential for capital accumulation. The two methods are complementary and valuable for understanding a multidimensional complex dynamic, as is the peasant's struggle against rentierism.

In analyzing these initiatives, the author critiques the different theoretical prepositions about the peasants' disappearance as remnants of precapitalist, or as expressions of primitive, capitalism. Contrary to the dominant economic thinking, the author offers a perspective that he shares with other recent studies (e.g., van der Ploeg) that recognize the resiliency of family-based farming. Moreover, the author's concepts coincide with the ecosystems theories, which emphasize the adaptation capacity of the peasants' economies.

Richani studied two Peasant Reserves Zones, two Indigenous *resguardos*, and two Afro-Colombian Community Councils. The experiences of those communities revealed that their responses were not homogeneous and depended on the interdependence between the nature of the menace, their respective cumulative historical experiences, and their level of organization. Still, they shared a common characteristic as peasants: their capacity to adapt and resist. Richani's discussion of those experiences is set within the broader historical context of the state's adoption of the liberal model, which privileged the dominant position of the cattle ranching *latifundios* and the systematic use of violence that characterizes war rentierism. This latter was represented by the combined actions of the state, agribusinesses, conglomerates, speculators, finance capital, and the narcobourgeoisie. According to Richani's line of analysis, the intensity of conflicts and spaces varied as the cases showed. Yet, the studied communities shared similar dynamics and outcomes in enhancing their respective levels of consciousness (knowledge) and building local, cross-national, and global solidarities. Those, in turn, helped them in the process of resisting subsumption, offering a positive outlook for noncapitalist formation to survive.

The author begins his discussion with the core question: Why is Colombia, with so many fertile lands, increasingly importing its food needs while, in contrast, more fertile land is used for pasture? The analysis of the rich information gathered by Richani's fieldwork reveals the diversity of the social organizations of the explored cases and how they were impacted by neoliberalism and its subjugating strategies. Three questions guided the research: How are they surviving? What are the sources of adaptability and resiliency? What characterized their responses and strategies? Those questions are posed against the background that peasant economies still supply food while facing adversarial state policies, the violence of the rural elite, and an enduring land-grabbing process. With these questions in mind, the author unpacked the sociohistorical characteristics of the communities, how they were affected by the policies and politics of the dominant class, and the forms of resistance deployed by each community. Those forms of resistance might have been rooted in their cultural systems.

The study explores two factors explaining the resilience of those groups, which could determine their future. One is their capacity to adapt to the mechanism of subsumption of the neoliberal rentierism; and two, the degree to which their success depends on the resistance to land grabbing and enclosure.

Zones of Peasant Reserves

The Zones of the Peasant Reserves discussed are represented by middle-sized to small land ownerships of the Valley of the Cimitarra River and Pato-Balsillas. The first is located in the Middle Magdalena, and the second is in the Amazon border region. Law 160 of 1994 created the figure of Peasant Reserves. It is noteworthy that the historical roots of the peasant reserves lie in the land struggles of the 1920s that heightened the hegemonic crisis of the large landownership dominating the peasant communities of mestizos, Indigenous, and Blacks configured during the colonial time. The 1920s class tensions were fueled and exacerbated by some changes and factors, including the indemnifying funds paid by the United States to the Colombian government for its intervention in Panama before the construction of the canal, alongside the increasing investments of the oil companies and cash crop exports of the United Fruit Company.

During the 1920s, the modernizing efforts proposed initiatives to create a rural middle class as the means to developing an internal land market (Londoño 2011). Consequently, Law 47 of 1926 was introduced to facilitate access to small land properties to create "peasants' colonies" as stipulated by decrees 839 and 1110 of 1928. The mentioned law and decrees allowed the creation of peasant communities organized in territories recognized by the state with rights to access credit and supplies. Within this modernizing effort, the agrarian regime of the "agricultural colonies" was created in 1930 and ended in 1948 with the assassination of Jorge Eliecer Gaitan, the leader of the Liberal Party. Gaitan's assassination ignited a civil war known as *La Violencia,* during which the first peasant colony in the municipality of Villarica, Tolima, was bombarded (LeGrand 1987; Londoño 2011). As a result, the peasants had to flee, regrouping and colonizing new areas in the Amazon piedmont. To end the civil war, a political arrangement was devised in which the two warring factions alternated power. A land reform proposal was recommended by the U.S. government, which later became law 135 of 1961.

However, Law 135 of 1961 was never implemented, due to the fierce opposition of the agrarian elite that culminated in the Pact of Chicoral of 1972, in which the large land ownership was conserved while access to land for the landless and poor peasants was closed. This forced peasants to become wage laborers in the large-scale agribusiness or seek alternative economic venues. As a result, they commenced cultivating and processing illicit crops such as marijuana, coca, and opium poppies.

In such an environment, the bases of neoliberal economics that were sown by Colombian economists formed in this perspective started taking roots. Those economists, oriented and influenced by the Washington Consensus agencies (World Bank, IMF, IDB), designed the economic and political path of the country, weakened the state, and dismantled the productive sectors, starting with the agricultural industry supplanting food crops by mining and agrobusiness. Furthermore, these policies helped consolidate the financial sector, which benefited from the deposits of narcodollars. Finally, rentierism constructed its legal/judicial system adequate for such an economy.

A critical characteristic of this neoliberal process was consolidating violence in all ambits of national life, from rural areas to labor relations and political intercourse. The cases investigated in this book illustrate aspects of war rentierism and their impact on the peasants' communities and the forms of resistance developed by those communities, their respective processes of learning about the old and new conditions of domination, weakness, achievements, vulnerabilities, and peasants' communities' prospects.

Indigenous *Resguardos* (Reservations)

Indigenous peasants represented those from the department of Meta in the Orinoco and Cauca in the southwest. The commonality between the two is their status as peasants subjected to the conflicts that the state policies brought on them, alongside the pressures and violence inflicted on them by large landowners, agribusinesses, and in more recent times by multinational corporations interested in the extraction of minerals, especially gold.

One central element of the Spanish colonial administration was the extraction of mineral resources from the colonies. For the extraction purpose, the administration of the territories was to secure the labor power needed for the gold and silver mines and to administer the food supply for the workforce and administrators. This meant that ensuring food production and distribution were pivotal for the sustenance of the mining upon which the colonial system was organized.

The dispossession of the Indigenous through war and tribute paying provided lands and labor power for mining and agriculture, pavement of roads, and production for the cities. Their subjection to colonial control was established through multiple institutions, including the military, policing, ideological-political, educational, religious, and reservations. The latter was set in lands granted by the crown to the surviving Indigenous, where they were allowed to have some self-rule through a governor-*cabildo*. Every reservation had to pay tribute either in the form of labor power or produce to the colonial administrator. This way, the colonial government secured labor for the mines, transportation, and maintenance.

After the independence from Spain, the transition contemplated a land tenure regime maintaining the *resguardos* despite the pressures of sectors interested in appropriating the Indigenous lands and their labor power. Some reservations were lost, and others saved, many of which were in Cauca. In 1890, the state introduced Law 89, in which *resguardos* were recognized as imprescriptible, with autonomous characteristics (Ministerio de Gobierno 1983).

The Indigenous of Cauca resisted the Spanish rule, the usurpation of land, and the exploitation of the *hacendados* and their Spanish descendants' (*criollos*) agribusinesses. During the colonial period, Spain's Crown policy was to establish reservations to secure Indigenous' labor power, and they obtained a form of self-rule (*cabildos*) and inalienable rights. The postindependence republic kept the *resguardos* as a social system embedded in the new order's racist and exclusive differentiated power structure. Law 89 of 1890 and other norms secured their continuity. Nevertheless, the author points out that the pressure to appropriate Indigenous lands has persisted over the years. Land conflicts were not only limited to those between large landowners but also included land disputes with Mestizo peasants and Afro-Colombians. Most of those conflicts may be attributed to the social configurations inherited from colonial times sprouting from land usurpation and expressed in violent forms.

Since the beginning of the 1970s, the Indigenous increased their resistance in Cauca, coinciding with a more prominent peasants' mobilization movement spearheaded by the National Association of Peasant Users (ANUC), supporting the land reform proposed by Law 135 of 1961. In this dynamic and agitated political milieu, the Cauca Indigenous held their second congress of the Regional Council of Indigenous of Cauca (CRIC), which comprehensively represents the different *resguardos*. The set goal of the CRIC congress was to activate the process of recuperating the lands usurped by the *hacendados* and bringing their claims to the national level. One distinctive element of the Cauca Indigenous was the institutional consolidation of *resguardos* and their authority: the *cabildo*. These two elements were remnants of the Spanish colonial legacy. Nevertheless, under the evolving conditions of war rentierism, the Indigenous were capable of building different forms of resistance that permitted, to a certain extent, defending their legally assigned territories and some measure of autonomy.

Afro-Descendants and the Community Councils

The Afro-descendant peasants were represented by Community Councils created by Law 70 of 1993, promulgated in the spirit of the 1991 Constitution, and established in the department of Cauca. The labor power of enslaved Africans was used in mining and plantations. It was mainly located on the Pacific and Caribbean coasts, alongside the banks of the Atrato River and San Juan. After the emancipation in 1851, a good portion of free Blacks found refuge in the already established *palenques*. In Cauca, Blacks settled in the north and the west in lands close to the old haciendas where they used to work, which were transformed into sugar cane plantations supplanting food-producing peasants' crops. The owners of the old haciendas exercised their power and influence through the local authorities, such as the mayors, who put pressure to appropriate the lands of the Afro-Colombian community, as was the case with the Indigenous: displacement and the transformation of their ecology and production systems (Velez 2013).

Aprile-Gniset (1994) described that Blacks' settlements after 1851 became subject to attacks and massacres. This unfortunate situation was only exacerbated decades later after the assassination of Gaitan in 1948, which sparked the 1948–1958 civil war. Another aggravating factor that affected the socioeconomic conditions of the Blacks was the noticeable increase in demand for Colombia's sugar after the United States banned sugar importation from Cuba in the wake of its revolution. The growing sugar demand enhanced the aggressiveness of the owners' sugar plantations to expand their lands at the expense of the Afro-community's communal properties in the region.

Alongside the expanding sugar plantations, the extraction of gold by multinational corporations was also increased, which were granted mining concessions by the state, assisted and protected by right wing paramilitary groups. In addition, the extractive multinational corporations have increased their encroachments on territories assigned by Law 70 of 1993 to the Black community.

In this mode, two contradictory processes concurred. First was the spatial reduction of lands available, undermining the community's food security, undercutting their traditional artisanal mining in a process that illustrates the working of war rentierism, which was propelled by the state's policies and exacerbated by large landowners, sugar cane agro industrialists, and the multinational mining corporations. The second was the promise of applying land reform as stipulated by Law 160 of 1994, in which access to land would be complemented by technical assistance, credit, and infrastructure yet to materialize.

Regardless of ethnicity, whether Indigenous, Black, or mestizo, peasants confronted war rentierism, found different challenges, and chose modes of resistance, adaptation, and survival, depending on their accumulated historical experiences. At the same time, a convergence of other processes whose impacts are difficult to determine, such as the one derived from the peace accord between the FARC and the state, reached in November 2016. The first point in the agreement was the Integral Land Reform, which contained the essential elements of Law 160 of 1994.

Finally, in considering the author's discussion of the continuous risks posed by war rentierism and the resistance of the communities it is vital to note Richani's perspective of re-peasantization as a path not only to deal with food insecurity in Colombia but also to build an integral sustainable peace.

References

Aprile-Gniset, Jacques. *Los pueblos negros caucanos y la fundación de Puerto Tejada*, Gobernación el Valle del Cauca. Cali, 1994.

LeGrand, Catherine. *Colonización y protesta campesina*. Universidad Nacional de Colombia, Bogotá, 1987.

Ministerio de Gobierno. *Fuero Indígena,* Bogotá, 1983.

Londoño, Rocío. *Juan de la Cruz Varela. Sociedad y política en la región de Sumapaz (1902-1984)*. Universidad Nacional de Colombia. Bogotá, 2011.

van der Ploeg, Jan Douwe. *The New Peasantries. Rural Development in Times of Globalization*. Earthscan Food and Agriculture. New York, 2018.

Vélez, Irene et al. "Agroindustria y extractivismo en el Alto Cauca. Impactos sobre los sistemas de subsistencia Afro-campesinos y resistencias 1950-2011," Universidad Nacional Colombia. Bogotá, 2013.

Acknowledgments

This book is the product of six years of research of the rural political economy of Colombia. During this stimulating intellectual query, I have incurred countless debts to individuals who shared generously their knowledge, invested their time, and risked their personal security in order to respond to my persistent inquiries. Their support and guidance helped me sift through significant and rich literature mostly written in Spanish zeroing in on a set of questions that if tackled properly might elevate the discussion to a higher theoretical level.

One of those persons is Dario Fajardo, a leading Colombian sociologist whose research and advice elucidated nuances of the agrarian question; his insights and conceptual contributions are reflected in this book. I thank him for his patience and guidance. Another towering figure was Orlando Fals Borda with whom in the mid-1990s I shared adjacent offices at the Institute of Political Studies and International Relations (IEPRI), at the National University in Bogotá. Orlando passed away in 2008, but his ideas on active participatory research and the sociology of the peasantry in Colombia opened new dimensions that informed this research. I am very thankful to Catherine LeGrand who took the time to review chapters of this book, providing me with very detailed comments and suggestions that significantly sharpened the discussion, and closing gaps in the manuscript's historical analysis.

I am also thankful to Alejandro Reyes whose work and insights provided a guideline that helped me in defining the contours of the agrarian question and its centrality in the conflict. I am also deeply indebted to several other Colombian scholars who became dear friends over the years such as Eduardo Pizarro, Gonzalo Sanchez, Francisco Leal Buitrago, Ricardo Peñaranda, Rocio Londoño who helped me understand the intricacies of Colombia's history and its nuances. I am forever thankful for their support and guidance, for sharing their thoughts and ideas, and for their generosity and opening their homes to me.

Many officials from the UN offices in Bogota, Villaviciencio, Barrancabermeja, Popayan facilitated and helped me conduct my research particularly in areas of conflict such as in the department of Meta, North Santander, and Middle Magdalena. To all those individuals I am thankful for their time and efforts, especially to the late Lucy Wittenberg, deputy representative of UNFPA country office (2004–2017), who strongly supported my research. I am also indebted to all of those that accepted to be interviewed whose identities are for most part kept in reserve unless the interviewee specified otherwise.

I am very thankful to the peasant reserves organizations (ACVC) leadership in Cimitarra and Pato Balsillas that facilitated this research as well as representatives of the mestizo peasants, Indigenous, and Afro-Colombian in Meta and Cauca. I hope that this book helps in shedding light on their daily struggle against all injustices and violations of their way of life and self-determination. In this vein I am indebted to the several peasants that I interviewed in Meta who taught me valuable lessons about agroecology and the efficiency of the peasant economy.

My research assistant Santiago Martinez, a former student, and a former UNDP employee accompanied me in different phases of this research. He helped in the organization and the conduction of interviews in Pato Balsillas and assisted me in Cimitarra and Barrancabermeja, Puerto Gaitan, Acacias, and Cauca. Santiago assumed great personal risks while helping me in achieving my research objectives. Our running joke was *"todo por la ciencias,"* "all for the sake of science." *Muchas gracias estimado Santi.*

I am thankful to my colleagues in the political science department that supported me in my arduous struggle to obtain a sabbatical so I can finish this book. My thanks to the president of Kean University Lemont Repollet who graciously took the time to learn about my research and granted me a sabbatical. In this respect, I express my gratitude to the Open Society Foundation that funded the initial phase of this research project.

Finally, I am profoundly indebted to my wife Mona Kaidbey whose insights, rigor, and critical reading of the manuscript at times generated heated discussions that were instrumental in making this book more accessible and more comprehensible.

I am also thankful to the SUNY team that helped bring this manuscript into a book. In this vein it is important to mention Michael Rinella, senior acquisition editor, who supported this book project since I proposed it to him few years ago. Our professional relationship started in the late 1990s, which culminated with the publication of the first edition of my book *Systems of Violence* in 2003. I also thank Jenn Bennett-Genthner, manuscript editorial manager, for her dedication and rigor.

Introduction

Peasants in the Neoliberal Age, Theories and Research Questions

Family-based farming has been gaining global attention. The United Nations (UN) proclaimed 2014 as the International Year of Family Farming to recognize family farms' critical role in enhancing food security and later developed a platform that identified the urgent actions required by governments to support especially small farmers. In addition, new research continues to reconfirm small farming's significant contribution to fighting hunger and starvation: five of six farms worldwide are small family farms of less than two hectares, producing one-third (33 percent) of the world's food.[1] Unfortunately, however, neoliberal economics is upending family-based peasant economies. The latest plight of peasants in India opposing the removal of state subsidies and new laws favoring agribusiness is a good example.[2] Thousands have taken to the streets, bringing their grievances to New Delhi and the international community, demonstrating a fault line accentuated by ending the state-supported model of the 1960s Green Revolution.[3]

What is the status of small, peasant family farming in the Colombian context? How do Colombia's small farmers, that is, subsistence peasants, Indigenous people, Afro-descendants, compare to their counterparts elsewhere in the world? At a glance, we see that Colombia mirrors the global scenario: 32 percent of its fifty million people live and depend on the rural economy.[4] But, most significantly, it is estimated that the family peasant economy produces more than 51 percent of the food in Colombia.[5] So they are equally successful, but their challenges run deeper and are quite formidable. This research describes the Colombian peasants' reality, their success in farming while in constant resistance and mobilization to claim their rights and fight the state's economic policies, large landowners' violence, forced displacement, and land grabbing. It focuses on three specific questions: (1) How did the Colombian peasants survive under adverse conditions? (2) What are the sources of their resilience and adaptability in the face of the onslaught of neoliberal war rentierism? (3) What distinguishes the responses and strategies employed by the Indigenous groups, Afro-descendants, and the peasant reserves in dealing with the state and managing the threats they face.

This research analyzes the processes and mechanisms of the subsistence peasant economy practiced in the peasant reserves, Indigenous *resguardos*, and the communal councils of Afro-Colombia. The analysis explores two factors that explain peasant groups' ability to survive and might determine their future: one is the capacity to adapt to the changing mechanisms and dynamics of capital subsumption of the neoliberal rentier economy, and two, the degree of success in resisting the increased encroachment on their lands, livelihood, and way of life. Subsumption occurs when rentier capitalists and agribusiness resort to grabbing land and hiring labor from peasant communities without totally dismantling their economy. The book presents the historical, socioeconomic, political, and security conditions experienced by the three peasant communities. It examines their adaptability strategies and resistance to subsumption processes and the prospects for the sustainability of their modes of production, culture, and livelihood. In addition, it explores the communities' level of agency that has allowed them to respond to the encroachments of rentier economy by devising adapting strategies and building collaborative networks, forging new partners at the national, regional, and global levels. This analysis is essential since the process of capitalist subsumption not only threatens a mode of production, given the massive environmental degradation associated with it, but also threatens the sources of life security: food, water, and land.

A key aspect of this study is recasting the political economy of the twenty-first-century peasantry as a function of the peasants' expanding capacity to resist subsumption literally under the guns of war rentierism. It focuses on seven case studies: two peasant reserves (Cimitarra and Pato-Balsillas), three Indigenous *resguardos* (in Meta and Cauca), and two Afro-Colombian communal councils in Cauca. Though limited, the research sheds light on the dynamics of the broader peasants' struggle against war rentierism waged to grab their communal lands. The area at risk represents about 26.8 percent of the country's rural territory that the state has distributed to the Indigenous reservations, African Colombian descendants' communal councils, and peasant reserves. Currently, the Indigenous population holds 23 percent of the 26.8 percent, the Afro-descendants 3 percent, and the peasant reserves have 0.8 percent.[6] Depending on their location and mining potential, these are strategic areas in high demand by various local and international actors. At the heart of this research is the impact of the aggressive pursuit of these lands by the different actors seeking to secure concessions for mining (gold, coltan, coal, among others), oil extraction, agribusiness, and speculation. For example, the "solicited" mining concession spiked to 59 percent of the country's 114 million hectares between 2000 and 2010.[7] At the end of 2012, 9,400 mining titles were granted that covered 5.13 million hectares, almost the size of the country's area dedicated to agriculture.

Review of Relevant Theories
on Peasantry and Peasant Economy

This study's conceptual framework draws upon three main theories that address capitalist subsumption, development, and the peasant economy: (1) the Marxist tradition, (2) the modernization approach, and (3) hybrid theories that draw on these two. These are elaborated on in the following sections of this chapter.

This section has four subsections. The first presents a brief panoramic critical analysis of some vital aspects of the peasant studies literature relevant to this book's purpose. The second subsection discusses the long-lasting effects of the "modernization theory," which underpinned the foreign policy of the United States and its Agency for International Development (AID) alongside the International Monetary Fund (IMF) and the World Bank for several decades. This approach has contributed to severe economic distortions in the Global South countries, including Colombia. The third subsection sheds light on Karl Marx, Rosa Luxemburg's theoretical contributions, and others pertinent to this book's conceptual edifice. The fourth subsection analyzes the transformations of the peasant economy resulting from the introduction of capitalism and market economics in postsocialist Poland. This subsection's relevance stems from the argument of the prominent sociologist Halmaska. Her theory intersects with Bernstein and his "vanishing peasant" thesis. Yet, she presents an empirical case showing that today's peasants in Poland are not "entrepreneurs," nor are they succumbing or subsumed to the logic of the capitalist market, which is an argument most instructive to the cases explored in the coming chapters.

PEASANT STUDIES LITERATURE

This book builds upon the contributions of various traditions, including the different stripes in peasant studies such as (Ploeg 2018; Bryceson et al. 2000; Scott 1998, 1985, 2020; Shanin 1990; Popkin 1979; Bernstein and Byre 2001; Wolf 1966; Wolf 1969) to name just a few.[8] The contributions of peasant studies are impressive and helped answer core questions about the development of rural economies in the Global South. Yet, there are many more to address, precipitated by the changing global political economy and its interplay with local peasants' responses to the change, thereby emphasizing the agency of resistance and adaptability.

Shanin (1971; 1984)[9] identified four attributes distinguishing peasants from other social classes or groups: (1) the peasant family farm, which constitutes the primary unit of social organization, production, and consumption; (2) land cultivation as their means of livelihood; (3) specific cultural norms stemming from their lifestyle in small communities and villages; and (4) peasants' resistance to outside domination or subordination.[10] Shanin's peasants' attributes need amendments in light of this study's findings. Peasant economies depend on multiple sources of income to sustain their existence. Therefore, they do not only depend on land cultivation. Chapters 3, 4, and 5 demonstrate that the peasants are much more than that, and their economies are more diverse, so they depend on producing their food to subsist. They also engage the capitalist market by selling products such as milk, cheese, wood, meat, and coca.

Scott shifted his attention to the norms and values underplaying the economic factors. Scott's (1976) book *The Moral Economy of the Peasant* drew on Chayanov's thesis that norms, values, and traditions carry more weight than economic considerations in the peasant communities' decision making and relations with the market.[11] In his study of lower Myanmar (former Burma) and Vietnam, he concluded that peasants' fear of "food shortages" undercut any drive for innovation alongside an aversion to taking economic risks due to their precarious food security. Scott defined "moral economy" as the peasants' notion of economic justice and exploitation. In contrast with Scott's moral argument, Popkin posited that peasants are rational economic actors following a profit-driven logic. In *The Rational Peasant: The Political Economy of Rural Society in Vietnam*, he argued that what is rational for the individual may not be rational for the community or village. As Meillassoux (1972) put it, "both Scott and Popkin drew different conclusions from their studies of Southeast Asia's rural societies."[12] Meillassoux continued that Scott claimed that peasants used violence and rebellion against capitalism that threatened their moral system. In contrast, Popkin thought that rebellion occurs when peasants solve their collective action problem since their motivation is individual self-interest.[13]

Popkin embraced the economists' rational choice model in which collective group behavior is the sum total of rational individual preferences, interests, and choices.[14] In my early study of Colombia's civil war, I argued that the peasants in Colombia, since the 1920s, have established defense leagues to protect their lands and way of life against the state and the landowners. The tipping point came in 1964 when they were dislodged from core areas in Tolima and Meta, forcing them to form a guerrilla movement.[15] My findings do not support Scott's thesis that peasants rebel when their "moral system" is threatened. Instead, peasants rebelled when their source of livelihood, upon which their moral system was based, was threatened; in this case, it was land.[16] This finding is in tune with Popkin's argument. However, Scott's argument that the invisible hands of the markets constitute a security threat to the peasants' subsistence economy is more in tune with this book's findings, with one caveat.[17] The Colombia case represents a peculiar one in which the peasant population faces the "invisible hand of the local-international market nexus" and the "visible violent hands" exercised by violent actors working at the behest of local and foreign capital. Since the 1950s, those violent actors, including state agents and paramilitaries, had committed most of the massacres, forceful displacement, land grabbing, intimidation, and other illegal methods complementing the working of the "market's invisible hands." Today, the interplay between those two characterizes several rural areas of Colombia, such as Cauca, Choco, North Santander, Narino, and Caqueta.

Henry Bernstein (1979) argued that simple commodity production designates a form of production, the logic of which is subsistence in the broad sense of the simple reproduction of the household and the unit of production (the household).[18] What distinguishes the simple mode of production from the capitalist one is its logic of subsistence as opposed to appropriation, accumulation of capital, and realization of surplus value.

Bernstein claimed that the peasants in the subsistence economy are not a proletariat because they retain some control over the production process (land, tools, and other means of production) and are not subject to a rigid division of labor like workers in a factory. Nonetheless, he stressed, peasants are "wage-labor equivalents" producing surplus value for the capitalist. Years later, Bernstein (2003,4), tackling the peasant mode of production, contended that the actors in this mode are both "capitalist and workers" at the same time because they own or command their means of production and employ their labor. He concluded that peasants become commodity producers when they cannot reproduce themselves outside the relations and processes of capitalist commodity production.[19] In this manner, Bernstein thought that such an outcome of peasants becoming entrepreneurs brings their end.

Bernstein (2016) did not change his "vanishing peasant" thesis in the current global capitalist system. Instead, he insisted on his posture by lashing out at the second and third wave of peasant studies focused on the food regime and the "return of the peasant way," or the "peasant turn." He argued that the most salient thrust of the criticism of "the peasant turn" is not to condemn it for utopianism but rather how it short-circuits the analytical and empirical demands of advancing knowledge of the moment of world capitalism we inhabit.[20] The jury is still out in assessing both the historical significance of the "peasant turn" and Bernstein's analysis of it within the context of global capitalism's contradictions, anomalies, and complexities. In my view, a two-pronged interlinked approach is needed, one from the Global South drawing on contemporary rural societies and the other focusing on the changes of capital and the accumulation processes.

This book challenges Bernstein's contention by presenting empirical evidence showing that the subsistence peasant economy in Colombia remains family-based and is noncapitalist. Such a finding is consistent with Ploeg (2018, 9), who argued that one of the distinctive features of peasant agriculture is the organic unity of the means of production and the labor force. In other words, those who toil on the land own the means of production. Furthermore, wage labor is absent or plays a minor role during seasons; class exploitation and accumulation are not part of this economy.

Other essential strands in the peasant literature are relevant to this book's conceptual framework, which is a genre that tackled the bias in modernization theory embraced for several decades by USAID, the World Bank, IMF, and U.S. foreign policy. The importance of this critical genre is questioning the premise of these theories and their grave implications on the Global South. Chapter 1 of this book illustrates the far-reaching conse-quences of modernization theories on Colombia's skewed and violent path.

Polanyi's seminal book *The Great Transformation* (1957) revived the discussion on understanding peasant economies in developing countries. Following Chayanov's findings in his Russian study, Polanyi confirms that peasant economies were based on subsistence logic. He, therefore, questioned the "universal rational choice utility theories" of the resource allocations and exchange of capitalism. In the same vein of critical analysis, Banerjee and Duflo observed that in many developing countries, "a part of the land (for example, the forest abutting the village) is always held as common property. As long as the land is used sparingly, it provides a resource of last resort for those villagers whose own economic plans have hit some headwinds; foraging in the forest or selling grass cut from the common land helps them survive. The intrusion of "private property into these settings, generally inspired by liberal and neoliberal economists who do not understand the logic of the context (and love private property), has been a disaster."[21] Banerjee and Duflo based their stance on empiri-cal evidence from the Global South showing the disappointing results of the modernization drive and its corollary, the "Washington Consensus" developed in the 1980s, which rested on the sanctity of privatization and securing private property as the springboard for development while over-looking socioeconomic inequalities.[22] Banerjee and Duflo's critical stance vis-à-vis mainstream economic capitalist theory that idealized private property negates the possibility of development without it. The primary stream current assumes that these formations are backward remnants of precapitalism, or, at best primitive capitalism, which will disappear. On the contrary, as the opening paragraphs showed, family-based farmers offer much more resilience than the dominant economist thought.

McNetting (1993) brings the dimension of ecosystems. He argues that subsistence and common properties economies depend for their survival on an equilibrium similar to a "biological ecosystem" whose stability and reproduction depends on the balance between equality and hierarchy.[23] In light of Colombia's experience, it is possible to redefine this ecosystem: its balance can be disturbed or distorted when outside powers (state, multinational corporations, violent entrepreneurs, narcotraffickers, and/or global market pressures) exacerbate the tension between actors in the hierarchy, producing more inequality. This, in turn, poses a threat to the boundaries between common properties and private ones, between capitalist modes and noncapitalist ones by having the former subsume the latter.

McNetting raised a point relevant to this research: government interventions that institutionalize state or public land contribute directly to inequality and permanently prevent the more equitable outcomes of local communal control. To the degree that exclusion impoverishes community members and limits their legitimate role in decision making, it is a true "tragedy of the commoners." That is, the people living in communal lands in noncapitalist relations.[24] Similarly, Kerrou (2021) and Tahri (2022) discussed the case of Jemna, Tunisia in which local peasants reclaimed their usurped farm of palm trees from two private operators in 2011, a few days before the fall of the Zein El Abedin autocratic regime, transforming the harvest of dates to the benefit of the community.[25] The local community and their Association for the Protection of Jemna's Oases (APJO) gained control of 185 hectares of public land. This example is spreading, it is estimated that sixty thousand hectares are being reclaimed by communities in different rural areas of Tunisia.[26] My book draws on these cases, focusing on the fault line between the communal drive for autonomy and the state's policies introduced in Colombia between the 1950s and 2021 that bear on the internal balance dynamics between "hierarchy and equality" within peasant reserves, subsistence peasant economies, and the communal mode of the Indigenous and Afro-descendants. I examine the internal dynamics within these modes and the viability of their chances to subsist.

Finally, Karatani (2014) and Samir Amin (2011) discuss the dismantling of communal land and other forms of property in developing countries due to capital accumulation, expansion, and the crisis of overaccumulation. Karatani contends that the commodification of land and labor is interlinked. Land privatization leads to the dissolution of the agrarian community and the destruction of the environment, whose preservation was predicated on the functioning of that community (Karatani 2014, 198). Samir Amin (2011) adds that the continuous dismantling of the peasant economy has led to increasing pauperization and proletarianization, shantytowns, and misery belts in most major cities such as Caracas, Rio de Janeiro, Medellin, Bogotá, Calcutta, Nairobi, and Cairo, to name a few, which are outcomes of the same process of dispossession, displacement, and marginalization. Finance-monopoly capital and imperialist rent shape the contours and tempo of this process through foreign direct investments and multinational corporations. Both Karatani and Amin analyzed the driving force behind capital encroaching on the rural frontiers of the Global South, an invaluable approach to framing the context. However, neither addressed what keeps subsistence peasant and communal economies surviving in the twenty-first century, a topic explored in this book.

The Modernization Theories: Peasants and the Post–World War II Literature

The modernization paradigm championed by Walt Rostow theorized a unilinear five-stage process of development: traditional peasant societies, transitional pre-takeoff, takeoff, and industrialization, drive to maturity, and finally, high mass consumption. This model proved to be a fallacy that never materialized in developing nations.[27] Nonetheless, his modernization myth became dominant within mainstream political science and development studies in the 1950s and 1960s. Even when Rostow's influence weakened, his views on the private sector continued to influence models that promoted solid market-friendly states and public-private partnerships, fomenting capitalist development. Rostow's ideas shaped John F. Kennedy's Alliance for Progress, which promoted agricultural capitalism in Latin America's rural areas to spearhead development to avert the spread of Cuban-like revolutions. His ideas continue to shape the neoliberal economic policies of the World Bank and IMF until today. However, the modernization paradigm's hegemonic dominance has been challenged by several waves of new studies and theories that have questioned the unilinear assumption of development considering its uncertainties and the complexities of the cases. The effects of the modernization paradigm in Colombia were far-reaching. They were articulated by World Bank experts such as Lauchlin Currie, who in 1959 led an economic mission to help the Colombian government formulate a policy toward its rural sector, which proved disastrous. The effects of this policy are discussed in the following chapter. But here, suffice to mention that Currie also played a critical role in laying the foundation of neoliberalism and war rentierism that undermined the peasant economy and food security.

The challengers of Rostow's modernization unilinear thesis did not wait long to respond. I discuss some of these responses related to the theoretical questions explored in this book. For example, Wolf (1966; 1984)[28] shifted the focus of analysis to the microlevel, dispelling the premises of the modernization theory that ignored the perils of peasants suffering from underdevelopment and dependency. He recognized the subsistence peasants as a social class who produce for their own consumption and whose retreat to subsistence production is threatened by capitalist encroachment. Furthermore, he identified family and kinship ties as providing an important support system that helps peasants absorb shocks of dislocation. As presented in the following chapters of this book, my research findings support Wolf's argument, particularly the behavior exhibited by the peasants in the reserves I studied alongside the Indigenous *resguardos* and Afro-Colombian community council. These three noncapitalist formations are chiefly subsistence family-based economies, yet they did not retreat but were proactive in their strategy for resisting the encroachments of war rentierism.

Moreover, the peasantry depended on monoculture cash crops such as coca, logging, and African palm oil. In other words, the peasantry reinvented their class. This type of change poses a challenge to some of the theories discussed in this chapter.

Marxist Theory of the Peasantry

The Marxist tradition is the second strand in the literature on which the conceptual framework draws. I found the concept of subsumption (actual and formal) elaborated by Karl Marx (*Capital*, Vol. 1, 1861) helpful 160 years later. Formal subsumption denotes a historical dialectical process where capital subjugates (i.e., subsumes) noncapitalist formations as its expansion necessitates more labor to exploit in order to accumulate surplus value. Marx may have not expected that noncapitalist peasant economies survive that long nor that capitalism in the Global South could be as deformed and heterogeneous as it has become. However, Marx's historical materialist dialectical method rejected unilinear developmentalism and Eurocentricity in his analysis of indigenous populations in the Americas, Africa, and Asia especially after the late 1850s when he became familiar with these international experiences.[29]

Rosa Luxemburg (1913) elaborated on Marx's concept of subsumption in her attempt to shed light on the workings of colonialism and imperialism as systems of domination, making capitalism a world system. Luxemburg's seminal book *The Accumulation of Capital* (1913) discussed the significance of primitive accumulation in capital expansion. She wrote: "non-capitalist organizations provide a fertile soil for capitalism; more strictly: capital feeds on the ruins of such organizations, and although this non-capitalist milieu is indispensable for accumulation, the latter proceeds at the cost of this medium nevertheless, by eating it up."[30] She added, "Historically, the accumulation of capital is a kind of metabolism between capitalist economy and those non-capitalist methods of production without which it cannot go on and which, in this light, it corrodes and assimilates."[31] She concludes: "Thus capital cannot accumulate without the aid of non-capitalist organizations, nor, on the other hand, can it tolerate their continued existence side by side with itself."[32] Luxemburg defined the relationship between capital and non-capitalist modes of production and their dialectical relationship. She stated that capital could not accumulate without non-capitalist modes because it provides a strategic depth for its expansion and the creation of new markets, leading to the gradual dissolution of non-capitalist relations. More important is her analysis of the relationship between imperialism and militarism. She defined imperialism as the political expression of capital accumulation in its competitive struggle for what remains of the non-capitalist areas.[33] She argued that militarism fulfills a decisive function in the history of capital, accompanying every phase of capital accumulation. It played a crucial role in the first stages of European capitalism, in the period of so-called primitive accumulation, as a means of conquering the New World and the spice-producing countries of India.[34] Luxemburg's theory of the importance of noncapitalist relations to the expansion of capitalism constitutes a principal theoretical pillar for this book. It provides a way to contextualize Colombia's integration of noncapitalist economic structures into the process of subsumption of capitalism that has been taking place since the conquest that brought mercantilism and slavery as modes of extracting surplus value. The present war rentier–capital modality extended this labor exploitation, affecting land and the environment.

A recent (2017) book by Harootunian revisited Marx's conceptualization of formal and real subsumption and the difference between the two by studying Japan's historical experience.[35] In Japan, old work associations and Shinto beliefs survived well into the Meiji period and beyond. It is reasonable to think that this kind of description might apply to other colonized and semicolonized countries where formal subsumption of capital absorbs/or subordinates noncapitalist forms to the logic of capital accumulation and surplus value based on wage labor. A formal subsumption is a form that marked the moment capitalism encountered older economic practices. In the first edition of *Capital*, Marx further explained the incompleteness of development throughout Western Europe as reflected in the passive survival of archaic and outmoded modes of production. In India, formal subsumption started in a noncapitalist mode of production in which usury played an important role. The Indian lender gives money to the peasant for cotton-growing expenses and charges 40 to 50 percent per year in interest on the debt. In this relationship, the peasant remains a self-sufficient, independent producer who is not yet subsumed by wage labor nor dispossessed of the means of production and reproduction: land. But the usurer still appropriates the surplus labor and the surplus value that this family-based labor creates. This example dated to the late nineteenth century when India formed part of the colonial system and its main product, cotton, became tied to England's colonial imperial industrializing machine.

In formal subsumption in the peripheral areas of the global economy, past practices are subordinated to capitalist domination in a hybrid system; for example, Uno Kozo (cited in Harootunian [2017, 72]) recorded the persistence of feudal mentality and customs in capitalist Japan.[36] Jose Carlos Mariategui noted the Incas' land arrangements and practices in Peru that the peasants adopted in the 1920s.[37] The implications of having those mixes of old and current economic systems within an overarching capitalist mode are complex and multidimensional. They reveal how formal subsumption incorporates the old modes, which neither eliminates contradictions and asymmetries nor produces homogeneity. It is a continuous dialectical process. The core element in this analysis inspired by Marx's conceptualization allows us to better understand contemporary societies in the Global South with all the residues of their distant past embedded both in their present and way into their future. After laying out the broad contours of the conceptual framework, the interplay between its two main pillars, subsumption and agency, is central to the book's analysis. Finally, I will discuss other contributions that helped construct the different concepts that the framework draws on.

Two authors stand out whose contributions to peasant studies are relevant to this book framework. Kautsky described the dissolution of peasant production as a slow process whereby peasant petty commodity producers co-exist with agrarian and urban-industrial capitalism, gradually shrinking over time under the force of urban migration and the introduction of mechanized agriculture. In this process, subsistence peasants are transformed into wage laborers. In *The Agrarian Question* (1899), Kautsky wrote: "Despite conclusive evidence of inherent superiority of large farms, we also must explain the existence and sometimes proliferation of small farms beyond Germany, including those in England and France. Even bourgeois economists from Adam Smith and Sismondi have expressed their approval of small farms over existing latifundium where tenant farmers precariously lived under duress. In England, small farms did not decline; in Germany, mid-size farms increased; in France, small farms proliferated from 1840 to 1890. The number of large farms increased only in the USA, which had a different history. These contradictory statistics indeed suggest there is no necessary link between the size of the farm and capitalist relations in agriculture. They indeed call for the need for further research. We must understand that even in industry, there is no linear decline or demise of small enterprises. There are always pockets where small enterprises survive, taking advantage of their survival abilities."[38] Kautsky's insights are helpful for this book in two key areas: they dismiss the notion of capitalist development as a linear process and shed light on the agency of the small commodity producers and people engaged in non-capitalist modes and in their abilities to survive. The focus of this study is the ability of these social groups involved in the subsistence peasant economy to adapt and resist capitalist subsumption.

Chayanov, an agronomist, made a significant contribution in his meticulous study of the Russian countryside, which he based on decades of detailed rural survey data.[39] He concluded that the peasant economy's driving force was not profit but satisfying their subsistence needs.[40] Central to Chayanov's theory is the precept of balance between labor and consumption, whereby the labor time of small peasant producers is based on the calculus of satisfying their basic needs of food, shelter, and improvement in living conditions.[41] The rational calculation of poor peasants aims to balance their labor time for sustenance with surplus to improve their living conditions but not accumulation.[42] The cases explored in this book approximate Chayanov's description of petty commodity production (subsistence peasant economy based on family labor).

Bartra's (1975),[43] Taussig's (1978), and Mariategui's (2011) studies of cases in Mexico, Colombia, and Peru respectively drew on Kautsky, Chayanov, and Lenin's studies of the relationship between capitalist farming and the peasants' economies and the survival of this latter in Latin America. For example, Bartra's Mexico study conclusions were similar to Lenin's as presented in his book *Capitalism in Russia*, which argues that the survival of the peasantry in any capitalist society is not due to the "technical efficient superiority" of the peasant's subsistence economy, but is because peasants reduce their livelihood requirements far below wage workers and tax their energies more than this latter.[44] Therefore, according to the analyses of Lenin, Kautsky, and Bartra, the peasant economy survived despite its inefficiency compared to capitalist agribusiness because of the extreme sacrifice peasants incur.

Taussig (1978), in contrast with Bartra, Lenin, and Kautsky's, in his empirical study of Colombia argued that the three mentioned authors did not base their comparative studies on empirical cases where capitalist farming and peasant economies coexisted in one space and area. That is, their studies were not comparatively designed to measure efficiency. Contrary to modernization and traditional Marxist theory arguments, Taussig discovered in southern Cauca Valley that small peasant production is more efficient than capitalist agribusiness in several core areas if it was not only attributed to land monopoly.[45] He contended that big agribusiness exercising control over land accomplished two interrelated objectives. One exerts economic and political pressure to appropriate more land, thus reducing land available to the peasants' farms below the minimum level required to sustain their families' food needs and reproduce their mode. The second related objective was to create a surplus rural wage-labor force for peasants who needed to sell their labor to sustain their livelihoods. Therefore, the subsistence peasant economy can reproduce itself if the land lots are protected from further declines in size.

According to Taussig, this condition was exhibited since the beginning of 1900 in Cauca, which used the impetus of U.S. capital incentivized by the construction of railway and the prospects of the Panama Canal linking this region with the global economy.[46] Such opening up to foreign markets led to the forcible appropriation of peasant lands to expand their agribusiness, forcing peasants to become wage laborers and semiproletarians whose subsistence depended partly on their plots and the wages needed to sustain their farms.[47] For their part, agribusiness, by employing these quasi-proletarianized peasants, can extract higher rates of surplus value than would be possible if the costs of the maintenance and reproduction of the labor force had to be covered by the capitalist production alone. That is to say, the subsistence peasant economy subsidizes the creation of surplus value by reducing the costs of their own reproduction and maintenance as a quasi-proletarianized peasant force. Taussig's description captured an essential feature of the Global South–dependent capitalist development in which a rural semiproletarianized peasant and an urban informalized labor force keep wages down, enhancing capital accumulation by helping in the extraction of more surplus value. Such a contradictory and "mutually beneficial" relationship in which the subsistence/quasi-proletarianized labor in rural and urban-periphery (shantytowns) areas suppresses wages to the level of surviving with the bare minimum. Such a description captures the underlying forces driving the historical dialectical processes of subsumption that have been taking place in Colombia and many parts of the Global South.

Taussig's insightful analysis did not consider the role of agency. Peasants' agency in organizing, coordinating activities, strategizing, and resisting—as the agencies of the CEOs of capital—helped them dodge the bullet and survive. Therefore, subsumption as a historical process is mediated by agency, which explains that peasant economies and noncapitalist formation remained a feature of the current international political economy. Agency is highlighted in this research, complementing some of the main arguments of the reviewed authors. The following section on the peasants of Poland sheds light on the experience of the subsistence peasant economy from which some insights can be drawn that are relevant to this book's purpose.

Taussig's findings and observations coincided with Mariategui's study of Peru's rural economy. Mariategui (2011), writing on Peru's rural productivity in the early decades of the twentieth century, found that large landholdings compared unfavorably with community productivity. The production of highland estates was generally the same as that of communities, and, more critically, production figures were no different.[48] In support of his argument, he summarized statistical data presented by Castro Pozo on the 1917–18 wheat harvest, which averaged between 450 and 580 kilos per hectare for communal and privately owned enterprises, respectively.[49] This was despite the fact that—as was the case in Colombia— large landowners occupied better, more fertile lands. Such occupation of the best lands in Peru was a violent process of dispossession punctuated by massacres against the Indigenous people. Mariategui, like more recent scholars such as De La Cadena (2015) and Escobar (2020), invoked the spiritual element in the communal Indigenous peasant culture, which kept them alive, adding a component for its reproduction. Mariategui concluded that if anything has been missing in Marx, it has been "an insufficient legal spirit."[50]

THE POLISH EXPERIENCE AND THE MYTH OF THE VANISHING PEASANT

The subsistence peasant economy in Poland survived not only capitalist development before its socialist experience but also the attempts of collectivization of the 1960s and 1970s and (since 1990) adoption of the neoliberal economic model. The hybrid Polish peasant economy can help explain the built-in adaptability and resistance mechanisms of these formations in Colombia within changing local and global market environments.

Leading Polish sociologist Maria Halamska described the process of dismantling the peasant economy since 1989 in her home country: "Poland's economic transformation, initiated in 1989, ushered in market economics with all the consequences thereof, including for family farms—entailing changes in the entire existing system of farms' external relations and internal mechanisms. Farmers were subjected to a brutal adaptation process to the new conditions, felt by their owners to be a kind of 'oppressive liberty.'"[51] She raised the possibility that peasants might become a vanishing social group. "The notion of the 'end of the peasants' then gradually spread throughout Europe: it signifies a vanishing peasant way of farming and the gradual absorption of the peasant economy into the capitalist economy, as farm functioning and reproduction become subordinated to the mechanisms of market economics. Out of the vast numbers of farms, a smaller group of robust, strong, entrepreneurial, 'professional' farms emerge and end up absorbing other farms, whose users then abandon agriculture. Once there are no more peasant farms, with their specific functioning and reproduction, there are likewise no more peasants."[52]

Halamska described "quasi sustenance peasant economy quasi peasant," which she thought did not function according to any familiar rationale.[53] She found that "the group of strong market-oriented farms now emerging (including also privatization of the state sector) is not absorbing the small farms because the latter are not succumbing to market rationale, having other, non-agricultural sources of financing."[54] Halamska added that this "group represents a new type of peasants overlooked by Western modernization theories." She explained that "the timing of agricultural modernization is crucial here: in the West, it occurred during times of forced industrializations that absorbed migrants abandoning agriculture, while in Poland, it has come during a post-industrial phase and a period of economic transformation involving high unemployment." "Poland's quasi-peasants 'absorb' part of that unemployment, easing social tension."[55] Halamska describes the quasi-peasant and quasi-sustenance peasants "as (producing food solely for the family), functioning—or rather existing—thanks to a specific rationale, neither peasant nor entrepreneurial."[56] Halamska's analysis dismissed the rationality of the peasants in disagreement with McNetting, Wolf, Scott, and Chayanov's theories and findings. She also disagrees with the thesis if the "vanishing peasant."

Finally, Halamska contended that the survival of four hundred thousand farms owned by 3.7 million people, with three-fifths of them comprising fewer than five hectares, was primarily due to political considerations.[57] One must wonder whether she gave sufficient weight to the agency of peasants to make decisions influencing the state's policymakers and their capacity to adjust to adversarial socioeconomic and political conditions. Peasants' rationality and agency, which she acknowledges is "different" from the one assumed by modernization theories, attempts to balance adaptability to the market's pressures and the conditions of subsumption while resisting them. It is a dynamic dialectical process in which outcomes are unpredictable and ever-changing. In my opinion, Halamska's analysis underplayed this factor. As this book demonstrates, the peasants in Colombia demonstrated extraordinary ability to organize and build their networks outside the orbit of the capital.

Peasant Economy:
The Struggle between Rentier Capital and Noncapitalist Mode

This book contributes to the literature on peasant economies by focusing on the agency of the affected noncapitalist and subsistence family–based peasant communities and their capacity to adapt and resist the encroachments of neoliberal global actors and their local rentier collaborators. In addition, it focuses on how local and international capital has been reshaping the political economy of rural Colombia since the mid-twentieth century by dismantling communal land properties, which allowed the expansion of capitalism in the forms of agribusinesses and the extraction of resources such as oil, coal, gold, and emeralds. This process has led to one of the most violent periods in Colombia's turbulent history. I call this period war rentierism, leading to violent rural transformation processes. A process unleashed during the civil wars of 1899–1902, the War of a Thousand Days (*La Guerra de Mil Dias*)[58] continued throughout *La Violencia* in 1948–1958 and 1964–2016, respectively.[59] Violence with ebbs and flows happened against the backdrop of profound transformations in the country's political economy from an agrarian-based economy in the late nineteenth century to the 1950s and 1960s development of manufacturing of consumer goods, expansion of capitalist agriculture, to deindustrialization and the enlargement of the rentier economy since the 1980s.[60] Despite the changes, two salient features remained to characterize the polity: (1) appropriation of land; and (2) the expansion of the rentier political economy.

Rentier economy was defined by David Ricardo as a margin of market price over cost value, unearned revenue that flows from land ownership, which also includes mining (see chapters 1 and 2).[61] For a wider use of the rentier concept than the one suggested by Ricardo, Michael Hudson expanded the concept to incorporate the industrial economies such as the United States, where more wealth is created from financial speculation and rents than from production. Hudson defined rentier income as economic rent and interest or other financial charges, arguing that this form of capitalism is polarizing the U.S. and other economies. He added, "The bulk of this rentier income is not being spent on expanding the means of production or raising living standards. Instead, it is plowed back into the purchase of property and financial securities already in place[62]—legal rights and claims for payment extracted from the economy at large." This research adopts the presented theoretical contours of a rentier economy, chiefly its service–financial capital base, with a crucial qualifier. That is, the rentier transformation of Colombia has been playing out in a dependent postcolonial economy. Consequently, the rentier transformation process in rural areas has been particularly painful, creating socioeconomic and environmental dislocation, which are elaborated on in the following chapters.

In this vein, and to capture the nuances of the rentier political economy in the Colombian context, I introduced "war rentierism," which is the use of violence to promote and accelerate the expansion of rentierism—altering land use from food production to agribusiness, mining, oil, coal, and gold extraction, unproductive cattle ranching, services, tourism, and speculation. War rentierism is examined as an effective instrument in the process of subsumption through which eight million hectares (circa 7 percent of the country's surface area) of land were usurped, dispossessing in the process more than seven million peasants and killing more than 220,000 between 1948 and 2012.[63] The different outcomes of dismantling noncapitalist relations and subsistence peasant economies are beyond the scope of this book, which focuses on illustrative cases. It examines the core changes in the rural political economy that affected the peasants living in the two reserves of Pato-Balsillas, Cimitarra, and the Indigenous *resguardos* in the departments of Meta and Cauca. This is alongside the struggle of the Afro-descendants in Cauca to establish their autonomous community councils.

In the investigated cases, capitalist and noncapitalist communal modes of production and the subsistence peasant economies coexist and dialectically interact.[64] This book explains these two salient trends—removing peasant economies in some areas and retaining an uneasy coexistence between subsistence family–based peasants and capitalist economies in other areas. Furthermore, this research attempts to answer why capitalist and noncapitalist economies interact violently in some areas and nonviolently in others, how the subsumption processes occur, and how capital extracts surplus value from noncapitalist communal and subsistence peasant economies without necessarily annihilating them. Answering these questions helps present a historical narrative as truthful as possible to the messiness of social change in which social actors have competing class interests and agencies.

The following section discusses a fundamental construct of this book: the definition of who is a "peasant" in twenty-first-century Colombia. It explains the underlying political and ideological currents behind the state's decision to grant juridical recognition of the Indigenous and Afro-Colombians as political subjects while denying their social class as peasants alongside the mixed-race (Mestizo) peasants. Privileging identity over class is not accidental but consistent with liberal ideological dogmas. This issue is discussed in greater detail in chapter 1.

From Identity Politics to Class Identity

In mainstream social science, it has become in vogue to characterize social fault lines and conflict in terms of identity/cultural politics overlooking or ignoring class, which might inform and shape identities, including race, ethnicity, and gender. However, in the case of the peasant, it shows a feedback loop in which a class agency capitalized on the success of ethnic/gender/racial groups in gaining legal rights to claim its demand for recognition.[65] That is to say, peasant groups and organizations such as La Via Campesina, which include hundreds of groups, learned from the success of the Indigenous groups in claiming protection rights in the era of neoliberal ideological hegemony and "savage capitalism."[66]

Since the nineteenth century, land conflicts between peasants and landowners have become the main fault line of societal divisions in Colombia, defining the contours of most of its civil strife and wars. However, the Colombian state, in its two constitutions of 1886 and 1991 constitution, did not recognize the peasant as subjects. Consequently, they were left in a normative twilight zone without legal rights and protection. In sharp contrast, the 1991 Constitution granted the Indigenous and Afro-Colombians political rights. The question is why the 1991 constitution did not recognize the principal peasant character of the Indigenous, Afro-descendants, and mestizos that constitute most of the rural population while acknowledging them as ethnic groups.

One explanation is attributed to the weakness of the peasant movement after the systematic extermination of its leadership during the 1980s, which killed more than three thousand activists. Another is the crisis within the insurgent groups, which ended with the demobilization of the M-19, EPL, and Quintin Lame in 1989. This demobilization of segments of the insurgency weakened the negotiation position of the radical armed Left and the peasants alongside the working-class movement in urban centers.[67] While the large land-owning elite who historically wielded significant political influence retained their power in both the Conservative and Liberal parties, encouraged by the enhanced dominance of the neoliberal economic thinking that embraced land-market, an anti–land redistribution strategy led by the then newly elected Cesar Gaviria (1990–94) of the Liberal Party (see chapter 1) exacerbated land conflicts. Those groups became the critical mass within the Constituent Assembly that drafted the 1991 Constitution. Then it was logical that the 1991Constitution disregarded the peasantry, denying this social group/class any legal rights, which might also have brought a measure of protection and, more importantly, opened the door for claims of land distribution. This lack of recognition remained unresolved in spite of the fact that in 1994 the state promulgated Law 160, which created peasant reserve zones, constituting a measure that did not require any redistribution of large landholdings and thus preserving the class interests of the powerful landed elite while seeking to contain the peasant organizations' pressure for land access.

The peasant as a legal subject remained unrecognized until 2018, when two events concurred. One was the UN declaration of the Rights of Peasants and Other People Working in Rural Areas, which responded to the activism of Via Campesina (VC) and peasants' groups in Indonesia and elsewhere. The UN declaration was a watershed in extending protection to the peasants' way of life. The declaration spelled out that "States shall take appropriate measures to provide legal recognition for land tenure rights, including customary land tenure rights not currently protected by law, recognizing the existence of different models and systems. Furthermore, States shall protect legitimate tenure and ensure that peasants and other people working in rural areas are not arbitrarily or unlawfully evicted and that their rights are not otherwise extinguished or infringed. Furthermore, States shall recognize and protect the natural commons and their related systems of collective use and management."

Against this landmark UN declaration, the Colombian Constitutional Court ordered the Ministry of Interior, the Administrative Department of National Statistics (DANE in Spanish acronyms), the Presidency of the Republic, the Ministry of Agriculture and Rural Development, and the Colombian Institute of Anthropology and History to append supplementary questions to the Agricultural Census of 2014 that would permit the introduction of the peasant as a social category in the future population census. This court decision led to the formation of a commission to define the identity of a peasant. The commission was formed and ended up defining the peasant as an "individual that identifies herself/himself as such; involved in the direct work in the land and nature; immersed in family and community-based unenumerated work or by selling his/her labor."[68] This definition of a peasant in today's Colombia and the UN declaration on peasants' rights came after a long and arduous global and local struggle to recognize and grant the peasant communities across the globe protection from the encroachments of capital, state policies, and violent nonstate actors. The introduction of the peasant as a subject in the 2018 population census did not extend to the constitution. However, the Colombian state has not yet recognized the peasant as a subject, as required by the UN declaration. This book describes the peasant's struggle for recognition with its successes and failures within the processes of resisting and adapting to capital subsumption focusing on agency as observed in the empirical cases investigated. The postscript of this book discusses the radical changes that the new Gustavo Petro (2022–26) government is bringing forward in its recognition of the peasantry by extending to them legal protection and support. For the first time in the country's turbulent history, a government weighs the peasant economy's strategic importance for the country's food and environmental security. One can note that a new economic paradigm is in the making, which offers some hope.

Book Map

The introduction of this book discusses the conditions under which liberal market ideology began guiding state policies since the 1950s, sidelining land distribution and reform demands. This chapter analyzes the ascendance of rentier capitalism with far-reaching implications for rural economies. Chapters 1 through 5 are the cases considered in analyzing the socio-economic and environmental effects of rentierism and its corollary war rentierism. Chapter 1, originally published by the *Journal of Latin American Research Review* (2012), was updated for this book. It delves into a salient and perplexing phenomenon in the rural sector's political economy: cattle ranching expansion despite its notorious inefficiency and low profit margins menaces food production and the peasant family–based economy. This chapter argues that cattle ranching was propelled by two intertwined and mutually reinforcing factors: war rentierism and political economy, which stimulated speculation in land prices and the repatriation of narcodollars that were laundered during the examined period. Chapter 2 analyzes the peasant reserves and the subsistence family–based economy. It focuses on the adaptability and resistance that allow that economy to survive under adverse socioeconomic and political conditions punctuated by violence, as illustrated in the cases of Pato-Balsillas and Cimitarra. Chapter 3 explores the adaptability and resistance strategies employed by the Indigenous groups in Meta and Cauca to contain the process of subsumption of capital. Chapter 4 examines the obstacles confronting Afro-Colombians in the department of Cauca seeking to access land to establish their communal councils. This chapter is important because it shows the diffusion of political learning of resistance between and among communities. The cases explored in this research are predominantly subsistence peasant economies struggling with capital subsumption, instrumentalized and represented by multinational corporations, agribusinesses, cattle ranchers, narcobourgeoisie, and land speculators. Finally, the conclusion sums up the book's main findings and its recommendations for future research.

Chapter 1

The Emergence of the Neoliberal State, Rentier Economics, and the Agrarian Question

> The fundamental right of the Colombian was not direct ownership of the land they occupied or worked on but a decent standard of living.
>
> —Lauchlin Currie

Since the mid-1980s, neoliberalism and rentier capital started ascending into the dominant economic model in Colombia, threatening millions of peasants' livelihood and way of life. This chapter provides a brief historical analysis of the factors that led to the neoliberal economic model's hegemony as an ideology that has shaped the country's rentier economic growth, sharpening income inequalities, social conflicts, and, most notably, land use. It focuses on the emergence of neoliberalism and the rentier model by the mid-1980s and its consolidation in the 1990s, thus shaping the state's policy toward rural development, the peasantry, and landless peasants (*colonos*), leading to extreme levels of concentration of land ownership. It analyzes the pivotal role of the above-cited, Canadian-born economist Lauchlin Currie, who led the first World Bank mission to Colombia in 1949, and the mission' far-reaching consequences on its socioeconomic capitalist path.[1] His mission stemmed from the increasing importance of Colombia for U.S. regional policy and security. The United States sought to make Colombia a showcase for capitalist development and an anchor of stability.[2] The chapter also describes the few ill-fated land reform attempts championed by presidents Lopez Pumarejo (1934–38) and Carlos Lleras Restrepo (1964–68). Both failed attempts were based on the limited distribution of inefficiently used *latifundios* and providing public land to landless peasants (*colonos*).

According to Currie's liberal economic paradigm, the problem crippling Colombia's rural economic development was not the distribution of land and its concentration in the hands of few landowners, but the absence of land markets due to lack of capital, a problem compounded by the surplus of labor in the agricultural sector.[3] His views reflected the dominant thinking of the hegemonic power triangle: the U.S. government, the U.S. academe, and the World Bank. Currie's paradigm and its rentier model variant that emerged a few decades later rested on three pillars: extraction, agribusiness, and services. Research has demonstrated how these activities have been undermining the country's food security and the livelihood of the almost 32 percent of the country's population that depends on the agricultural sector.[4] Between 1965 and 2020, the agricultural sector's contribution to GDP declined steeply from 27.2 percent to 7.6 percent (see Figure 1.1). Among the most affected social groups are those that depend on family-based farming, including Indigenous, Afro-Colombians, and poor mestizos, peasants occupying about 25 percent

Figure 1.1. Agriculture 1965–2019 percentage of GDP. *Source*: World Bank, public domain.

of Colombia's total area, equivalent to 34 million hectares (40 percent of which is forested).[5] As such, they became a target for dispossession by rentier capital in its multiple forms: extractive multinational corporations, agribusinesses, cattle ranching enterprises, narcobourgeoisie investments, and land speculators. For example, cattle ranching enterprises expanded exponentially during the last two to three decades (discussed in chapter 2). This problem is one of the most perverse results of the rentier economy that has a devastating impact on the environment, food security, and livelihood, by exacerbating land dispossession and grabbing,

The State, Landed Elite, and Land Reform

An essential characteristic of Colombia's state formation since colonial times is the formidable political power of its large landowning elite.[6] This power was most evident in its ability to prevent the state from undertaking meaningful land reform to solve the intractable land conflict. Those conflicts have marred the country's history from the early twentieth century up to this time. The stiff opposition of the large landowning elite (*hacendados*) to any land reform led to repeated failures by the central government to introduce land reform, as demonstrated by the demise of Law 200 of 1936, Law 135 of 1961, and Law 1 of 1968.[7] In those cases, the local elites, primarily large landowners, heavily represented in both Conservative and Liberal parties, hindered the implementation of the laws by using intimidation and violence, as was the case in 1936 against "land judges" appointed to adjudicate land disputes. Similarly, violent methods were deployed against peasants in the wake of Law 1 of 1968.

In the words of Francisco Leal, a prominent Colombian political scientist: "The land problem and its concentration in a few hands is an old one that has been safeguarded by an oversized representation of landowning oligarchy in congress and compounded by the state's inability to tax rural land properties due to the landowning elite manipulation of land registries and underreporting property values" (Leal 2020; Richani 2012; Richani interviews).[8] Similarly, Berry (2017) identified the agrarian elite in Colombia and its class interests as central to all governments since the nineteenth century. He contended that their role was not well understood even by technocrats. Leal and Berry agreed on the disproportionate political influence of the landed elite on land policies and beyond. The landed elite, along with the multinational mining companies, agribusiness, cattle ranchers, and narcobourgeoisie, have become a formidable force that shaped the rural areas' political economy, fueling the civil war and limiting the inclusiveness of the political system and the democratization of property rights.

The landed elite's primary sources of power continue to be their strong representation in both the Liberal Conservatives parties, their powerful representation in parliament, achieved by controlling the Caribbean bloc (Bolivar, Sucre, Cesar, Magdalena, La Guajira, Cordoba), alongside their representation in state institutions dealing with the rural sector. They also exercise their political influence at the local level in congressional elections and the elections of mayors and governors in areas where they retain significant power (Romero 2003; Reyes 2010; Berry 2017; Duncan 2007).[9] The landed elite's powerful influence can explain why in more than 120 years only two liberal-minded presidents attempted to introduce land reform in the rural economy by redistributing primarily public land without breaking the unproductive *latifundios*.[10] The failure of these two moderate attempts closed the path of land distribution, curtailing access by landless peasants (*colonos*) to land. In particular, Misael Pastrana, the successor of President Lleras Restrepo, under the pressure of the landowning elite, signed the 1972 Pact of Chicoral. The large landowners reversed the changes made by Lleras Restrepo, ending the reformist drive. The subsequent two decades witnessed the gradual ascendance of rentier economics and neoliberal changes that aggravated land conflicts and violence and enhanced land property concentration. As discussed below, the landowning elite benefited from the policy recommendations of the World Bank Commission, led by Currie, which were based on the opinion that the concentration of land ownership was not an obstacle for development,[11] a typical strand in the pro-capital modernization paradigm.

The following section discusses the failure of Law 200 of 1936 to defuse the landless peasants' struggle for land, which led to the bloody civil war of 1948–1958, referred to as "La Violencia." It is followed by a description of the last attempt at land reform in Colombia, as championed by President Carlo Lleras Restrepo's introduction of Law 135 of 1961 and Law 1 of 1968.

Law 200 of 1936: The Promise and the Fall of Land Reform

When Lopez Pumarejo, a Liberal party leader, introduced Law 200 during his first government (1934–38), he sought to reform the skewed distribution of landholdings to incentivize agricultural production. Law 200 was introduced in the midst of the critical juncture of a massive *colonos* mobilization and the looming Great Depression, forcing the dominant elite to prioritize agriculture to satisfy food demand and promote industrialization. In addition, the Liberal Party wanted to enhance its support base and tried to settle the competing claims of *colonos* and large landowners in frontier areas such as Meta, Caqueta, Choco, and Cordoba.

Law 200 stipulated in Article 12 that whoever occupied the land for five years might claim it as their own. Law 200 also gave evicted *colonos* the right to be compensated for whatever improvements they might have made to the land. Law 200 was significant because it stipulated the creation of *jueces de tierras* (land judges) with the responsibility of arbitrating land disputes. From 1937 through 1943, the judges acted expeditiously, and according to the Ministry of Industries, more than 80 percent of existing disputes were settled by 1938. However, Law 200 of 1936 did not affect property relations in any fundamental way. Still, the law was designed to rectify the "defects" of the preceding law, which required landowners to provide land titles in the event of a dispute over ownership. Law 200 eliminated this requirement with the condition that land had to be used for ten years or it would be transferred to public ownership. None of these properties were returned to the state, and very few were recovered with compensation.

Berry noted that Pumarejo's was the "first and most serious approach to an agrarian reform of significance in Colombia." In his review of the escalating land conflict between the *colonos* and large landowners in the1930s, Berry (2017) stated that "all of the standard arguments in favor of helping and defending the small settlers were aired at this time in Colombia and various approaches were tried to deal with the two problems perceived by policymakers—inadequate agricultural production and violent conflict." Fajardo (2008; 2012; 2019), a leading Colombian expert on the agrarian question, contended that Colombia came closer to a genuine reform than any other country of the region at the time. He argued that the law would have facilitated *colonos'* access to land and legalized their land acquisition. However, conditions changed, forcing the central government to pull back at the critical moment.[12] The large landowning class was strongly represented in both dominant parties, and Congress outmaneuvered Pumarejo and sabotaged his attempt. This was not the first time they imposed their will: three years before Pumarejo's reform plan, the landed elite, in a show of force, defeated in Congress a proposal that would have given the state control of 75 percent of the country's privately held property (Madrid 1944 as quoted by LeGrand 1986).

To contain the *colonos'* unrest, the government purchased three huge haciendas in the areas of the most serious conflict and initially provided free title to *colonos* who had occupied them in the late 1920s and early 1930s (Berry 2017; LeGrand 1986). While this measure did calm social unrest, the fiscal cost was high, and the government later decided that peasants should pay full market value (Berry 2017). When the peasants refused to pay, the initiative failed. On their part, landlords, fearing that the *colonos* would press claim on the lands they occupied, responded by expelling them. *Colonos* took their cases to court collectively—though usually unsuccessfully, as the landlords coordinated with local authorities. Berry (2017) points out that when Law 200 of 1936 was approved, the balance of power had already shifted in favor of the landlords. The *colonos* movement had lost some political influence and political steam due to the cooptation of some of its political leaders by the traditional parties, compounded by internal dissension around the parcelization program. Although land struggles continued, the *colonos'* representatives sought accommodation with the Liberal Party in power. President Lopez attempted to build a power base among urban labor and *colonos* to outbid his opponents in the Conservative Party by embracing some of the *colonos* demands. On the other hand, large landowners remained suspicious of Lopez's plans and the *colonos* challenge; they made sure to limit the implementation of Article 12 of Law 200. To avoid the loss of their lands, they started to expel their sharecroppers and tenants. This process of expulsion was, in most cases, was accomplished through violent methods.

Consequently, Law 200 increased polarization between political actors, especially with the emergence within the Liberal party of a left-leaning populist leader, Jorge Eliécer Gaitán, who challenged both traditional Liberal Party leaders and the more recalcitrant members of the Conservative Party.[13] This socioeconomic polarization, together with the unresolved land conflict, exploded in 1948 in a civil war between the two main political parties, Conservative and Liberal, cited by historians as "La Violencia.

Land Dispossession and Displacement
during La Violencia (1948–1958)

Even before the emergence of the insurgency in the 1960s, the two traditional parties that dominated Colombia's political system had been embroiled in a bitter competition since the country's independence. This competition led to a series of civil wars that ended without developing an institutional mechanism to secure the interests of the different factions of the ruling elite. But by the end of the 1946–1958 conflict (La Violencia), the National Front had been formed, an institution engineered to guarantee an equal representation of both political parties and a rotational presidency until 1974.

During La Violencia, forced displacement and dispossession of peasants occurred, generating the massive exodus of people to new colonization areas in the south in departments such as Meta, Caquetá, Putumayo, and Guaviare. As discussed in chapter 2, the largest number of displaced people expelled were from the department of Cauca, followed by Tolima and Antioquia.[14] Approximately seven hundred thousand civilians were displaced from three departments, home to 6 percent of the country's total population in the 1950s. During this same period, the total number of people forcefully displaced was 2,003,600, or 16 percent, of the country's twelve million population in 1950.[15] This profound demographic shift of predominantly small and poor peasants generated all sorts of socioeconomic dislocation and tension. The new settlements, or colonies, of displaced people, became hotbeds of resistance against the state and large landowners. Massive violent dislodging of the rural population has been a continuous process in the country's history since the 1930s, as the following section will show. The rate of privatization of public land rose precipitously during La Violencia from an average of 60,000 hectares(ha) per year over 1931–1945 to 150,000 ha over 1946–1954 and to 375,000 ha over 1955–59 (Legrand 1989, 13, citing Diot 1976). Using Oquist's data on the number of lots appropriated, Machado calculated that during La Violencia, circa 1.9 million hectares were abandoned, representing 11.2 percent of the country's used agricultural land in 1960.[16]

La Violencia then became a mechanism that helped a few accumulate more lands at the expense of the small and medium-sized landowner. More importantly, large landowners continuously appropriated the *colonos'* lands after the *colonos* had cleared new frontier areas for cultivation. La Violencia most affected the Andean region of the country. On Colombia's Caribbean coast, cattle ranching activity predominated and has expanded since the 1950s (Richani 2012). The expansion of the *latifundios* exacerbated land conflicts in some departments (such as Cesar, Bolivar, Sucre, and Córdoba), increasingly limiting land access to landless and poor peasants, which created the favorable conditions for the left-leaning radical challengers that emerged in the 1960s. President Carlos Lleras Restrepo

(1966–1970) introduced an initiative to address the concentration of land that La Violencia had aggravated. But the Restrepo administration was no more successful than the Pumarejo administration had been three decades earlier.

Carlos Lleras Restrepo's (1966–1970) Law 135 of 1961 and Law 1 of 1968

In 1966, Carlos Lleras Restrepo's Liberal reformist government took over from the Conservative Party according to the alternation of power arrangement of the National Front (1958–1974). Lleras Restrepo was keen on mitigating the escalating land conflict by doubling down on his commitment to Law 135 of 1961 and introducing Law 1 of 1968.[17] The leadership of both parties negotiated Law 1 of 1968, but the Conservative Party was objecting to its provisions that could affect large landowners.

Law 135 of 1961 established the Institute of Colombia for Land Reform (Spanish acronym INCORA). INCORA attempted to mitigate the increasing land disputes by offering landless peasants public lands in the frontier areas for colonization. More than 50 percent of the INCORA projects and 75 percent of the land titling were done in high conflict areas. But the most revealing aspect of the limitations of INCORA's performance was its negligible effect on large land properties. It only used 8,3 percent of its funds to compensate for large landholdings appropriated by the state, leaving *hacendados* virtually untouched. INCORA's low investment in large landholdings demonstrated that Law 135 was designed primarily to direct the colonization process of public lands, mitigating land conflicts and addressing the rising demands of landless peasants.[18] The irony was that most of the colonized areas, including frontier areas, ended up in the hands of large landowners, including cattle ranchers, agribusinesses, narcobourgeoisie, speculators, and multinational corporations, that is, the agents of rentier capital.[19]

The other important law introduced by Lleras Restrepo's government was Law 1 of 1968, which sought to activate the agricultural sector by incentivizing owners of large properties to use their lands. Law 1 of 1968 granted ten years of proper and continuous land cultivation as a requirement for land titling. However, large landowners, fearing that Law 1 of 1968 might give their sharecroppers or land lessors legal rights to claim part of their landholdings expelled land tenants and discontinued sharecropping.[20] As a result, thousands of peasants lost their livelihoods and homes, thus exacerbating grievances and leading to land conflicts, violence, and political polarization amid an increasingly fractured elite at the central level. In contrast, local elites and large landowners remained united.

During that period, the World Bank incessantly promoted the argument that the problem in Colombia was not the land tenure system and the concentration of land property but rather the stagnation in agricultural production and development.[21] Lauchlin Currie, a Canadian working for the World Bank, was the influential adviser who recommended policies to governments. Furthermore, he was instrumental in creating the Department of National Planning (DNP) in 1959, successfully marketing his view that land reform is not essential for development.[22] According to the economist Salomón Kalmanovitz, Currie's influence was not limited to the diagnosis of the agrarian problem, but extended to the promotion of the economic theories dominant in the United States, chiefly those of Milton Friedman and Frederick Hayek. These theories were also introduced in the economics department at the Andes University and the National University, the two leading universities from which the country's future economists graduated.[23]

In 1960, President Alberto Lleras named Currie to the permanent Council of National Planning, which he declined. Currie was convinced that the economic problem of Colombia was not its monetary policy (high-interest rates, circulation of money) but the maldistribution of human and technical resources, which generated high unemployment in the rural areas. The solution, he proposed, was the migration of surplus rural unskilled labor to the cities where they could be employed in construction and other sectors. In addition, agriculture and cattle ranching (an activity he was involved in) must be modernized to increase production and wages in the rural economy. In 1960, Currie authored a document titled "Operation Colombia." He projected that the redistribution of human resources would create five hundred thousand new jobs in the cities within two years. In Currie's opinion, Colombia lacked high demand. So, industrial production was not stimulated to its full potential to attain economies of scale and consequently reduce production costs.[24] Therefore, increasing demand and the expansion of the market were imperative to stimulate growth.

Lleras Restrepo rejected Currie's thesis that the problem in the rural sector was one of poor distribution of human resources. The paradox then was that Lleras's land reform project was in some respects in tune with Kennedy's Alliance for Progress while Currie's proposal ran against it. The extreme right-wing faction of the Conservative Party led by Laureano Gomez Hurtado in parliament used Currie's thesis to attack Lleras Restrepo's land reformist policy.[25] This reveals the unintended consequence of a policy recommendation in the context of polarization and land conflict. The right-wing factions and the landowning elite used Currie's recommendation to safeguard their land properties against any argument calling for land distribution.

A decade later, in 1971, Currie was asked by Director of National Planning Roberto Arenas Borulla to help him formulate a national development plan. Currie's old liberal convictions had not altered much since the publication of "Operation Colombia." He thought that the construction sector in the cities could generate employment for rural migrants; the construction sector must be privately financed without depending on the state. In addition to construction, he proposed that three sectors be promoted: the export sector, the agricultural sector, and progressive taxes and reduction of tax incentives to industry. Currie's development plan, outlined in 1971's "Four Strategies," again dismissed the idea of land distribution, just as he had in 1961.

By rejecting distributive land reform, Currie benefited the most recalcitrant and "backward" segment of the dominant class as well as its most "modern." Large landowners, the extreme-right faction, and service-oriented entrepreneurs (construction, real estate, banks, finance, beverages, insurance) had a stake in the plan.[26] Currie's "development" plan (based on housing construction, facilitating housing credit, and the export economy) laid the basis for Colombia's rentier extractive political economy. As one Colombian scholar put it, "His ideas and plans to resolve Colombia's economic problems had a profound impact not only in academia but also on the nation's socio-economic development."[27] Currie's ideas helped create an institutional framework for liberalization and the rentier economy, mainly through his focus on strengthening the construction sector to absorb surplus rural labor, with the assumption that this would create demand for building materials. The twin goals of de-peasantization and urbanization were the objective. To achieve these two goals, he devised his eclectic economic policies. In defense of his economic thinking, Currie was quoted as saying, "Although I have great respect for the power of economic incentives and the efficacy of decentralized decision making, I am still an inveterate planner. Despite my good intentions, the State reappeared, I hope in acceptable collaboration with the use of economic incentives." He added, "The 'invisible hand' became two hands, the traditional one working silently through economic incentives and the more visible one of national economic policymaking. The resulting strategy is a mixed one, difficult to classify." Currie concluded that "I would not call myself a monetarist nor a Keynesian, nor a believer in intervention nor the market, nor a structuralist nor a neo-classicist but a little of all of these, and am prepared to use policies involving elements of all these approaches when the attainment of certain goals appears to make their use appropriate"[28] Currie's elaboration demonstrated the use of the state policy to strengthen the capitalist market and to accelerate urbanization, which was his doctrinal focus.[29]

Currie did not shy away from expressing his strong bias against the peasants, which was a view dominant in the development and modernization literature of the time.[30] He argued that the "real rural problem was an excess rural population. This excess must be transferred, forcibly, if need be, to the large cities and employed in public work to create increased consumer demand, which in turn would be met with industrialization. Colombia agriculture in the meantime, would be intensively mechanized and the remaining rural population would be these large, mechanized farming operations."[31] Such an extreme view approximates the language of class cleansing in our time.

Against the backdrop of Currie's view on the peasants and Lleras Restrepo's failure to break the *latifundios* power, the *latifundos'* dominance in the rural political economy was certified by their triumph under the historical Chicoral Pact in 1972. The reactionary coalition of *hacendados* (large landowners) of both political parties and their backers sealed the prospects of land reform for decades to come. In this regard, by downplaying the role of land property concentration as an obstacle to development, Currie's and the World Bank's view provided a powerful argument for the reactionary coalition to defend their class and political interest. In the following chapters, the impact of neoliberal economic policies on the political economy of the rural sector will be discussed.

The Chicoral Pact: Law 4 of 1973 and Currie's "Four Strategies"

President Misael Pastrana (1970–74), a conservative follower of Hurtado, put an end to Lleras Restrepo's reforms. He formed the Chicoral Pact, which had three objectives: to suppress the most radicalized Sincelejo faction of the National Association of Peasant Users (ANUC), an organization that Carlos Lleras Restrepo created to help him promote popular support for his land reform; to promote cash crop exports as advised by Currie's "Four Strategies"; and, to reassure the large landowners and other investors that their properties would not be appropriated.[32] Subsequently, Law 4 of 1973 reversed Law 135 of 1961 and set the contours of the rural political economy dominated by a few thousand large landowners. It reduced the number of years of productive land use from ten to three, allowing large landowners a significant leeway to dodge the inefficient land use provision. Law 4 also extended protection for cattle ranchers seeking to prove the adequate use of their land to satisfy the norms of productivity and social function, by granting a vague requirement of "productivity" that was not based on liquid or presumptive income.[33] Additionally, Law 4 created "communal enterprises" administered by INCORA and was designed to contain and defuse the ANUC's mobilizations. By 1974, 1,177 communal enterprises had been created, with 11,832 members. However, most of these "communal enterprises" collapsed due to inadequate land size, quality of land, access to credit, and the uncertainty of land titling.[34] The idea of creating "communal enterprises" was in concert with Currie's capitalist market economic dogma. More importantly, it was a smokescreen that neither contained nor defused but instead exacerbated the social conflict in rural areas.

Rafael Pardo, minister of defense under the Cesar Gaviria government (1990–94), and the first civilian to occupy this position after the National Front gained power, reflecting on Carlos Lleras's attempt at land reform, succinctly summed up the experience: "The ideological controversy—which is still relevant today—was between a trend led by professor Lauchlin Currie, inspirator of the Conservative Party, who argued that the problem of Colombia is not the land tenure system but the agricultural production which needs to increase. The other tendency led by Lleras considered the redistribution of land as necessary not only for moral and social justice issues but to expand the internal market."[35] Pardo emphasized that "half a century later, President Lleras has been the one that contributed the most to redistribution of land." According to the Contraloria General, between 1962 and 2004, 6,620,000 hectares were adjudicated, and 72 percent of the extinction of dominion and 25 percent of land acquisitions were carried out by Carlos Lleras Restrepo.[36] In 1961 there were an estimated one million families tilling land who remained without land titles. Decades later, only 10 percent of those were granted land titles.[37]

According to the Institutes of Agustín Codazzi and Corpoica, in 2002 15,273 persons owned 47,147,680 hectares; in other words, 4 percent of landowners owned 61.2 percent of rural lands. This indicates that since the 1960s, the concentration of land ownership has increased. According to Felipe Fonseca, director of the Rural Agricultural Planning Unit of Colombia (Spanish: UPRA), 82 percent of the country's productive land is in the hands of only 10 percent of the total owners. In comparison, 68 percent of the farms have fewer than five hectares, and only 50 percent of the landowners have land titles.[38] In 2009, the GINI coefficient of land amounted to 0.86, one of the highest in the world.[39] Figure 1.2 shows the evolution of the concentration of land plots in fewer hands.

Land distributions slowed after 1973 and then increased again in the1990s as a result of changes associated with the 1991 Constitution. Shifting gears again, Law 160 of 1994 promoted a market-oriented approach to land reform that sought to lower the cost of land for poor peasants and provided publicly subsidized loans, which, according to Mondragon (2001), led to decreased peasants' access to land.[40]

Currie's Legacy and the Consolidation of the Neo-Liberal Doctrine

By the 1970s, the coffee economy and import substitution, the cornerstones of the country's political economy, lost ground, creating favorable conditions for developing new ideas and currents of thought. Theories

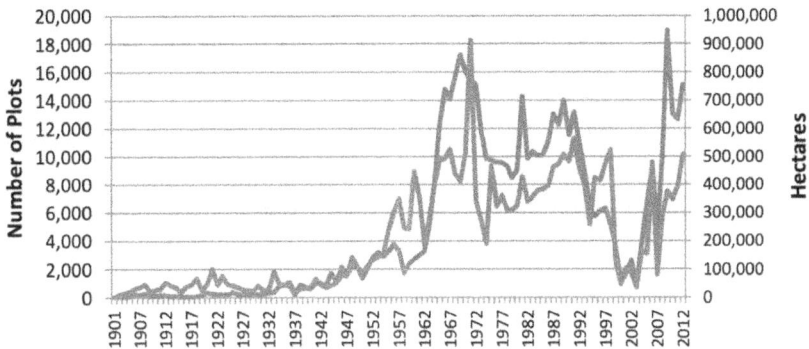

Figure 1.2. Land distribution in hectares. *Source*: LSE, public domain.

regarding liberalization, deregulation, and trickle-down economics started influencing local currents of thought in Colombia, though they were not strong enough to reorient state policies. During the presidency of Misael Pastrana (1970–74), a dispute emerged between neoliberals and structuralists in the Department of National Planning regarding the economic policies that Currie was proposing in his "Four Strategies" doctrine. Currie's policies prevailed, and his opponents resigned. This episode in 1971 demonstrated Currie's more decisive influence than those emerging neophyte economists.[41]

Pastrana's government adopted Currie's Four Strategies and introduced policies to encourage housing construction to absorb the rural oversupply of labor. Currie argued that construction, a labor-intensive sector, would also provide higher salaries to urban workers and enhance demands from other sectors for construction, creating a "virtuous cycle" that would incentivize industrial development. Currie was focused on providing financial instruments to encourage the emerging urban middle class to deposit their money in savings accounts. He recommended creating the constant purchasing power unit (*Unidad de poder Adquisitivo*; UPAC) to assure depositors that their savings were secure irrespective of fluctuations in interest rates and inflation. Steady interest rates, according to Currie, would increase deposits, which, in turn, would give them capital to use in a mortgage.

Banks responded positively to Currie's proposal, and President Pastrana declared a state of economic emergency to allow him to issue two presidential decrees in 1972, decrees 677 and 678, calling for the establishment of new financial systems for housing and construction, respectively. Decree 677 created a fund for saving and housing (FAVI), and Decree 678 created housing and saving corporations (CAVI) stipulating the saving and mortgage system for fifteen year terms and adjusting to fluctuations in the currency's purchasing power. In a short time, CAV succeeded in securing funds for its operation and investment in construction, garnishing significant profits to private banks (Lopez-Pradero 2019, 233).

In 1972, the Colombian Corporation of Saving and Housing (Coldeahorro) was founded, with branches in the cities of Bogota, Medellin, Cali, and Barranquilla. In 1973, Coldeahorro changed its name to Davivienda, a bank that by 2016 had total assets estimated at $31.2 billion. The Pastrana measures expanded the social base of the urban middle class. They created a new housing market, which expanded the role of the financial sector in the economy. This laid out the basis of the rentier economy, in which finance capital and the real estate market were pivotal.[42] President Lopez Michelsen adopted the "Closing the Gap" plan and President Turbay Ayala the "National Integration" plan (Lopez-Pradero 2019, 223); both promoted economic policies that moved away from import-substitution industrialization (ISI) to expand cash crop exports and consolidate the service-oriented base of an emerging rentier economy. They laid down the institutional and ideological foundations of market economics, which in the 1980s gained more followers within academic circles and those who occupied strategic positions in deciding national planning and economic policy, including agrarian policy.[43]

Foreign investments in Colombia remained very limited between 1960 and 1990 due to the lack of laws that protected these investments. In 1967, Decree 444 required that foreign or local investments be registered with the Exchange Office of the Central Bank. In 1971, another resolution was introduced, which required that the Department of National Planning authorize all foreign investments.[44] These measures did not encourage foreign capital investments. Between 1979 and 1990, foreign investments in Colombia totaled about $500 million (Colmenares and Pardo 2015, 45). Between 1970 and 1979, foreign direct investments averaged 0.36 percent of the GDP; it increased to 1.30 percent of GDP between 1980 and 1989, and 2.14 percent between 1990 and 1999 after the apertura (economic liberalization).[45]

In the 1970s, service and financial conglomerates reconfigured the country's political economy and its positioning within the global economy; the coffee sector was still important but was losing ground. During the same period, a professional elite, mostly trained in the United States and local elite universities such as the Andes University, started occupying high positions in the government and the private sector. Fedesarrollo (Foundation for High Education and Development) was founded in 1970 and funded by Manuel Carbajal, the owner of one of the main conglomerates, Carbajal & Cia, who became its president.[46] The economic views of Colombian and foreign economists found an outlet in *Coyuntura Economica*, a specialist magazine that served as a forum for debate, education, socialization, and promoting ideas in conformity with the interest of the dominant class. Certainly, the emergence of a "local intelligentsia" marked a departure from the past, in which the state depended on foreign missions and experts such as the one that Currie led or the last one, the Musgrave Mission established during Lleras Restrepo's tenure to chart its economic plans and policies (Estrada 2005, 269).[47] An "organic intelligentsia" (to use Gramsci's concept) started to articulate the interests of the different factions of capital and translate them into policies. This process took more than two decades to mature into a full-fledged commitment to the neoliberal orthodoxy that has dominated the state and elite ideological formation and cultural production since the 1990s.

President Gaviria had earned a degree in economics from the Andes University, a citadel of neoliberal doctrine. He explained how the *apertura* and neoliberal economic ideology made their way to his government.[48] It all started when Gaviria was minister of economy in Virgilio Barco's administration (1986–1990). He employed two economic advisers, Rudolph Hommes and Armando Montenegro, who had received their PhDs in the United States, one from the University of Massachusetts in Amherst and the other from New York University. These two were neoliberal ideologues who edited the influential economic magazine *Estrategia Economica y Financiera* and occupied nodal government positions.[49] When Gaviria became president in 1990, he hired both to join his economic team.[50] Three months after Gaviria's election, Conpes 2494 was released, in which the administration spelled out its *apertura* economic policy and its gradual elimination of tariffs on imported commodities from its 33.5 percent recorded in November 1990 to 14.6 percent by 1994.[51] Reflecting on this period, Gaviria believed that these "neo-liberal measures" were not at fault but that the gradual elimination of tariffs created disincentives to import; the expectation was that further reductions were underway, which slowed down economic growth.[52]

International organizations such as the World Bank and the IMF played a role through their missions, including the one led by Currie, in pushing their neoliberal "recipes," as Joseph Stiglitz called the structural adjustments package that the Washington Consensus enforced among the developing nations.[53] Thanks to its neoliberal technocrats in Colombia, the *apertura* was facilitated by the local intelligentsia, primarily economists (Urrutia, interview with author 1996; Junguito, interview with author 1996).[54] Gaviria stated that, in contrast with other countries in Latin America, "the *apertura* was not a result of an economic crisis or was demanded by international organizations but because we did not want to stay behind from the direction that the world was taking."[55] Gaviria identified one crucial component: Colombia's main economic conglomerate, the Antioquia Syndicate, not only endorsed the economic *apertura* but called on Gaviria to accelerate the process.[56] Gaviria stated that the late Nicanor Restrepo, the president of Suramericana (which formed part of the conglomerate), asked him to expedite the process by a faster reduction of the tariffs on imports, replacing the piecemeal approach that was hampering the economy. Gaviria's government followed the recommendation of Restrepo.

Gaviria identified two factors that made the economic *apertura* of 1990 possible. The first was the ascendance of U.S.-trained economists versed in the post-Keynesian theory of market economics into a position of power in the finance ministry. The second, happening simultaneously, was the consolidation of a globally connected faction of the dominant class represented by the Antioquian Syndicate and other conglomerates, particularly those linked with international finance capital and commercial banks. Colombia's liberalization path had far-reaching effects. It ended import substitution industrialization, creating a new political economy whose main pillars were rentier/agribusiness. The rentier has two sectors—the extractive sector of oil, coal, gold, emeralds, and agribusiness, and the speculative sector that accumulates lands to hedge economic risks, taxes, anticipating price appreciation represented by the increase in lands for pasture and cattle ranching, as discussed in chapter 2. (Richani 2012).

In the 1990s, tariffs protecting the manufacturing sector were reduced to 11.6 percent, less than half of the 1989 level, and import quotas were eliminated. By 2000, a host of other measures were introduced, which led to the reduction of average nominal tariff protection for the agricultural sector, as defined in terms of the Uruguay Round, to an average of 10.7 percent, or less than one-third of its 1989 level, as well as the relaxing of import restrictions.[57] Combining these measures made the Colombian economy more dependent and vulnerable to changes in the international political economy. The consequence of this dependency on the global economy compelled the different sectors to either comply with Colombia's role in the global division of labor or suffer the consequences of foreign competition. The manufacturing and agriculture sectors were impacted negatively by the opening of the Colombian economy in the 1990s and 2000s. Subsequently, many actors in these sectors went out of business, and the rural economy declined.[58]

The "Neoliberal Organic" Economists and Questions of Social and Land Inequality

Gramsci introduced the role of the "organic intellectuals" that provide the state's ruling elite a coherent ideology that asserts its class interest while persuading society at large that it is for their own good.[59] According to Gramsci, this group may include scholars, administrators of enterprises, and technocrats that occupy the upper echelons of the state's administration.[60] In more recent times, think tanks and mass media might be added to the body of organic intellectuals that cater to the dominant class. Ideally, the organic intelligentsia produces policies that orient the economy with an ideological underpinning persuasive enough to convince the different factions of the dominant class that their interests are being promoted. Since the 1980s, Colombian neoliberal intellectuals have formulated Colombia's economic policies. Most of them embraced Currie's ideas, laid out in the 1960s and 1970s, regarding inequality and the land question. Here, I review the neoliberal intellectuals' views on inequality and land tenure and the trajectory of this group as exemplified by a few individuals who became key players in designing economic policies. These policies led to shifts in land use and rentier capital subsumption within noncapitalist family-based peasant production relations.

The economic opening and political reforms implemented by President Cesar Gaviria (1990–94) had their roots in the preceding administration of Virgilio Barco, in which Gaviria served as minister of finance (1986–87) and minister of justice (1987–89).[61] The "Kinder Group," as these like-minded technocrats came to be known, were the closest to what Gramsci had in mind.[62] What distinguished the members of this "Kinder Group "was their social-class and educational backgrounds different from the traditional 'caciques,' " as Gaviria wrote. According to him, the traditional elite, that is, the *caciques*, "did not speak English, none had a master's degree, they did not study abroad, they were orators in public squares and with little knowledge of how to manipulate modern mass communication." Gaviria concluded that by the late 1980s, the old generation had been left behind and a new one installed that was well versed and knowledgeable about the *apertura*, globalization, constitutional reforms, and pluralism. Equally important, Gaviria noted that during his term as finance minister he introduced institutional changes to facilitate the development of financial markets, an essential step for inserting Colombia into global financial markets.[63]

In the 1990s, prominent economist Juan Luis Londoño, the leading player in the inner circle of Gaviria's economic team, embraced the mantra that Colombia's development needed a "social infrastructure" that could lead to growth and at the same time mitigate inequality. This social infrastructure depended on three pillars: free international trade, less state intervention in the economy, and free markets. He dismissed consequences such as social inequality because they were seen as irrelevant to development and growth.[64] Londoño argued that in the 1990s, inequality in Colombia remained at an internationally acceptable level (Londoño 1992, 62). Consequently, inequality was no longer structural, and economists had to think of new strategies for poverty reduction. He claimed that distributive inequality and absolute poverty were no longer a social problem during the last quarter-century. Londoño described this advancement as "spectacular,"[65] a description not supported by the GINI index of the income distribution.

Velez's (2015) study refutes Londoño and the predictions of his neoliberal companions, Hommes and Montenegro, both of whom were the architects of Gaviria's neoliberal policy. In fact, according to Velez, income distribution in Colombia became more concentrated at the top 1 percent. The recessionary period of the mid-1990s, followed by one of the most severe economic crises in Colombian history, dwarfed top income shares. Since 2003, high economic growth had contributed to a surge in top income shares, especially among the ultra-rich (i.e., the top .01 percent). Colombia currently stands as one of the most unequal countries in the world, as the top 1 percent accounts for more than one-fifth of total income.[66] The GINI index of land distribution also indicated an increase in the concentration of land ownership since the 1980s, reaching 0.88 percent in 2009 (Oxfam 2016).

Colombia's neoliberal economists—Londoño, Rudolph Hommes, Roberto Junguito, Armando Montenegro, and others—embraced the idea that the country's problems were not related to income inequality and land tenure system. Instead, they blamed the lack of growth on the failure of Colombia to integrate into global markets (Estrada 2005; Araujo 2015). Londoño and his cohorts believed that neoliberal reforms would eventually reduce social inequality. Londoño became minister of health in Gaviria's government and remained committed to his "social infrastructure" theory. Yet, over time, Colombia's growth increased income inequality; only when the state increased public housing, which benefited the urban poor, did social inequality decrease. The GINI index declined from 60.68 percent, recorded in 2002, to 51.7 percent in 2018.[67]

Londoño (1992, 64) supported the structural adjustment policies suggested by the Washington Consensus, which guided Gaviria's and successive administrations. He claimed that the state must allow local authorities to manage public services. He argued that decentralization might create opportunities and conditions to help the local population generate income. The "Social Infrastructure" plan includes enhancing basic services in education, capacity building, health, nutrition, sewer systems, and aqueducts (Londoño 1992, 62).

Londoño and his neoliberal companions overlooked the implications of their neoliberal policy on income inequality in the urban areas and the ongoing rural conflicts generated by the high concentration of land properties in unproductive *latifundios*.[68] Early signs of this problem became apparent with the emergence of narcotrafficking, with the so-called Bonanza Marimbera of the marijuana (golden variant) grown in Santa Marta(1975–1985) coinciding in the coca economy in the late 1970s and early 1980s, discussed in the following chapter. Of course, a contingency such as narcotrafficking would have been difficult for anyone to predict, let alone to foresee the social tsunami it created in the country's political economy and especially in the rural areas.

The Political Power of the Landed Elite

The current landed elite comprises a much wider group than the traditional *hacendados* or *latifundios* of the 1920s; the group's expansion reflects the profound changes in the country's political economy since the mid-1980s, chief among them the growing importance of agribusiness, speculators, and multinational corporations. Business groups, including large cattle ranchers (discussed in chapter 2), share common concerns, especially in the wake of the peace accord with the FARC signed in 2016. Those concerns were listed by Rafael Aubad: land use, land rights, land restitution, land reform, subsoil rights of the Indigenous and Afro-Colombians on their communal properties, and environmental laws and regulations.[69] Then-president of ProAntioquia Rafael Aubad explained that business groups feared a legal change that might undermine their "freedom of land use and exploitation."[70] These contentious issues have become as complex as the global changes in the capitalist political economy precipitated by the interplay of the imminent threats of deforestation (discussed in the following chapters), global warming, and the growing demand for land, of which Colombia's land serves as an object.

The first part of this chapter explained the emergence of neoliberal thinking that became dominant in the late 1980s as the main ideological force that helped the landed elite maintain the land tenure system intact.

In the neoliberal ideology represented by Currie and then by Montenegro, Holmes, and Londoño, unequal land distribution did not prevent the country's economic takeoff; instead, the economy required the stimulation of demand and creation of capital markets. Although the landed elite benefited from this thinking, it relied on its political power, resources, and paramilitaries. It promoted its interests through government and state bureaucracies.

The landed elite chiefly represented by the Caribbean coastal politicians constituted a formidable lobbying bloc. "The weight of large landowners in the Colombian political system is one of the apparent reasons that Colombia has not witnessed a significant change in its agricultural property structures. Through opposition or foot-dragging, large landowners could sabotage reforms from above. They could neutralize pressure from below through outright violence—even in the National Front period, which was relatively pacific. Even in the most redistributive moments, big landowners had vital access to decision-making bodies, including the Institute for Agrarian Reform (INCORA 1961–2003) replaced by the Colombian Institute of Rural Development (INCODER) board."[71]

The Pact of Chicoral in 1972 demonstrated a correlation of forces among the bourgeois factions favoring the landowning elite. The defeat of Restrepo's land reform attempt marked the end of land reform for the next few decades. The landowning elite was supported by ministers of agriculture who hailed from the Caribbean coast departments of Atlantic, Antioquia, Bolivar, and Magdalena, reflecting the political weight of Barranquilla, Cartagena, and Santa Marta.[72] In addition to controlling the Ministry of Agriculture, the landowning elite was also represented in INCORA and then Incoder, state agencies in charge of land issues, thus affecting decision making. Its representatives in Congress (twenty-three seats in both houses, out of 280) secured for the landed elite a reliable veto power.[73]

Another telling example of the undue influence of the agribusiness elite was their relationship with President Ivan Duque. Soon after his inauguration in 2018, President Ivan Duque's second activity as president was to visit one of the significant African oil processing plants, owned by Carlos Margas, an agribusiness mogul who supported Duque's presidential campaign.[74] This sector's cozy relationship with Duque provided it with significant leverage to appoint individuals in Incoder and the Ministry of Agriculture that represented their interests.[75] This was reflected in the appointment to critical positions in the administration of two former Fedepalma employees, Andrés Castro and Myriam Martínez. Castro was appointed as director of the Land Restitution Unit and Martinez as director of Land National Agency, two pivotal organizations regarding any land policy. By controlling these two alongside the Ministry of Agriculture and Incoder, the agribusiness elite secured its class interest, ensuring the 2016 peace deal with the FARC would not touch the extensive land possessions of the landowning elite. Consequently, it would not affect the expansion of the rentier economic model in the Rural Sector.

The two main lobbying groups, Sociedad de Agricultores de Colombia (the Association of Agricultural Businesses), comprising the most powerful agribusinesses in the country, and Fedegan, which represents the cattle ranchers, have been the pillars of the reactionary coalition and articulators of their class and political interests.[76] They worked to steer the state away from policies that might infringe on land properties. To consolidate its power at the local level, Fedegan formed strategic relationships with paramilitaries, which continue to this day.

The landed elite of today include powerful new economic forces: local and foreign multinational corporations involved in the extractive sectors and agribusinesses seeking to expand their land acquisitions in new frontiers. These new players in the country's political economy were the logical outcome of its neoliberal development economic policies and institutional and legal changes. All of which stimulated the rentier/agribusiness hegemonic mode shaping the country's political economy. Despite the fragmented hegemony at the political level, the neoliberal rentier model determines the contours of capital accumulation, and resource allocation of land and labor at the economic level. In other words, the existence of fragmented political hegemony did not prevent the emergence of a neoliberal state, or the consolidation of an economy whose service sector (rentierism) grew exponentially during the last four decades, overshadowing agriculture and manufacturing. The following section sheds some light on the process and its perverse aspects: crony-rentier capitalism and its infringement on the 1991 constitutional pledge to protect food security.

Rentier-"Buddy Capitalism," Mining, and the Quest of Land

The spread of "buddy capitalism" in the biofuel sector led to increased gas and diesel prices. Oligopolies made deals to exploit the consumers without caring about exporting. "Some enterprises have become simple *maquilas* and packagers for imported commodities" (Kalmanovitz)[77] (See Figure 1.3).

Figure 1.3. Manufacturing 1965–2019. *Source*: World Bank, public domain.

Salomon Kalmanovitz, a former member of the Central Bank directorate and a prominent economist, and once a leftist, referred to the profound structural changes in Colombia's economy. In a few decades, the country's economy shifted from an agriculture- and manufacturing-based economy to services. Service economy's share was 46.5 percent in 1965 and took off in 1985 when neoliberal ideas and policies started flourishing, peaking in 1998 when it accounted for 58.9 percent of GDP; it dropped slightly (by 1.7 percent) in 2019, due to a slowdown in the economy; by then, it employed 64.5 percent of the formal labor force and was becoming the backbone of the economy. In sharp contrast, agriculture, which accounted for 27.8 percent of GDP in 1965, has fallen consistently; by 2018, it accounted for a meager 6.2 percent of GDP and employed 16.2% of the workforce. Manufacturing/industry used 19.3 percent of the labor force (see Table 1.1). As mentioned earlier, Colombia's agricultural share of GDP decreased during the 1990s by less than it did in many of the world's countries at a similar level of development.[78] In sum, the share of agriculture in GDP has been falling consistently for more than fifty years, as services have expanded exponentially and, to a much lesser extent, some manufacturing entities—the *maquilas*—have "repackaged" themselves, as Kalmonovitz termed it.[79] However, the decline of agriculture's share meant that land use witnessed significant changes. More lands became used for

Table 1.1. Distribution of Workforce by Sector

Breakdown of Economic Activity By Sector	Agriculture	Industry	Services
Employment By Sector (in % of Total Employment)	16.2	19.3	64.5
Value Added (in % of GDP)	6.3	26.7	55.7
Value Added (Annual % Change)	2.1	1.2	2.8

Source: World Bank, Latest Available Data. Because of rounding, the sum of the percentages may be smaller/greater than 100%. As cited in https://santandertrade.com/en/portal/analyse-markets/colombia/economic-outline.

speculation in cattle ranching (discussed in chapter 2) and for mining, biofuels, and agribusiness, befitting the rentier economic model.

Kalmanovitz's "rent-seekers" characterization of the ruling class is telling because they are the ones presiding over the state's economic policies. He said: "What has been missed is a state's policy that helps stimulate agricultural and industrial production. This has become a difficult task after 20 years of rentierism."[80] What Kalmanovitz is alluding to can be summed up in three main points: the dominance of a rentier economy resting on raw material extraction, biofuels, and services; the close-knit relationships among the ruling elite that created an oligopolist market structure; and finally, the country's market specialization and dependency on global markets. These three characteristics are interdependent with the country's insertion into global markets, the dismantling of import substitution industrialization (ISI), and the embrace of neoliberalism in the early 1990s,[81] to the detriment of the productive sectors in agriculture and manufacturing. Figures 2.1 and 2.4 demonstrate the precipitous decline of the productive sectors: agriculture and manufacturing since 1965. In contrast, Figures 1.1, 1.3, and 1.4 and Table 1. 1 show the structure of the evolving rentier economy, with the increase in the services sector.

Another prominent economist, Garay (2013), alongwith Rudas (2013), and Alzate (2013), pointed out that if the neoliberal economic policy and its rentier accent sought to increase the state's income the results were disappointing. They argued that tax policies related to the extractive sector were denying proceeds to the state's coffers. These authors noted that the state's exemptions, tax allowances, risk sharing, and low royalties to the

Figure 1.4. Service sector size 1965–2019. *Source*: World Bank, public domain.

extractive multinational companies were leaving only a meager $1 billion return on foreign investments.[82]

Moreover, most relevant to this book's focus is Garay's observation that the 1991 Constitution privileged the agricultural sector due to its importance in guaranteeing food security and land to the peasant population.[83] Henceforth, Garay argued, mining, in its function as a public utility, could not claim the right to predominate the agricultural sector since the 1991 Constitution gave agriculture a priority. He emphasized the need to establish a "hierarchy" of rights, privileging communities, land and subsoil rights, and the exploitation of the land's surface, land restitution, and environment,[84] and to review the mining laws to reflect such a hierarchy.

Garay contended that one of the problems of the existing mining laws lies in the normative-legal aspect legitimizing the neoliberal rentier process discussed in this chapter. A case in point is article 332 of the Constitution, which establishes that subsoil is the property of the state. Consequently, the Mining Code gives those with mining titles the authority to exploit minerals. Article 332, alongside article 13 of the Mining Code, declares that mining is a public utility of social interest, pressuring the owners of lands whose properties lie within areas subject to mining interests to sell, fearing appropriation. Such a situation created insecurity and displacement of people in targeted areas such as La Guajira, Cesar (coal extraction), or Santander, Antioquia, Tolima, Caldas, Cauca, Choco, and Cordoba (gold mining), undermining the constitutional hierarchy that privileged agricultural production and food security, which cannot be remedied by paying mining interests for the acquired lands.[85]

Mining has been one of the significant sectors upon which the neoliberal economy has rested. This sector is the most problematic due to its severe impact on the environment, water resources, and land use. The area under mining concessions increased from 1.1 million hectares in 2002 to 5.7 million in 2015, equivalent to 5 percent of the nation's territory,[86] and when we add the areas sought by mining companies (forty million out of the country's 114 million hectares), the total use of land by mining amounts to 28.5 percent of the nation's territory.[87] The extractive rentier economy is where the crux of the land use and subsoil conflict lie, particularly since the Pact of Chicoral (1972) and its exponential increase since the 1990s, which had an inflationary effect on land prices, land rents, labor, wages, and subsequently on food production. That is to say, the negative impact of mining, oil, gold, and coal extraction is not only measured by the number of hectares under use or potentially conceded to mining but also by the multiplier effects of this activity on the livelihoods and environment of the communities where it is taking place.

The neoliberal economic model that the state embraced in the mid-1980s and reinforced in the 1990s rested on three pillars, all of which threatened the country's food security and the livelihood of the almost 35 percent of its population that depends on the agricultural sector to earn a living. Among this population are the most vulnerable groups: the peasants, the Indigenous, and Afro-Colombians,[90] whose land is the target but not as much their labor, as was the case in England in Marx's time.

Conclusion

The emergence and consolidation of the neoliberal economic model and its rentier political economy had a multidimensional effect favoring its three foundational pillars, as pointed out by Kalmanovitz: extraction, services, and agribusiness. The path that led to this economy was not unilinear, nor was it coherent regarding land reform. The two instances that stood out in the story of land reform have been discussed above: first, Lopez

Pumarejo's attempt to facilitate *colonos'* access to land, which led to distortions and unintended adverse consequences that the powerful landed elite exploited; and the second, and last, attempt by Carlos Lleras to introduce some structural change into the land tenure system, whose likelihood of success became nil with the triumph of Currie market economic dogma in the 1960s and 1970s, fueling the gradual ascendance of the neoliberalism paradigm into hegemony that still governs the state's economic policy and that of its organic intelligentsia. In this way, the fate of the rural economy, its lands, environment, population, and conflicts became intimately tied to the state's chosen economic development model. The last four decades showed little rural development, as has been reflected in the prevalence of poverty, inequality, and lack of access to clean water. The country's economic growth did not translate into an improved quality of life for the millions in rural areas and their peripheries, as well as the peripheries of the cities: slums, shantytowns.

For more than three decades, the state's economic policy rested on the assumption that economic growth depends on the extraction of raw materials (such as oil, coal, and gold), cash crops (African palm oil, bananas, cut flowers, timber, sugar), and an expanding service sector. This rentier growth led to what have I coined elsewhere as "growth without development."[91] Empirical evidence shows that the dividends of the rentier model economic growth did not trickle down but essentially profited the rentier agents: the multinational extractive corporations (oil, coal, and gold); agribusinesses—especially African palm oil; land speculators seeking to establish cattle ranching; and services (such as banks, telecom, insurance, tourism, hotels).[92] In rural areas, the advancement of the rentier sector decreased the areas of food production by 22 percent from their 1990 levels, increased the prices of land, making them among the highest in Latin America and the world, and in turn increased tenant land leases and hiked prices of food (see Figure 1.1).[93] Amid the rural economic crisis of the 1980s, the coca economy emerged, creating a new dynamic in rural Colombia and at the national level. Paradoxically, this coca economy helped the family-based peasant economies while advancing the rentier mode, that is, introducing destructive elements into the peasantry's food production. Although this subject is beyond the scope and focus of this book, the following chapters tackle it when deemed necessary.

In the rentier mode, the rural population and the lands they use for their family-based economy are obstacles to its extractive drive to expand toward new areas, including frontier areas in the plains and Amazon region. The dilemma of the state is that a critical mass of the country's population—almost 32 percent—still live in rural and quasi-rural areas that depend for their livelihood on agriculture and related activities of this sector. As the rentier capital accumulation expands, it confronts a diametrically opposing logic: a fight for survival, resistance, and adaptability embodied in the rural peasant communities and families as they see their lands come under assault by the state and a cohort of multinationals, agribusinesses, cattle ranchers, large landowners, and speculators. In the following chapter, I discuss one of the rentier model's most perverse effects: cattle ranching and its most inefficient land use.

Chapter 2

Rentierism, Cattle Ranching, and Food Insecurity in Colombia

Why does Colombia, with all its fertile land, continue increasingly to import its food supply and experience alarming rates of food insecurity? This chapter analyzes the history, the conditions, and the policies that have led to the shrinking of lands dedicated to crop production while, in contrast, the allocation of fertile land to pasture and livestock has expanded exponentially. It argues that the answer lies in the land laws approved since the 1930s, coupled with the state's economic policies, which have reduced the opportunity costs of investing in this sector. Both have provided an institutional matrix that has transformed parts of the rural economy from food production to a rentier political economy spearheaded by cattle ranching. It explains why cattle ranching has become increasingly prominent since the 1950s for a segment of the dominant classes predisposed to invest in this endeavor despite the risks and low economic returns. This chapter also explains how, since the mid-1970s, this institutional matrix (laws and policies) and precarious property rights in rural areas have provided the incipient narcobourgeoisie[1] with a pivotal incentive to choose cattle ranching as one of its favorite means to launder, speculate, exercise political power, and consequently cement in place rentier capitalism.

The first section and subsection of this chapter elaborate on the concepts of rentier capitalism and the commodification of land. The second section provides a brief history of cattle ranching. The third section is subdivided into two subsections examining the institutional setting that is the set of land laws and economic policies which reduced the opportunity costs of cattle ranching and consequently fomented a rentier capital. The third section, on narcoinvestments, complements and expands on why the narcobourgeoisie invested in cattle ranching. The fourth section discusses the set of land laws introduced in the last few years that dealt with the displaced population and how these laws legitimized "land grabbing," thus consolidating the rentier political economy. The final section provides examples of the lucrative land market reflecting those investments in land in some core regions that are based on expected capital gains due to increasing prices and the expected impact on food production and security.

This chapter attempts to answer pertinent questions regarding the widespread cattle ranching phenomena nationwide, including in the studied areas of this book, chiefly in Cimitarra, Meta and Cauca. Finally, in this chapter as in this book the terms *rentier* and *speculation* are used interchangeably. Speculation is defined in this chapter as the expected returns on land which at least meet and or exceed investors' opportunity costs.

Defining and Amending "Rentier" Capitalism

In the growing complexity of capitalism in the late twentieth and early twenty-first century it is very difficult to find a pure rentier economy. Nevertheless, every economy has some elements of rent. According to Beblawi (1990), a rentier economy might be defined as one where rent situations predominate, where the economy relies on substantial external rent, and where the state is the main recipient of rents and consequently the actor distributing rents among the dominant benificiaries. Beblawi (1990), along with Anderson (1987), Yates (1996), and Karl (1997), focuses on oil-exporting nations where oil revenues (rents) dominate the political economies. This chapter, however, deals with a different type of rentier economy, and consequently it amends the use of the concept to explore specifically the problematic of agricultural land that has been transformed increasingly from productive to unproductive purposes: rents and speculation (for a discussion on the rentier oil economy in Colombia see Richani 2005). In this chapter, the definition of "rentier" is more in tune with David Ricardo (2006) and Karl Marx (1991: 944) who discussed land rent as a revenue that does not involve production and labor.[2] That is to say, investment in land is mainly based on expected rent revenues that is to say, speculation, rather than on the land's current productivity.

Notwithstanding the importance of the expected increase in land values in making investment decisions, state policies and laws have provided the institutional contours for the development of rentier rural capital, that is, by favoring large cattle ranchers and permitting them to use land properties both as a hedge against inflation and to evade taxation. This conceptualization of rentier and the institutional factors allows for a focus on the interplay among policies, agents, and agency that has evolved since the 1930s and how it contributed to speculative behavior that became salient during the 1980s.

The Commoditization of Land

Capitalism in its current phase, which many have labeled globalization, signifies the hyper connectivity of finance capital and its dominance in the process of global capital accumulation and its corresponding institutions, such as WTO, IMF, and World Bank. This process has produced important and disturbing changes in developing countries, particularly in those that have significant rural populations. Colombia belongs to this cohort of countries, with a rural population of twenty-three million that is close to 31.6 percent of its population, 60 percent of whom rely for their livelihood on agriculture (UNDP 2011). The remaining 40 percent depend on service-related employment, artisanal mining, fishing, tourism, laboring in multinational extracting corporations, and other jobs.

The core challenge to rural economies is the transformation of land into a commodity subject to the laws of circulation and exchange, which according to Marx is the practical result of the development of the capitalist mode of production: "The price of land is nothing but the capitalized and thus anticipated rent." In fact "what is paid in the purchase of land, just like the money spent on the purchase of government bonds, is only capital in itself, just as any sum of values is potential capital on the basis of the capitalist mode of production" (Marx 1991, 944, 945). What the buyer expects is rent or interest on the money he used to buy the land. Marx's description captures the nature of how land acquires value regardless of agricultural production. More than a century later, a World Bank study on Colombia zeroes in on the specific conditions that have motivated some capitalists to invest in farmland for livestock, pasture, and other uses, given that this sector was not competitive and produced low profit margins. The study concluded that

> the price of land typically exceeds the capitalized value of farm
> profits. This occurs because land value is based only partially
> on its agricultural potential. In all areas, land serves as a hedge
> against inflation. Its immobility makes it a preferred form for
> collateral in credit markets conferring additional utility when
> production risks cannot be insured, and lands close to urban
> centers offer the prospect of higher returns from real estate
> development than from farming. (Heath and Binswanger
> 1999, 28)

These characteristics discussed by Marx and later by the World Bank study
define important aspects of the political economy of the rural economy
in general, as well as how it applies to the Colombian case.

This process of transforming land into rentier capital started during
colonial times with the privatization of Indian reservations, creation of
public lands (*baldios*), and in sharecropping and land rentals. But due to
the meager time series data available one cannot construct an analytical
narrative looking at the continuities and discontinuities of this historical
process of rentier capital. Acknowledging this important shortcoming, this
chapter focuses on the twentieth century and particularly the post-1950
years when data has become more available, particularly in light of the
first agrarian census of 1960.

The strengthening trend of rentier capitalism illustrated by the
continuous dismantling of small peasant production, sharecropping, and
subsistence farming helps explain why since 1950 cattle ranching based
on large land ownerships has expanded while traditional agricultural
production declined. The only exception to this was a limited number of
commercial cash crops that increased only until the late 1970s when it
entered into crisis (Ocampo 1994, 284–85). During the period between
1950 and 1979, mainly commercial cash crops such as sugar, cotton,
bananas, cacao, sorghum, soya, African palm oil, and flowers were given
government protection (Perfetti 1994).

The crisis in cash crops was in part triggered by appreciation of the
Colombian peso, increased governmental subsidies, and protectionism in
the United States (the main market for these crops), which strengthened
a new trend that had been unfolding and became dominant in the 1990s.
Considering that less than 5 percent of the 16 percent of the territory that
is suitable for food crops is cultivated, compounded by decreasing food crop
production, it is not surprising that there has been an eightfold increase

in its food imports since the 1980s to feed the growing urban population. In contrast, livestock production has expanded dramatically. Only 13 percent of the country's territory is deemed suitable for pastureland, and 35 percent of that is utilized knowing that the productivity of livestock remains very low, about 50 or 60 percent of that achieved in Argentina and the United States, respectively (Heath and Binswanger 1998, 26). Since the 1980s, these trends in agricultural production in Colombia have led to the obvious conclusion: it is the expected or speculated land rent/price increase, and not the land's productivity, that largely motivates investment.

Cattle Ranching in Colombia's Historiography

A brief recap of some of the central strands in the extensive literature on cattle ranching and the agrarian question might help contextualize this chapter. Livestock and pasture use expanded in the nineteenth century but was limited because of the density and inhospitality of forestry and the sparsely populated urban centers. By the mid-nineteenth century, there were only 1.5 million head of cattle in the country, about 75 percent of them concentrated in five main regions: Cundinamarca, Boyacá, upper Magdalena River, upper Cauca River, and the inlands of the Caribbean Coast (Van Ausdal 2008). Since then, cattle ranching has ebbed and flowed with the changing rural political economy and the country's capitalist development and its relationship with global markets.

Most scholars studying the agrarian economy and the role of the large landowning class during the first half of the twentieth century have presented various alternative explanations for the continuity of ranching, which they assume to be at best precarious (Van Ausdal 2008). One prevalent explanation is that the decision to invest in cattle ranching is related to the "prestige" and "power "status it confers by virtue of its entrenchment in traditional values (Kalmanovitz 2003; Reyes 2009; Gómez 1987; Perez 2001). Another explanation has focused on cattle ranching as a mean of expanding and acquiring more land, which also increases political influence (Reyes 2009; Romero). Gómez (1987) and Feder (1975) argued that the control of territory and agrarian resources were the main function of cattle raising. One of the classic arguments in Colombian historiography is that in a country with a large agrarian frontier, "the monopoly of available land was the only way to control labor" (Van Ausdal 2008; Reyes 1978; Reyes 2009; McGreevey 1971). Furthermore, by dominating the peasantry, landed elites ensured that the state remained under their hegemony (Fals Borda 2002; LeGrand 1986). Van Ausdal (2008, 91) posits the profit motive without discounting the speculative aspect for cattle ranching to better explain why a segment of the dominant classes opted for such an activity, particularly between 1850 and 1950. These explanations are not mutually exclusive; in fact many are complementary, such as the nexus among land acquisition, power, prestige, and labor/peasant control and profit; they present useful pieces that help solve the puzzle. But often this literature does not accord land laws and state policies the weight they merit because they are either assumed or underplayed. This shortcoming becomes evident in explaining why narcotraffickers chose this economic activity as opposed to others and why this activity expanded exponentially during the second half of the twentieth century and increasingly since the late 1970s (see figure 2.1).

Power, control, profits, and prestige might be part of their objective, but these were made possible by laws and policies that favored large land-owners, especially cattle ranchers. More importantly, these laws contributed to lowering the opportunity costs for cattle ranchers (although not for *colonos* or poor peasants) who chose the accumulation of land as a venue by which to accumulate capital, as discussed by Marx and Ricardo. Consequently, as this chapter argues, the incentive of cattle ranchers alongside

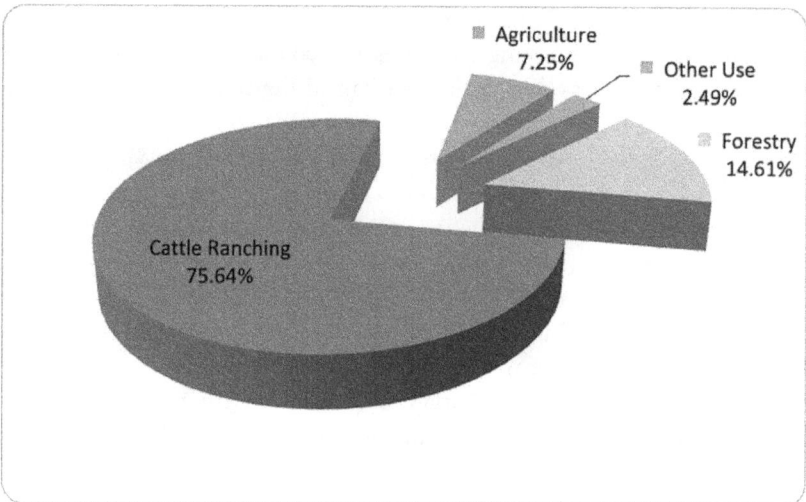

Figure 2.1. Land use. *Source*: DANE, public domain.

other owners of capital seeking lands is this: the net present value of their claims to land will most likely exceed their opportunity cost. Keep in mind Marx's and Ricardo's contention that land speculation has been associated with capitalist development since the nineteenth century, if not before. What are changing, however, are the historical context, the magnitude of speculation, the laws that facilitate or inhibit speculation, and the impact of all of these on land use (e.g., food production) and exchange value. This chapter attempts to examine and explain these changes.

The Institutional Setting

Land Laws

Chapter 1 discussed the main laws that have provided the institutional framework for the development of rentier capitalism in the countryside at the expense of millions of subsistence-reliant small peasants and *colonos*. This section does not examine all the laws and decrees related to landed property. Instead, it reviews a subset of laws that constitute the principal institutional contours of the land question and that have been critical in determining the path of rural development.

Most of the different governments that have ruled Colombia since the turn of the twentieth century have displayed an institutional bias toward large landowners given the economic structure of the country, which this sector has dominated with its pronounced overrepresentation in Congress as well as other governmental sectors, including the military (Reyes 2009; Richani 1997; Richani 2002, ch. 2; Berry 2004, 128–35; Zamosc 1986). Perhaps one exception was the short-lived attempt of the government of Lopez Pumarejo (1934–38), a banker, to promote the capitalist transformation of the rural political economy, which was characterized by backward social relations among production remnants of the earlier regimes, such as land colonization, squatting, and sharecropping, alongside inefficient *latifundios*. This was during a period of heightened peasant mobilization during which twenty thousand peasants participated in rural struggles in eighteen different areas of the country (Pearce 1990; see also LeGrand 1986).

In order to dismantle sharecropping and squatting and defuse the volatile situation, the state introduced a series of laws, starting with Law 200 of 1936, with the idea of stabilizing property relations by granting land titles after an occupation of ten years (for a background of this law see Berry 2000; LeGrand 1986). The intention was to phase out squatting (colonization) by landless peasants and eliminate sharecroppers by transforming them into either small landowners or wage workers, thus incorporating them into the orbit of capitalist relations (Kalmanovitz 2003, 351; LeGrand 1986; Ocampo 1994, 230–33). LeGrand (1986) argued that Law 200 tended to favor *colonos*/small holders, although large landowners managed to use local and regional authorities and resources to get their way.

More important for this chapter's purpose is decree 0059 of Law 200, which protected cattle ranchers' idle and/or underused large landholdings from any state intervention (Arango 1994, 131–32). Arango argues that as a consequence of this decree, alongside the state's failure to award public lands to sharecroppers and *colonos*, as Law 200 stipulated, favorable conditions were created for the expansion of cattle ranching, which was coupled with massive expulsions of *colonos* and sharecroppers (1994, 131). Another crucial element of Law 200 was the legalization of large-scale appropriation of public lands when proof of use was provided. Malagon (2008, 132) explains that what facilitated this grabbing of public lands were the easy conditions under which title might be obtained, specifically, proof of use. As a case in point, Law 200 of 1936 maintained a stipulation that had been established in 1926, which required only one cow per hectare in prime productive land, one cow for every two hectares in lands of medium quality, and one cow per three hectares in areas classified as low quality. Thus, the law not only permitted the land grab but created an incentive for cattle ranchers and other capitalists in many areas of the country to accumulate more capital in the form of land: the law reduced their opportunity costs. This in turn might have inspired a trend designed to accumulate more land for speculation rather than productive purposes.

Large landowners, particularly cattle ranchers, preyed on *colonos* who invaded and improved lands that subsequently were titled and then later bought up by large landowners. More importantly, in order that they not lose title to "unused" lands after a period of five years, as Law 200 stipulated, landowners claimed them as lands dedicated to pasture and cattle raising (Kalmanovitz 2003, 353). With little if any state oversight, large landowners cited "cattle ranching," real or fictional, as a mechanism to preserve and expand their *latifundios*, and it worked. This explains why, by 1960, only 16 percent of the cattle ranchers in Colombia owned 58 percent of the pasture lands, grazing them with herds that exceeded five hundred animals, and of those 712 ranchers owned 30 percent of the land; whereas 84 percent of the small cattle ranchers (those with fifty or fewer head of cattle) owned 16 percent of the pasture land (Van Ausdal 2008, 84).

This model became salient in the Atlantic coastal areas where *colonos* were allowed to colonize lands and gain titles only to be bought out or chased out by large landowners. The underlying logic of the process was to allow the *colonos* and sharecroppers to cultivate subsistence crops that expanded pasture growing and then facilitate the large landowners' acquisition of the same land with the additional bonus of new pasture, which the sharecroppers had sowed. In effect, Law 200 created a dialectic in which *colonos* and large landowners were united in their antagonism, yet both helped expand the frontier of capitalist development in the form of cattle ranching. Restrepo (1994, 131–32) notes that Law 200 had another interrelated consequence that is central to this chapter. It contributed to a reduction in food production and thus instigated food shortages, which led to a 73.5 percent increase in agricultural food imports between 1938 and 1939 (Restrepo 1994, 132). He attributed this decline in traditional crop production to the incentive to transform sharecropping lands into pastures. Law 200 was followed by three other laws that attempted to remedy its shortcoming in promoting capitalist development of rural areas: Law 100 of 1944, Law 135 of 1961, and Law 1a of 1968.

To safeguard landowners' property rights, Law 100 prohibited sharecroppers from planting permanent crops on the landowners' property (Ocampo 1994, 232). This law provided an additional five years to that stipulated in Law 200 for improving idle *latifundios*. This period was extended by nearly two decades, until 1961. According to Kalmanovitz, if Law 200 attempted in some respects to provide *colonos* and sharecroppers access to land, Law 100 demonstrated the state's full support for the interests of large landlords (Kalmanovitz 2003, 377). Between 1940 and 1946, the state increased its subsidies to all commercial agriculture but, most importantly, to cattle ranchers, whose subsidies were increased fivefold, while the agricultural reforms of the first Pumarejo government were reversed (Kalmanovitz 2003, 377–78; Pearce 1990, 43). Thus, law 100 reflected the power that this sector exercises over the state's rural policy.

As discussed in chapter 1, the second law was introduced by reform-minded President Alberto Lleras and was influenced by the agrarian reforms of the Cuban revolution, as well as by U.S. president John F. Kennedy's Alliance for Progress, which was designed to avert Cuba-inspired revolutionary change in the region (Diaz-Callejas 2002,

127). Law 135 distributed and titled some lands for sharecroppers, and *colonos*. It was a moderate reform attempt negotiated with large land-owners' representatives in Congress. Nonetheless, this did not ease their resistance to its implementation. If, as Hartlyn argued, the Colombian state at times showed relative autonomy in introducing policies (e.g., under Pumarejo and Lleras), business associations, with their multiple connections—including those within the two dominant political parties, Liberals and Conservatives—blocked their implementation and thwarted reform, yet succeeded in obtaining valuable state assistance (Hartlyn 1985, 121–22). Hartlyn (1985) sheds light on the role played by the SAC and the cattle ranchers in aborting the land reforms proposed by Lleras—notwithstanding the wide support that he enjoyed within other sectors of the dominant class—through their representatives on the government board established to carry out the reforms, the Instituto Colombiano de La Reforma Agraria (INCORA).[3]

Before discussing Law 1a of 1968 and its repercussions, it is important to note that in 1963, the cattle ranchers established their own business association, the Federation of Cattle Ranchers (FEDEGAN), which artic-ulated the class interest of large cattle ranchers. Prior to that, large cattle ranchers had expressed their class interests through the Association of Agriculturalist (SAC), founded in 1871, and Accion Patriotica Econom-ica Nacional (APEN), which was established by the dominant economic groups—including large cattle ranchers—to fight Pumarejo's (1934–38, 1942–44) reforms (Ocampo 1994, 231–32).

Lleras Restrepo's Law of 1968 was negotiated with the powerful bloc of congresspersons representing FEDEGAN and SAC. This law again attempted to distribute land by providing more legal instruments for the abolition of sharecropping (Diaz-Callejas 2002, 134). But the reaction of the large landowners was dramatic: they expelled thousands of sharecroppers and tenants from their *latifundios,* fearing that their work could provide them with a legal basis to claim property rights. Large landowners' resistance continued unabated until they obtained government guarantees regarding land tenure, particularly lands dedicated to cattle ranching and pasture (Diaz-Callejas 2002). They got their way after the election of the Con-servative president Misael Pastrana, who was more inclined than Carlos Lleras to abandon the quest for land reform. Pastrana, along with most of the segments of the dominant classes, felt threatened in the wake of 812 invasions of large properties motivated by the Carlos Lleras land reforms spearheaded by the ANUC (Restrepo 1994, 139; Richani 2002, 32; see also

Zamosc 1986). Consequently, Pastrana called for a meeting in Chicoral of representatives of both parties, along with business groups, to deal with the increasing radicalization of the peasantry, particularly after the emergence of the radical faction of the ANUC in Sincelejo. At this meeting, the two parties and the business groups' representatives sought to protect large landowner's possessions, and considering the peasant mobilization they wanted to make sure that these lands were classified as "productive" in order to avoid taxation and redistribution, and also to obtain favorable credits and protection (Diaz-Callejas 2002, 135). These concerns were negotiated and later formulated into Law 4a of 1973 (Diaz-Callejas 2002, 134–35; Leal 1984; Kalmanovitz 2003, 463; Pearce 1990, 122; Bagley 1979). In effect, the cattle-raising faction of the large landholding class was one of the principal winners in the Chicoral agreement. This pact, I believe, ushered in a new phase, in which the most conservative faction within the dominant classes—large landowners, led by cattle ranchers—became the backbone of a "reactionary configuration" of social and political forces that, on one hand, fomented rentier capitalism and, on the other, devised a counterinsurgency strategy based on repression, massacres, and expulsion.[4] In the 1980s and 1990s these two intertwined processes gained the crucial impetus imparted by narcotraffickers and their private armies, the paramilitaries (see Richani 2009; 2002).

These laws have produced a series of effects, both intended and unforeseen, on land tenure and the developmental path, which subsequently became institutionalized. In the coffee regions and in the Caribbean coastal areas, sharecroppers and *colonos* were the hardest hit by the measures (Ocampo 1994; Heath and Binswanger 1998). Rural employment continued to decline by 3.9 percent annually between 1970 and 1975, which Heath and Binswanger (1998) attributed to the impact of Law 1968. This decrease was not offset by a meaningful land redistribution; instead, the law had a slight impact on the concentration of land. Between 1960 and 1988, the areas occupied by small holdings of fewer than five hectares declined from 6 to 5 percent; whereas the medium-sized properties (between five and fifty hectares) increased from 24 to 26 percent, and large landholdings (fifty and more hectares) fell from 70 to 69 percent (Heath and Binswanger 1998, 27).

This change was not enough to mitigate land conflicts, and soon the concentration of land increased unabated (see section below about The Displaced and New Land Laws). Land invasions increased during the 1970s, championed by *colonos* and small peasants affecting between

1,500 and two thousand farms situated in about two-thirds of the country's departments (Heath and Binswanger 1998, 27; LeGrand 1986; Zamosc 1986; Kalmanovitz 2003).

The Colombian Institute of Land Reform (INCORA) did little to address the issue of land distribution to offset the increasing crises in the rural economy. With Law 30 of 1988 the fate of land invasions was sealed. Law 30 banned INCORA from adjudicating or redistributing lands invaded by *colonos,* in effect safeguarding the economic interests of large landowners. In 2003, INCORA was replaced by The Institute for Rural Development (INCODER), which, with only 20 percent of INCO-RA's original budget and a more diffuse mandate (not exclusively land reform), reflected not only the economic and political changes but also the desires of the "reactionary configuration" to defeat once and for all the idea of land reform. Minister of Agriculture Andres Filipe Arias, in a self-congratulating remark, reflected the spirit of the Uribe government (2002–10) when he announced the dismantling of INCORA by saying, "No more land reform" (Murrillo 2009, 29). INCODER is also criticized because one its main missions is to oversee the dismantling of the collective land titles of the Indigenous and Afro-Colombian communities in order to facilitate both foreign and local capital investment in extraction projects, as well as supporting agroindustry and land speculation (http://colombia.indymedia.org/news/2005/10/32516.php; Murrillo 2009, 25–29).

Peasants' Agency and Trade Liberalization

Ideas might be as important as structural constraints, including class interests, in shaping and influencing policies, but ideas are neither born in a vacuum nor do they fly alone. As eloquently explained by Kalmanovitz (2003, 470), economic ideologies do not prosper on their own merits, but they can prevail when members of the dominant sectors of capital who are not content with their condition discover that the bourgeoisie of other countries, who are applying a different economic model, are in fact better off than they are; when that happens, then most likely they will try to emulate that model. Consequently, he observed, in Colombia, sectors of the local bourgeoisie began listening to proponents of neoliberal economic ideology and gradually urging it upon other sectors of the dominant class and politicians, until it established its hegemony within the realm of ideas (Kalmanovitz 2003, 471). In this same spirit, two main economic ideologies or "sets of ideas" are relevant to the development of rentier capitalism.

The first is attributed to Lauchlin Currie of the World Bank, discussed in chapter 1. We have seen that his recommendations were widely translated into the state's economic policies during the 1960s and 1970s (Kalmanovitz 2003; Misas 1997), particularly in the development of agroindustry as a means of propelling the capitalist mode of production into the rural economy though the creation of economies of scale. This translated into government support for the exportation of cash crops, along with protection, tax exemptions, and credits for cattle ranchers (Kalmanovitz 2007, 141–67).

A 1998 World Bank study of Colombia's rural economy drew important conclusions. One was that implementation of Currie's 1960s recommendations had failed to result in the anticipated development for several reasons, particularly the inability of agroindustry and other sectors of the urban economy to absorb rural surplus labor. Secondly, *colonos* and small peasants proved to be more resourceful and resilient than Currie had contemplated, and they resorted to colonizing new frontiers whenever capital evicted them from their former sites (Heath and Binswanger 1998, 25–26). The arrival of marijuana in the 1970s (known as the Bonanza Marimbera) and the surge in coca production in the 1980s offered subsistence peasants another means of weathering the storm of Colombia's rentier development and subsequent trade liberalization of the 1990s.[5]

These groups depend upon the plantations for financial support for their subsistence farming by working as wage laborers, collectors, or by planting coca alongside their food crops (Richani 2002).[6] It is noteworthy that 60 percent of coca production in Colombia is in the hands of small peasants (Montoya 2005). This explains how the millions that depend on the subsistence economy are yet to "disappear" from the socioeconomic map, an important point to keep in mind that is further elaborated in the remainder of this chapter.

In addition, the 1998 World Bank study argued that Currie had failed to consider the class bias embodied in the government's policies, which were oriented toward large farmers. The study referred specifically to the pattern of public investment and trade orientation that favored livestock. Credit policies tended to discriminate against small peasants— only one-third of small peasants obtained loans—and tax policies converted agricultural land into a shelter for both income and capital gains taxation, providing incentives for holding land as a tax shelter rather than for agricultural production (Heath and Binswanger 1998, 25). This is an important incentive that has encouraged both owners of capital and high-income groups, including narcotraffickers, to use land as a commodity that embodies capital, thereby sheltering their fortunes from taxation. But more important these tax incentives, when applied against the backdrop of the Land Laws, diminished the opportunity costs for capitalists that usurp/invest in land and livestock, since the latter does not require heavily capitalized and costly mechanized farms but rather involves traditional low-cost cattle ranching.

It is no accident that the narcobourgeoisie opted to invest around 45 percent of its narcodollars obtained between 1980 and 1988 in this sector; the remaining narcodollars were invested in commerce (20 percent), construction (15 percent), services (10 percent), and recreation (10 percent) (Richani, 2002, 118).[7] The irony is that the state's economic policies and land laws offered the narcobourgeoisie an excellent incentive, which explains in part why between 1985 and the end of the 1990s it sought aggressively and violently to acquire between 4.4 million (Rocha 2000, 146) and 6 million (Comisión de Juristas 2006) hectares that were mostly dedicated to cattle ranching. These landholdings constitute between 10.7 percent and 17 percent of the total 41 million hectares dedicated to this activity. It is safe to say that by 2009 this percentage might have been much higher given the income of narcotraffickers and their past investment preference, as discussed in the section below. This in turn has cemented the process of rentier development in the rural economy.

There is yet one more finding that might explain why livestock was chosen by an important segment of the dominant classes that was not related to narcotraffickers, which is supported by the World Bank study and corroborated by more recent investigations (Machado 1994; Machado 1999; Fajardo 1994; Reyes 2009; Guigale, Lafourcade, and Luff 2003, 562). The "beef sector has been protected more than the crop sector, helping to account for its rapid expansion" (Guigale, Lafourcade, and Luff 2003, 562). Between 1980 and 1992, beef and milk absorbed 82 percent of the total support (price and other forms) that the government provided to a group of nine farm commodities (Guigale, Lafourcade, and Luff 2003, 562).

The foregoing offers a better understanding as to why land suitable for agricultural production increased between 1950 and 1986, from 2.6 to 4.6 million hectares, and then steadily decreased after 1987, to 3.9 million hectares in 1999 (Guigale, Lafourcade, and Luff 2003, 562) and 3.7 million hectares in 2004 (DANE 2004). This represents about 7.25 percent of the total agrarian land (21.5 million hectares), of which the area cultivated in nonpermanent crops such as maize, potatoes, and beans constituted only 45.95 percent, while permanent crops (coffee 740,030 hectares; plantains 407,034 hectares; African palm 243,038 hectares; sugar cane 234,870 hectares) occupied 51.30 percent (DANE 2004; see Figure 2.1 above).

Coca production witnessed a sharp increase in the 1990s, from thirty-four metric tons in 1987 to 520 metric tons in 1999, while in terms of land it encompassed ninety-three thousand hectares, which is about 3 percent of the suitable crop land (UNDOC 2000; Rocha 2000, 15).[8] Thus, by 2000 less than one-third of suitable agricultural land was used for that purpose (Guigale, Lafourcade, and Luff 2003, 562), while land dedicated to pasture rose steadily after 1950, going from 12.1 million hectares in 1950 to 17.5 million by 1970 and increasing to 20.5 million in 1978, 40.1 million in 1987 (Heath and Binswanger 1998: Ocampo 1994, 283), and reaching 41.2 million hectares in 1999 (Guigale, Lafourcade, and Luff 2003, 562; Balcazar 1994, 323).

The increasing trend might have begun before 1950, especially after the introduction of Law 200 of 1936, but, unfortunately, data compiled prior to 1950 is anecdotal and inaccurate, which make it difficult to establish a time series analysis. Keep in mind that the first agricultural census wasn't conducted until 1960. Given this important limitation, I can only hypothesize the ascending trend since the 1950s. This trend witnessed a significant increase between 1978 and 1987, when lands used for pasture more than doubled. This increase might be explained by the favorable land laws discussed above (such as Law 1a of 1968 and the Chicoral Agreement of 1972) and in part by the influx of narcotrafficking investment after the introduction of the popular variant, the "Golden Marijuana" of Santa Marta that led to the so-called Bonanza Marimbera (1974–80), which was itself followed by an even longer-lasting bonanza, of cocaine. In part, the reason is that by 1998 the narcobourgeoisie's agricultural land possession was estimated to encompass six million hectares, and assuming that all these lands became marijuana pastureland they constitute only 30 percent of the twenty million hectares added to this activity between 1978 and 1998. The remaining 70 percent are in the hands of other cattle ranchers and owners of capital who joined the frenzy.

Thereafter, the major expansion in pasture lands (1978–1987) coincided with favorable political conditions created by the reactionary configuration that made the Chicoral Agreement possible. This was also against the backdrop of the discussed land laws, capital shelters, and low-ered land tax[9] and complemented by the influx of the proceeds from the marijuana trade, followed by a significant increase in cocaine production, which started in the mid-1980s and increased in earnest in the 1990s.[10] These trends caused the expansion of pasture land to reach 75.64 percent of the total agricultural area (DANE 2004), half of which is not suitable for cattle ranching but mostly for food production (UNDP, Hechos del Callejon 2008) (See Figure 2.2).

Given this expansion in land dedicated to cattle ranching one might expect a proportionate increase in livestock. The data, however, reveal that in 1978, the total herds comprised 18,399,000 head, which increased to 20,073,000 in 1987. That is an increase of 1,674,000 head of cattle while the lands dedicated to cattle ranching increased by 20 million hectares, achieving an average of 11.9 hectares/cow. By 1995 the herd size amounted 25,551,00 decreasing to 25 million head in 2005 and further declining to 23 million head by the end of 2009 (FAO Data Base 2006; FEDEGAN 2010, Plan Estrategico de La Ganaderia Colombiana 2019).[11] This dis-proportionate increase in the ratio of cows/hectare during 1978–1987 alongside the declining trend in herds between 1995 and 2009 calls into question the reasons behind increasing the area of land assigned for this economic activity.[12] The populations of ther main livestock such as goats,

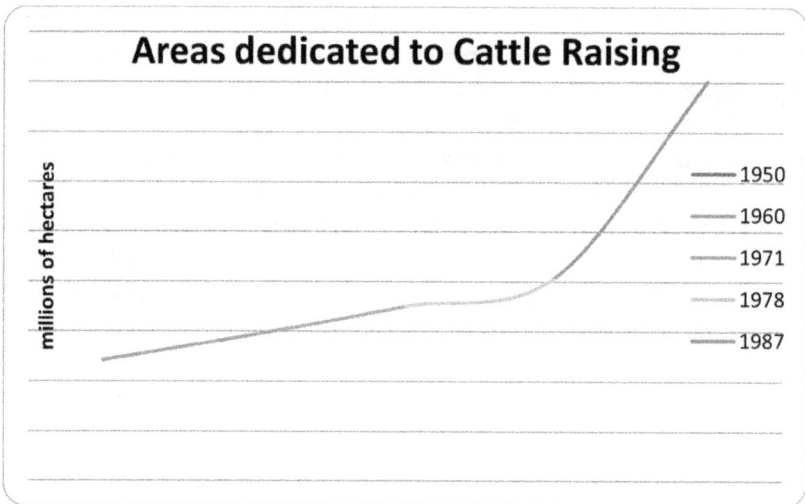

Figure 2.2. Land for cattle raising. *Source*: Data from UNDP, chart by author.

sheep, and horses slightly changed: horses increased from 2,451,000 to 2,750,000, goats increased from 965,000 to 1,200,000, while the number of sheep declined from 2,540,000 to 2,180,000 (FAO Data Base 2006). Yet, the economic contribution of cattle ranching sector does not exceed 25 percent of the total rural economy (3 percent of the national GNP), whereas food production, despite its diminishing land area, contributes 67 percent of rural income (Machado 1998, 98). FEDEGAN 2009, 4) reported a contribution of 27 percent of the rural economy for 2007.

Finally, if land value is only determined by productivity, the empirical evidence for Colombian agriculture suggests otherwise. On average, one hectare of extensive cattle ranching produces an annual net income of about three hundred thousand pesos (US$ 150); meanwhile one hectare of food crops produces between two and five million pesos—US$1,000 and US$2,500 (UNDP, Hechos del Callejon 2008, 5). What is noteworthy is that small and subsistence peasants produce 63 percent of the total food production (UNDP, Hechos del Callejon 2008).[13] This contribution by small and subsistence peasants,[14] who own plots of less than two hectares, is higher than the Latin American average for small peasants' properties of 1.8 hectares, responsible for 41 percent of the agricultural output for domestic consumption and producing at the regional level 51 percent of the maize, 77 percent of the beans, and 61 percent of the potatoes (Altieri 2009, 104).[15]

Therefore, the difference in economic return and productivity between small peasants' food production and large-scale cattle ranching validates my argument that the expansion of extensive cattle ranching post-1950 and especially since the late 1970s has not been motivated primarily by expected economic returns on such activity but rather depends upon the expected speculative rent from land, that is, land as capital. Additionally, "fringe" benefits are also associated with these types of landholdings, namely, income sheltered from taxation, subsidies from the government, and the exercise of political power. The first two benefits relate to the accumulation of capital and the last translates into influencing policymaking.

Narcoinvestment and the Rural Economy

This section and the following one attempt to bring into a sharper focus the question why land was chosen by the narcobourgeoisie as their main money-laundering mechanism. After discussing some land laws and policies that encouraged the narcobourgeoisie, along with other speculators, to invest in cattle ranching as a means to shelter their fortunes while betting on expected future rents, there is also another important factor that must be considered. That is the precariousness of rural property rights, which made it much easier for narcotraffickers to launder money by acquiring land, rather than through the financial system, urban real estate, or other businesses where the state's monitoring and anti-money laundering mechanisms became stronger during the 1990s (Thoumi 2003, 185–87). Consequently, according to Reyes (1997; 2009), narcodollars were invested in land in recently settled areas where property rights were dubious or in dispute, and where the state's regulatory machine was weak. Rocha (2000, 146) estimated that by 1998 the narcobourgeoisie had acquired 11 percent of the country's agricultural lands, with a dollar value of about $2.4 billion. This trend continued, and by 2009 one could project that the number of hectares involved might have been more than six million as a consequence of the continuous influx of narcodollars ($2 billion to $4 billion yearly), and assuming that prior investment patterns of the narcobourgeoisie remained constant (Steiner 1997; Thoumi 2003, 150). (See Table 2.1.)

The influx of narcodollars during the 1990s coincided with the trade liberalization policies of the Cèsar Gaviria administration (1990–94), which made it difficult for traditional crop producers to compete with cheaper imports. This in turn provided an additional incentive to shift from traditional crops into sectors that remained protected, such as cattle ranching or investment in agroindustries that cater to the international markets, such as African palms and cut flowers. The 1990s ushered in an increasing specialization of Colombia's economy, restructuring it to accommodate its position in the global division of labor and the increasingly dominant speculative component of its rural economy.

Economic transformation is by its very nature destabilizing, particularly in a socioeconomic and political context in the midst of armed conflict that has been exacerbated by a long history of struggle over land. This transformation process, as one might anticipate, was violent: it has been characterized by massacres, massive displacement, and resistance. This section explains what is pertinent for the consolidation of rentier capital, a process characterized by the resurgence of violence and massive displacement, which exceeded what some of these same rural areas had witnessed during La Violencia (1948–1958).[16] The earlier process resulted in the displacement of more than two million people, the appropriation

Table 2.1 Narcotraffickers' Acquisition of Lands per Department 1980–1995

DEPARTMENT	% of Municipalities with Purchase	# of Municipality with Purchase	Total # of Municipalities in Dept
Valle	85.7	36	42
Córdoba	84.6	22	26
Quindío	75.0	9	12
Risaralda	71.4	10	14
Antioquia	70.9	88	124
Magdalena	66.6	14	21
Guajira	66.6	6	9
Tolima	63.0	29	46
Caldas	56.0	14	25
Caquetá	53.0	8	15
Atlántico	52.2	12	23
Bolívar	51.4	18	35
Casanare	43.0	8	19
Meta	39.2	11	28
Cundinamarca	37.3	43	115
Cesar	33.3	8	24
Vichada	33.3	2	6
Chocó	31.5	6	19
Sucre	29.2	7	24
Guaviare	25.0	1	4
Amazonas	25.0	2	8
Putumayo	23.0	3	13
Santander	22.0	14	87
Cauca	15.8	6	38
Boyacá	13.0	16	123
Huila	10.8	4	37
Nte de Santander	7.5	3	40
Nariño	4.8	3	62
TOTAL	42%	409	1039

Source: Alejandro Reyes Posada, Guerreros Y Campesinos: El Despojo de La tierra en Colombia (Bogotá: Editorial Norma, 2009), 75.

of 393,648 land holdings, and approximately 180,000 deaths (see Table 2.2 in the following section). Berry (1998, 35) noted that in certain areas of Valle, for example, thousands of *colonos* were massacred, leaving their homesteads to urban speculators who took up cattle raising. There was a relative respite between 1958 and the 1970s, but even then, there were serious land conflicts, expulsions, and territorial invasions from which the insurgency evolved, particularly FARC, which was originally a defense group consisting of small peasants attempting to protect their acquired lands from the encroachments of large landowners and the state.

The Displaced and New Land Laws

Another set of laws dealt with lands lost by the approximately four million displaced persons, 60 percent of whom were small and subsistence farmers (COHDES 2000). The new land laws legitimized the violent dispossession of peasants and reinforced the trends toward increasing land concentration and rentier capitalism by forcefully removing people and land from subsistence and small peasant production. Most of these lands were appropriated by speculators, cattle ranchers, and the narcobourgeoisie.[17] In this vein, it is noteworthy that 67 percent of the cultivated land is planted by small and subsistence peasants and, more importantly, 90 percent of what subsistence peasants produce goes to the market, while less than 10 percent is for the peasants' actual subsistence. (UNDP, Hechos del Callejon 2008, 5).

There is no accurate estimate yet as to the magnitude of the land lost by around four million forcibly displaced persons since the 1980s. Figures oscillate between 2.6 million and 6.8 million hectares. According to the Controlaría General de La República 2.6 million hectares were lost between 2000 and 2005, (Revertir, 25). Based on current rates of displacement, Betancourt (2008) extrapolated that between 6.9 and 7.4 million hectares are needed to restitute those forcibly displaced between 2008 and 2010. These figures were derived by estimating the number of expulsions by municipality.[18] One last and more rigorous empirical study led by the economist Luis Jorge Garay presented an estimate of 5.5 million hectares that were usurped between 1998 and 2008, which constitutes 10.8 percent of the country's agricultural land (*Semana*, Sept. 22, 2010).

Although for the most part the state did not alter its inherent bias in laws that historically have favored large landowners and cattle ranchers (chiefly after the Chicoral Pact), Alvaro Uribe's administration (2002–10) reached a new level of permissiveness. The administration's legal response to this historical calamity in effect legitimized a land tenure structure that

Table 2.2. Number of Displaced and Landholdings Abandoned in Selected Departments in 1997–2007 and During "La Violencia" (1946–1966)

Department	Number of Displaced	Abandoned Hectares	Number of Displaced (1946–1966)	Number of Abandoned Landholdings (1946–1966)
Cordoba	74,784	60,851		
Sucre	82,299	14,254		
Bolívar	197,431	180,030		
Atlántico	2,865	1,785		
Magdalena	122,957	22,217		
César	116,767	74,742		
Guajira	36,700	10,120		
Antioquia	309,815	97,182	116,500	16,020
Tolima (2001–06)	79,450	N/A	224,700	54,900
Cauca (2001–06)	59,592	N/A	368,900	98,400
Putumayo* 2001–06)	78,521	N/A		
Meta* (2001–06)	74,171	98,396 declared by only 21,519 people, that is 29% of the displaced	16,800	800
Caqueta* (2001–06)	91,569	416,288		

Sources used: Reyes (2009) uses the figures of Acción Social for the number of displaced, which is less than the ones reported by CODHES. The source of 1946–1966 forceful displacement and abandoned lands is Apolinar Diaz-Callejas, Colombia Y La Reforma Agraria: Sus Documentos Fundamentales (Cartagena: Universiad de Cartagena 2002), 126.

*It is important to note that in Meta, Putumayo, and Caquetá the mass displacement may have to do with the state's offensive launched in the wake of the collapsed peace talks in 2002.

resulted from one of the most violent phases of Colombian history. Law 812 of 2003 sets the tone for a series of other measures outlined in the National Development Plan. This law and Decree 1250 stipulated that the government would subsidize land purchases if the land involved were used for the development of an agribusiness during a period of no less than five years. The law was tilted toward those with enough capital to afford the costs of creating an economy of scale favoring their agribusiness. Given the poor infrastructure conditions in the countryside, it is costly for small peasants to create an economy of scale profitable enough to offset the costs of transporting their produce to local market. Critics of the 812 Law argued that Uribe's government, along with congresspersons backed by large landowners, promulgated the law in order to enforce a model of agrarian development that undermines the subsistence peasant economy. Critics also maintain that the National Development Plan does not consider or protect the property rights of the forcibly displaced population. Instead, the plan reinforces the trend toward transforming the rural economy at the expense of food production.

Law 812 must be explored in the context of other relevant laws that in effect did not reverse but rather enhanced the ongoing "counterrevolution" in the rural economy. Law 975 and Decree 3391, passed in 2006, did not differentiate between restitution for properties lost by the peasants and compensation, but they refer to symbolic collective compensations (Comision de Juristas 2006, 41). Neither Law 812 nor Law 975 and its regulatory decree address compensating individuals who suffered from state-sponsored terrorism.

Law 1182 of 2008 was perhaps the one that most reflected the class interests of the "reactionary configuration" in Congress. This law expedited the registry of land titles by authorizing not only judges but notary publics and other personnel to perform these tasks. This provided more venues for narcotraffickers, paramilitaries, and landowners to legitimize their historic land grabbing by pressuring, threatening, or bribing notaries and public officials if judges refused to title the land. In addition, the law made it difficult for those who lost their land to challenge the appropriation of their properties, particularly when these properties were not included in the registry of lost lands and properties, as they related to displaced persons. This registry reflects an incomplete record of all displaced people and, more importantly, a large proportion of the displaced population does not hold proper title to their land.

A study revealed that the main problem confronting the displaced population relates to dubious land titles. The study reported that only "31% of the abandoned hectares have legal title to the land; 15% have legal title but the title is either lost or not available, whereas the remaining 56%

of the hectares, landownership and titles are precarious" (Comision de Juristas 2006). Law 1182 makes it easier for opportunists and speculators, particularly narcotraffickers, to capitalize on these loopholes to expand their land acquisitions (Garay 2008). Another important loophole is that a claimant must have a minimum of five years' title to his/her land. Garay (2008) argues that putting the minimum at five years ignores the fact that the largest amount of displacement and land grabbing occurred between 2001 and 2002, during which 343,698 and 392,920 people were displaced, respectively, amounting to about 28 percent of the total forcefully displaced population through March 2008. By the terms of this law, the "legitimate owners," who were forced either to sell or abandon their lands, forfeited their rights, thereby allowing new owners to lay claim to the land.

Another important shortcoming of Law 1182 is that it fails to take into consideration that many peasants pass their properties from one generation to another without bothering with public registration, because of bureaucratic hurdles and the costs of the land registration. A major proportion of land properties are formalized by verbal agreements or by signing a contract, and these types of land transfers have facilitated the usurpation of properties from poor peasants (Garay 2008). Keep in mind that more than 56 percent of the displaced have no formal registered titles and another 15 percent have lost or do not have access to their titles to register claims against usurpers.

The relationship between these land laws, the displaced, and the concentration of land property may not be linear, but an arrow of causality can be inferred. Salgado (2008) demonstrates that between 1984 and 2003 the concentration of land in the hands of large cattle ranchers increased significantly. The percentage of those holding properties of less than twenty hectares increased from 85.15 percent to 86.3 percent, whereas the total area of the properties of less than twenty hectares decreased from 14.6 to 8.8 percent. In contrast, Salgado (2008) reported that land ownership of five hundred hectares or more increased from 32.7 percent of the land to 62.6 percent. These are in the hands of 0.4 percent of the landowners. The most significant increase (18 percent) occurred between 1996 and 2003, the period during which the paramilitaries expanded their radius of operations into most parts of the national territory (See Richani 2002; Richani 2001; Richani 2007; Duncan 2006; Romero 2003). Fajardo (2002) showed a strong correlation between the increase in the value of the GINI land index and displacement. Ibanez and Querubin (2004) corroborated this by showing that between 2000 and 2002 the municipalities that witnessed an increase in forceful displacement also recorded an increase in their land GINI index. In 1984, the land GINI was 83.9, rising to 88.0 in 1996 (Machado and Suarez 1999, 11), whereas in 1970 its value was 74.0. (Benetiz 2001, 5)

The Instituto Geográfico Agustín Codazzi (IGAC) presented its assessment of the trends in land tenure and found that 94 percent of the 3,346.445 small and middle-size peasants hold titles that account for only 18.7 percent of the 12,683,640 agrarian hectares, which equals about 2,411,399 parcels of lands with extensions of fewer than fifty hectares each. By contrast 1.4 percent of landowners, roughly 48,212 individuals, own 65.4 percent of the total area of 44,260,931 hectares, consisting of 29,342 parcels with sizes that exceed two hundred hectares each. In the same vein, Reyes (2009, 367) highlights the economic gap that separates the two million small peasant owners of fewer than 1.3 million hectares, and the 2,300 owners of thirty-nine million hectares. It is plausible to claim that many of the 2,300 owners are a social class hybrid of cattle ranchers, narcobourgeois, land speculators, and to a lesser extent agroindustrialists, representing the main social class base of the reactionary configuration that staunchly resist land reform.

In the Colombian context, an individual might alternate between each of these roles; that is, one can start as a narcotrafficker and then end up as an agroindustrialist farming African palm, with another parcel for cattle ranching used for speculation and for sheltering capital gains. Cases in point, Salvatore Mancuso, a leading paramilitary figure, is a cattle rancher and owns a rice agribusiness; Cuchillo, now commanding a paramilitary force of 1,100 fighters (*El Tiempo*, Sept. 20, 2009) and other narcotraffickers, became owner of several African palm agribusinesses; Jorge 40, another paramilitary commander, owns extensive businesses, including Coolechera, the most important milk-producing company on the Caribbean coast, with more than five hundred workers and over 2,700 cattle ranchers as associates or contributors (*Semana*, Oct. 14, 2006). Jorge 40 also acquired landed properties in several departments.

The laws introduced during the past few years clearly did not mitigate or protect the interests of the dispossessed. Instead, they legitimized their losses by providing legal instruments (a requirement of five years of occupation) for the "new owners" to register their claims, and made it more difficult for the displaced to claim and prove ownership. Hence, millions of hectares might have been illegally appropriated and put to use by the narcobourgeoisie and its paramilitaries in accelerating the processes of land concentration and solidifying rentier capitalism as the dominant mode of capital accumulation in the rural political economy. Most of these lands are utilized for cattle ranching, which is one way to launder money and protect capital in the form of landholdings.[19] Moreover, this path of rentier/speculative economic "development" has been largely set forth by the land laws and policies that have taken hold since the early twentieth century and gained strength since the late 1970s.

The old as well as the new (narcobourgeoisie) cattle ranchers found in this new institutional/legal setting an incentive to invest and an opportunity to enhance their political power within the configuration of the dominant classes. This in turn provided them with even more leverage to influence policy. That process unleashed a dynamic in which class power and policymaking became mutually reinforcing, especially when this faction of large landowners contracted and sponsored private armies (paramilitaries).[20]

Lucrative Land Market–Enhancing Food Insecurity

This section reveals that the process of land grabbing did not follow a uniform pattern across time and space. While the previous sections argued that violence and intimidation were employed, this section reveals that land was also grabbed by offering high prices that made it difficult for poor peasants and even medium-sized property owners to resist, given the dire economic conditions resulting from cheaper food imports since the early 1990s, limited access to credit, global warming (el Niño), and ongoing conflict.

One of the main consequences of rentier land use is the increasing price of the land itself, which in turn offers additional incentives to shift more land from production to speculation. This section provides some evidence related to the valorization of land and how a host of entrepreneurs are increasingly seeking land deals in areas where guerrillas are present and prices are low. Then they hire paramilitaries and/or the military to secure the area, which significantly escalates prices. But in some other areas, ironically, narcotraffickers have offered exorbitant amounts of money above and beyond market prices to purchase land. Keep in mind that by buying land and registering titles narcodollars enter the "legal" circuit of capital.

Currently there are about 3,044,067 hectares enrolled in a governmental program called the Land Protection Program which prohibits selling land in conflict areas. Of these, 1,694,331 hectares were abandoned by their owners. But given the dire economic conditions of these peasants, compounded by their fear of returning to their landholdings, they sought the government's permission to sell their land.

In Oveja, Sucre, for example, about 3,000 hectares were sold in 2008, which was a 50 percent increase from the annual average rate (*El Tiempo*, Aug. 10, 2009). A few years ago, a hectare was valued at around US $300; today it is worth US $2,000 (*El Tiempo*, Aug. 10, 2009). This is a better return for a buyer than speculating in the stock market, even prior to the world financial crisis. In the high-conflict area Montes de Maria, Wálter Ahumada, the secretary of government in San Juan Nepomuceno, said that one forestry company from Medellín—Tierras de Promisión—bought circa 5,000 hectares (*El Tiempo*, Aug. 10, 2009). He explained that five years ago nobody would have bought even if the hectare was valued at one peso, whereas now this company was offered a million pesos per hectare, and the displaced peasants were willing to sell because they were afraid to return to their holdings. According to the local government, a hectare ranged in price between $50 and $100, and after the death of the Martin Caballero, commander of the FARC's 37th Front, the hectare fluctuated between $2,000 and $3,000 (*El Tiempo*, Aug. 10, 2009).

This overpriced market reached El Salado in the department of Bolivar, where in February 2000 the paramilitaries massacred one hundred civilians. Sixty-seven permits were issued to sell around 2,500 hectares between October 2008 and January 2009 (*El Tiempo*, Aug. 10, 2009; Garay 2008, 37). In Catatumbo, North Santander, more than ten thousand people were killed in the course of the conflict, mostly by the paramilitaries and the armed forces, who displaced one hundred thousand people in all. Similar land markets prices prevailed there as well.

Since the 1980s, in Meta, with an area of 5,406,601 hectares of which only about 381,798 (7.06 percent) are under cultivation, with the remaining 4,337,291 (80.2 percent) utilized for cattle raising and pasture (Reyes 2009,271), Victor Carranza, an emerald baron with close links to the paramilitaries, in league with notorious narcotraffickers such as Gonzalo Rodriguez Gacha purchased areas that are suitable for cattle raising, paying prices well above the going market rate. This constitutes a part of their money laundering operation. In 1997, Reyes (2009, 265) noted, emerald entrepreneurs and narcotraffickers bought land in the municipalities of Villavicencio, Acacias, Castilla la Nueva, Cumaral, and Restrepo among others. These are illustrative examples of a growing trend that encompasses most of the country, especially noteworthy in Antioquia, Guajira, Cordoba, and Bolivar. Thus, commoditization of land continues. One of the most notable features of the buyers is that they are front companies for money-laundering schemes based primarily in Antioquia (*El Tiempo*, Aug. 10, 2009).

These examples of land valorization in a context of perpetual violence and laws favoring large landowners—chiefly large cattle ranchers—suggest that the forces promoting displacement[21] are likely to prey on the weakening subsistence and small peasant economy, thereby further exacerbating food shortages. Keeping in mind that small and subsistence peasants produce 63 percent of the country's total food production (UNDP, Hechos del Callejon 2008), it is evident that if current displacement and rentier patterns persist fewer people and less land will be dedicated to food production, and consequently food production will continue its decline, as shown in the next section. As established in this chapter, since the 1980s displacement and rentier economic "development" have become two intertwined processes underpinned by violence.

LAND PRICES AND FOOD PRODUCTION

The increasing prices of land distort the allocation of resources and affect food production, making land rents in Colombia among the highest in Latin America and consequently reducing the country's competiveness (see Table 2.3). Garay (2004, 49) explains that "in Colombia land far from being a factor of production is used for capital accumulation which generates "extra-rents" which affects the competitiveness of the agrarian sector." In this chapter these "extra-rents" are identified as "rentier," because investments are in part to launder money (in the case of narcotraffickers), shelter capital gains from taxation (for large cattle ranchers and other capitalists), and all converge on the common expectation of increased land prices (as discussed by Marx and Ricardo, i.e., as a rentier motivation).

The speculative behavior (i.e., their expected valorization of land value) of owners of capital has grave economic consequences on food production. A case in point is rice, which illustrates some of the core arguments of this chapter. Garay (2004) and Fajardo (2008) note that the price/hectare of rice production in Colombia reached $202/hectare in 1999 while in Ecuador (1995) it was $131; Uruguay (1999) $78; Brazil (1999) $157; and Argentina (1999) $73.[22] According to both authors this land cost is considerably above the regional average (Table 2.3). And

Table 2.3. Costs of Land Rent/Hectare of Rice
Production (1999) in U.S. Dollars*

Colombia	202
Ecuador	131 (year 1995)
Uruguay	78
Brazil	157
Argentina	73
USA**	34

Sources: Garay (2004) and Fajardo (2008).

*exchange rate = 1,816 pesos/dollar

**This is estimated as opportunity cost of production/hectare

more important, the overall land price—ground rent—in Colombia is also considerably high, averaging 15 percent of the production costs of sugar and tomato de Arbol, soya, and other food crops.

One explanation is that since the mid-1980s narcotraffickers bought significant amounts of property in a great number of municipalities, including those containing rice production (see Table 2.1 above). This was the case in Espinal, one of the main rice-producing municipalities in the department of Tolima (Reyes 2009). It is notable that Tolima is the eighth most favorite location for narcotraffickers' investments (Table 2.2) and is where 27 percent of the nation's rice is produced, the highest proportion in the country (FAO 2009). As a consequence of narcobourgeoisie investments alongside others, the cost of land (ground rent) increased to 30 percent of the total cost of production, which, according to Garay (2004, 49), is extremely high by both regional and world standards. Since the mid-1980s, it's worth mentioning, the mafioso and emerald baron Victor Carranza has also bought lands in the agroindustrial region of Tolima, which in turn contributed to this increase in land prices and rents (*Panorama Actual del Tolima* 2002, 224–27).

Keep in mind that 51 percent of the rice growers are renters and are affected by the increasing costs of land rent (FAO 2009). Now consider that the overall cost of land is high in Colombia, which increases significantly the costs of production—including dairy products and meat, which affect mainly small producers with small landholdings. This is mainly attributed to the unrelenting trend in the concentration of land property, leading to the formation of a landed oligopoly, economic dislocations, and land market inelasticity. This in turn inflates land prices and rents and diminishes incentives for production (See Machado and Suarez 1999, 151–56). This in part explains why the amount of rice harvested in this area has declined. It mirrors a decline in most harvest areas and consequently in food production in other regions, such as: soya –14.0 percent; wheat –12.5 percent; rice (overall) –4.1 percent; sorgo –14,0 percent (Fajardo 2008, 29). It represents a net loss of food harvest lands to large cattle ranching, as Fajardo (2008) pointed out. According to Montoya (2005), one million hectares of food-producing land have been predominantly transformed into pastureland for cattle ranchers in the last few years.

Concluding Remarks

Since the 1950s, the zero-sum game contested between rentier capital—manifested in cattle ranching—and food production has increasingly tilted in favor of the first. During the 1950–1987 period agricultural crops enjoyed tariff protections that stimulated an expansion of land under cultivation. But since 1987 the amount of land used for food crops has undergone a significant decline. Many causes are offered to explain this continuous decline exacerbated in the 1990s, including: the liberalization of the economy, oil discoveries and production (see Kalmonovitz and Lopez 2007, 145–46), the increasing influx of narcodollars. Taken together, these factors contributed to an increase in commodity prices, including land, alongside an appreciation of the peso. This in turn offered a comparative advantage to land speculators and rentier capitalism.

This rentier trend within the cattle ranching economy ebbed and flowed with the oscillations of land laws, which swung between land reform (championed by Pumarejo, and Carlos Lleras) and conservatism (led by Pastrana and Turbay [1978–82]). The first two attempted to advance agrarian capitalism, and the latter protected the interests of large landowners such as cattle ranchers. Conservatism and "the reactionary configuration" prevailed in Chicoral 1972, with the reinforcement of both the provisions of Land Law 200 of 1936 and the subsequent laws protecting cattle ranchers under used lands. Land Laws—including those introduced after 2002—alongside low land tax policies diminished considerably the opportunity costs to those capitalists—including cattle ranchers, entrepreneurs, and the narcobourgeoisie—who invested in land. For these landowners their opportunity cost of using their land today is the higher rent price or profit that can be gained tomorrow. Consequently, more land is kept for speculation and is underused and/or withheld altogether from food production. This explains, for example, the disproportionate increase in the ratio of 11.9 hectares/cow recorded between 1978 and 1987 alongside the decreasing investment in livestock manifested in the declining number of herds between 1995 and 2009.

This chapter demonstrates that the role of the narcobourgeoisie only complemented and reinforced a trend that had started decades before their emergence in the 1970s. This sector of capital might have accumulated circa twelve million hectares of agricultural lands,[23] or about 30 percent of the forty-one million hectares currently dedicated to cattle ranching. This is a significant percentage, but there is also the remaining 70 percent to consider, located in the hands of cattle ranchers that realized that their opportunity costs are measured against what they expect in rents and/or the price of land. Combined, these forces are among the major players shaping the rural rentier political economy.

However, I think this rentier trend suffers also from an inherent contradiction between the high concentration of property and the inelasticity of land markets. For instance, in 1984 landholdings greater than five hundred hectares were owned by 0.5 percent of landowners comprising 32.7 percent of agricultural land, while in 2001, 0.4 percent of landlords expanded their acquisitions to 61.2 percent of agricultural land, most of it occupied by extensive cattle ranching (Fajardo 2008, 33). This concentration created a monopoly in land markets, increasing prices and rents as discussed and allowing large owners to distort market forces. An FAO (1998, 31) study, for example, shows that large landowners prefer to sell to wealthy urban dwellers rather than break up their properties, due to higher profit margins. According to this study, large landowners make improvements, such as luxurious fences and houses, that can increase the value of land twofold. These phenomena, obviously, would neither improve the country's food security nor produce sustainable development, but the equally important question is not when but for how long this contradiction between land concentration and the inelastic land market might be expected to maintain the ratio between low opportunity costs and high expected gains. The next chapters focus on the impact of the rentier economy on the peasants' reserves, the Indigenous and Afro-Colombian communities, the weakest ranks in the socioeconomic political hierarchy.

Chapter 3

Peasant Reserves' Adaptability, Resistance, Subsumption, and War Rentierism

Thus, capital cannot accumulate without the aid of non-capitalist organizations, nor, on the other hand, it can tolerate their continued existence side by side with itself

—Rosa Luxemburg

Capitalism in Colombia, alongside many other Global South countries, has become dependent on extracting raw material, cash crops, and services. That is to say their economies have become predominantly rentier-based after abandoning import-substitution industrialization and agriculture. As discussed in chapter 2, rentier economies and their laws of capital accumulation have created a shift in the rural economy from one based on food production to one geared to satisfy global demand for commodities such as biofuels, ethanol, African palm oil, and crops for animal feed. In Colombia, the forces of rentier capital boosted by narcodollars created an unprecedented wave of massive violent displacement with the objective of land grabbing. Between 1982 and 2013, about six million Colombians were forced off their land and became internally displaced persons (IDPs), which ranked Colombia second worldwide after Syria (2012–19) in this category, followed by Nigeria, the Democratic Republic of Congo, and Sudan. In 2013, these six countries recorded 63 percent of 33.3 million IDPs worldwide.[1]

To date, we do not have a historical account that classifies and differentiates the specific causes of the six million Colombian IDPs' forced displacement. Nevertheless, what is relevant to this book is the amount of land that has changed hands due to such exodus: eight million hectares in the past fifteen years, representing 17 percent of the agricultural land of Colombia.[2] A host of private armies, working at the behest of large landowners, narcobourgeoisie, cattle ranchers, agribusinesses, speculators, multinational corporations, and the state, have been deployed to force peasants off their land. I characterize this forced and violent dispossession phase as neoliberal "war rentierism," a war against peasants, forcing them out of their economically strategic lands to foment a rentier model of capitalism that rests on three pillars: extracting raw materials, land speculation, and export-oriented agribusiness. Since the 1990s, this war has prevailed, particularly after 1997 when United Self Defense (AUC), an umbrella organization, was founded and sponsored by the actors mentioned above.[3]

The tumultuous period that followed La Violencia (1948–1958) and the failure of the last attempt at land reform, led by President Lleras Restrepo (1966–1970), ushered in the triumph of Currie's view of capitalism, setting the stage for the "neoliberal war rentierism" (see chapter 1). Currie's theory was further consolidated by the neoliberalism of the late 1980s and 1990s. The twin ideas of establishing land markets alongside capitalist agribusiness development in rural areas were the main pillars of what had become the ruling rentier economic paradigm. This chapter poses the overarching question, How does the creation of peasant reserves fit within this hegemonic rentier capitalist mode? It examines the struggles of two communities: the peasant reserves in Pato-Balsillas in the department of Caquetá in the south, and in the Plain of Cimitarra. It describes how these communities are coping with the challenges of capitalist subsumption and illustrates the two types of colonization processes that have characterized Colombia's history since the eighteenth century. One is the internal process of colonization, employed in the "inner frontier" of the "Andes region," the plains and the Caribbean shores, as Fajardo (2012) has explained. Cimitarra, in the Middle Magdalena, lies in the inner frontier. By contrast, the other, "outer frontier" colonization process, that is, the expansion away from the Andes, ranges toward the Amazon and Orinoquian regions represented by Balsillas.

This chapter is divided into three main sections. The first presents a brief history of the peasants' struggle since colonial times to access land and establish autonomy vis-à-vis the process of capitalist subsumption. This brief historical account aims to identify the dialectic between the peasants' struggle for autonomy and their dependency on the colonial hacienda system and its mutations in the postcolonial state. The unfolding of this dialectic process between autonomy and dependency is discussed in section two leading up to Law 160 of 1994, which legally sanctioned the creation of peasant reserves. This section also sheds light on the agencies that collaborated in creating the peasant reserves in Balsillas and Cimitarra, defining the peasants and squatters' (hereafter referred to as *colonos*) struggle in drawing the boundaries of their geographic areas. These two peasant reserves, and four others, were created in areas where the *colonos* have succeeded in establishing their colonies and have managed to retain some control since the 1950s.[4] These reserves may be considered part of the "geography of conflict" determined by the struggle of the *colonos* to access land, a phenomenon characterizing rural areas in the Global South.[5] The third and last section discusses the prospects regarding the reserves' expansions and subsistence.

Methodology and Research Questions

Field trips were carried out in 2018 and 2019 to Cimitarra (2018) and Balsillas (2019). Thirty unstructured interviews with open-ended questions were conducted, allowing the interviewees to explain their personal experiences and concerns related to each reserve's history, inner dynamics, challenges, and governance. The interviews have four goals designed to evaluate the adaptability and resistance of the reserves to the encroachment of capital subsumption, as it has been carried out by actors such as multinational corporations, agribusinesses, and credit-granting financial institutions: (1) to examine how the peasants articulate their identity and assess their relationship with peasant economies outside the reserves; (2) to explicate their relationship with multinational corporations and agribusinesses operating near their areas; (3) to identify coping strategies for dealing with market forces over which they have little control, such as land prices, speculation, costs of fertilization, herbicides, and wages; (4) to assess the strengths and weaknesses of the reserves' governance bodies, and to investigate for signs of fatigue, desertion, and financial stress.

Most of these goals were accomplished, and the findings are discussed in the following sections. The identities of the interviewed individuals have been kept confidential unless the interviewee was an official and granted permission to cite their name. The book's appendix provides further information about the methodology of the oral interviews.

Peasants, Growth, and Uneven Development

The literature regarding the peasant economies is extensive, incorporating studies within all fields in the social sciences, as was briefly discussed in the first chapter. This subsection discusses an aspect relevant to this book, situating it within this myriad of international literature by examining the shiftings and mixtures of collective communal land ownership and individual family holdings during early industrial capitalism and their uneasy coexistence and dialectic. Many social scientists have dismissed the unilinear modernization thesis of development from ancient tribal territory through clan holdings to individual ownership.[6] Peasants' land ownership became more pronounced in the nineteenth century in Western European countries. Evans (1956), for instance, contends that before the nineteenth century private land ownership was not part of peasant societies.[7] Engels (1972), in his study of the peasant economies in Germany, considered the pressure of population on land resources and the lack of sufficient lands to support shifting cultivation, which generated conflict but did not result in privatizing all land. Instead, meadows and arable lands were reserved as single family holdings, while pasture areas and bodies of water remained common.[8] This division between private and common land ownership that characterized parts of Europe's rural areas in the nineteenth century has survived into the twenty-first century.

More importantly, as economists and Nobel Prize winners Abhijit Banerjee and Esther Duflo have argued, mainstream economists have a clear bias toward private property.[9] This is not surprising, given that the dominant paradigm in development economics is based on the assumption that securing property rights is essential for "growth and prosperity," forming an integral part of the Weberian edifice of the "modern" capitalist state.[10] Banerjee and Duflo questioned the validity of this assumption and its ideological underpinning, particularly the notion that this type of growth had benefited the majority of the global population. They wrote, "blinkered economics told us trade is good for everyone. And faster growth is everywhere. It is just a matter of trying harder and worth all the pain it might take. Blind economics missed the explosion in inequality all over the world, the increasing fragmentation that came with it, and the impending environmental disaster, delaying action, perhaps irrevocably."[11]Pointing out the problem with the notion of unqualified "growth," Banerjee and Duflo wrote, "When the benefits of economic growth are captured by a small elite, growth can be a recipe for a social disaster (like the one we are currently experiencing). We argued before that we should be wary of any policy sold in the name of growth; it is likely to be bogus. Perhaps we should be even more scared if we think that such a policy might work because growth will benefit only the happy few."[12] I will add to this critical view of growth two analytical factors that are important to the theoretical framework of this chapter, as underscored by Mandel, Novack, and Amin. First, capitalist development is not a homogenizing process; it creates uneven development within and between countries.[13] Novack argues that capitalism creates faster or slower growth, imparts varying rates and extents of growth to different people, different branches of the economy, social institutions, and fields of culture. These differentiations precipitated by capitalist growth represent the "law of uneven development."[14] Second, that any homogenizing process is compounded by the position of the country/region (urban-rural) in the global division of labor.

This chapter, like the next two, follows the unevenness and distortion of capitalist development in Colombia, as evidenced by the existence of different dynamically interacting and interdependent modes of production, discussed in the introduction of this book: the simple commodity of production represented by the family-based subsistence economy mode of the peasant reserves, the communal properties held by the Afro-descendant and Indigenous communities, and finally the agribusiness-rentier mode that is subsuming the former three. This chapter tackles the peasant reserves, analyzing family-based subsistence farming and its relationship with the capitalist market. Most of the reserves' population is made up of poor, landless *colonos* that engage with the market in order to sustain their subsistence economy by selling their excess milk, meat, cacao, yuca. The meager sustenance provided by the subsistence economy is their principal means of resisting subsumption within capitalism and avoiding their own proletarianization (i.e., the commodification of their labor power) and dispossession of their means of production, including their land.

Historical Background

Peasant Struggles and Laying the Foundation for Peasant Colonies

Darío Fajardo (2019)[15] contends that the historical precursors of the peasant reserves might be found in the colonial period, when blacks, Indians, army deserters, and landless peasants escaped the Spanish forced labor regimes, slavery, and brutality to establish their own communities, which they coined as *rochelas*. During the nineteenth century, *rochelas* became refuge areas and continued as such into the twentieth. Fajardo noted that the *rochelas*, alongside *palenques cimarrones* created by blacks escaping slavery, occupied areas on the peripheries of the colonialist-controlled areas bordering the haciendas, to enable them to secure labor. This goes to the heart of this investigation: the working of the subsumption process. Since the nineteenth century, if not before, a dominant mode of production drew on other modes (i.e., free labor) to obtain the labor power of those that had escaped slavery. For the sake of this research, it is noteworthy that the process of subsumption predates the rentier mode. The haciendas needed labor to keep tilling the soil and maintaining the estates, labor that was available in the *rochelas*. This division of labor between two economic systems (hacienda and free labor) in the eighteenth and nineteenth centuries laid the foundation for the new political economy promoted by the postcolonial state with the emergence of agribusinesses based on coffee, tobacco, sugar, and cattle ranching.

By the early twentieth century, Colombia's economy witnessed significant changes triggered by several factors, including the expansion of coffee production due to increased global demand, which added pressure to develop roads, infrastructure, and ports to facilitate exportation. This development was made possible by credits that the government secured from foreign banks. The expansion of coffee exports and growth of the country's infrastructure in their turn put pressure on the labor market. This pressure intensified with industrialization, which was encouraged by increased access to credit, the expansion of internal markets facilitated by new roads, and exports during this same period.[16] Combined, these factors contributed to the increasing demand for access to the "surplus labor" in rural areas. However, this labor was tied to the hacienda system, which became an obstacle to capitalist development.[17] Coffee haciendas and other agribusinesses increased their worker's wages by 30 percent to mitigate labor migration to urban areas.[18] But this did not stop the migration.

Salomon Kalmanovitz (1994) describes Colombia's rural political economy in the 1920s. He identifies a rural social system consisting of large haciendas, medium-sized property owners, peasants, small family-based farms, and a floating population of landless squatters seeking access to land. Kalmanovitz explains that "in the large haciendas of Cundinamarca, Boyacá, Tolima, Huila, Valle, Valle del Cauca, the production was chiefly performed by tenants (permanent or aggregated) who paid rents for their lots, which they used for producing food for their subsistence while laboring other functions in the hacienda." Kalmanovitz calculated that for their labor the renters received 30 percent less than the wage paid to seasonal workers. The haciendas concentrated on cattle ranching, cereals, sugar, and rice cultivation for exports. At the same time, coffee production combined the hacienda system and the small coffee producers.[19] Kalmanovitz argues that alongside the hacienda system, the peasant economy of small producers was concentrated in lands of lesser value than the ones occupied by the large haciendas yet whose production satisfied the cities with their basic food needs.[20] It is important to keep in mind that the small-family-based peasant has remained a significant provider of the cities' food needs up until this writing.[21] In the 1920s, the peasantry was class-differentiated into three main social groups: small-family-based, middle-class peasants with better fertile lands and easier access to the cities than the poor, and the *hacendados* (*latifundios*: large landowners) who dedicated their land use to cattle ranching, sugar cane, cereals, and rice.[22]

The haciendas decreased in size over time as they became divided among family members, which had no significant effect on the concentration of land ownership nor on improving access to the land for poor and landless peasants, *colonos*. Consequently, in the 1920s, Colombia witnessed an intensified struggle by *colonos* to acquire land, culminating in the emergence of peasant colonies. The peasants' pressing demands and the creation of peasant colonies led to a state policy of granting public lands to organized peasant groups in leagues. Law 47 of 1926 and its regulatory laws 839 and 1110 of 1928 laid the legal foundation for establishing the peasant colonies (*colonias campesinas*), by providing them with legal protection. Despite the state's conceding to the peasants, its overall policy remained committed to the old hacienda system due to the heavy representation of the large landowning class in congress, government, and both dominant political parties, Liberal and Conservative.[23] Peasant colonies were created in different parts of the country, and with their creation, social struggles intensified. Peasant-based organizations emerged during the period culminating in 1928, with the foundingof the Agrarian National Party, led by Erasmo Valencia, the National Union of Revolutionary Left, led by Jorge Eliécer Gaitán, and the Socialist Revolutionary Party. From this latter, the Communist Party emerged.[24] Peasant leagues were created in Tolima, North of the Valle, Santander, North Santander, and Bolivar.[25]

THE GREAT DEPRESSION OF 1929–1932 AND RE-PEASANTIZATION

In 1929, the Global Depression changed Colombia's economic landscape.[26] It brought a sudden decrease in economic growth to an average of 1.6 percent from an average of 3.6 percent before 1929.[27] The demand for coffee plummeted, affecting the price of coffee and depressing wages in rural areas by 50 to 60 percent. Previously approved credits were canceled and food prices in cities increased by 100 percent.[28] Workers hired to work in infrastructure projects lost their jobs, which increased the levels of unemployment in the cities. But one of the notable aspects of the Depression was the state policy adopted to satisfy the food needs of the cities considering the amount of decreasing imports, which was to encourage unemployed workers to return to rural areas, thus incentivizing the colonization of public lands. The Liberal government of Enrique Olaya Herrera (1930–34) offered to pay workers' train fare. In Bogotá alone, 1,700 workers took advantage of the government's offer, as was the case in other cities.[29] What was noted from this plan of re-peasantization of urban workers was that those who returned to the countryside empowered by their urban experience, better wages, and exposure to unions and leftist ideology started to resist the harsh working conditions the hacienda owners (*haciendados*) wanted to impose. The *haciendados*, pressed by the economic crisis, tried to pay lower wages and extract more labor. Contrary to what the government expected from its re-peasantization plan, this led to more conflict in rural areas and did not mitigate the urban crisis.[30]

Among the main consequences of the Great Depression in Colombia were the expansion of both frontiers (one pushing toward Amazonia and the other fostering internal colonization near urban areas) and the consolidation of a trend among the returnees to become independent family-based peasant producers rather than rural proletariat.[31] These changes aggravated the class conflict between the large *haciendados* who owned most of the land and the squatters who sought to protect their acquisitions of public lands. LeGrand contends that the intensification of land conflicts in the 1930s was precipitated by the Depression and the lack of progress in solving the land issue.[32]

In the 1930s, peasants succeeded in establishing colonies with legal protection (Law 47 of 1926 and laws 839 and 1110 of 1928) when they organized into leagues. Thus, the laws incentivized *colonos* to organize leagues to facilitate access to public lands. Between 1930 and 1935, for example, 567 peasant leagues and unions were formally registered.[33] Mondragon

(2002), LeGrand (1998; 2016), Richani (2002; 2018), and Munera (1998) concur that the 1930s was a decade of a growing level of organization, articulation, and activism by the peasants, which led to the occupation of large landowners' lands. In 1931, Jorge Eliécer Gaitán presented a land reform. He called for abolishing the *latifundios* (large landholdings) without compensation and distributing the land to the peasants' cooperatives supported by the state. The land reform proposal included the distribution to landless squatters of land free of charge to those who had cultivated their lots for five consecutive years without landlord intervention. Gaitan's project included a one thousand hectares' maximum limitation on land ownership according to their regional locations and also called for a general review of rural land ownership. Law 200 of 1936 incorporated most of Gaitan's project with the notable exception of the one thousand hectares' limit, which was vehemently opposed by the landed elite.

THE "INDEPENDENT REPUBLICS" BETWEEN RIGHT-WING SLOGANS AND PEASANTS' RADICALIZATION

Liberal Party and pro–land reform leader, Jorge Eliécer Gaitan, was assassinated in 1948, triggering a partisan-based civil war between the two parties founded after independence. This war, named "La Violencia" by historiographers, led to the killings of more than two hundred thousand people, which amounted to 1.6 percent of the total population (12.6 million in 1958) and displaced another million people, 10 percent of the population.[34] As a result, two million hectares (11 percent of the agrarian frontier in that period) of lands were appropriated illegally.[35] This phase of the country's turbulent history did not end the peasant colonies or their organizations and radicalization. It led the thousands of displaced to seek lands in frontiers areas in peripheral departments such as Meta, Guaviare, Putumayo, and Caquetá. In the absence of state protection, the colonies established defense leagues for protection against conservative forces. Armed peasant leagues sprouted in various areas, including Viota, Marquetalia, El Pato, Rio Chiquito, La Troja, Guayabero, Natagaima, and Purificacion.[36] The peasant reserves came about against the historical background of *rochelas, cimarrones,* and leagues. These armed peasant leagues were defensive and supported by the Communist Party and radicalized Liberal partisans who had not surrendered their weapons during the amnesty of Rojas Pinilla. The reasons behind their decision not to give up their weapons were twofold. The peasants had little confidence in the state's intentions, and second, they wanted to retain their weapons for self-defense. Given this radicalized peasant stance, the right-wing forces championed by Conservative Party leader Alvaro Gomez Hurtado[37] launched a vigorous political campaign against the peasant leagues in the 1960s, which culminated on May 27, 1964, in the infamous military attack against Marquetalia's peasant league in the department of Tolima with the support of the U.S. military.[38] This attack was a watershed event that marked the beginning of the FARC insurgency that waged war against the state between 1964 and 2016, in the second-longest insurgency war in the world, after Myanmar's. The experiences of the "independent republics" had left their marks, upon which the peasant reserves were constructed three decades later. It is important to note that Hurtado's son called the peasant reserves the "independent republics," inviting the violence of the death squads and state agents, who perceived them as the antithesis of the landed elite and the neoliberal rentier mode.[39]

The 1970s witnessed two critical developments that ended the path to land reform. One was the land reform attempted by President Lleras Restrepo that sparked a grassroots peasant movement led by the National Association of Peasant Users (ANUC), who championed 316 occupations of private lands in thirteen departments, with the participation of sixteen thousand families during February 1971. This massive movement forced some landowners to sell their properties to INCORA. The landed elite and other sectors of the dominant class, alarmed by the rising radical specters of such grassroots movement, decided to close ranks in a pact wherein the state committed once and for all to repudiate redistributive land reform. This was the essence of the 1972 Pact of Chicoral, discussed in chapters 1 and 2. Consistent with Currie's "Four Strategies" for rural capitalist development, the pact reaffirmed the state's commitment to creating a land market and expanding the agricultural frontier, instead of land reform. This economic policy laid the foundations for the neoliberal thinking that evolved in the late 1980s and has remained in force up to this writing.

One can conclude that since the mid-nineteenth century, the state's economic policies have been central to the skewed distribution of land properties. It started with the state selling or granting public lands to wealthy individuals as public bonds to extract income to service its high debts incurred during the war of independence. At the same time, it denied access to the predominant majority of people. Consequently, the peasant population had limited options, one of them colonizing frontier lands either in the country's interior or on the country's border-region frontiers. In the 1930s, the land struggle and squatting intensified, as LeGrand (1988) explains, but again, the state failed to solve the core issue: land redistribution. The state unwittingly or wittingly encouraged colonialization of public land as a mechanism through which millions might escape political repression and economic violence.

Consequently, colonization became a "safety valve" to mitigate class conflict and rural unrest, as Fajardo (2012) contends.[40] Fajardo (2018) also pointed out a critical component: the colonized frontiers became reservoirs for exploiting natural resources. More critically, colonizing new territories put more pressure on the state to provide these outpost frontiers (internal or outbound) with basic services such as mail delivery, roads, electricity, education, public health, credit, and technical help, which in turn expanded the state's reach and authority.

It is puzzling that, on the one hand, the state acknowledged and legalized the peasants and the Indigenous reserves as well as the Afro-descendant communal lands yet, on the other, remained steadfastly committed to the rentier model that threatens their very existence. The state attempted to mitigate land conflicts and the coca growers' mobilizations of the 1970s and 1980s by encouraging colonization of public lands to avoid the thorny issue of land distribution. The state's policy, wittingly or unwittingly, drove the expansion of the agricultural frontier and, simultaneously, it facilitated the expansion of extraction, accumulation, and rentierism.

THE PREAMBLE TO LAW 160 OF 1994 THAT CREATED THE PEASANT RESERVES

The signing of a peace accord in 1990 with the M-19, an insurgent group that emerged in the wake of the electoral fraud that denied Rojas Pinilla from winning the presidency in 1970, ushered in the process of democratization of the rigid, exclusive political system that had been cemented in place during the National Front experience (1958–1974). In this new environment, the idea of creating peasant reserves prospered by allowing its incorporation into Law 160 of 1994.[41] This idea originated in the peasant organizations themselves, including ANUC, insurgents, and other progressive forces embraced by intellectuals such as Alfredo Molano, a prominent progressive sociologist, along with Dario Fajardo, a leading expert on the agrarian question, as well as Hector Mondragon and Manuel Ramos Bermudez. The concept of peasant reserves also won the support of many others, including the then-minister of agriculture Jose Antonio Ocampo, a leading neoliberal economist, and from peasant movements, the National Council of Agrarian Reform, Incora's chief, and from an emissary of the Executive Committee Fund of Peasant Capacity Building and Organization. The alignment between those actors and the then-prevailing political conditions made the peasant reserves a normative reality. The challenge then became how to translate the idea into practice.

One might ask why the "reactionary coalition," which included participants of the 1972 Pact of Chicoral such as cattle ranchers, alongside new owners of large cut-flowers businesses and banana plantations, the narcobourgeoisie, and the African palm oil agribusiness, allowed the passage of a law that permitted the creation of peasant reserves. The "reactionary coalition" retreated temporarily during that critical juncture due to a shifting balance of power and the overwhelming popular support for the change. This temporary partial retreat facilitated the passage of a new constitution and Law 160 in 1994. In hindsight, it is apparent that this "retreat" was only to regroup and rethink. The "reactionary coalition" realized that it needed to depend on its own resources and local power to defend its class interests, which ushered in a new phase in Colombia's conflict: the emergence of paramilitarism as a countervailing force. I think 1990 was a critical juncture in Colombia's turbulent history, which allowed the election of a constituent assembly, creating an unprecedented opportunity for nonestablishment forces—such as M-19—to participate in drafting a new constitution. The reactionaries responded by assassinating the leader of M-19, Carlos Pizarro, who was poised to win the 1990 presidential election. The "reactionary coalition" did not regain the political/military initiative until 1997, when, under the Pastrana government, the national paramilitary project became formalized in the creation of the Auto defenses United of Colombia (AUC), whose strength increased steadily until their theatrical demobilization in 2005.[42] Paramilitarism created the environment in which the landed elite regained their status within the dominant class, securing that no political arrangements could be reached at the expense of their class interests. Jorge Visbal, president of Fedegan—the Colombian Federation of Cattle Ranchers, which represents the most recalcitrant reactionary sector of the dominant class—explained in an interview that "no peaceful settlement is possible at our expense, we would not allow it, let them go to hell 'Ni del Carajo.'"[43] Referring to the then ongoing failed peace talks between the Andres Pastrana government

(1998–2002) and the FARC, Visbal voiced his social class cohorts' concern about the prospects of an agreement in which their large land ownerships might be compromised.

Peasant Reserves 1994–Present

One of the leading architects who helped articulate and establish the peasant reserves in Colombia was Dario Fajardo, a sociologist specializing in agrarian issues. In one of our interviews, he provided a synopsis of the creation of the reserves. He had been contacted by the World Bank seeking his advice regarding the founding of "peasant enterprises," as the Bank called them. Fajardo suggested a number of communities as possible locations, including Pato-Balsillas, whose peasants had acquired extensive organizational experience, having engaged in struggle since the 1920s.[44]

The Colombian Communist Party and peasant unions such as FENSUAGRO were instrumental in developing the organizations of the peasants' colonization movement in several areas of Colombia, including Pato-Balsillas, Cabrera, and Guaviare. Cabrera, located in the department of Cundinamarca, became a peasant reserve in 2000, having established an agrarian colony in 1928 and become a powerful school for the colonization movement that developed in the 1930s and afterward. Guaviare, located in the Guaviare department, was founded in 1997, the same year as Pato-Balsillas, with whom it shared a long history of *colonos* struggling for land. Cimitarra, recognized in 2002, benefited from the experiences of Pato, Guaviare, and Cabrera. The institutional memory of these peasant experiences is guarded and transmitted by organizations such as the National Association of the Peasant Reserves (ANZORC), created in 2010 (see Map 3.1, of peasant reserves).

During the Ernesto Samper (1994–98) presidency, little progress was made in applying Law 160 of 1994. Samper's administration was engulfed by the scandal of narcodollars funding his campaign, which weakened his political standing vis-à-vis his detractors on the right, who were adamantly opposed to any concession to the peasants. The Samper plan to distribute one million hectares to 75,764 families was never carried out,[45] and the execution of Law 160 of 1994 stalled at its inception. The succeeding governments of Pastrana (1998–2002), Alvaro Uribe Velez (2002–10), and Juan Manuel Santos (2010–16) did not advance much. Since 1997, seven reserves have been established, the last of them Montes de Maria

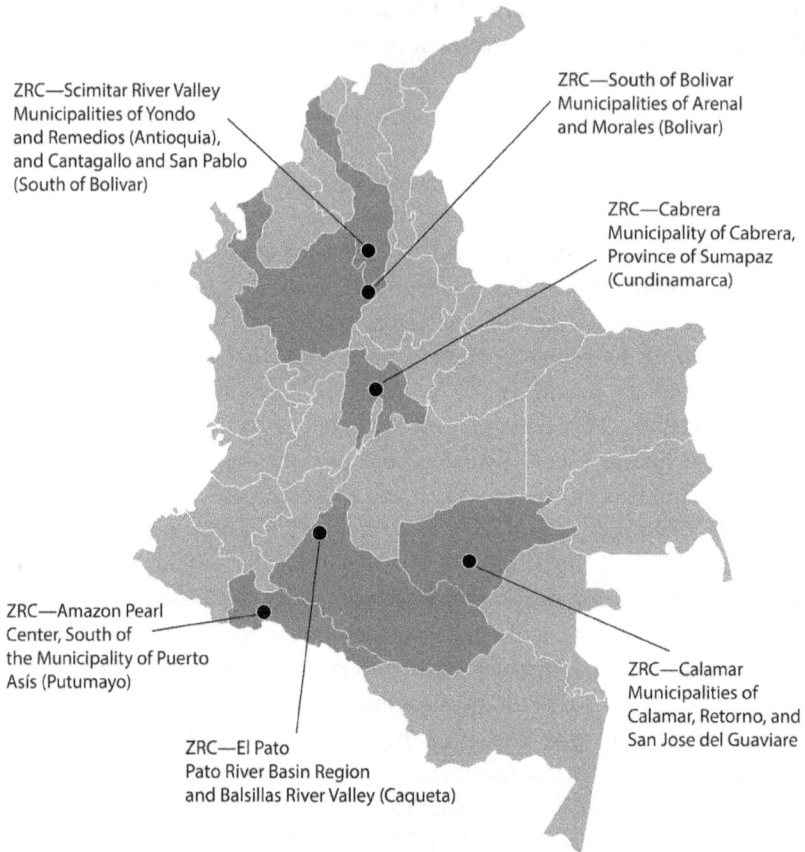

ZRC—Scimitar River Valley
Municipalities of Yondo
and Remedios (Antioquia),
and Cantagallo and San Pablo
(South of Bolivar)

ZRC—South of Bolivar
Municipalities of Arenal
and Morales (Bolivar)

ZRC—Cabrera
Municipality of Cabrera,
Province of Sumapaz
(Cundinamarca)

ZRC—Amazon Pearl
Center, South of
the Municipality of Puerto
Asís (Putumayo)

ZRC—Calamar
Municipalities of
Calamar, Retorno, and
San Jose del Guaviare

ZRC—El Pato
Pato River Basin Region
and Balsillas River Valley (Caqueta)

Map 3.1. Zonas Reservas. *Source*: Created by the author.

2018 (which is not the map). The first six reserves amounted to 830,000 hectares, in which 75,000 people live. The biggest is located in San Jose del Guaviare, with an area of 463,000 hectares, followed by Cimitarra with 184,000 hectares and Balsillas with 88,401 hectares.

Reflecting the ebbs and flows in the institutional development of the peasant reserves since they were created in 1994 with Law 160, they have remained in a continuous daily struggle. Their inhabitants have created their own space and environment and, incrementally, tried to create boundaries, which have been fluid, in flux, and, more critically, permeable. Boundaries have been contested by large landowners, the state, multinational corporations, among other challengers. Law 160 of 1994 set the geographic boundaries demarking the reserves' limits, but this has not protected the people inhabiting those territories from subsumption by capital. The discussion below of the two peasant reserves has five primary areas around which the narrative is constructed. The first is a simple description of the process, defining the geography and social composition of the reserve since its creation. It describes the social backgrounds of those that inhabit those territories, their places of origin, the dates and causes of their migrations, and their class backgrounds. The second part discusses the relationship between the reserves and their economic environment: local and international markets, multinational corporations, banks, lending institutions (World Bank, NGOs). It describes and analyzes the economies of the peasant reserves and their susceptibility to market forces. The third tackles the process of subsumption, defining its forms, mechanism, dynamics, and dialectical synthesis with the agency of resistance posed by the communities. The fourth part elucidates and evaluates the policy responses of the reserves' governing body, its coping, adjustment, and resistance strategies in dealing with subsumption. The fifth and last section synthesizes the empirical findings informing the subsumption theory and assesses the viability of the peasant reserves as an alternative, noncapitalist path to consolidating family-based farming and agroecology.

Pato-Balsillas and the Colonization of the Caqueta

HISTORICAL BACKGROUND

If there were a Ground Zero for Colombia's civil war and land disputes, it would be found in El Pato-Balsillas, Caquetá, which embodies its antagonistic contradictions. Pato-Balsillas has been a hotbed of landless peasants' colonization processes and struggles since the late nineteenth century, culminating in the FARC's birth in 1964. *Colonos* were initially attracted to this remote frontier area by the surge in rubber production, quinoa, and cattle ranching that occurred in the early twentieth century. But Caguan remained largely sparsely inhabited, with the exception of San Vicente del Caguan. In 1921, the first *colonos* from the department of Huila occupied public lands in El Pato; they reported that the trail was scarcely transited over the course of six months.[46] In the 1930s and 1940s, new waves of migration originating from Tolima and Huila established new villages such as Rovira, Pueblito, and San Luis de Oso, which became *colonos*-populated centers.[47]

During La Violencia (1948–1958), Tolima, Huila, Antioquia, Valle, and Caldas became battlegrounds between the Liberal and the Conservative parties, forcing thousands of people to flee. Some settled in today's El Pato, and others founded Vista Hermosa. Between 1953 and 1957, the government of President Rojas Pinilla launched a military offensive against the communists in what was called the war of Villarica, which led to the exodus of *colonos* into the mountainous region of Sumapaz. Some of those *colonos* organized in groups under the leadership of "Comandante Richard" and continued their march toward the plains of Ariari, el Guayabero, El Pato, and Duda. This "march" of *colonos* was christened by historian William Ramirez (1981) as "armed colonization."[48] Armed insurgents accompanied the *colonos* in their journey to find lands in new frontiers. In 1952, they established the first nucleus of the Armed Revolutionary Forces of Colombia (FARC) in El Pato and gradually expanded into the high Caguan and River Guayas. These armed formations were disbanded by the end of the 1950s. Instead, an agrarian movement was established, which eventually led to the infamous "independent republics" as the extreme Right, led by Leureano Hurtado, who called for their elimination, characterized them.[49] All along, the dominant landowning elite feared the implications of an expansion of such a *colonos* movement on the security of their land properties.

The agrarian movement championing the cause of the *colonos* gained strength in the late 1950s and early 1960s, especially in El Pato, Riochiquito, Marquetalia, Guayabero, and Sumapaz. Guayabero, like El Pato, became emblematic, with a powerful peasant movement. In El Pato, "Comandante Richard" established an organization recognized by the state, as explained earlier, and succeeded in obtaining credits for constructing roads. Collective land property and democratically elected peasants' councils were the dominant modes of political and economic organization and production, inspired by Marxist ideology and experiences, including the Chinese and Soviet peasants' communal property.

This peasants' experiment in communal property, production, and way of life was considered a national threat to a social order based on private property and its extreme concentration in the hands of a few, as manifested by the archaic hacienda system. Consequently, in the early 1960s, state forces alongside conservative and liberal militias working at the behest of the landowning elite launched several military campaigns to dislodge the peasant organizations in Marquetalia and elsewhere. The campaigns intensified until June 14, 1964, when the offensive, as it became more coordinated, culminated in the so-called LASO offensive in April 1965. With this offensive, the state, with U.S. support, launched its infamous attack against the peasant communities, as a consequence of which the dislodged peasants transformed their disjoined leagues into a mobile insurgent movement, which became the FARC. According to the 1964 census, El Pato had a population of nine thousand people before the 1965 offensive; in 1976, it had fewer than 890. Most of its peasant population had been forcefully displaced.[50]

The state established a military base in Balsillas, intensified its repressive policy targeting the peasant leagues—their organizing tool—restricted their mobility, impeded land titling (as a retribution/deterrent measure), and enhanced its surveillance. In protest against those aggressive measures, 1,500 *colonos* marched through the treacherously inhospitable Eastern Cordillera with its unpaved road, to Huila, the adjacent department, to raise their complaints about the constant harassment and threats by the army. They pleaded their case before the public, and as a result, the governor of Huila and state officials committed to improving their conditions. As soon as peasants returned to their villages, the army bombarded the Pato region. The *colonos'* struggle against state violence continued.[51] Pato remained a bastion of *colonos* resistance and struggle for land, inspiring the wrath of the state and the landowning elite, including the then-emerging narcobourgeoisie, represented by Pablo Escobar, Rodrigo Gacha, the Castano clans, and a host of others. When the state initiated its offensive against the FARC after the collapse of the peace talks with the Pastrana government in 2002, this area became a major theater of operation under Plan Patriota. Ironically, despite all this, Pato-Balsillas remained a symbol of *colonos* resilience, resistance, and adaptability to the process of subsumption, as explained in the following subsections.

FUMIGATION OF COCA CROPS, MOBILIZATION, AND THE CREATION OF THE RESERVE

The global prohibition regime promoted by the United States has severely impacted Colombia and Latin America by targeting the subsistence peasant economy affecting their coca crops and other crops, livestock, health, and water.[52] The prohibition regime has inflicted considerable pain on the peasantry, leading to mass mobilizations in which thousands of *colonos* have participated, bringing their plight to the national and international stages. In 1996, the coca growers in Putumayo, Caqueta, Cauca, South Bolivar, and the Guaviare massively mobilized to protest the fumigation of the crops and restrictions imposed by the state on the distribution of cement and gasoline, both used in the production of cocaine. They also pressed for creating four peasant reserves, which the government accepted. Consequently, the reserve of Pato-Balsillas was founded, followed by that of Cimitarra discussed in the next section.

When Law 160 was passed, the *colonos* in Pato-Balsillas initiated contact with the Corporation for the Sustainable Development of the Amazon (CORPOAmazonia), seeking a solution to the logging problem and the titling of lands lying close to the protected national park of Los Picachos. The state, through Incora, offered to relocate the 289 families that were occupying lands within or close to the Picachos Park to a large landholding known as Abisinia in the plain of Balsillas, dividing it into lots of fourteen hectares per family. However, at least six hundred lots within the reserve remain occupied without legal titling.[53]

General Description and Characteristics of the Reserve

At the end of 1997, the Pato-Balsillas peasant reserve was established, which in 1998 became part of the forty-two thousand square km distension area ceded to the FARC to start the peace talks. The reserve area comprises eighty-eight thousand hectares inhabited by 6,200 people distributed in twenty-seven hamlets. Although most of its peasant population are peasant *colonos mestizos,* there are two Indigenous *cabildos*: Altamira and Coreguajes. The peasant reserve of Balsillas borders two protected natural parks, Picachos and the Miraflores *paramo*. Like the reserves in Cimitarra and elsewhere, Balsillas is committed to protecting the environment, governed by agreements with the state.

The Balsillas reserve is divided into three parts, at different elevations (high, medium, and low), and is made up of three main centers: Balsillas, Guayabal, and the Andes. The variations in altitude give the reserve different climates and soils accordingly encourage the cultivation of suitable crops. The reserve's funding depends on various sources of financing, including projects, cooperation with other groups outside the reserve, and Popular

Action Committee/Juntas de Accion Comunal (JAC) contributions; each JAC contributes ten thousand CP/month to a common reserve fund.

In the wake of the failure of Pastrana's peace talks with the FARC in 2002, the area of contention became the main theater of a ferocious war launched by the Alvaro Uribe's government with the support of the United States' Plan Colombia. According to peasant informants: "Many social leaders were imprisoned or killed after the collapse of the peace talks in 2002."[54] The Municipal Association of the Pato Colonos (Spanish: AMCOP) that emerged during that period became a principal target of the state's persecution.[55]

AMCOP is now the organization that directs the reserve. It is the equivalent of the ACVC in Cimitarra. AMCOP is composed of nine associations; every village has its own JAC and elected representatives in the General Assembly. The General Assembly, in turn, elects the leadership of the reserve. This latter execute the policy recommendations of the General Assembly and is composed of a president, vice president, treasurer, and a spokesperson. AMCOP also has an attorney and a tax auditor.

Landless peasants of Balsillas received parcels of land to plant and harvest within a given time, monitored by the JAC. The reserve is guided by its sustainable development plan, similar to the ACVC. AMCOP has committees dealing with politics, youth, human rights, peasant women, public health, land issues, mass media, environment, and finance. There are written norms that govern the reserve's population and the protection of the environment. These norms are safeguarded by the peasant guards, who are not armed but equipped with communication systems. Their main task is to protect the environment by preventing illegal deforestation, logging, or hunting violations. The reserve's norms must be respected by all, including newcomers, and peasant guards oversee compliance with them. New *colonos* are subject to a probation period during which their behavior and compliance are observed, after which, if they are in good standing, they are admitted.

Peasant guards were adopted in the wake of FARC's disarmament in the aftermath of the peace agreement in 2016. Years before the formal creation of the reserves in 1998, during the civil war, FARC organized the territory. Pato-Balsillas and Cimitarra had been areas of colonization since the 1920s. The Communist Party of Colombia and later FARC were the leading forces in these processes of colonization.[56] As stated by one of the AMCOP interviewees, "Currently we have an ongoing process of reconciliation, the army and former FARC's fighters are working together, but what we are missing is state's investments."[57]

WOMEN'S PARTICIPATION

The peasant reserves represent a socioeconomic alternative to the renti-er-agribusiness model that attempts to improve the living conditions of women and men within the frame of sustainable ecology. Oxfam (2016) estimated that about five million peasant women, mestizos, Indigenous, and Afro-descendants, predominantly live in poverty in Colombia.[58] Due to a concerted effort, the peasant reserve of Cimitarra has witnessed a significant increase in women's participation in the reserve's decision-making process after 2014.

In Pato-Balsillas, a similar process has taken place in AMCOP, the highest representative organ; women represent 20 percent of its leaders. Women occupy key decision-making positions: the president of JAC in Pato-Balsilla, the treasurer, the person in charge of natural parks, and the public representative of AMCOP. It represents an important step forward, although still a less than gender-equal representation.[59] In addition, the women interviewed in Pato-Balsillas expressed optimism in the expansion of their representation and the attention to issues such as domestic violence, agroecology, and the protection of the environment.[60]

It is important to emphasize that the empowerment of women in the reserve of Pato-Balsillas, as in Cimitarra, alongside the Indigenous and Afro-descendants, have received great encouragement from other women's groups in Colombia, Latin America, and the world.[61] It represents an issue that cannot be understated in any serious discussion about women's empowerment and their role in the alternative project to capitalism that might secure life, dignity, and the environment.

PEASANT PRODUCTION SYSTEMS AND THE INTERPLAY OF ADAPTABILITY, RESISTANCE, AND SUBSUMPTION

Protecting the environment is central to AMCOP. One primary purpose of the reserve is to prohibit the colonization and deforestation of the two natural reserves: Los Picachos and Forest Reserve of the Amazonia, of which Pato-Balsillas reserve is part. Those goals resonate with the plethora of agroecological literature (Weis 2007; Gasquet et al. 2014; Buttel 2001; Sevilla Guzman 2006; Ellis 1993; Van der Ploeg 2018). As in the case of the Cimitarra, the Pato-Balsillas reserve is a project in creating a peasant mode of production based on organic practices, including diversity, balanced food production, and the sustainability of natural resources. The successes and limitations of this reserve experiment are assessed below. The reserve of Cimitarra is examined, based on field research in which fifteen unstructured interviews were conducted in December 2019, followed up by more interviews conducted in 2020. Primary sources supplied by the reserve and other governmental sources were also used.[62] This section and the chapter also drew on other studies of the reserves and the peasant economies.

By 2016, the reserve's population had reached eight thousand peasant *colonos* and was still increasing.[63] The reserve produces milk, cheeses, beans, *solanum quintoenses* (naranjillas), peas, coffee, and plantains, alongside livestock, mainly cattle. The reserve produces more than one thousand tons of coffee and three thousand tons of beans/year. "This latter is the most important crop that the reserve produces, and because of that, the reserve created a committee to organize the production and preserve the environment."[64] The reserve's products are transported to San Vicente del Caguan, Neiva, and Bogota. The reserve economy is tied in with local markets integrated into the capitalist commodity chain, yet it maintains its communal peasant social structure and norms without introducing relations based on labor exploitation. AMCOP uses accumulation and profits to cover its costs. This important characteristic defines its communal social production mode in which the producers share profits. Surplus value in the Marxist sense is absent because the producers themselves are the owners of the means of production. Wage labor is mostly absent in this peasant mode. In Pato-Balsillas, there are "five systems of production," according to the Sustainable Development Plan, depending on their elevation, the nature of the soil, and topography, which can succinctly be summed up into two main categories: the family-based peasant economy and the capitalist model.

FAMILY-BASED PRODUCTION

According to the Pato-Balsillas Development Plan, four of the five "production systems" operate at an elevation between eight hundred and 2,200 meters, with family-based units of production ranging from twelve and fifty hectares (see Table 3.1). These four systems cultivate based on climate and soil conditions, producing yucca, coffee, cacao, plantains, corn, and beans. Milk and dairy products are also produced. All four systems are family-based, in which the peasants are the producers and the owners of their own means of production. They engage the market by selling what exceeds their needs.[65]

Capitalist Farms: The "Fifth System"

The large landholdings are in the fifth system, at 2,200 meters' elevation (MSA). Their owners are absentee landlords, and administrators and "*mayodornos*" manage their holdings. These landholdings range between 150 and 250 hectares, with some reaching 950 hectares. These are classi-fied as capitalist farms. Cattle ranching is the dominant economic activity, and the LLU load within the kikuyu pasture paddock of between twenty and twenty-five hectares is between 1.5 and 2 per hectare. The rest of the landholding comprises a wooded area with the same LLU as the cow/ hectare ratio found in the fourth system. Fifty percent of those large farms' income is derived from milk production and the other half from selling meat.[66] In this system, 480 liters of milk are collected every day and sold primarily in Neiva through a local collector with a bulk hauling truck; also, some milk is sold on the roadside in Balsillas.[67] Under the first four subsistence farming systems, peasants cultivate the transient crops that were mentioned before alongside coffee and plantains. The small properties are located in the Pato area, and the few large landholdings of system 5 are limited to Balsillas (see Table 3.1).

Table 3.1 shows that 79 percent of the landholdings are classified as small; the family provides the labor and owns the means of production.

Table 3.1. Land Holdings According to Size (UAF),* Pato-Balsillas Peasants' Reserve

Very small land properties less than 1/2 UAF	50%	Systems 3 & 4
Small land properties (0.5 UAF to 2)	29%	Systems 1, 2, & 3
Medium-Sized land properties (0.5 to 10UAF)	14%	System 5
Large land properties (More than 10UAF)	7%	System 5

Source: Plan de Desarrollo Sostenible, 112–13.

*UAF stands for the family production unit. It is a landholding unit created by the state to distribute public land to landless peasant colonos. The unit varies according to land fertility, type of soil, and access to water. In the reserve of Pato-Balsillas, the UAF is between 58 hectares and 78 hectares, as stipulated in Resolution 041 of 1996.

Production is for subsistence and is only partially market oriented. System 5 is market oriented and driven by market forces, depending on labor, and it entails a process of industrialization. This system is also incentivized by the state's economic policies and credit availability.

Table 3.2 below on land tenure type reveals that 84 percent of landholdings are titled, which is relatively high compared to the peasant reserve of Cimitarra, where the titling of land has been hampered by legislation such as Law 1728 of 2014, which prohibits the adjudication of lands within a radius of 2,500 meters surrounding areas of extraction of oil and minerals. Law 160 of 1994 had put the radius at five thousand meters. With these restrictions, the state laws privilege the rentier model at the expense of the peasant reserve. The Pato-Balsillas reserve was not affected by the mentioned laws nor by the encroachments of the extractive activities as of this writing. Still, the threat persists, from both the cattle ranching *latifundios* and the ever-present potential for fracking for oil extraction.

Peasant Agroecology as an Alternative Model

AUTONOMY AND THE SOCIAL FUND

In Pato-Balsillas, the *colonos'* ties to the capitalist chain are obvious, signaling the historical process of subsumption. At the same time, the *colonos'* noncapitalist agency is evident in their attempts to adapt and resist. One striking example is the communal fund, which the peasants established following unsuccessful attempts to get credit from commercial banks. As explained by a *colono* and founding member from Balsillas, "When the

Table 3.2. Land Tenure by Type

Land Tenure type	Number of landholdings	Percentages
Tenant	26	3%
Usufruct	48	5%
Owner without land title	52	6%
Owner with land title	766	84%
Total	912	100%

Source: Plan de Desarrollo Sostenible, 115

commercial banks refused our repetitive attempts, we thought of an alternative. We decided that each family contributes one percent of their coffee, beans, milk, and plantain production. Then this one percent is sold, and the money goes to a common fund. That is how we started. Initially, we were twenty families. Now three hundred families are contributing to the fund. Credits are offered to the peasants that need them. Currently, eighty families are benefiting from the credits that are offered at an interest rate of two percent." He added, "We are planning to increase our participants in the fund so interest rates can go down to one percent or lower."[68]

This communal fund, among other strategies such as establishing production and marketing cooperatives, creating local agroecology, and practicing environmental protection illustrate the community's effort to sustain the reserve's peasant economy and way of life. The interviewees argued that their goal is to offer elements for resisting market pressure and thus provide continuity to their peasants' subsistence economy and their mode of life. Another important observation is the struggle for autonomy described by Miguel Cordoba, the treasurer of AMCOP: "We maintain with pride our autonomy over this territory after forty years of struggle."[69]

To achieve autonomy, AMCOP developed different strategies, including creating a social fund. The significance of the creation of a communal fund, which AMCOP called Administrative Social Fund, as a cooperative mini bank was that it "consolidate[s] our autonomy," as one peasant described it.[70] The fund has helped expand production of coffee, beans, fruits, and milk, contributing to the consolidation of the subsistence peasants' economy. It has supported the peasants in diversifying their production base, to avoid fluctuations in the market, crop failure, and climate change. It offers an example of the agency of resistance to the subsumption process and the peasants' drive to negotiate their relations/position within the market. Perhaps one of the most successful strategies has been to seek outside sources to boost the social fund. It has raised financial support from local and international agencies such as UNDP, the Agrarian Bank, and DIAN.[71] Diversifying its financial base is both a blessing and a curse, inasmuch as it runs the risk of creating dependency and inviting political pressure from the donors, which might weaken the peasants' resolve in resisting capitalist subsumption.

One of the most important functions of the communal fund is filled by the JAC, who recommends the individuals that would benefit from loans and plays the role of the mediator in case of a dispute with the fund. With the JAC's participation, the role of the social fund has been expanded to benefit all the individuals affiliated with the fund. With the help of UNDP, the JAC has expanded the categories of beneficiaries to include youths and women.[72]

The community social fund provides an alternative to the capitalist banks and offers an alternative path of agroecological socioeconomic development grounded in the community's interests and dedicated to protecting the environment. The fund is incorporating new projects that contribute to the enhancement of agroecology, including encouraging agrodiversity and designing sustainable agrosystems alongside supporting auto-consumption and access to local markets.[73]

AGROECOLOGY: AN ALTERNATIVE PATH

The peasant reserves have two interdependent strategic goals. One is to create a sustainable agricultural model to protect the environment and preserve a noncapitalist peasant way of life. According to Darío Fajardo, agroecological sustainable production was the fundamental goal of the peasant reserves, and in pursuit of this goal many achievements have been accomplished.[74] Although the peasant reserves have a long way to go to formulate a fully coherent agroecological model, the experiences of the peasant reserves substantiate a mode of production, reinforce the cultural identity of the peasantry, and provide an alternative model for the agricultural sector.[75] In Pato-Balsilla Reserve, activism was responsible for controlling deforestation inside the reserve and the adjacent municipalities, including San Vicente del Caguan, which had recorded one of the country's highest rates of destruction, which activists succeeded in bringing down to the national average. Similar results have been observed in the peasant reserve of Cimitarra, where the norms of controlling deforestation have been effective, and peasants are observing the rules. Those norms are considered by the peasants essential for the preservation of both the ecosystem itself and their livelihood and subsistence.[76]

Every JAC in the reserve contains an ecological committee in charge of protecting the forest, water, and fauna, and prohibiting hunting of wild animals. Fishing for commercial purposes is also prohibited, as is cutting native trees and slashing weed and stubble near water springs. Penalties for violation of these ecological norms include confiscating the offender's hunting rifle and imposing a penalty of between one hundred thousand and two million CP. The norms prohibit the burning of bushes, which is only permitted by the general assembly. Violators are penalized.[77] Those strict norms, some of them introduced by the FARC, have caused tensions within the reserve, because hunting and fishing, among other practices, had been common before the reserve was created. Currently, under the auspices of JAC, the expansion of the agricultural frontier is under strict control. Consequently, the reserves have become important actors limiting deforestation and environmental degradation. Many other frontier areas are witnessing an exponential increase in deforestation, most notably after signing the peace accord in 2016 between FARC and the Santos government.[78]

The Pato-Balsillas became an important player in preserving two core areas that had been threatened by the uncontrolled expansion of the agricultural frontier subject to a typical modality.[79] These two strategic areas in the ecosystem are the National Park of the Picachos Nacional Natural in the Andes Mountains and the Special Management Area of the Macarena, which is of paramount importance for its biodiversity within the confluence of three ecosystems: the Andes, Amazonia, and the Orinoquía region. Thus, Pato-Balsillas's location and role in protecting those ecosystems enhanced its position and validated the existence of the peasant reserve as the site of an agroecological grassroots movement where the organic links between production, lifestyle, and sustainability are constantly negotiated.

The experience in the Pato-Balsillas has been shared with other peasant reserves, and this has served as an example to emulate.[80] The agroecology peasant mode that the Pato-Balsillas promoted has reached new levels of acceptance. In a public ceremony in which the National Reserve Park participated, peasant subsistence farmers pledged to conserve the Picachos. The actions seek to enhance the conservation of the environment, with peasant-based grassroots organizations leading the charge in pressuring the state agencies, including the National Reserve Park, to accept the norms that the reserve put in place prohibiting slashing and burning croplands, hunting and fishing, and logging, and instead replanting the affected areas with native trees and bushes.

Resistance to the Extractive Rentier Economy in Caquetáa

The state's strategic National Development Plan 2019–22, which guides Colombia's overall economic policy, articulated that its goal was to transform Caquetá's economy from agriculture into oil production.[81] That is, to incorporate this peripheral department, which had remained on the fringe of capital and its laws of accumulation, partly because of its resistance history, the dominance of the FARC insurgency, and its socioeconomic and ethnic composition of peasants, *colonos,* and Indigenous. Now that resistance history is facing up to one of the major challenges posed by the state's extractive rentier drive. The way of life of its entire population and ecology system is in the balance, not only the Pato-Balsillas reserve.

Oil exploration in Caquetá started in 2006, and by 2009 the production was concentrated in San Vicente del Caguan. The number of multinational oil corporations and national oil companies interested in oil extraction is noteworthy and includes Emerald Energy, Meta Petroleum Corp, Canacol Energy Colombia, C&C Energy Group, and Barbados Sucursal Colombia, Hupecol Operating, Ecopetrol, Pacific Stratus Energy, and the Consortium Optima Range, all of them drawn by the potential oil reserves that they have detected. The main problem that these companies and the state are facing is the resistance of the local communities to the extraction of oil, knowing the environmental devastation that this activity entails.

In addition to increasing political consciousness of what oil extraction has caused in other departments and its disappointing socioeconomic returns, the communities' stiff resistance stems from a long history of contestation politics in Caquetá, a hotbed for the FARC. In 2015, the communities of Caquetá blocked the employees of Emerald Energy, owned by the Chinese state-owned multinational Sinochem Group. They succeeded in stopping the oil extraction and other exploratory activities for fifteen days, after which the state executed its policy by removing the protestors forcefully, which was expected, given the state's commitment to this extractive rentier model. Continuation of the extractive activity is not likely to stop unless the mobilization makes it impossible for the companies to operate. The peasant reserve of Pato-Balsillas constitutes part of the movement, whose whole objective is to conserve the delicate Amazon ecology of the department. They declared Green Caquetá as a slogan to halt the advancement of extraction.

So far, sixteen Colombian and multinational oil companies have been granted fifty-one contracts allowing them to study the area and carry out exploration and drilling activities in the Amazon region. In the western Caquetá and Putumayo municipalities, thirty-seven of these titles overlap with eighty-one Indigenous reservations. According to the native Colombians from the region, these reservations have not been consulted as required by the law.[82] At the Nogal, a 240,000-hectares bloc encroaches on the Caquetá's Amazon municipalities of Morelia, Milan, and Valparaiso.[83] As expected, in June 2020 an oil spill contaminated the Caquetá River between Yapura and Currillo, alarming environmental groups in the department who had voiced their concerns earlier during the mobilization against Emerald Energy, the Sinochem affiliate.

In its National Development Plan 2019–22, the state reaffirmed its commitment to a rentier economy in which oil extraction is one of the key pillars. Unfortunately, Caquetá and Putumayo are the new epicenters. The targeted area is 110,304 km2 in Caquetá (north) and Putumayo (south).[84] According to Ecopetrol, the expected oil reserves are about five hundred million barrels. At the same time, the National Agency of Hydrocarbons estimates it at three billion barrels, and the National University puts the figure at six billion barrels.[85] Whatever the actual figure is, the state's decision makers are zeroing on this untapped Amazon area.

Leonor Bravo, a social leader in Cartagena del Chairá, said that the extractive economy is against the community's wishes. He continued, "It has been many years of struggle in which we have been trying to make the state understand that we have to be part of the decision-making process when it comes to a development plan."[86] On her part, the coordinator of the environmentalist group Coordosac voiced similar concerns and added that the multinational corporations' bottom line is profit, and the state does not protect the peasants or the environment.[87] These testimonies illustrate Caquetá communities' collective effort to construct an alternative economic model in which the priority is to protect the environment and the peasant economy, resisting the oil enclave economy.

Resistance by the communities was not limited to Valparaiso against the Chinese company Emerald Energy; it expanded to the municipalities of Puerto Rico, Paujil, and Doncello, where the peasant communities established preventive resistance to block entry by the multinational into Nogal, which Emerald Energy eventually accomplished only with the intervention of the state's coercive power. The state granted Emerald Energy 239,414 hectares in the Nogal bloc.

What is evident is that among the communities of Caquetá, there is strong opposition to the rentier drive and that their aspiration is a communal collective ecology model consistent with what the Commission of Water Life, which opposes the extraction of oil, espouses, a model in which the soil, ecosystem, biodiversity, and sociocultural diversity are central.[88]

The agency representing the communities advanced a series of "green projects" to establish links with the capitalist market on the agency's own terms: preserving the environment, resisting the rentier model, and protecting the peasant economy. The communities launched alternative green energy proposals in which the human needs and environmental protection are concentrated. In the sixteen municipalities of the Caquetá, environmentalist groups, peasants, youth, and civil society organizations joined forces to raise awareness of the green economy and its importance to their survival. In 2028, Belen de los Andaquies will be formally declared a "green territory," in which its use of water and soil in rural and urban areas adequately guarantees environmental sustainability alongside strengthening the people's capacity to recover their culture and the Andaquis' traditions.[89]

The communities embrace green economy based on biomass renewable energy. The idea is to transform this ecological practice into service by increasing its use as an energy source and establishing political contours promoting it. The green economy hoped for by the Caquetá communities includes more efficiency in energy generation in terms of using resources, avoiding the loss of biodiversity, and providing ecosystem services.[90]

In sum, at this moment, two diametrically opposed models are in confrontation: one representing the past, led by the state and rentier sector, and the other embraced by the peasant communities representing the progressive green forces in the global economy fighting global warming and fossil fuels. Paradoxically, although they constitute a presumably dying or dead class, the peasantry leads the charge into the future, ushering the new global trends. This is while oil companies, such as the behemoth Exxon Mobil, are in crisis. For decades one of the most profitable corporations in the world, in August 2020 Exxon Mobil was tossed out of the Dow Jones industrial average, replaced by Salesforce, a software company.[91] This change symbolizes a shift from "Big Oil" to an information technology where alternative clean green energy might have a niche. Considering this search for cleaner energy as an opportunity for capital accumulation by finance capital, one might ask: Would this phase offer the peasants a break from the pressure of the rentier/extractive-based economy?

The second section discusses the peasant reserve of Cimitarra, contrasting its experience with that of Pato-Balsillas, especially in their struggle for autonomy, and charting agroecology as a path to consolidate their family-based subsistence economy.

Geography and Social Composition: Cimitarra

Geographically, Cimitarra's peasant reserve is located in the eastern part of the Central Mountain range and parts of the plain of the Magdalena River and south of the Serrania de San Lucas. It comprises four areas (Yondó, Cantagallo, San Pablo, Remedios) drawn from three municipalities located in two departments: Antioquia and Bolivar. It has an area of 188,259 hectares, primarily located in the municipality of Yondó, Antioquia. In total, the reserve has 134 hamlets (*veredas*). The area slope terrain is classified as comprising low, medium, and high.

The plain of the Cimitarra River is a subregion of the Middle Magdalena, which includes the municipalities of Santa Rosa, Simití, San Pablo, Cantagallo, and Yondó.[92] This subregion was populated in the late nineteenth century by cattle ranching *colonos,* followed in 1941 by the oil multinational Royal Dutch Shell. Then came people escaping violence in the late 1940s and 1950s, from different parts of the country (Prada 2006, 168–69; interviews 2017). There were three distinct waves of migration. The early wave, in the 1920s, was caused by land struggles, as identified by LeGrand (1986) and validated by Murillo; it was followed by the wave created by La Violencia 1948–1958, which brought a massive influx of peasants and *colonos* escaping the onslaught of the Conservatives in Tolima, Caldas, Antioquia, Santander, Bolivar, and the Plains. The first wave of migrants originated spontaneously in other parts of the Middle Magdalena and settled in the southern part of the subregion. The second wave was coupled with the judicial awarding of public lands to *colonos* in the northern part of the subregion (Fajardo 2008; interviews 2018). Most *colonos* of the second wave that populated Cimitarra settled on land conceded by the state to the Shell Oil Company in La Rampira. Some of these *colonos* were Liberal partisans amnestied by the Rojas Pinilla military junta in 1957 or were peasants who had been forcefully removed from their lands. The third wave of peasants that settled in Cimitarra in the 1970s and 1980s were forced off their lands by the military counterinsurgency operations and the paramilitaries. Some were peasants and artisan miners displaced from Segovia and Remedios in Antioquia, areas known for their large gold reserves and mining.[93]

The formation of small villages started in the 1960s in the lower and the middle part of Cimitarra, in small villages such as Felicidad and Cuatro Bocas, where the first Popular Action Committee (JAC) was formed. To populate those terrains, peasants snuck in during the night to build their hamlets and claim possession, an endeavor that required group support and solidarity. In Cuatro Bocas, for instance, after the guards employed by Shell had made their rounds, the squatters came in to build their hamlets, with the help of others who expected the beneficiaries to return the favor when needed. The peasants followed a traditional rural system known in Spanish as *mano de vuelta*, return the favor; it is an act of reciprocity inherited from ancient practices.[94] In Cantagallo, a similar colonization process took place. Initially, the Anglo-Dutch oil company Shell returned some of these concessions to the state, to accommodate the peasants, but as it became a pattern, the state unleashed its coercive force to protect Shell and its land concessions.[95] It is noteworthy that all of the peasants, except the native Indigenous who inhabited areas close to River Ite in Cimitarra, were *colonos* and poor peasants displaced from various other departments, including: Antioquia, Santander, Sucre, Choco, Cesar, Cordoba, Atlantico, Valle, Boyaca, Cundinamarca, Tolima, Caldas, Huila, Meta, and the eastern Plains. The Cimitarra reserve absorbed internally displaced persons from as many as fifteen of the thirty-two departments that make up the country's political geography. What is notable is that many of the *colonos* were veterans of social movements in their places of origin and had gained a remarkable capacity to organize, adjust, resist, and subsist in adverse conditions.

In this vein, Amparo Murillo's (1999) study of the history and social background of the peasants in the Middle Magdalena offers some useful insights that might have influenced their political adaptability and resistance. She underlines three main "constitutive attributes" that characterized the colonization processes in Yondó and the valley of Cimitarra.[96] The first was the social rupture that the displaced peasants suffered when they were caused by the violence to settle in the forest away from the onslaughts of capital, including war rentierism. The second attribute is the continuity of social conflict in the new environment. The third attribute is their experience of resistance that might help them face the new challenges. Then, one must add an important sociological and political component that Fajardo observed (2012, 2): the "tradition of colonization" of those that originated from the department of Tolima.

Subsequently, the cumulative experience of expulsion, violence, adaptability, resistance, retained in a collective memory shared by the *colonos*, gave "the tradition" of colonization meaning and guidance for collective praxis.[97] Those experiences, according to Fajardo (2012, 2), translated into political, union-like organization. In this line of analysis, the colonization movement, although it does not exclude individualism, is primarily a group act motivated and incentivized by experiences of dispossession, resistance, and displacement. In the case of Cimitarra, I observed the praxis of "Mano Vuelta," which validated Fajardo's contention that a colonization tradition exists that forms part of the collective experience accumulated over the years by peasants in adverse social conditions.

Governance: Popular Action Committees (JACs)

The JAC[98] has a long tradition in Colombia as a basic unit of social organization at the community and village levels, dating back centuries. In the late 1950s, legislation was passed to give JACs legal status and regulate them as instruments of community development under the authority of various government ministries. Consequently, for the leftist groups and the right-wing parties, JACs became a contested forum. JACs became the main channel for communicating local demands to the municipality, governorship, and other state institutions more highly placed than local communities. When the peasant reserves in Pato-Balsillas and Cimitarra were founded in 1997 and 2010, respectively, the JACs became pivotal forums for governance and organizing the affairs of the communities.

In the 1980s, the Cooperative of Small and Medium-sized Farms of Antioquia (Coopemantioquia) was formed, which included small- and middle-sized property owners in Cimitarra, Pueblo Nuevo, and on the banks of the Ite River. This cooperative played a pivotal role in Cimitarra's conflict resolution among *colonos* regarding land claims, and represented the community vis-à-vis the authorities. The growth of Coopemantioquia led the army in 1989 to bombard its headquarters under the pretext that the insurgency had established a military base within the reserve. From 1989 onward, the army considered the cooperative an enemy of the state, initiating a campaign of killing, torturing, and imprisoning its members. During this period, the paramilitaries were deployed in coordination with the army to continue the "counterinsurgency" strategy,[99] resulting in the killing and disappearance of many peasants (ACVC 2009a). The cooperative stayed active until 1996, when the paramilitaries intensified their offensive in Magdalena Medio as a national-level counterinsurgency strategy. In 1997, the Auto defenses of Colombia (AUC) was created as a confederation consisting of most paramilitary groups; its spokesperson and nominal leader was Carlos Castano.[100] In the early 1980s, the spearhead of the AUC was located in Puerto Boyaca, 136 km from Cimitarra in the Middle Magdalena region. Puerto Boyaca became one of the main epicenters of "counterinsurgency" in the region and a rallying national symbol for the right-wing forces in Colombia.[101]

In this connection, it is important to note what then-president Belisario Betancur (1982–86) said in his celebratory visit to Puerto Boyacá in the wake of the inauguration of its paramilitary in 1985: "Now, every resident of the Middle Magdalena have risen to become a defender of peace alongside the army and the police. Forward people of Boyacá."[102] Betancur was not the only one; almost all presidents of Colombia invariably have supported paramilitaries, because their creation corresponded with the Cold War security doctrine to which the country's military had adhered since the 1950s as a feature of its collaboration with the United States. Betancur's predecessor, President Julio Cesar Turbay Ayala (1978–82),[103] invoked the state of siege and fully embraced the National Security Doctrine, which legalized the creation of paramilitaries. President Virgilio Barco (1986–1990) attempted to scrutinize the use of paramilitaries by the military.[104] The links between the state's coercive apparatus with those groups changed over the following decades but never stopped.[105] They witnessed a revival under President Alvaro Uribe Velez (2002–10). Uribe's counterinsurgency strategy was typical of the Cold War's National Security Doctrine and its manual for involving "armed civilians" in defense of the state. To that end, organizations such as the Convivir recruited civilians and armed them in cities and suburban areas alongside "Peasant-Soldiers" in rural areas and informant networks in the cities. The idea is simple: take the fish out of its water. That is, deprive the insurgency of its peasant base by forcefully displacing civilians, a tactic used in most phases of the civil war. However, the deployment of the population displacement tactic increased exponentially during the Uribe period. As a case in point, 2008 marked the highest displacement rate in twenty-three years, amounting to 270,000 internally displaced persons.[106] Hundreds escaped from Cimitarra to Barrancabermeja, while most peasants held their ground and resisted the onslaught supported by the FARC's units that historically had operated in these areas.[107] The Following subsection delves into the Peasant Association of the Plain of the Cimitarra River (ACVC), and its leadership and economic activities in the Cimitarra reserve.

The Peasant Association of the Plain of the Cimitarra River (ACVC) Leadership

It is important to emphasize that the population of the reserves consists predominantly of men and women *colonos* displaced from other regions of the country who constitute the Peasant Association of the Plain of the Cimitarra River (ACVC). According to Irene Ramirez, president of the ACVC, 80percent of the population in the reserve of Cimitarra are *colonos*.[108] The ACVC has led and organized the process of colonization. It received all new *colonos* arrivals and assigned them a place to stay, and the rest of the community helped until they could make it on their own.[109] Consequently, the ACVC has created social norms and practices that have strengthened solidarity among the reserves' inhabitants and protected the environment.[110]

Women in leadership positions in the ACVC and JAC have increased since 2018. Currently, five women and four men constitute the leadership of ACVC, and in JAC women's representation has increased from 15 percent to almost 40 percent.[111] This significant increase in the number of women in leadership positions reflects a commitment to eradicating patriarchy, paving the way for democratizing gender power relations.

Women in the reserves play a leading role in two major areas: conserving native seeds to secure agroecology and sustainability, and recuperating native trees and plants following decades of state neglect and environmental degradation caused by the oil companies and mining; and second, strengthening food security and food sovereignty by devising and monitoring the peasants' use of their small home lots to plant food crops and helping those peasants who are interested in livestock, chickens, and pigs. Women have also been instrumental in opening community shops where local products may be sold.[112] In Pato-Balsillas, women play a similar role in promoting agroecology, creating a seed bank, cementing food sovereignty and autonomy, and protecting the environment.

ECONOMIC ACTIVITY

The ACVC has attempted to develop norms to protect the forested areas and recommended plans for soil. For example, for the families that depended on logging, the borders of their respective areas are defined for each family according to their needs and the sustenance of the forest. ACVC continues accepting new *colonos*, since large swaths of public land are still available. One challenge that the ACVC has faced has been to prevent the concentration of land in the hands of a few *colonos* by defining the maximum number of hectares allowed per family. If a *colono* decides to sell their land, the ACVC must approve it.[113]

The 6,457 families (circa 32,285 people) inhabiting the Cimitarra peasant reserve depend on six main economic activities: logging, agriculture, cattle ranching, fishing, coca growing, and artisanal mining. The reserve is divided into three agroecological areas. High Cimitarra is where the two rivers, Ite and Tamar, originate. Parts of the municipalities of Yondó and Remedios lie in this part. *Colonos* inhabiting this area depend chiefly on cattle ranching and logging alongside cultivating yuca, corn, and plantain for family consumption.[114]

The middle Cimitarra includes parts of Yondó and Cantagallo. *Colonos'* subsistence in this area depends on the crops of yuca, plantains, and corn, as well as fishing, logging, small-scale cattle ranching, and coca plantation.[115] In Low Cimitarra, people make their livings from fishing, planting yuca, plantains, and corn, and cultivating coca, alongside small-scale cattle ranching. It is noticeable that the coca plantations are cultivated in the middle and lower parts of the agroecological area, an activity that is largely correlated with subsistence family–based farming. Most peasants sell their surplus food production and crops in the regional city, Barrancabermeja.[116]

Figure 3.1 below shows a particular picture of the principal activities in the region: logging (26.9 percent), followed by mining (14.44 percent). Agriculture makes up barely 2.22 percent of the activities pursued by the

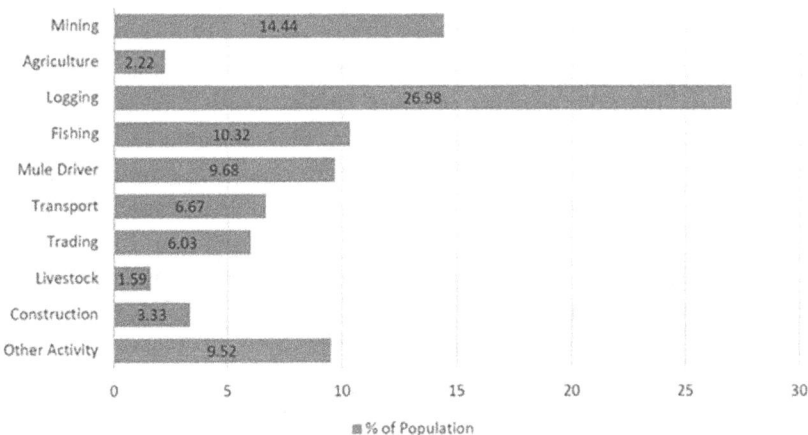

Figure 3.1. Population by activity. *Source*: FAO, public domain.

reserve's population.[117] Most of the *colonos* plant crops for their own consumption, however, a fact that is important to keep in mind to understand the nuances of the peasants' political economy as they try to balance the processes of subsumption exercised by not-so-"hidden hands of the market" against the need to subsist. The same economic practice applies to the cultivation of coca plants, which generate a flow of cash that supplements the meager incomes generated by the family-based subsistence economy. This will be discussed below.

Between 2000 and 2010, the land tenure system favored properties of larger than five hundred hectares, which increased from occupying 0.9 percent of the available land to 3 percent. The quantity of medium-sized landholdings (one hundred to two hundred hectares) declined from 31 percent to 18 percent. Small landholdings of one to ten hectares increased from 10.2 percent to 35 percent due to extreme fragmentation of landholdings. The medium-sized landholdings had been distributed during 1980–89, when the first peasants' reform plan was introduced. The changes in land distribution are attributed to several factors. One was the suspension of the reserve system between 2002 and 2011, which gave rentier capital (multinational corporations, agribusinesses, cattle ranchers, land speculators) almost a decade to freely encroach upon and influence the internal dynamics and distribution of land, whose leaders were either in prison or in hiding due to the intensified state repression. At the same time, the state's offensive and its investments in road infrastructure incentivized and lured rentier capital and increased land prices, especially in Yondó.[118] During that period, twenty-five thousand hectares that had previously been assigned to the reserve were grabbed by large landowners.[119] In addition, the neighborhoods of La Congoya, El Ite, La Cienaga, and La Virgen land were (like Yondó) subsumed by capital. These lands now are owned by one individual, and the previous *colonos* owners have become his day laborers, which is to say, they have been proletarianized. During the time of the reserves' suspension, the demand for mining titles increased, including within the protected Yellow Zone. Combined, these factors caused a significant decline in agricultural economic activity, which by 2012 constituted only 2.22 percent of the total, as Table 3.1 shows, mostly dedicated to subsistence farming.[120]

One of the main problems that the ACVC confronts is the rise of *latifiundios* in Yondó, where thirty-four landholdings of five hundred hectares or more occupy more than 20 percent of Yondó's rural area. In comparison, 1,040 landholdings of twenty or fewer hectares occupy less than 3.85 percent of the Yondó rural area. The 1,519 medium-sized (between twenty and two hundred hectares) landholdings occupy 56.3 percent. This extreme concentration is generating the social tensions and conflicts that the ACVC faces and which, as of this writing, remain unresolved.[121] In this respect, it is important to note that landholdings that exceed five hundred hectares are in blatant violation of the legal definition that stipulates seventy-two hectares as the maximum amount of property any individual may possess: Resolution 028 of 2002, under which Yondó was established as a municipality in 1978,[122] allows only landholdings between fifty-three and seventy-two hectares. Before that, Yondó formed part of the forest reserve governed by Law 2 of 1959, which prohibited colonization within its area, until agreement was reached with the *colonos* in 1972. The state accepted the adjudication of 172,000 hectares to the *colonos* in the area, but decades later the problem not only persists but is exacerbated by the expansion of large landownership, chiefly for cattle ranching.[123]

More alarming has been the change in land use from food crops to rentierism, in the form of land speculation. Yondó presents one of the major challenges it presents to the reserve and its sustenance. This is a contradictory dialectical relation caused by to their different, competing logics. Rentierism is governed by the law of value-accumulation, while the reserve embodies peasant subsistence.[124] An ACVC leader interviewee explained that Yondó African palm projects did not prosper because the peasants put up strong resistance, whereas, in San Pablo, this agribusiness expanded, menacing the peasant economy.[125] The peasants' success in Yondó may be attributed to a number of factors, including their level of organization and solidarity, while in San Pablo, the forces of capital in mining, narcotrafficking, and multinational corporations fueled war rentierism by weakening the resistance of peasants, artisanal miners, and fishermen by the use of targeted assassinations, massacres, and displacement, as well as debilitating the ELN, which had acted for a while as a countervailing force.[126] Combined, those factors tore apart the social fabric, debilitating the organizational capacities of subsistence peasants and artisanal miners to resist, and thereby facilitating the process of subsumption.

Adaptation, Resistance, Subsumption, and Multinational Corporations

The multinational corporations who have spearheaded the advance of capitalism worldwide have been leading players in Colombia since the early twentieth century. Multinational corporations abound, from the extracting rubber boom (1912–1929) and the United Fruit Company's banana plantations in Santa Marta, to the many extracting companies seeking gold, coal, oil, timber, and African palm oil. Throughout the history of Colombia, those companies have inflicted suffering and terror, from the massacres of the Indigenous in the Chorrera, Amazon, region, where rubber barons killed one hundred thousand people, to the infamous massacre in the 1920s by the United Fruit Company against its striking workers.[127] In more recent times, the direct involvement of multinational companies in Colombia's war system has included funding paramilitary groups to protect their installations and personnel from insurgents' attacks, as seen in cases involving Chiquita, Coca-Cola, Drummond, Pacific Rubiales, and AngloGold Ashanti, among others.[128]

In Cimitarra, the multinational corporations' subsumption role has been multifaceted and multidimensional. This subsection tackles the most salient activities that have disrupted the consolidation of the peasant reserve and continue to constitute an existential threat to its subsistence: chiefly preventing land titling and distribution, in a zero-sum game by which, if peasants lose their lands it means losing their very survival as a community owning the means of production, that is to say their means of sustaining an independent livelihood. Consequently, their culture and way of life are threatened. The discussion below unpacks the basis of the critical view of rentierism. This subsection tackles the employment of legal mechanisms by the companies, the dynamics unleashed by the menace of the multinationals, and finally, the issue of food security

There are two sides to the threat posed by the extraction of resources. One is the legal aspect embedded in Law 160 of 1994 and Decree 2644 of 1994 of the Ministry of Agriculture and Rural Development, which says that public lands within a radius of five kilometers cannot be adjudicated in oil extraction areas. According to the UNDP, the problem stems from the National Oil Agency (ANH), which does not distinguish between the specific coordinate points of the exploration and the exploited bloc.[129] Decree 2644 stipulated five kilometers from the end of exploitation, but the ANH does not distinguish between exploration and production in practice. This situation places in limbo the land titling of a large portion of the reserve, undermining the possibility for the peasants to access credit, loans, and other state assistance. This is the situation of 80 percent of the area of Yondó, which falls within the extractive plan. The same applies in San Pablo, Remedios, and Cantagallo.[130]

Multinational corporations, agribusinesses, and other commercial interests are increasingly investing in peripheral areas as the margins of returns are higher, particularly after the global financial crisis and recession of 2007. The agents of capital joined forces to amend Law 160 of 1994. A draft bill 003 of 2018 attempted to modify two critical parts of Law 160 of 1994. First, it sought to limit communities' "prior consultation" in areas of interest for exploration and extraction. And second, it introduced the "Legitimate Confidence" article that allows the state to give public land to individuals or companies that it deemed "legitimate" in line with the state's economic rentier policies (as Law 2 of 160 1994 stipulated regarding business zones). Those consultations had often succeeded in halting several multinational projects, and the state, and various national and multinational corporations, were attempting to circumvent them.[131] The most important defining issue has been the "right of ownership of the land surface." The state is, on the one hand, claiming its "sovereign power" to grant public land use rights and exploitation to private companies and corporations.[132] Yet on the other hand, following Law 160 of 1994, the state was required to prioritize *colonos* and poor peasants in its allocation of public lands.

Irene Ramirez, president of the ACVC, explained that land titling is the main problem facing the reserve and that there is no progress on this issue.[133] The ACVC is committed to pressing to obtain land titles; its remit includes restricting land sales by individuals to other individuals within the community and not to corporations or agribusinesses, in full adherence to the norms of the Yellow Line.[134] Law 1728 of 2014 decreased the radius from five thousand meters to 2,500 meters, which is still an encroachment into the reserve area, impeding the titling of land and exercising virtual control over large swaths of land within its parameters. According to the FAO 2019, both Decree 2644 of 1994 and Law 1728 of 2014 have negatively impacted colonization and limited the expansion of food production.[135] Law 1728 of 2014 threatened the survival of the reserve and the environment by guaranteeing the expansion of oil extraction and gold mining. The following subsection discusses the expansion of the coca plantations in the reserve, their driving force, and their impact on the peasant economy.

Coca Production and Capital Subsumption

In San Pablo and the lower parts of the reserve, the presence of coca plantations has fluctuated over the last two decades. It is worth knowing that coca plantations increased in Bolivar—mostly in San Pablo and Santa Rosa del Sur—from 3,324 in 2010 to 7,964 in 2019.[136] That doubled the number of hectares under coca cultivation and created a new economy and new dynamics affecting the region. The peasants of the reserve attempted to mitigate the negative impact of the easy money and the temptation that ties the peasantry to the circuit of capital and its chain of production. ACVC is aware of this menace to the communal way of life and the peasant economy that coca, African palm oil plantations, mining, and oil extraction poses by subsuming the peasants' labor and their land.[137] According to Jesuit Refugee Service (JRS), whose main work centers on San Pablo, "Since 2015, not only the production of coca skyrocketed but also the consumption of cocaine."[138] The consumption of cocaine added another challenge that the peasants' leadership must address. The coca/cocaine economy incorporates in its production chain peasants, day laborers (*raspachines*, seasonal workers hired to pick the leaves of coca), merchants, processors, transporters to points of export, and finally, those in charge of shipping the product to regional and international markets.

The coca economy is transforming the subsistence economy, eroding it, and making peasants a floating semiproletarian group shifting their activities between cash crops, mining, and fishing. They are also joining organized criminal organizations that are active in most parts of the Middle Magdalena or joining the ELN, which is also active in most parts of the Cimitarra's reserve, including in Yondó, Serrania de San Lucas, and San Pablo.[139] Chohan (2018) reports that the move from coca production to alternative crops and economic activities was manifested by the fact that only seven hundred of the twenty thousand farms that make up the reserve cultivated coca in 2017.[140] But by 2019, the coca trade had picked up again, as mentioned before. The fluctuation in coca plantations indicates no clear trend because this depends on the viability and sustainability of alternative crops.

Conclusion

As mentioned at the outset of this chapter, seven reserves were recognized by the state and governed by Law 160 of 1994; the last is Montes de Maria, established in 2018. In total, 875,000 hectares are recognized by the state as peasants' reserves. Seven more reserves are awaiting approval, representing an area of 1,253,000 hectares.

Since the late 1920s, the Colombian Communist Party and later its military branch, FARC, have been pivotal actors in leading the peasants' defense leagues and colonization processes in different departments, some of which have materialized as peasant reserves since the 1990s, for example, Pato-Balsillas, Cimitarra, Cabrera, Guaviare, and Putumayo. As a peasant-based insurgency, FARC was committed to defending the class interests of the poor peasants and *colonos*.[141] This was evident in the peace accord that it signed with the state, in which the agrarian question was the first item of the agreement. FARC sought to obtain ten million hectares, which the ANZORC struggled to formalize.[142] Moreover, the FARC's environmental protection legacy, forged and socialized by its peasant base and fighters, formed the base upon which a new agroecological system was developed to preserve the peasants' economy and farming and to secure for them a sustainable mode of life.

The formation of the peasant reserves and their sustainability continues to be a daunting task within the orbit of an adverse rentier political economy. The subsumption of the peasant economy and subjugation of the reserve's lands and peasants' labor to the rules of capital accumulation is taking place simultaneously with peasants' attempts to organize and resist, as demonstrated in Pato-Balsillas and Cimitarra. The struggle by subsistence peasant farmers to remain economically afloat has been successful. Most of the peasant reserve farmers remain committed to the cause, and their number has increased with the influx of new *colonos*. The reserves have become regional focal points attracting a floating population of poor and landless peasants.

This study has presented several observations that capture the current juncture. The expanding rentier mode in the rural sector is transforming the local economy shaped by the extractive sector, agribusinesses, and the service-oriented sector. This expanding hegemonic mode championed by the state and the dominant class puts the peasants in a defensive posture and defines the contours, scope, and dynamics of the struggle against rentier capital. The peasants' options are to migrate to cities and join the marginalized populations there, proletarianized as in San Pablo, for instance, or to join the existing peasant reserves and struggle to establish new ones. This might explain the demands to construct fifty-seven new peasant reserves in addition to the existing seven reserves, which reflects the increasing number of peasants choosing to stay in rural areas, as well as others seeking to return and reclaim their usurped lands.[143]

The two reserves explored in this chapter have shown resistance to the state-supported encroachments by corporations, large cattle ranching, cash crops, and agribusiness. The reserves' leaders and their agency have resisted with significant adaptability. They have capitalized on agroecology and built alliances with other peasants' groups, international organizations, some state agencies, universities, academics, and social media. These peasant communities are not a social class of the past refusing to die, but rather a modern social class rising to harness the marketplace and global networks to serve its peasant mode and ecology. The "eco-buffalo" exemplifies this case in Puerto Matilde. In Pato-Balsillas, the communal bank, the cooperative system, community shops, and the marketing of milk and other commodities in nearby markets are examples of the peasants' abilities to adapt and use the market to sustain their peasant economy, mitigating the process of subsumption if not subverting it. The experiences of the eco-buffalo of Puerto Matilde in Cimitarra and the communal fund in Pato-Balsillas are success stories. The representatives of both reserves are learning from one another and from other reserves and peasant communities nationwide.

The peasants' activism and agency are omnipresent, as illustrated in the reciprocity relationship of the "Mano Vuelta," through which the peasants of Cimitarra and Pato-Balsillas help new *colonos* build their homes and settle, or as exhibited by the JAC's communal decision-making processes. In this way, the peasants of Cimitarra and Pato-Balsillas are not only surviving but developing an agroecological mode that subverts the various institutional obstacles, including the lack of state support and the advancement of the rentier economy propelled by war rentierism. Most significantly, the agency of the peasants has reached the level of sophistication that allows them to draw on new scientific knowledge and incorporate it in their production process, including the eco-buffalo, dairy products, and green energy. In conclusion, one can safely say that the peasants of these two reserves are a new generation of peasants who are not relics of the past, validating Chayanov's, Van der Ploeg's, and Escobar's thesis of the "peasant mode," as opposed to Bernstein's. The latter disqualified the possibility of a peasantry that engages the market or engages in labor activity while staying outside the orbit of capitalist accumulation and exploitation. As this research shows, the peasants of the two reserves struggle to maintain their autonomy while engaging market capitalism, resisting their proletarianization by maintaining control of their land and labor as the core ingredients of their production, reproduction, and autonomy. So far, they have succeeded in solidifying the reserve's autonomy, developing cooperatives to market their products, and expanding their exchange with other peasant communities.[144] The peasant reserves are also drawing on the support of universities, scholars, and international groups that are fighting for clean energy and promoting noncapital formations. This vast network of support is helping the peasants in coping, adjusting, and resisting.[145]

The two cases discussed in this chapter demonstrated agile resistance and adaptability to the subsumption processes triggered by rentier capitalism's encroachments in rural economies. This brings to the forefront Marx's and Luxemburg's conceptualizations in which they explained the dialectics of subsumption. One can safely conclude that the subsumption process in Colombia is far from over. The peasants and their subsistence economy are threatened, but they are changing and adapting in an uneasy coexistence with the rentier mode.[146] The struggle continues in Colombia, alongside the Global South and the Global North where peasant farmers are making a comeback.

Chapter 4

The Struggle for Survival

The Indigenous People

We are not content with demanding the Indians' right to education, culture, progress, love, and heaven. We start by categorically demanding their right to land.

—Jose Carlos Mariategui

The Peruvian philosopher Mariategui framed the past and future struggle of the Indigenous people in Latin America as one that primarily revolves around their right to land, which is the source of life, reproduction, and autonomy. Starting in 1492, the Indigenous peoples of the Americas endured centuries of carnage and enslavement due to the Spanish Crown and Portuguese colonial extractive enterprises. There were five hundred years of organized looting and bloody projects. The Indigenous groups of Colombia had their share of death and enslavement, which led to their virtual extinction. These cases illustrate some of the core aspects of subsumption, resistance and adaptability, and the contextual political economy of war rentierism. This chapter does not dwell on colonial history; instead, it briefly introduces aspects deemed relevant to this inquiry. Two sites are the focus of this chapter. It focuses on Meta and Cauca, which I have studied intermittently over the past ten years, and on the challenges the Indigenous people there are confronting due to the increasing encroachments of the rentier political economy at the site of the Wakoyo *resguardo* in Meta, and in municipalities such as Corinto, Toribio, Tejada, and Santander de Quilichao in Cauca.

In 2019, the number of Indigenous people in Colombia was 1,905,617, constituting 4.4 percent of the total population (DANE in Spanish).[1] There are 115 different Indigenous groups (sixty-five different languages) spread over twenty-seven of the thirty-two departments, which include Cauca, Choco, Arauca, Magdalena, Vichada, Guainia, Tolima, Meta, and Nariño. In 2018, the largest concentration of Indigenous people was settled in La Guajira (394,683), followed by Cauca (308,455). Meta department had 20,528 Indigenous.[2]

The Indigenous peoples in Colombia did not have a centralized empire structure, such as the Incas and Mayans had, but instead occupied somewhat scattered communities in what became Colombia. This situation might have influenced the cohesiveness of their movement due to the heterogeneity of their experiences, composition, and different languages. After six hundred years of struggle, there are two central, that is, national and thirty-six regional Indigenous organizations today in Colombia. The start of the Indigenous movement in Colombia is associated with the formation in 1971 of the Regional Indigenous Council of the Cauca Department (Consejo Regional Indigena del Cauca, CRIC). Eleven years later, in 1982, the Colombian National Indigenous Organization (ONIC) was established as an umbrella federation representing the Indigenous groups. Finally, the Organization of the Indigenous Peoples of the Colombian Amazon (OPIAC) was formed in 1995. It represents the Indigenous peoples of the Amazonian Basin and is part of the Coordination of Indigenous Organizations in the Amazonian Basin (COICA).[3] In addition, two national Indigenous political parties were formed in the 1990s: ASI, the Social Indigenous Alliance, and MIC, the Colombian Indigenous Movement.[4] Finally, the advisory councils are structured at the local level as the "Cabildos," and at the regional-national levels as the "Mingas." The first is an Indigenous council that forms the leadership of the Indigenous reserves. For example, in the department of Cauca, there are 127 *cabildos*. *Minga* is an Indigenous word that initially meant collective work or a mutual agreement between neighbors to build a house, road, bridge, or government. The Minga functions as a labor union or syndicate. In more recent times, Minga acquired the meaning of collective, contentious political movements spearheading massive national mobilization to bring their demands into national focus.[5]

The Threat: Expansion of War Rentierism

The primary source of conflict between the Indigenous peoples and the Colombian state is the existence of the rentier political economy. As promoted by the state since the 1990s (see chapters 1 and 2), the rentier economy has facilitated land grabbing from the Indigenous people, who legally own 30 percent of the national territory. Throughout Colombia's history, multiple actors have targeted Indigenous lands in order to pursue megaprojects such as hydroelectric plants, mining, oil, gold, cobalt, coal extraction, and agribusiness, which are fundamental pillars of a rentier economy.

As in the case of the peasant reserves, the Indigenous way of life, communal land ownership, and peasant culture constitute obstacles to expanding rentier capitalism. Although communal life, norms, culture, and the collective ownership of land are the antithesis of capitalism, capitalism cannibalizes—subsumes—these noncapitalist structures as capital accumulation and circulation necessitate. As discussed in the introduction, the literature has analyzed the dialectical existence of noncapitalist relations and the capitalist mode of production in the same space and time, generating conflicts, resistances, and coexistence, forcing both sides to adjust, adapt, and strategize.[6] The following sections analyze these relations and their threats to Indigenous groups in Meta and Cauca. The rentier mode was adopted in the early 1990s and consolidated by core state agencies and ministries such as the state's Department of National Planning (DNP), Ministry of Mining and Energy, INCORA, and local governments. This policy has unleashed the forces of rentier capitalism, facilitating the expansion of economic conglomerates, multinational corporations, mining, oil companies, agribusinesses, and the cocaine and service sectors. The actions that express rentier socioeconomic and political power in the departments of Meta and Cauca are similar, but there are significant differences between them in the scope and magnitude of the overall conflict. In Cauca, the Indigenous population constitutes a critical mass that exceeds 20 percent of the department's population, whereas, in Meta, they constitute 1.28 percent of the population.[7] In addition, their *resguardos* are located in strategic corridors leading to the Pacific Ocean, an important exit route for narcotraffickers and important lands for mining gold and other minerals. Consequently, the Indigenous *resguardos'* exposure to the rentier economy and its agents is more complex and violent in Cauca than in Meta.

However, since 2008, Meta, like Cauca, has witnessed an expansion of "megaprojects" in its southern municipalities, chiefly involving African palm oil, mining, and oil extraction. Before 2008, Meta had 172 mining licenses, which covered 536 square kilometers. However, in that year, the number of mining licenses jumped to 326, covering 5,331 km² or 6.2 percent of the department's area (85,770 km²), which represents a tenfold increase. Moreover, this rapid expansion occurred amid the U.S.-backed military offensive seeking to dislodge FARC from its historical strongholds in Meta and Caquetá.[8] The growth of the rentier economy coincided with the offensive, demonstrating the interplay of war escalation and the development of rentierism. More specifically, *war rentierism* denotes that the goal of violence was to help expand rentier capital by eliminating all social forces and individuals that opposed it, as was the case in Meta, as well as Cauca, Middle Magdalena, Caqueta, Bolivar, Arauca, Cesar, Casanare, and others.

Historical Context

Colombia's path to becoming one of the most socially unequal countries in the world lies in its colonial history and the elite that came to rule after it gained its independence in 1819. This chapter very briefly presents the historical context of the subjugation of the Indigenous population and their struggle for autonomy against servitude, exploitation, and the postcolonial state. The historical narrative starts with the Indian *resguardos* established by Spanish colonial authorities in an attempt to exterminate the Indigenous in the late seventeenth century. The most crucial phase in the land struggles relevant to this book's central question started with the Bourbons Reforms of the eighteenth century, their dismantling, and the reinstitution of the Indigenous *resguardos*. This process has happened within the complexities generated by Colombia's capitalist development since the eighteenth century.

The chapter is organized into three main sections. The first section gives a brief historical background explaining how and why the Indigenous were granted legal rights, culminating in the 1991 Constitution. The second and third sections discuss the empirical cases from the Meta and the Cauca, illustrating the core challenges that the Indigenous people are confronting vis-á-vis the advancement of rentier capitalism. The case studies are based on forty unstructured interviews with representatives and leaders of Indigenous groups, peasants, local government officials, human rights activists, and local church officials. Those interviews have been supplemented by official data, statistics, and secondary sources. Some of the interviews were recorded with the consent of the interviewee. Most of the interviewees' identities are not disclosed, upon their request. Instead, they are identified as informants, with their respective official titles.

DEFINING THE "PATH OF ECONOMIC DEPENDENCY" OF COLOMBIA 1750–1900

The Spanish colonial regime changed with the Bourbon Reforms, which attempted to introduce institutional and political changes in Spain by rationalizing and modernizing its state institutions. These changes impacted its colonies' exploitation mechanisms, particularly by devising more effective ways to extract and transfer resources to the metropolis.

The Bourbon Reforms marked significant changes from the previous two centuries of the colonial conquest, according to prominent historian William Paul McGreevey (1971). First and foremost was their gradual reduction of protection accorded to the aboriginals by the Bourbons' predecessors, the Hapsburg kings, and they extended the authority of crown officials over the *criollo* elite. As a result, foreign trade, gold extraction, and export increased by between2 and 2.5 percent per year. This expansion was attributed to the free trade measures introduced within the Spanish empire, beginning with the elimination of the Cadiz merchants' trade monopoly in 1778.

Consequently, the mercantilist policy pursued by Charles III in the colonies was designed to secure more transfer to the metropolis. It rested on two core elements: expanding the number of exportable items, which would enlarge the taxable surplus, and transferring any economic growth back to Spain. By the second part of the eighteenth century, exports exceeded imports thanks to gold extraction and its transfer to Spain. Colombia was the primary source of gold throughout the colonial period and produced one-quarter of the world's output in the eighteenth century.[9] McGreevey (1971) treats 1760–1845 as one historical period marked by policy continuity more than discontinuity given the ouster of Spanish officials and their replacement by the *criollo* elite. The most crucial policy continuity pertinent for this book is land policy and its development over time. In this respect, I discuss two core policies: establishment of the *resguardos* and the formation of the institution of *baldios* (public lands) and the politics of public land distribution.

The *Resguardos* under Colonial Rule and Postindependence

The *resguardos* as an institution were designed in response to the decimation of the native population in Latin America, which declined from one hundred million on the eve of the Spanish conquest to fewer than twelve million by 1650.[10] In 1595, the Spanish government granted the Indian communities land titles and restricted native labor to stymie their decimation. The land titles given to the Indigenous communities came to be known as *resguardos* and remained legal and unchallenged until the eighteenth century's Bourbon Reforms. The critical issue for the large *hacendados* in the eighteenth century was not the acquisition of land but securing labor for their *haciendas*; they needed the Indigenous to work as *Conciertors*. As a result, forced labor in the form of *Concierto* became a common practice in the lands of the *hacendados*, along with public works projects such as road construction.

The forced labor of the Indigenous was justified by Don Antonio de Mans, the Audience President of the New Kingdom of Granada. He stated, "It is good for those who serve because there does not reside in the Indians the desire to have; if we were to leave them at liberty, none would work voluntarily."[11] Indian labor was pivotal for the haciendas, and colonial power sought to secure it to the white and Spanish *hacendados*. Thus, the colonials created a system of resident laborers who produced their foodstuffs while dedicating most of their labor to the landlords.

The *Concierto* system imposed on the Indigenous contributed to the depopulation of the *resguardos*, and consequently, their lands were abandoned. The large landowners could not gain control of the deserted lands because the Indigenous communities did not have the right to sell them. Instead, they rented the lands from the Indigenous; a similar practice remains prevalent in more recent times.[12] The administrative reforms of Charles III (1759–1788) did not introduce rural changes but instead recognized the changes in the land tenure, particularly the disintegration of the *resguardos*. For example, the visitor Don Andres Berdugo y Oquendo found that the Indians had been renting their land to whites, which left only a tiny portion of the *resguardos* to themselves. "Not only were the whites occupying most of the land, but some were living, illegally of course, in the pueblo itself."[13] It is noteworthy that the pressure to usurp Indigenous lands did not stem from large *hacendados* but rather from small Spanish landholders, themselves incipient immigrants, as Orlando Fals Borda has observed.[14]

Fals Borda and Ots Capdequi argue that in 1754 a new phase in land tenure started with the promulgation of the Real *Cedula* (Decree) of October 15. The royal decree 1754 was introduced to repeal the role of the courts; instead, it authorized the local notables to dispatch confirmation of land titles. Decree 1754 was designed to provide a new legal basis for expanding private property at the expense of communal land ownership such as the *resguardos*. The decree of 1754 required landowners to present the appropriate land title to the authorities to remove any undue occupant. The occupant had the choice to pay a modest "compensation," which legalized de facto occupation of public land in violation of the law.

The new land policies and the attack on the *resguardos* had more to do with changes in the metropolis than with internal class dynamics in the colonies, which has been underplayed in the historiography of the times. In the eighteenth century, capitalism entered a new phase in Europe, including laying the foundations of industrial capital in its Iberian periphery. As a result, new modalities were introduced to exploit the colonies, spearheaded by England and France. In this context, Charles III's government was no longer interested in social justice for the Indigenous. Instead, it focused on extracting more from tax money and other sources from the colonies. To levy more taxes and increase rent extraction, the Crown gave more lands to the *criollo* elite, particularly in areas close to urban centers such as Bogotá, which explains why, between 1777 and 1778, the viceregal arranged to sell most of the nineteen *resguardos* in Boyaca.[15]

Thus, the end of the eighteenth century marked the accelerated dismantling of the Indigenous land rights that had been established earlier. The driving economic incentive behind the dispossession of the natives and the dismantling of the *resguardos* was not so much the acquisition of land but, more importantly, to "liberate labor power" that was much needed by the *hacendados* and other property owners. Dispossessing peasants was a typical primitive accumulation process similar to what Marx observed taking part in England and other parts of Europe since the sixteenth century with the incremental advancement of capitalism that increasingly necessitated labor power. Sociologist Orlando Fals Borda underscores the importance of this shift in the exploitation system of labor power to the *Concierto* system, in which peasants received in part wages and a piece of land on which their family could settle. In return, the peasants worked for large landowners for free on certain days of the week. According to Fals Borda, for the landowners the *Concierto* system was 30 percent cheaper than the "peon: wage labor" system that existed then.[16] Hence, the *Concierto* system of exploitation was more effective for capital accumulation.

Driving the Indigenous out of their *resguardos* in the late eighteenth century created a floating rural population seeking employment, which increased vagabondage. Furthermore, with laws prohibiting vagabondage, this depressed wage forced the unemployed to work under harsh conditions benefiting the landowning elite. These laws served the elite well in times of harvest when they needed the most labor power. Vagabonds were rounded up and forced to work because they violated the vagrancy laws.[17] A critical and complementary law to the vagrancy laws was the Crown's acceptance of the Roman law of simple fee land tenure reflected in the August 2, 1780, Royal Decree. According to the simple fee tenure system, unused land can be kept idle for as long as possible. Therefore, the 1780 decree incorporating the simple fee land tenure was designed to prevent the Indigenous from using lands for subsistence farming, forcing them to wage labor. The equation was explicit: limiting access to land to force peasants to wage labor on the *criollo* haciendas by using vagrancy laws as an instrument to discipline and enforce wage labor. However, a puzzle remained, which the following pages try to unravel: How did the *resguardo*, an institution created by the colonial power and phased out by them in the eighteenth century, manage to survive all the way into the twenty-first century?

In the postindependence period, Simón Bolívar, with his liberal thinking influenced by Montesquieu, issued several decrees to protect the Indigenous population, including the decree of May 20, 1820. Bolívar insisted that no Indian remain without land (Decree of April 4, 1824). He restored *resguardos* in Cundinamarca and linked the size of land distributed to each family to their capacity to cultivate it.[18] His goal was to support Indigenous farmers and liberate them from all forms of discrimination and exploitation at the hands of *caciques*, state officials, landowners, and priests. However, landowners and the Church circumvented Bolívar's well-intentioned policies designed to promote equality and imbued with humanistic instincts. One important element emerged from the relationship between Bolívar and the Indigenous. He wanted to eliminate their payment of tributes as part of his attempt to redress the injustices committed against them. The Indigenous, Bolívar revealed, requested to be allowed to make personal contributions.[19] I believe that by making payments to the government coffers the Indigenous sought to retain the right to press for demands, as exhibited in the years that followed.

In the decade that followed Bolívar's tragic death in 1830, there was a push to divide the *resguardos*, but as described by Safford and Palacios (2002), that division was not easy. This push was driven by several factors, including the belief among the ruling elite that if "Indians" that held common lands were not permitted to sell, they could not prosper and actively share in the free market, thus straining the national economic development.[20] This liberal capitalist thinking started taking hold in the early nineteenth century. However, the dismantling of the *resguardos* ran into serious problems, among them the resistance of the Indigenous to such an effort and the dispute over who had the right to the divided land, as well as logistical problems such as the lack of surveyors to do the job. Some Mestizos lived in *resguardos*, and some Indian lived outside their territory.[21] The Creole elite in Bogotá was unhappy with the Indigenous resistance, in contrast to the elite in Cauca, who were based in Popayan. The latter had a different relationship with the *resguardos* due to their existing labor arrangement, which was to the satisfaction of the *hacendados* because they could exploit the labor power of the *resguardos* to sustain their haciendas. That is, the subsumption process became evident in the political economy of Cauca in the 1830s. According to Safford and Palacios, many *resguardos* close to the Central Cordillera bordering the Cauca Valley were also able to preserve their communal land until the end of the nineteenth century,[22] the most plausible reason being that the landed elite could draw on the cheap labor that the *resguardos* offered, as Taussig (1978) demonstrated in his research on the Valle del Cauca.[23] Consequently, *resguardos* survived the reforms of the 1850s, and in 1890 Law 89 was introduced, which recognized land rights granting a certain autonomy to the Indigenous peoples.

However, law 1890 also created an ethnic/racial basis for excluding the Indigenous peoples from the general legal system by formulating special "savage and semi-savage" laws. For example, Ariza (2020) writes that Article 1 of Law 89 states: "The Republican general legislation will not apply to the savages brought into civilized life through missions. Therefore, according to the religious authorities, the government will define how such incipient societies must be governed."[24] As quoted by Ariza, "Law 89 of 1890 stated that the Indigenous person was outside the legal system while remaining in a state of savagery, or semi-savagery. Therefore, in this case, the Indigenous must be regarded as catechumens and sheltered under the missionary's wing."[25] Law 89 of 1890, despite its racist conceptual foundation, provided a legal instrument for the Indigenous to protect their *resguardos* and their way of life. One hundred and one years later, in 1991, a new Constitution was introduced, abandoning the condescending racism of Law 89 and offering more legal guarantees suitable to neoliberal thinking.

Nevertheless, during a long interim period, Law 89 of 1890 was used effectively by the Indigenous leaders, as discussed in the second part of this chapter. According to McGreevey (1971), the "Indian," a subject without agency, resisted, stood his ground, and occasionally outmaneuvered the *criollos*. However, today, since the *apertura* in the early 1990s unleashed the expansion of rentier capital, the *resguardos'* existence is again threatened as they have become economically, socially, and culturally challenged. This chapter examines their successes and their weakened capacities in adapting and resisting the subsumption processes. In the nineteenth century, under enormous pressures from the *hacendados,* the Indigenous leased their lands and sold their labor power in acquiescence, surviving the onslaught. Today, despite the 1991 Constitution's legal protection, the threats to the Indigenous people's land, communal way of production, and life have become more complex and multidimensional. This chapter tackles the question not of whether they will survive but how.

The Indigenous Lands and the Expansion of the Rentier Economy

The 1991 Constitution recognized the Indigenous and Afro-descendants as ethnic groups, granting them communal property rights, including collective rights to their ancestral lands. Such recognition was a watershed in the legal history of Colombia, in which the political establishment accepted the multiethnic composition of the society.

This section argues that the heart of the conflict between the Indigenous groups, the state, and other actors is their land's rights.[26] The Indigenous right to manage their *resguardos,* communal land property, production, language, and culture are central to their struggle to exercise their autonomy. Nevertheless, some Indigenous lands are in extraction areas (oil, gold, coal) or subject to subsumption by agribusinesses. Lands of the *resguardos* put the communities of the Meta, Cauca, and elsewhere in the eye of the rentier hurricane. Remember that about 54 percent of the Amazon region and 27 percent of the national territory are classified as Indigenous lands.[27] A good swath of these lands have been the target of rentier capital, local and foreign.

While in the previous centuries Indigenous labor power was the target of the large landowners (*hacendados*) who needed their labor for tending their cultivation and cattle, in the late twentieth century and into the twenty-first, the new dominant groups and economic conglomerates have sought only their land, in which their effort is compounded by the support of the state who is also seeking to increase its rents and assert its "sovereign" right to the subsoil.[28] The "right" to the subsoil has emerged as the main fault line of contentious politics in the rentier political economy, defining the relationship between the state, the dominant class, Indigenous groups, and the Afro-descendants. The latter groups reject the state's claim of sovereign rights and their transfer to third parties such as multinational companies. The emerging lines of conflict affecting the Indigenous groups can be summed up into two principal categories/groups: (1) the state, the dominant class, multinational corporations, illegal mining interests, and agribusinesses; and (2) illegal plantations, organized crime, and insurgents' groups.

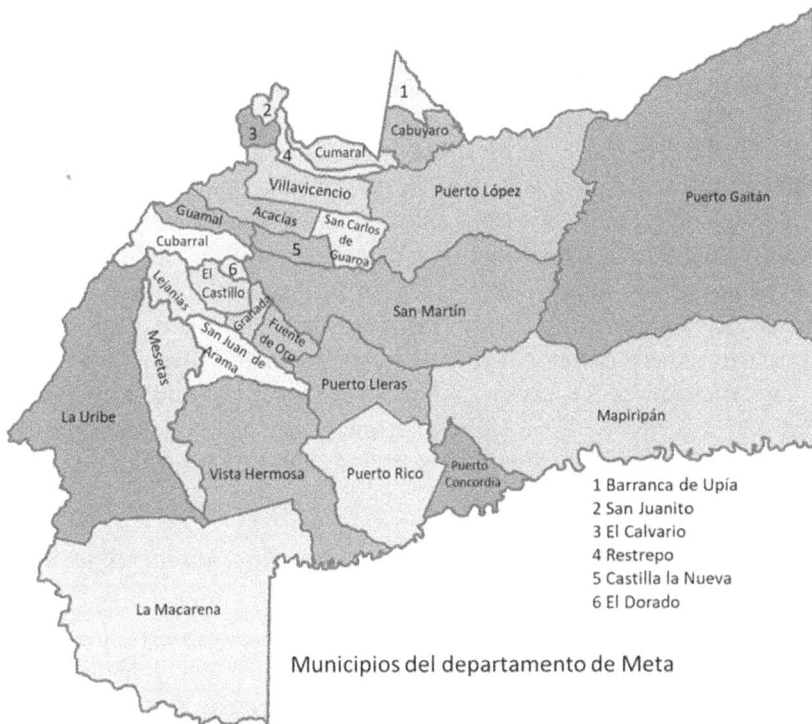

Map 4.1. Meta. *Source*: Public domain.

Since the 1990s, Puerto Gaitan, Meta, has been one of the chief peripheral places in Colombia transformed by the interplay of oil economics and the expansion of the agribusinesses and land speculation under cover of cattle ranching, as discussed in chapter 2, which is to say, the main pillars of the rentier economy. The Indigenous groups and the family-based peasant economy within Puerto Gaitan and its surroundings were impacted the most by the advent of the rentier economy and the expansion of agribusinesses, which included African palm oil, rubber, timber, and livestock. The state's economic policy articulation is spelled out in CONPES 2011, elaborated by its Department of National Planning (DNP). In this plan, 13.5 million hectares in the Meta and Vichada are the targeted areas for megaprojects in the three mentioned sectors. The capitalist enterprises come from many countries, including China, Brazil, the United States, Argentina, and Bolivia.[29] Keep in mind that the average daily oil production in 2011 amounted to 420,777 barrels produced by Meta, the leading national oil producer. The increase in oil production in the Meta changed its economy radically, by attracting foreign capital as well as migrant labor from other departments, and increased commodity prices, land values, and the cost of housing. These contributed to the decline in agricultural lands dedicated to food production. As a result, Meta's population dwindled until the late 1970s, thus laying the roots of the rentier political economy.

In the department of Meta, there are close to 20,500 Indigenous of three main ethnic groups: Sikuani, Saliba, and Piapocos, distributed into nine *resguardos,* and invariably all of them have difficulties in coping with the rapid political economy reconfiguration that the department has been undergoing since the second half of the twentieth century. It is too simplistic to classify this relationship with only one aspect or two. My goal is to provide the most accurate description and analysis of the multidimensionality of the relationship between *resguardos'* political economy and those encircling them in a department that has been transformed from agricultural production to oil extraction, agribusinesses, and services.

Colombia's Conglomerates and War Rentierism in Meta

Conglomerates are agents whose core objective is to insert Colombia's economy into the ranks of the global division of labor, which increasingly rests on a rentier triad consisting of services, extractive industries, and agribusiness. Meta and the other peripheral frontier departments such as Vichada, Caquetá, Putumayo, Vaupes, and Guainía possess strategic natural reserves, water resources, and minerals, making them attractive to local and foreign capital. Expanding investments into frontiers represents a leap of the rentier capitalist development in Colombia. Consequently, the conquest of these lands and their incorporation into the circuits of capital have become an imperative to the "decentering spatial fix," as defined in this chapter.[30] Organized crime is active in the departments mentioned above; its study is beyond the scope of this chapter.

The following section is divided into four subsections. The first three discuss the Colombian conglomerates that increased their investments in the Meta during the past two decades, namely: Sarmiento Angulo Group, Santo Domingo Group, and Fazenda, all based in Colombia. These three are among many others that capitalized on the violent changes that organized crime accomplished in the 1980s: chasing out the FARC and its peasant bases. The fourth section has one subsection discussing the relationship between Fazenda and the Indigenous and how Fazenda is subsuming a noncapitalist mode of social production.

SARMIENTO ANGULO GROUP

In 1974, Angulo's group had a market share of 9 percent of GDP. Then, it increased to 10.5 percent of GDP, with a capital of more than $7 billion. By 2016, its share in the country's $282.5 billion GDP had decreased to 4.28 percent, while its assets increased to $12.1 billion. Grupo Santo Domingo focused on the beer markets, globalized its business incursion through acquisitions and mergers, and ventured into other service-oriented sectors, including the media.[31] Its net worth was estimated to be $15.7 billion, about 5.5 percent of its capital in 2016. Despite this decrease, they still command the lion's share of the country's economy. They remained in the same classification as other monopolies such as Argos, the shapers of the country's political economy and its relationship with the global capitalist system. Sarmiento Group, which offers internet services, beverages, mass media, tourism, and banking, controls about 30 percent of the finance sector.[32] This group has launched ventures that include an infrastructure road project linking Villavicencio, Meta's capital, with Bogotá and Puerto Gaitan, enhancing the market integration of Meta and Altillanura with the capital, the rest of the country, and the global economy.

In the 1980s, Sarmiento Group was the first among Colombia's conglomerates to venture into Meta while the private armies of criminal organizations were still in the midst of their violent conflict with the FARC. It inaugurated its capitalist incursion with its branch Corficolombia in a joint investment with Unilever's Anglo-Dutch multinational, operated by Unipalma S.A. In this early investment, the group and Unilever acquired 4,500 hectares located in Cumaral, a municipality under the control of criminal organizations. This land has been planted with palm oil trees. In addition to this partnership with Unilever, Sarmiento is partnering through Cabriolet with three other companies owned by large investors.[33] Those associates owned 25 percent of 3,816 hectares located in the municipality of Primavera.

The 1997 offensive engaged in by organized crime, led by the United Autodefenses of Colombia (AUC)—an umbrella organization for narcotrafficking groups—against Mapiripan ushered in a new phase and forcing the FARC to retreat. The AUC offensive was followed in 2003 by the state's offensive with the support of the United States' S Plan Colombia. In this new, more secure environment with legal state protection, Corficolombiana expanded its investments in Meta by expanding its agroindustries, mainly rubber plantations. It acquired Mavelle and Pajonales, rubber agribusinesses of 4,600 and twenty-two thousand hectares, respectively. Its goal was the extraction of latex and cashing in on carbon bonds that the UN started issuing in 2005.[34] Pajonales secured a trade deal with the French multinational Michelin, which produces rubber and tires: Pajonales provides the raw rubber extract, and Michelin manufactures the material. Like most industries in the Eastern Plains, this project received financial support from the state. In 2009, Jorge Robledo, a senator and government critic, alleged that Sarmiento's agribusinesses received more than one-third of the state's funds paid to the department of Meta (six million Colombian pesos out of seventeen million).[35] Sarmiento's acquisition of Pajonales raised an essential question regarding the legality of the land ownership. The acquisition of lands of this size in areas reserved for poor peasants violated Law 160 of 1994, which limited the size of public land that an individual can own according to a scale called the Family Production Unit (Unidad de Production Familiar) (UAF).[36] Sarmiento's investments contributed to an astronomical increase in land prices, affecting the small peasant economy.[37] A hectare of land close to Pajonales sells for ten million CP, close to three thousand U.S. dollars. This land is planted with short-cycle crops such as corn and soybeans.[38]

Santo Domingo Group

The Santo Domingo Group has adopted the Brazilian "Enclosed Model," which includes grabbing large tracts of land to create economies of scale, which in most cases has required appropriating peasants' and public lands and planting cash crops for export.[39] The Group promotes agribusinesses' cultivation of corn and soya in Vichada (among the last available frontiers land), transporting the grains to Puerto Gaitan, Meta, for sale. Santo Domingo's business strategy depends on land leasing and subcontracting production. The Group has sought to rent twenty-three thousand hectares. This strategy is consistent with the group's historical experience in logistics, transportation, and storage gained from decades of beer production and marketing. Hence, its venture into storing, marketing, and distributing grains was a logical step. The means of transportation are the Meta River and a highway under construction.

Santo Domingo Group is a holding company with diversified investments, including breweries and telecommunications. The capital and assets of Santo Domingo Group amounted to 4.6 percent of the country's GDP in 1974 and had more than doubled (to $8 billion, or 10.9 percent of GDP) by 1999. By 2016, its capital had reached $12.1 billion. The Group went into Meta in the mid-1980s, during the narcobourgeoisie's ascendance in the department. It thrived even during the respective military offensives by organized crime (1980–2005) and Colombia's army, which sought to dislodge the FARC from the Meta, one of its historical strongholds, and make the area hospitable to agroindustry and oil extraction.

Fazenda and Indigenous

Fazenda, like the Sarmiento and Angulo groups, invested only after the organized criminal organization of narcotraffickers and the emerald Mafia had secured their hegemonic control over a large portion of the Meta. Fazenda is one of the major dealers in animal feed such as soy products and corn, and it owns the country's largest pork slaughterhouse and is the largest distributor of pork products. Since its establishment, Fazenda has faced questions about the land it acquired for its facility, land which the Mafioso Victor Carranza previously owned. Fazenda's disputes with the Indigenous have stemmed from its land acquisitions, encroaching on the lands assigned to *resguardos*. The Indigenous have also complained about the foul smell that the Fazenda slaughtering facility produces, which affects the Wakoyo *resguardo* that is across the street from the facility. Both contentious issues, among others, have led to several mobilizations, including the 2013 occupation of Fazenda's facility by the Sikuani Indigenous group that lives in the Wakoyo *resguardo*.

Fazenda is a joint capital venture involving two leading business enterprises, the Santander group Aliar, and the Medellín-based agribusiness

Contegral, owned by the Mesa family, which produces food for animals. In 2003, they joined forces and established Fazenda, making it the leading pork provider to the Colombian market. The land on which Fazenda has its facility and farm is estimated to occupy between eighteen and twenty thousand hectares and was previously owned by Victor Carranza, the "Emerald Mafioso," who has appropriated large swaths of land in the Meta.[40]

Fazenda brought with it ten other agribusinesses, some of which have the same owners in Santander and Medellin, and Jaime Lievano's son, Juan Pablo Lievano, who represents one of the companies that own the agribusiness Brazil. The Aliar group plans to expand its land acquisitions to one hundred thousand hectares by 2027, to increase its soy and corn production for animal feed. Capital and war in Colombia have been intimately interlaced since La Violencia. The four businesses discussed above have either increased or commenced their investments under the fog of war. However, Colombia's capitalism is not unique in this respect, as other world-historical experiences attest.[41]

The Englobed Indigenous: Clientelism and Subsumption

This subsection describes the multidimensional relationship between the *resguardos*' political economy and the multinational corporations and agribusinesses that surround them. Meta has been transformed from agricultural production to dependency on oil extraction, agribusinesses, and services, that is, a rentier economy. There are 13,760 Indigenous in Meta, belonging to three main ethnic groups: Sikuani, Saliba, and Piapocos.[42] They are distributed into nine *resguardos* occupying about 332,000 hectares. About 90 percent of the Indigenous population are Sikuani. They form part of the Unama Association, the organizational umbrella that includes governors elected by their respective *resguardos*. The governor is the community leader, and their function is to safeguard the cohesion and well-being of the *resguardos*' families and represent the *resguardo* before the state, the companies, and other communities.[43]

Most Indigenous ethnic groups have a complex relationship with the rapid economic reconfiguration that the department has undergone since the second half of the twentieth century. Their Indigenous livelihood, culture, social fabric, and subsistence peasant economy have been impacted. The advent of the corporations has produced two interlaced conditions: the creation of an enclave where economic power is centered; and second, a clientelisticdependent relationship in which companies pay for their influence and the acquiescence of the communities, most particularly when it relates to "Prior Consultation."[44] This observation is based on interviews supplemented by secondary sources.[45] The clientelistic dependency forms part of the subsumption system because its objective is to co-opt the Indigenous communities in cases where their lands are sought. The dependency relationship is especially pronounced on the Wakoyo reservation, where 370 predominantly Sikauni families receive provisions from CEPSA, a Spanish oil company.[46] But this is only part of a vast clientelist network created by the enclave economy. Pacific Rubiales, the leading multinational oil corporation operating in Meta, has built multiple relationships with the surrounding *resguardos,* by means that include funding projects and providing food.[47] In this regard, the Catholic Church plays a role in distributing assistance.

The "largesse" of the enclave economy has cemented clientelism and dependency, allowing it to penetrate the *resguardos,* sidestep the community's governors, and forge relations with other leaders. Such subversion of authority has served the interest of companies and the political ambitions of the local leaders seeking to challenge the governor.[48] Some leaders in various communities such as Domo-Planas, Awaliba, and Alto Unuma, among others, have challenged the governor's authority and sought to tap into the "fringe benefits" of power that a close relationship with the big businesses brings.[49] Furthermore, the clientelistic relationship that the companies have built with some local leaders has activated family- and kinship-based divisions, which have undermined the social cohesion of the *resguardo.*[50]

Land Leasing, Adaptability, Resistance, and Subsumption

Adaptability

Fredy Galino, a teacher and member of the Sikuani ethnic group, explained the effects of land leasing on his community. According to Galino, the Wakoyo reservation occupies an area of 8,050 hectares. "As a result of the twenty-thirteen Indigenous strike, Fazenda agreed to pay us three hundred million CP/year in rent [about US$100,000/year], which is distributed equally to the three hundred and sixteen families of the community."[51] Since 1975, he reported, the Sikuanis have become more sedentary and less nomadic.[52] He attributed this change to several factors, but chiefly to the advocacy of "some teachers sent by the government social services that started convincing the community to settle down and take up agriculture rather than hunting and fishing."[53] By 2015, the Sikuani were using bricks and cement in construction, which reflected the profound changes in their lives; as Galino put it, "Those workshops organized by the teachers led us to adopt a Western mode of life."[54]

RESISTANCE

Several factors explain Fazenda's offering money and other incentives to the Sikuanis, including securing the rental of three thousand hectares from Wakoyo *resguardo,* which they used to produce corn to feed Fazenda's pig farm. Monetary incentives were also employed to defend the company against the community's complaints that the Fazenda pig farm generated contaminants and offensive smells, affecting them and allegedly causing the deaths of seven children.[55] In fact, in 2012 there was a strike, and members of the Wakoyo *resguardo* occupied the Fazenda facilities.[56] Renting reservation land to agribusinesses is a relatively new phenomenon, which increasingly links Indigenous communities with the circuits of capital. More importantly, it enhances the community's dependence on such land rents, thereby monetizing their economy. Members of the Sikuani noted that the rental relationship with Fazenda undermined their communally based economy and led to growing tensions within the community as it tried to formulate a coherent response to the challenges it faces.[57] Labor and, more importantly, the land has been incrementally appropriated by Fazenda and its agribusinesses allies. This case exemplifies what Marx referred to as subsumption, which might endure for generations and which does not necessarily imply a linear change due to multiple variables, including capital structure, community agency, resistances, climate change, public policy, and economic crisis. The following subsection tackles an intergenerational problem that is evolving.

THE YOUNGER GENERATION AND THE PROCESS OF SUBSUMPTION

To further elaborate on the erosion process within the Indigenous groups' social fabric, the informants explained the tension in intergenerational relations, particularly between youths, who have acquired some education and have learned to read Spanish, and the older authorities (the captains), who do not read Spanish. The Indigenous youths, who know how to read, have established relationships with the oil companies, while their older leaders could not, which, in turn, has subverted power/authority relationships within the ethnic group and created tension, as in the case of the governors discussed above. The youths can work with the oil company and generate income, while their elders could not. An informant from the Piapoco community noted that young people are now being employed by the oil companies in the area: "Six young men abandoned the Piapoco *resguardo,* and eight young women left the Saliba reservation to work with oil companies. This destabilizes our way of life and threatens its continuity."[58] According to this informant and others interviewed, the Indigenous communities have a great challenge in addressing the needs of the younger generation that are more educated and plan for a future outside the Indigenous culture, its norms, and its traditions. The following section discusses war rentierism in Meta following the achievement of the 2016 peace accord with the FARC.

War Rentierism 2016–

Since the mid-twentieth century, the department of Meta has been a major theater of conflict and violence. The interplay of insurgency, counterin-surgency, and the U.S.-supported Plan Colombia has shaped its political economy and had its toll on the department population, Indigenous and *mestizo* peasants. In sharp contrast, in Meta, as in Arauca and Casanare, multinational corporations have thrived as they invest and increase their oil extraction, manifesting the role of multinational corporations in the Colombian war system

An illustrative case is Pacific Energy, the Canadian-based multina-tional oil corporation, which expanded its oil production during the most challenging years of civil war leading up to 2016. The mechanism that allowed it to continue its operations was the creation of a security web composed of state forces (special forces or battalion-strength), paramil-itaries, private security, and indirect payments to rebels.[59] That was how such actors as multinational corporations became involved in a systemic relationship called a war system.[60]

By 2008, Rubiales had acquired more lands around its largest Quifa oil fields, reaching fifty-five thousand hectares.[61] These lands remained owned by Pacific until 2016, when it sold them to Catalyst Enterprise and its Quifa's oilfields to Ecopetrol, the Colombian oil multinational. Catalyst and Ecopetrol maintained almost the same security apparatus (minus the rebels). Officially, Rubiales was liquidated in 2016. The Catalyst Group now owns their properties, including the fifty-five thousand hectares usurped from local peasants.

The neo-paramilitaries that emerged after 2005–06 demobilization of the AUC continue to operate in Meta as of this writing. Two main groups were identified by multiple sources, including the informants interviewed: Clan del Golfo and Anti Subversive Revolutionary Army. Both operate in Puerto Gaitan and Vichada. Both are extracting protection rents from corporations and businesses.[62] They provide protection and impose a reign of terror to safeguard the post–civil war land tenure system by deterring land restitution claimants.[63] An example is a terrain of twenty-eight thousand hectares that was usurped by the late Mafioso Victor Carranza in the Porvenir, in the Puerto Gaitan metropolitan area. In June 2021, the Carranza family's paramilitaries assassinated peasants who had started reclaiming their lost land.[64] Furthermore, in January 2021, a group of Sikuanis attempted to reclaim their ancestral lands, from which paramilitaries had forcefully removed them in preceding decades. Once more, they were confronted by paramilitaries, who threatened them.[65] These cases are among many others that this research encountered in Meta and Cauca, Cimitarra, and San Pablo.

A picture is emerging in which two main issues become apparent. One, that paramilitary groups are still a force to be reckoned with. Two, they serve the function of safeguarding the gains of rentier capital acquired by usurping millions of hectares from Indigenous and *mestizos* peasants; now occupied by multinational corporations like the defunct Rubiales, mining companies, agribusinesses, African palm oil plantations, cattle ranchers, recreation resorts, and the energy-mining sector. Thus, the paramilitaries and their sponsors act to secure the gains of war rentierism, making sure that land assets are not given back, which explains the increasing number of assassinations of land claimants nationwide following the promulgation of Law 1448 in June 2011 regarding land restitution. Following the introduction of Law 1448 and until April 2018, forty-five leaders who sought to claim land restitution were assassinated; 27percent of those were Indigenous and Afro-Colombian, and 73 percent were *mestizos campesinos*.[66]

Cauca *Resguardos* between Resistance and Adaptability

Like the situation in Meta, Cauca's Indigenous are struggling to resist and adapt to the encroaching rentier political economy. However, there are four differences between the two cases that are important to note from the outset: The first is that Cauca has a much larger Indigenous population than Meta, punctuated by a very long history of struggle for autonomy; the second is the importance of its agroindustry, which exceeds that of Meta; third, the mining sector, chiefly gold, has been a mainstay of its economy since colonial times, while oil in Meta is a more recent addition; and the fourth and last is what I call the "geo-economy" of Cauca, that is, its geographic location as a corridor for trafficking cocaine, with its soil suitable for coca plantations. The interplay of those four factors gives Cauca's political economy a distinct characteristic that corresponds to a variant of rentier economies. The political economy of Cauca is characterized as "late capitalist development." Its capitalist development peaked after World War II, when it moved away from the hacienda/mining system into export-driven agroindustrial businesses such as the sugar cane mills, the extraction of gold, oil, and coltan, timber, and cattle ranching. This development was transformative in its scope and magnitude, like the oil boom in Meta. The following section discusses the Indigenous Council for Cauca Region (CRIC), which became one of its most influential organizations.

CRIC and the Articulation of Ethnic Identity

The Indigenous People of Cauca

The Indigenous people of Cauca, the largest concentration after La Guajira, are represented by different tribes: Páez (Nasa) 65 percent, Yanacona 15 percent, Guámbiano 13 percent, Coconuco 5 percent, and Embera and Inga 2 percent. (IGAC 1992). About 24.8 percent of its 1.2 million are Indigenous people and 22 percent are Afro descendants.[67] Combined, they occupy 32 percent of Cauca's surface area. The remaining land is in the hands of the landed elite, agribusinesses, multinational corporations, and narcotraffickers. The Indigenous population has witnessed a significant increase of 24.1 percent, from 248,532 to 308,455 people, between

2005 and 2018,[68] representing an average increase of 1.66 percent, which exceeds the national average of 0.39 percent. The GINI land index shows an increasing trend in the concentration of land ownership since the 1970s, making Cauca the second department in this category after Valle del Cauca: 83.7 and 84.7 percent respectively.[69]

The Indigenous inhabit a geostrategic crossroad to the Pacific Ocean endowed with natural resources. The lure of the department's rich natural resources attracted waves of incursions by multiple actors, including multinational corporations, illegal miners, armed nonstate actors, land speculators, agribusinesses, and narcotraffickers. During La Violencia (1948–1958), those incursions intensified and exacerbated land struggles between *hacendados* and the peasantry, who comprised the Indigenous, Afro-Colombian, and *mestizo* populations. As a result, the Consejo Indigena Regional del Cauca (Indigenous Council for Cauca Region/CRIC) was created in 1971 in the *resguardo* of Toribio, against the background of the struggles of the Indigenous in the villages of Silvia and Credo, both in the north of Cauca, and building on the long struggles of the natives elsewhere. CRIC has been instrumental in articulating and organizing the resistance of the communities and presenting national plans. Its objectives have been unity, land, and culture, which translates into an autonomous rule.

Historical Background of the Legalistic Approach

At the outset, it is imperative to shed some light on the litigation experiences accumulated by the Indigenous and their leaders during the seventeenth and eighteenth centuries as they learned that their precarious survival depended on whatever legal protection the King of Spain could offer. The historical records validated such a view.[70] For example, in the eighteenth century, the Nasas obtained a royal patent (*Cedulas Reales*) from the King of Spain that recognized the *cabildos* authority and granted them lands as aboriginals; this became a stepping stone that helped them acquire more lands for their *resguardos*. The majority of the titled lands were in the province of Paez, a Nasa native territory located within the jurisdiction of Cauca's capital, Popayan. The records indicated that the *caciques* played a core role in recuperating ancestral lands and expanding the boundaries of the *resguardos* that Corona had granted in the seventeenth century, securing the local colonial authority's recognition. They also revealed that the Nasa negotiated with Spanish hacienda landowners close to Popayan.[71] A case in point is the *resguardo* Tobayma, which was awarded in 1663, and the attempts of natives to expand it into a nearby Itaiby hacienda owned by a Spanish captain who was granted this land for his military service. The Indigenous presented a legal claim to the land and succeeded in annexing some of it to their *resguardos*. In presenting their claim, they combined litigation and direct action, which proved effective in the Paez province. This combination of litigation plus communal pressure became a recurring practice in the eighteenth and nineteenth centuries.[72] This salient legalistic tactic was manifested in several cases in which the Nasa natives used the argument that they were recognized as "direct vassals of the king" and consequently claimed more lands to expand their *resguardos*.[73]

Before drawing a premature conclusion, one must consider another core factor that helped the Nasa in Cauca have a comparative advantage over other natives in Colombia. The Cauca's Paez province was extremely inhospitable and predominantly inhabited by the Nasa ethnic group.[74] In the seventeenth century, this demographic composition did not change, which gave the Nasa a comparative advantage vis-à-vis other Indigenous groups with larger Spanish mixed populations. Geography, litigation, resistance, and negotiating skill helped the Nasa craft a policy that suited the Crown while obtaining gains from the local Popayan governors.

In 1708, Juan Tama Y Calambas, a Nasa chief, was granted land by the king of Spain in Vitonco, where his community lived. The title of the land became emblematic of defending their lands against any encroachments that remained important to the natives' political consciousness.[75] Caballero described the importance of Tama's successful experience in hammering out an agreement with the king of Spain, which resulted in the establishment of five *resguardos*. Centuries later, the importance of having land title remained palpable in the natives' modern political praxis, according to Rapaport's (1985) study. Caballero, in his turn, validated Rapaport's observation that the collective memory of the Paez (Nasa) still retained the importance of obtaining and having title over the land as a mechanism to protect their *resguardos*, as sanctioned by laws and norms.[76]

The legendary sharecropper and Paez leader Quintin Lame (1883–1967) employed past experience by emphasizing the legal path as a defense strategy against the state's stampeding their *resguardos*' rights, boundaries, and autonomy. A self-taught peasant, Quintin Lame understood the importance of calling on the "jurisprudence of the oppressed," for instance, to capitalize on the liberal notion of rights by reframing it to incorporate the plight of the marginalized. Julieta Lemaitre (2017) argued that this type of jurisprudence used by Lame might be identified within the genre of "minor jurisprudence."[77] Lemaitre contended that the minor jurisprudence of the oppressed and marginalized sought to subvert the dominant bourgeois racialized legal order. Lame's style and legal approach were described by Lemaitre as follows: "His writings, although profuse, are also fragmented, scattered in letters and newspaper articles, and interrupted by lapses into poetry and mystic visions, as well as extended paraphrases of well-known legal authorities, changing words to suit his needs. This form of writing has a disturbing and alluring effect, de-territorializing legal expertise by both claiming the authority to speak as a lawyer and performing that authority in tandem with appeals to poetry and emotion, and with odd forms of legal bricolage and innovative interpretations."[78]

An alternative jurisprudence sought to extract from the bourgeois jurisprudence as much as possible protection, particularly for the Paez's legal land titles, chiefly the *resguardos*. His appeal to justice alongside activism redressed the skewed nature of law biased in favor of the dominant classes. Lame and Tama shared the common idea of extracting as many legal protections as possible without necessarily destroying the system of domination and exploitation set up by the colonial powers or the post-colonial capitalist order. The following sections discuss the emergence of CRIC in Cauca. This most important Indigenous organization absorbed Tama's and Lame's legacies, chiefly their struggle for legal protection of their fundamental rights.

CRIC and Its Foundation (1971–present)

The development of political consciousness was a process that passed through countless historical experiences that remained in the collective memory of the groups, including those discussed above. Some individuals played unique roles, such as Pedro Leon Rodriguez, known as the "red priest," and Gustavo Mejia. Both were activists and played a significant role in articulating CRIC strategy.[79] Father Pedro Leon Rodriguez acted as a mediator between the local authorities and some of the Liberal guerrillas that had not yet disarmed. In 1966, he became the parish priest of Corinto and led a support group of landless peasants who occupied the hacienda Santa Elena, owned by one of the *hacendados*. He also led the United Popular Movement, which won representation in the local council. Father Rodriquez also supported the radical Agrarian Social Front (FRESAGRO) led by Mejia and called upon the Cauca priests to support CRIC and the Indigenous population.[80]

Gustavo Mejia was born in 1950 in Trujillo, Cauca, the son of a family escaping "La Violencia." In 1957 he spent some years in Herrera, South Tolima, a hotbed of insurgency. During his stay in Herrera he established a relationship with the Liberal guerrillas who recruited disgruntled liberals to a Left-leaning insurgency. He spent some time in prison, accused of the kidnapping, in 1965, of Harold Elder. After his release, he came back to Corinto, founding FRESAGRO, and promoted the first assemblies of CRIC. He was assassinated in 1974, and Father Rodriguez died in Cali under suspicious circumstances in 1970.[81] With the disappearance of those two leaders, CRIC and local activists started to consider the creation of armed auto defenses, which was an idea promoted by the Communist Party and became common among peasants' communities in Tolima and elsewhere. In addition to Mejia and Gomez, many others supported CRIC and contributed to the creation of an Indigenous movement,[82] including Edgar Londoño, Pablo Tattay, born in Hungary and living in Colombia, Luis Ángel Monroy, the teacher Graciela Bolaños, and the journalist Víctor Daniel Bonilla, in addition to three intellectuals from Argentina, Panama, and Chile. Luis Ángel Monroy, Afro-descendant, was born in Candeleria, Valle, and joined the Indigenous movement in the 1970s, becoming and radicalized after the assassination of Mejia and calling for the creation of armed Indigenous auto defenses.[83] Subsequently, he joined M-19 and became one of the founding members of the Quintin Lame insurgent group. Edgar Londono, was a teacher from Rionegro, Antioquia, who resided in Corinto and in the 1970s worked as a social worker in INCORA, whose role then was to help consolidate the incipient peasants' organization. Despite his position in INCORA, where he stayed until 1988, Londono actively supported CRIC and its leading ideological proponents such as Mejia.[84]

THE PACT OF CHICORAL AND THE CRIC

Pablo Tattay, one of the prominent leaders of the Indigenous movement, described the organizational process, saying that it all started during the presidency of Carlos Lleras Restrepo (1966–1970), when there was the optimism of possible land reform. CRIC was created at that moment. He explained that the goal was to articulate the Indigenous and peasants' concerns and demands. However, these efforts were soon dashed by the adoption of the Pact of Chicoral in 1972 (discussed in chapters 1 and 2), which ended and reversed Lleras Restrepo's reformist attempt.[85] Tattay explained that the Chicoral Pact put the Indigenous of Cauca again in the traditional confrontational mode against the large landowning class in the region.[86] Not only in Cauca, the reversal of Lleras Restrepo's reforms led to an intensification of conflict, expulsion, and violence in most rural areas around the country.[87]

Tattay summed up CRIC's three-pronged strategy since 1972. One is to recognize the state's norms; two, to pressure the state to fulfill its obligation toward these communities; and three, to empower the Indigenous groups' traditional structures to resist the system of domination that governs them. Initially, CRIC carried out its resistance activities quasi-clandestinely under the slogan "Unity, Land, and Culture." Tattay concluded that the resistance continued because, fundamentally, the system of domination persisted.[88]

The primary organizational tool has been the Indigenous *cabildo*, the governing body that each communal group has.[89] The *cabildo* became the focal point where the Indigenous learn to govern themselves, construct autonomy, and, more important, form their organic intelligentsia. When the CRIC was formed, some *cabildos* stood against the Indigenous tenants that were losing their lands, siding with the Church, traditional politicians, and landlords involved in this dispossession. Nevertheless, this unfortunate episode did not change the CRIC leadership's view of the historical importance that *cabildos* might play in charting the path of resistance and autonomy.[90] Subsequently, CRIC's effort has focused on regaining those *cabildos* and seeking to liberate them from the spell of the Church and large landlords and to rebuild the inactive ones. Those efforts paid off, resulting in a new leadership within the *cabildos* faithful to their group's collective interest.[91] The *cabildo* was consolidated as the primary organizational tool to build a national Indigenous movement, and the CRIC became the general assembly of *cabildos*.

THE STEPPING STONE: LAW 89 OF 1890

Two primary laws marked the history of the Indigenous peoples and their rights, providing tools to protect their culture and way of life: Law 89 of 1890, and, one hundred and one years later, the 1991 Constitution, which expanded the legal protection of the Indigenous and other minorities, including the Afro-descendants discussed in the next chapter. Tattay spelled out a three-pronged strategy: educating the Indigenous of their legal rights to raise their political consciousness; compelling the state to respect, acknowledge, and fulfill its commitment to those rights; and mobilizing the Indigenous to resist the system of domination. The first goal addressed political education and socialization about the groups' legal rights, articulating their distinct ethnic agenda regarding their history, tradition, customs, languages, and communal life. The last two goals proactively laid the grounds for contentious identity politics.

Law 89 of 1890 served as the linchpin to achieve these three goals. First, it recognized the *resguardos* as the legitimate right of the Indigenous to their lands and their autonomy to rule themselves by their customs and traditions. Secondly, the core legal element of self-rule within a particular territory gave the Indigenous communities some legal protection against violators. Although CRIC leaders noted that Law 89 of 1890 had a racist and condescending premise by treating Indigenous as "minors" and "savages," and created the "Division of Indigenous Relations" to act as a guide, they were also aware that other articles of Law 89, which were essential for their legal protection, established a sort of legitimacy. They opined that, with that legitimacy, they could build upon their political struggle to protect their culture and autonomy and recover the lands of the *resguardos*. CRIC used it as a tool for socialization and education of the communities.[92]

During the 1970s, a period of heavy persecution, CRIC developed its educational program and taught the *cabildos* about the stipulation of Law 89 of 1890 and practical issues of immediate concerns, such as ceasing the payment of land rents and the recovery of lost land. The interesting aspect of this education process was the breadth of its coverage, which included workshops to discuss land reform in Latin America, socialism, peasants' and workers' struggles, social conditions in Colombia and Cauca, and other themes, depending on the political circumstances and the organizational development.[93]

The Formation of a Political Identity: Class and Ethnicity

CRIC's three-tier program reflected the concentric circles of its modus operandi and national strategy. The innermost circle was made up of the *cabildos* and *resguardos*. Within this circle, the immediate issues related to the group were discussed, including Law 89 and the most current political issues. The second circle comprised the zones and focused on education about the history of Colombia, the history of the CRIC, analyzing the correlation of force between the friends and enemies, social class structures in Cauca, and assessing the current political situation. The last circle was the regional one, in which only the representatives of the organization participated. Discussion themes depend on the pressing political issues at the national, regional, and global levels. Among the themes that have been discussed were Indigenous peoples' relationship with the state, along with socialist theory and its praxis in Latin America.[94] The Indigenous communities are made up of peasants that depend on farming to make a living and enjoy the fruits of collective land property. This class characteristic has helped them define their identity vis-à-vis other peasants, who might be small landowners or be seeking individual land ownership.

In contrast, the Indigenous people do not seek private property. In addition, by not contesting the state's power, the CRIC and the Indigenous have distinguished their stance from that of other groups, including ANUC and the insurgent groups influenced by Marxist-Leninist ideology. CRIC's stance has been that power is constructed from the bottom up.

CRIC has focused on Indigenous groups in alliance with ANUC, while ANUC concentrated its efforts on non-Indigenous peasants. Disagreements emerged between the two organizations when ANUC attempted to fold CRIC under its leadership, overlooking the peculiarity of the ethnic component that CRIC represents. This ethnic component became more pronounced in the 1970s and 1980s, exacerbating those tensions, which led to friction between the Indigenous and FARC and other insurgent groups. The insurgents failed to reconcile the nature of the emancipatory revolutionary project with the autonomous claims of the Indigenous. As a case in point, FARC maintained a strong military presence in Cauca, including in the *resguardos,* and sought to impose their authority, which the Indigenous *cabildos* often rejected. Nonetheless, FARC had to negotiate with the *cabildos* to mitigate their resistance to the guerrillas' presence in their *resguardos.* The Indigenous sought to protect their communities by preventing the state forces and the rebels from trespassing within their territory or using it as a battleground, which had been the case on countless occasions during the civil war.

Autonomy, Governance, and the Westphalian State

By distancing its position from the warring actors in the civil war, including the state, the CRIC sought to achieve three core objectives: (1) consolidate Indigenous people's autonomy vis-à-vis other political actors, thereby underscoring their ethnic identity; (2) build Indigenous people's confidence in their capability of ruling their own territories, recovering lost lands, and governing the people by dispensing justice, services, and guidance; and (3) articulate an ethnic identity based on the ideological worldview of the Indigenous, which does not coincide with dogmatic modernization paradigms of the Left or the Right. Although Karl Marx understood that humans are the products of nature and are governed by universal laws, he acknowledged the progressive aspect of capitalism compared to previous social systems that had existed throughout history. But he did not present an apology for capitalism's savagery in enslaving people of the colonies and subsuming previous modes of subsistence economies. He simply laid out his own empirical historical analysis of the paths of socioeconomic change since primitive societies. Marx's in the 1844 Manuscripts wrote:

> Man is a species-being . . . because in practice and in theory he adopts the species (his own as well as those of other things) as his object. . . . Just as plants, animals, stones, air, light, etc., constitute theoretically a part of human consciousness, partly as art—his spiritual inorganic nature, spiritual nature, spiritual nourishment which he must first make palatable and digestible—so also in the realm of practice they constitute a part of human life and human activity. . . . The universality of man appears in practice precisely in the universality which makes all nature his inorganic body. (1975a, 275–76) [95]

Marx thought of capitalism as a system that subjugates humans and nature to its laws of accumulation. However, he remained committed to his historical view of capitalism as a revolutionary phase if contrasted with the previous socioeconomic systems: feudalism and slavery.

In contrast, the Indigenous worldview and philosophy rejects the whole modernization project of capitalism and dogmatic socialism. Yet, as this research uncovers, their communities have been permeated by the lures of consumerism, values, and diets.[96] The divergence between the Colombian Left, including FARC, and the Indigenous CRIC might have its philosophical and ideological roots in the difficulty of reconciling FARC's goal of taking power and the Indigenous' goal of autonomy and, more importantly, the dispute regarding the exercise of authority in Indigenous territories.[97] FARC insisted as a revolutionary movement that they were the authority in areas of their influence, such as in Cauca, where they enjoyed virtual hegemony.

In sharp contrast, CRIC's political agenda was never a revolutionary project, but instead sought to recover lost lands and conserve the Indigenous people's way of life. This "conservationist" project in a dynamic socioeconomic-political, cultural, and globalized neoliberal environment ran into conflict with multiple currents, social class forces, and interests, one of which is the conceptual foundation of the Westphalian state. CRIC proposed a post-Westphalian state in which the rights of groups to choose their own process of livelihood were encouraged, both respecting their differences and at the same time recognizing their need for mutual collaboration to secure their reproduction.[98] The construction of an ethnic identity is a "modern" concept based on recovering culture, languages, historical narratives, folk culture, and music, and building boundaries among the Indigenous communities themselves and between them and other social groups. In other words, the Indigenous' effort to construct and preserve their ethnic identity has carried with it another element similar to nationalism, inasmuch as each Indigenous group has sought to build and defend its own identity-turf and territoriality. In turn, this has generated tension between groups such as the Nasa and Embolenos and between the Misak and Nasa, not to mention conflicts with non-Indigenous peasants and Afro-descendants.[99]

Escobar (2020) discussed the roots of autonomism that stemmed from a broad range of tendencies, including decolonial thought, and subaltern and postcolonial studies, to the epistemologies of the South and political ecology.[100] He added that the political theoretical anchor comprises three concepts: autonomy, communality, and territoriality. Only the first, Escobar contends, has any grounding among leftist groups. The notion of community is shared with the peasant reserves and the Afro-descendants; however, these three groups are peasants struggling for a communal way of life based on subsistence farming, which is noncapitalist.

Territoriality is central to the Indigenous communities, as Escobar and Tattay explained. In a territory that is legally protected by domestic and international laws, communal life is made possible. The connection between humans and nonhumans is established, and the "Good Living" transcends economics.[101] This is where the main point of contention lies between the territoriality of the Indigenous, the Afro-descendants, and the peasant reserves and the neoliberal globalization and its perverse variant, war rentierism. In dialectical terminology, there are two antagonistic claims.

One stemmed from the Westphalian sovereignty concept that the subsoil belongs to the state and hence it has the exclusive right to extract resources anywhere within its national sovereign boundaries. This Westphalian sovereign argument overrides the territorial claim of any communal group, more so given the current neoliberal global economic and political order. However, the Indigenous people of Colombia are not alone. Indigenous groups across Latin America, from Mexico to Bolivia, Peru, Ecuador, and Brazil, struggle for autonomy, communality, and territoriality as they resist this hegemonic order and its rentier extractive model.

As the evidence from the peasant reserves shows, the dialectics between communal life and rentier capital coexist, and their relationship is calibrated between adaptability, resistance, and subsumption (ARS). The following sections analyze the relationships between the Indigenous of Cauca and the agents of rentier capital, contrasting their experience with those of the peasant reserves discussed in the previous chapter.

Rentier Capital, the Indigenous, and Subsumption in Cauca

Since its inception in 1971, CRIC has successfully mobilized and organized the Indigenous in Cauca even in times of heightened suppression when its leaders were being killed and imprisoned. As a result, they successfully reclaimed thirty-five thousand hectares that large landowners and the Catholic Church had previously occupied.[102] In the 1980s, building on their growing success and collaborating with ONIC promoted the Indigenous councils. In 1985, they presented the Vitonco Declaration, calling for autonomy, which would become a landmark among Indigenous communities. As discussed above, autonomy consisted of the management of natural resources, the election of their representatives according to their traditions, "all financed by funds available from the public budget (so-called 'transfers') and backed by a system of justice based on their customary law."[103] The Vitonco Declaration, which emphasized the Indigenous' right to autonomy, called on the Catholic Church to stop acculturation and respect their religious and cultural systems. The declaration also demanded that the warring actors, including the state, refrain from using their territory as launching pads for war.[104]

The Vitonco Declaration enhanced Indigenous assertiveness vis-à-vis the church, the state, the insurgency, and the right-wing paramilitary groups. In effect, CRIC embarked on a two-pronged strategy. One was to gain strength by organizing and mobilizing the communities, and the other was to strike agreements that would keep their lands and communities out of the conflict. In retrospect, it succeeded at mobilization but could not keep its communities out of the conflict because the warring actors invariably used the Indigenous territories as staging grounds for their military maneuvers, shipments of arms and munitions, extraction of protection rents, illegal mining, and narcotrafficking. Keep in mind that the Cauca strategic geographical location is a nodal point between Tolima and Valle del Cauca, an important narcotrafficking corridor to the Pacific coast.

CRIC managed to negotiate a controversial deal to recover lands usurped by large landowners. In return, CRIC assured the federation of cattle ranchers (FEDEGAN), known for their support of paramilitaries and representatives of large landowners, that they would not seek to occupy their haciendas. Leftist organizations described CRIC's deal as a betrayal of the cause of recuperating lands. Such a bilateral deal without state negotiators exemplifies CRIC's conviction that social groups can negotiate their differences and conflicts without resorting to violence. With the same conceptual reasoning grounded on the autonomous line, CRIC attempted to insulate its territories from a grinding and escalating civil war. However, since its inception in 1970 up until this writing, CRIC has failed to achieve this goal.

Below is a discussion of the Indigenous response to the advancement of five actors of rentier capitalism: sugar cane plantations, cattle ranching, multinational mining companies, coca plantations, and narcotrafficking.

Sugar Cane Biofuels' Monopolies and the Indigenous

The political economy of sugar production in the north of Cauca, where the sugar agroindustry has been concentrated, has consisted of four main phases, as Teodora Hurtado has described it. My findings are congruent with her periodization, with some amendments to the last two periods.[105] Hurtado presented the four periods of the history of the north of Cauca as: (1) 1851–1910, in which the abolishment of slavery occurred and the peasant economy was born; (2) 1910–1950, marked by prosperity and the autonomy of the peasant economy; (3)1950–1985, which saw the development of the sugar agroindustry, which led to decreasing land tenure and loss of autonomy and regional leadership, and; (4) 1985–2000, the proletarianization of the Indigenous. However, the last two periods witnessed significant developments that Hurtado did not assess correctly, one of them the success of the Indigenous in asserting their autonomous rights, starting with the leader Quintin Lame's quest for "Indigenous republics" in Cauca, Tolima, and Huila. Quintin Lame's legacy was then consolidated with the emergence of CRIC in 1971, which again cemented the drive by the Indigenous to establish autonomy on the management of their territory. The second development was the process of proletarianization, which mainly the Indigenous avoided by abandoning the plains and taking to the mountain slopes as their new settlements.[106]

As a result, agribusiness depended on the nearby Afro-descendant inhabitants to provide labor power, while the mainly Indigenous averted this process.[107] The other source of labor power was workers hired through the "associated cooperative work." Those workers were contracted as "independent entrepreneurs" and were denied any benefits that wage laborers received under the law. The "associated cooperative work" created a new form of flexible contractual relations. The owners may pay less and can fire and hire in a more unrestricted mode consistent with the neoliberal structural adjustment doctrine. Workers contracted under this modality enhanced surplus-value accumulation and were exploited to the point that made working conditions unbearable, which led to several workers' strikes in which the local Indigenous groups stood in support.

The economic monopolies and multinational corporations that have controlled most of Colombia's production of goods and services and their expansion into rural economies have been transformative, changing the political economies of the areas they operate. As seen in Meta with oil companies, in the Cauca the Ardila Lulle sugar mill and ethanol production have succeeded in consolidating the shift to a rentier-extractive model that the state's tax policies and exemptions have incentivized.[108] The model's logic of accumulation requires lands for expanding its plantations of sugar cane, much of it owned by the Indigenous. Agribusiness, cattle ranching, and mining have a very long history in Cauca, exceeding that of Meta, which has had short booms of cash crop exports that dissipated until the 1980s, when oil rents overwhelmed its economy.[109]

In Cauca, capital penetration, especially in sugar cane, mining, and cattle ranching, had a long history, beginning in the colonial era. Sugar cane plantations and mills are located in the valley of the Cauca River, which runs through fifty-one municipalities in six departments (Valle del Cauca, Cauca, Risaralda, Caldas, Quindío y Meta). The total area of sugar cane plantations is 241,205 hectares. Twenty-five percent of these hectares are used by sugar mills, and the remaining 75 percent are owned by 2,750 cultivators of sugar cane. Since 2005, five of the twelve operating mills have been extracting ethanol. Beginning in 2015, new mills joined in to produce ethanol. Given the climate, sugar cane production can be sustained for the whole year, according to Asocania, the sugar producers' syndicate. In the early twentieth century, Cauca political economy was based mainly on cattle ranching, soybeans, rice, food crops, and then, in the 1920s and 1930s, sugar cane was introduced. Since then, it has gradually become the mainstay of the economy.

The expansion of the sugar cane agroindustry generated two inter-dependent social conflicts. First, the sugar cane mills' quest for more land to expand its production facilities impinged on the *resguardos'* lands. Secondly, the mills conflicted with the agrarian working class over wages and working conditions. Since the 1991 infamous massacre of the hacienda El Nilo, in which paramilitaries killed twenty Indigenous children and adults, the grievances of the Indigenous have only grown, and the state's bias in favor of the mill owners has only aggravated the situation.[110] The government, after many years, granted the disputed areas to the sugar mill's owners. Several lots of El Nilo were later leased by Incauca to plant sugar cane for ethanol extraction. The victims of the massacre are still waiting for justice.[111]

Organización Ardila Lüle, one of the most powerful of the Colombian economic conglomerates, owned by the entrepreneur Carlos Ardila Lüle, became a core player in Cauca's economy, encroaching on the communal economy of the Indigenous peoples and endangering their way of life and their future. The conglomerate encompasses eighty diverse companies, vertically related, that employ forty thousand people in various sectors, from sugar mills, ethanol production, communications, soft drinks (Postobon), radio networks (RCN), to financial enterprises, insurance companies, and television channels. In addition, its soft drinks and chocolate company consumes 25 percent of the sugar market, and by 2015, controlled 45.5 percent of the sugar production in Colombia.[112] Manuelita, one of Lüle's companies, is the country's largest distributor of Coca-Cola. The conglomerate has expanded its business to include African palm plantations and biodiesel production in the department of Meta and other parts of the eastern plains.

Ardila Lüle's enterprises, such as Sucromiles, Alcoquimica, Providencia Band, and Risaralda produce 65 percent of the ethanol extracted from sugar cane in the country, positioning the group in a dominant market position that affects both pricing and pricing policy, which explains in part why ethanol production costs in Colombia are 50 percent higher than in Brazil. Furthermore, due to the high price of land in Cauca, the production cost per hectare of sugar cane there is one of the highest in the world, amounting to 82 percent higher than in China, 63 percent higher than in Brazil, 42 percent higher than in Guatemala, and 6 percent higher than in South Africa.[113] Production monopolized by a few (oligopoly) distorts the market, inflates prices, and inhibits efficiency, for all of which consumers must pay.

Law 693, passed in 2001, mandated that gasoline sold in cities of more than five hundred thousand inhabitants must contain ethanol. Given that the cost of ethanol production is higher than of gasoline, a gallon of ethanol costs $2.40 at the pump, while gasoline is $1.26,[114] which has allowed Lüle's group to increase its profit margins significantly. As if this were not enough, the Ministry of Mining prohibited the extraction of ethanol from gases or minerals, confining it to biomass, in a regulation that, coupled with Law 788 of 2002, eliminated the IVA aggregate value tax and other related taxes, thereby denying the state one hundred million dollars' income per year.[115] This background clearly exposes the favorable state policies that have helped Ardila Lüle's conglomerate retain its monopoly on ethanol production. Consequently, this dominant market position has led to disputes with sugar cane producers concerning the discriminatory, arbitrary pricing system imposed on purchasing sugar cane per ton. For example, if the cane is earmarked for sugar production, the conglomerate pays fifty thousand Colombian pesos per ton ($15), while if it is for ethanol, it pays only thirty thousand ($9.30). The sugar cane producers resent this arbitrary pricing, but they can do nothing to adjust it.

The following subsection discusses the communities' contentions with the above situation and the economic dominance of the Colombian conglomerates and describes the continuum of the communities' adaptability, resistance, and subsumption.

HORIZONTAL INTEGRATION AND LAND LEASING:
BETWEEN ADAPTABILITY AND RESISTANCE

Like most multinational corporations, the Colombian conglomerates adopted a horizontal model in their production chain, which offered more flexibility, reduced administrative and labor costs, and increased efficiency than the old vertical model.[116] Lüle's conglomerate adopted this horizontal model like its counterparts/competitors, such as Grupo Santo Domingo and the Sarmiento Group, that is to say, the members of the "Cacaos," as these conglomerates are referred to in Colombia. Ardila Lüle could procure the cheapest sugar cane by subcontracting and renting, employing horizontal land integration as a business tactic. Buying land was no longer necessary within the flexible administrative strategy of the conglomerates. Multiple sources have confirmed that the Lüle group has rented various lots from their owners in San Rafael, Santander de Quili-chao, Garcia Arriba, Corinto, Elvira, and Miranda. Some of those lots were claimed by Indigenous *resguardos* and Afro-descendants, as discussed in the following chapter.[117]

Sugar cane production requires a significant amount of water for irrigation, and the increase in the cultivated areas and the number of processing mills has multiplied the water demand. These conditions have led to the diversion of surrounding rivers such as the Mondono River that passes through Caldono, reaching the aqueduct of Santander de Quilichao. Therefore, the expansion of sugar cane production, cultivation, and processing into ethanol has increased the water demand exponentially. This, in its turn, has impacted the Indigenous people's access to water to satisfy their basic needs. Consequently, the competition for water and land has become the main, defining area of conflict between the conglomerate and the Indigenous. For example, in February 2021, Asana, and the Association of Agriculturalist and Cattle Ranchers of North Cauca (SAG), Procania, Andi-Cauca, complained that Indigenous groups had attacked and burned sugar cane crops in the municipalities of Guachené, Corinto, and Caloto.[118] Another illustrative example of the simmering conflict was reported in 2017 in Toribio, when Indigenous from the Nasa people attempted to occupy part of a large sugar cane plantation owned by Ardila Lüle's group, which resulted in the killing of one person and injuries to several others.[119] This was just one of many confrontations in which the Indigenous have tried to recover some of the lands usurped by agribusiness groups.

The intensified social tensions in Cauca can be measured by proxy indicators such as violations of human rights laws, targeted assassinations of social leaders, and other forms of political violence. Between July 1 and December 31, 2019, the department registered 139 occurrences, the highest nationwide, constituting 27 percent of the total, followed by Valle del Cauca, with ninety-three human rights violations, testifying to similar socioeconomic conditions and trends.[120] In 2020, Cauca's share of human rights violations increased to 33 percent of the national total, making the department the most violent in the country. Such a high rate of killing is the outcome of war rentierism's attempt to eliminate impediments to the advancement of rentier capital. This process is far from concluded given resistance by the Indigenous, Afro-descendants, and peasants.

It is important to note the Indigenous people's longstanding struggle to conserve what they already possessed and recover their lost land. Feliciano Valencia, an Indigenous leader, eloquently described the historical struggle that started with the "Pajaros" assassins in 1940 who targeted the Indigenous and Blacks at the behest of the large landowners in order to appropriate their lands. He continued, "Then came FARC, and also the large landowners and agribusiness reinitiated their push. In two thousand, the paramilitaries made their appearance by killing fifty of our community, punctuating their path with countless massacres starting in the municipality of Naya, targeting Indigenous and Afro-Colombians, where they killed one hundred people."[121] According to Valencia, the AUC's "Bloque Calima" (Calima Bloc) perpetrated the massacre. As described by Indigenous leaders, their purpose was to force people out of their lands to facilitate the expansion of agribusiness and the extraction of gold, minerals, and timber.[122] The Indigenous, for their part, fought back. Valencia remarked, "In the 1970s, we were six *cabildos* controlling two hundred hectares, now we are one hundred twenty-two *cabildos* with five hundred and seventy thousand hectares."[123] This description captures the process of war rentierism and the agency of resistance, indicating that this war rentierism process is not a forgone conclusion, as evidenced by the expansion of the hectares under the control of the *cabildos*.

However, it is not only violent antagonism that has characterized the relationship between the communities and the sugar conglomerates and other agents of capital. There has also been a subtle process of subsumption, exemplified by the Indigenous owners of the land, who did not have the resources to cultivate and grow sugarcane and leased their land to the mills; the mills planted and harvested the sugarcane, and secured the capital to grow and process it.[124] Then, when the sugar had been sold, the portion agreed on was paid to the Indigenous communities. "With a vision of sustainability, [the mills] realize that it is best to have good relations with those that surround them, and this is essential to ensuring that there is added value."[125] Incrementally the communities are sucked into the circuit of capital and dependency that fuel the economic subsumption process. Agribusiness has exploited the community's land with negotiated consent, by preying on their socioeconomic vulnerability and need. Leasing land is one of the mechanisms that companies are using to acquire land for long-term use without creating a conflict with the Indigenous.

Land leasing by the Indigenous has multiple effects. One is that it runs the risk of creating a dependent relationship, with the agribusiness creating an incentive to maintain dependency. A second injects cash into a subsistence peasant economy, distorting the allocation of their limited resources if not properly managed. A third opens up opportunities for corruption, nepotism, and class/status differentiation within the communities.[126] Consequently, leasing land is an important manifestation of the subsumption process, observed in Cauca as well as the Wakoyo *resguardo* in Meta (discussed above) and San Pablos in the peasant's reserve Cimitarra (discussed in chapter 2). The differences between subsumption processes lie in the question of which factor of production is needed the most by capital: labor, land, or both. In the Cauca and Meta, Indigenous lands were needed most for rentier capital (chiefly mining and oil extraction, respectively) and agroindustry expansion. At the same time, labor was procured from Afro communities and so-called worker's associations.[127] In the peasant reserves of Cimitarra and Balsillas, both labor and land were subject to the subsumption process, incorporating them into the law of value. It is important to note that 65 percent of the area of Cauca has been solicited for a mining concession.[128] This amount of land sought for mining exploration and extraction might essentially be what is at stake there, where the state's rentier model has become the main threat to the department's entire population and environment.

INDIGENOUS POPULATION GROWTH AND LAND CONFLICT: FROM ADAPTABILITY TO RESISTANCE

The strategy by the Indigenous to escape the sugar plantations' aggressive labor recruitment by seeking refuge on the mountain slopes reached its limits as the Indigenous population grew, as DANE statistics demonstrated. Between 2005 and 2018, the Indigenous population's growth rate, at 1.6 percent, exceeded the Cauca rate of 0.39 percent.[129] This growth is one of the driving forces behind the communities' efforts to reclaim lands in the plains that were more apt for food production, which they had ceded in the previous decades. The Indigenous population's increase is expected to continue, given that in 2018, 30.6 percent of them were between zero and fourteen years old.[130] A generation this young will be likely to exacerbate the conflict over land as the Indigenous respond to increasing population pressure, which will put them in a collision course with rentier capitalists and their violent systemic web.

An interview with an Indigenous male from the community of Yanacona who is a member of CRIC eloquently illustrated the issue, based on his family experience. He contended that, "In the early 1980s, my mother was granted a land lot of four hectares, which was then enough to sustain our family. But, with the increase of our family size due to marriages and more children reaching thirty, the produce of that land was not enough any longer to feed us."[131] He explained that his family experience illustrated the leading cause that pushed the Indigenous to reclaim their ancestral lands in the plains.[132] The *resguardo* Huellas in the municipality of Caldono exhibited a similar trend, propelled by an expansion of the population that pushed them from the mountain slopes with their limited areas for cultivation to the plains, where the possibility of growing more crops for subsistence is better and where consequently they came into conflict with the large landowners and the sugar cane agrobusinesses. The former Indigenous governor of the Huellas, Arcadio Mestizo, described the formation process of the *resguardo* since 1969, starting with "recovering," as the Indigenous conceptualize the process of retaking possession, of "mother earth, the estate of El Credo of five hundred hectares."[133] Since then, the *resguardo* had "recovered" 14,703 hectares, of which twelve thousand are either sacred land, sources of water, or slopes, unsuitable for food production. Hence, only 2,703 hectares have been divided among 3,450 families (10,500 inhabitants), an average of 0.77 hectares per family, way below what a family needs to reproduce and survive. Mestizo explained that he has less than two hectares, and the problem is that when the time comes to share his lot with his children, little if any land is left to share. Such a situation is common, which has motivated the inhabitants to acquire more land by invading adjacent private properties. In the case of Huellas, the community invaded a 2,500 hectares lot, burning the sugar cane crop there and filing their claim for land "recovery," which is still contested, with its legal status not yet decided.[134]

This, in turn, has led to increased confrontations with the landed elite, conglomerates, cattle ranchers, narcobourgeoisie, and mining multinationals. Those are all formidable players representing a myriad of local and global capital, which are mainly interested in the land itself and its natural resources, more than in labor, as were the colonial modes of exploitation. In this same vein, Henry Caballero, CRIC's senior leader, confirmed that the population increases have led the Indigenous to resettle on their ancestral lands under the slogan of "recovering lands" that had been granted to them during the Republican era in the eighteenth and nineteenth centuries,[135] a process that started in the 1970s and has accelerated in the subsequent decades. It is worth mentioning that the Indigenous have retained documents of land titles.

So far, the state and its land agencies have been reticent in distributing land to the Indigenous groups. The state's rate of distributing land to Cauca's Indigenous over the past fifteen years has been extremely slow and cumbersome, having amounted to only seventy-seven thousand hectares, measured against CRIC's calculation that Cauca's Indigenous need 218,000 hectares. CRIC estimates that if this rate of land distribution continues, it will take the state 245 years to distribute the remaining hectares.[136] Moreover, there are misleading figures about how much of the lands in the hands of the Indigenous are arable lands. According to CIRIC, only 18 percent (174,375 hectares) of the total area of 544,901 hectares, can be used for agriculture. Those 174,375 hectares, when divided by the Indigenous population in the *resguardos,* amounts to an average of 3.5 hectares per family,[137] less than the Unidad Agricola Familiar (Productive Family Unit, UAF), the standard amount required to sustain a family unit in the overwhelming majority of the municipalities where the Indigenous are concentrated.[138]

According to Resolution 041 of 1996, the UAF of Cauca and the recommendations for the municipalities where 70 percent of the Indigenous are concentrated fall short of the 3.5 hectares accepted as a benchmark to support a family. The list below shows municipalities and the corresponding hectares needed to sustain a UAF: Caldono and Caloto: seventeen to twenty-two hectares per family; Jumbalo, not available; Turibio: eight to eleven hectares; Paez: four to six hectares; Morales: four to six hectares; Totoro and Purace: eight to eleven hectares; Inza four to six hectares; Silvia: fourteen to nineteen hectares.

The available data are not disaggregated per ethnic group. Therefore, it is not possible to verify the actual sizes of UAF that the Indigenous have. Nevertheless, several informants interviewed estimated that the average landholding per Indigenous family hovers around 3.5 hectares or less. Keep in mind that more than 50 percent of the landholdings of fifty hectares or more are owned by 3 percent of the property holders, and 97 percent of the landowners of the remaining 50 percent have lots of less than fifty hectares. More striking, however, is that 1 percent of the landowners own 35 percent of the land, while 40percent of the landowners own one hectare or less and occupy only 2 percent of Cauca's land surface.[139] Such a concentration of land ownership in a dynamic and changing political economy that is influenced by multiple local and global forces and punctuated by the oscillations in the cocaine and gold markets is making the situation toxic. The Indigenous representatives and informants interviewed voiced a high concern for the increasing violence in Cauca, which is targeting their *resguardos* and their unarmed guards who are resisting the expansion of the coca economy and land grabbing.

The following subsection tackles the coca plantations in the *resguardos* and their impact on the subsistence peasant economy of the Indigenous communities.

COCA, MONEY ECONOMY, AND ADAPTATION

Starting in the early 1990s, coca was introduced into the political economy of Cauca. In 1999, coca was planted in 6,269.30 hectares, and by 2019 it had spiked to 17,355 hectares, the highest since its inception, following which it declined slightly in 2020 to 16,543 hectares.[140] Many factors help explain this dramatic increase in the expansion of coca crops. Coca as a cash crop helped hundreds of thousands of subsistence peasants stay afloat in many peripheral areas of the country. In Cauca, coca plantation penetrated Indigenous *resguardos* in several areas such as Silvia, Toribio, Tambo, Piamonte, Caldono, and Timbiqui, despite "the *cabildos'* objection," according to one CRIC official.[141] The coca economy enabled the peasants to buy consumer commodities such as cellular phones, TV sets, and other items that the subsistence economy, with its limitation, could not provide.[142] The advent of the coca economy and its money signaled adaptability to capitalism. A condition that, if continued without resistance, might implode the social fabric of the Indigenous and subsume their culture. In the Meta, such a condition was observed in the Wakoyo *resguardo* in the form of land leasing and other innovations.

Giovanni Yule, CIRC's Peace Coordinator, identified the severe threats facing the *resguardos* and their subsistence economy caused by the advancement of sugar cane plantations and the increase in cash crops such as coca and pine and eucalyptus trees.[143] Yule also articulated the dilemma that the CIRC and other peasant leaders are confronting as they seek to keep the youth attending schools and helping cultivate the land. Young people have high economic incentives for picking coca leaves compared to expected returns achieved by staying in school or helping on the family farm. They can earn up to 150,000 CP, equivalent to $40 (exchange rate of 3,700 pesos/dollar), per half-day spent picking coca leaves, whereas working all day in traditional food production might earn only thirty thousand CP, or about $8 a day. This staggering difference clearly illustrates the nature of the problem. Its resolution will require a radical change in the economic development model.[144]

The broader implication of the coca economy (planting, picking leaves, processing) is that the consolidation of the money economy might supplant the tradition of "gift reciprocity," or the barter system on which the Indigenous economy has depended for generations.[145] The money economy has injected a new element of capitalism that promoted the culture of consumerism, creating class differentiation between those members of the community that had access to money and those that didn't. The money economy within these communities started during colonial times, mutating and changing according to the extent of its incorporation by the Indigenous, which depended on their *resguardos'* locations vis-á-vis the economic/political center of power.[146] In the twentieth century, in areas of accelerated capitalist development such as Cauca, "the money economy became more pronounced in the 1950s and 1960s with the sugar mills and accelerating with the advent of coca in the 1980s."[147] But it is premature to conclude that the money economy has become the dominant mode of exchange among community members, or, more importantly, that it is irreversible. A case in point is the barter system such as the one in Poblazon, which remains flourishing and is gaining momentum across the cases investigated in this book.[148] In this same vein, it is noteworthy that in 2020 about six hundred Indigenous traders and representatives of nine nations from the southwest of the country attended a meeting in Cauca to consolidate the barter system and reject the money economy.[149] The coexistence in the twenty-first century of the money economy and the barter system within the same social formation demonstrates the agency of resistance and adaptability to the subsumption process, delaying it, and prolonging its completion.

CULTURAL SUBSUMPTION AND A COUNTERHEGEMONIC PROJECT

The Indigenous culture and its nature as a living entity with its human and ecological assets is under threat by the encroachments of rentier capitalism and its ideology and commodification process. The Indigenous, especially those living close to urban centers, are bombarded with consumerism. The violence of the guns is potent, but consumerism glitters like the gold of

Cauca and is equally threatening to Indigenous livelihood, culture, diet, social cohesion, and subsistence.

A CRIC informant highlighted the context and implications of consumerism: "Exposure to the consumption culture has an enormous impact on the younger generations and their world outlook."[150] He added, "We cannot deny that economic inequalities have emerged among us due to several factors, including, for example, that some families have resorted to the usage of pesticides and other chemicals to increase production while others did not, or that some became more educated and hence acquired better jobs. But these transformations have not changed our collective identity."[151] A related point raised by Caballero was the changing diet of the Indigenous, which has incorporated white people's food such as pasta spices and cooking methods. The CRIC Yanocona informant described the broader context against which these social changes have occurred over the last few decades, which included "the advent of roads, mechanization of the sugar cane production process, expansion of markets, more Indigenous children going to college, the increasing use of money instead of the barter system in the exchanging commodities, expansion of local farmers' markets in which Indigenous sold their produce, and the introduction of coffee in the *resguardos.*"[152] The Yanocona CRIC representative concluded that, with the advent of the coca plantations, which the Indigenous subsistence economy incorporated like peasants elsewhere, "capitalism permeated the Indigenous culture save those living deep in the Amazon."

The Indigenous established a university in Popayan (Autonomous Intercultural Indigenous University, UAIIN) to deflect these imminent threats to their way of life. Its primary mission is "to nurture, plant wisdom and knowledge" and train students to acquire knowledge that is of practical use to their communities. The government officially recognized the university in 2018. The university has 135 faculty members and seven hundred students enrolled in the university's ten different programs.[153]

CRIC started thinking of founding a university back in the 1990s. Now it is up and running. Establishing this university with a philosophical and ideological platform of preserving the Indigenous way of life and defending it against the encroaching threats is an effort by a subordinate group to break away from or resist the hegemony of the dominant capitalist culture. Indigenous resistance to cultural subsumption has entered a new phase, laying a solid foundation for a counterhegemonic culture with national, regional, and international implications. In Gramscian terms, creating an institution of higher learning, such as the one the CRIC established, challenges the core aspect of Western education and epistemology by representing a counterhegemonic effort by a subordinate group, the Indigenous.[154]

In the spirit of building a counterhegemonic project, the CRIC members interviewed emphasized that "our last line of defense against capitalism is our language and spirituality, which requires a new reinvigorated struggle for more autonomy."[155] Whether this line of defense will withstand the menace remains to be seen. Considering this study's findings, I would add the cultural dimension to Marx/Luxemburg's subsumption concept, which influences sociopolitical consciousness, consumption patterns, social relations, and attitudes affecting communal values.[156] The following subsection sheds light on the other forces at play in Cauca that impact its entire population's livelihood, especially the marginalized subsistence peasantry, including Indigenous, Afro-descendants, and mestizos.

INDIGENOUS WOMEN AND THE CRIC: "RESISTANCE WITHIN THE RESISTANCE"

The Indigenous women's struggle for autonomy, rights, and land has been permanent, but is underresearched and often overlooked by mainstream scholarship. This brief section does not do justice to the struggle of women, but it seeks to highlight some elements that are relevant to this enquiry. I attended a meeting organized by the women's division of the CRIC, assisted by twenty representatives of the different *resguardos* in northern Cauca, at which they highlighted the problems and challenges facing their respective communities. The issues raised ranged from sexual violence, interfamily abuse, drug addiction, discrimination against LGBT individuals, and machismo. Some representatives raised the issue that they as community leaders faced resistance from other women alongside some men. Most relevant to this investigation is that of ten members of CRIC's leading council only one is a woman.

The low representation of women in the leadership of CRIC was not attributed to a "glass ceiling" that is difficult to break, but lies instead at the grassroots level where communities elect their respective *cabildos* and those in turn elect their higher authority. In 2022, forty-four representatives from 139 authorities at the local level were women engaged in a process that they coined as "resistance within the resistance." In this resistance spirit, Indigenous women articulated their aims and described their uphill battles at the local level, not only to achieve more representation reflecting their demographic weight but, more importantly, bringing to the forefront social issues that are important to women's well-being, which are critical to the reinforcement of resistance enhancing solidarity and a good life.[157] At the 2021 CRIC congress the decision to equalize representation between the two sexes was taken, which is a significant step forward to achieve gender equality.[158] Now the issue has become building the bottom-up sociopolitical balance to accomplish that goal.

REPRESENTATION AND SCHISM: CRIC-ONIC

The increased activism of CRIC beyond Cauca has created tensions with the National Organization of Colombia Indigenous (Organization Nacional Indigina de Colombia, ONIC), which has had a national outreach since it was founded in 1982. This friction has increased due to many factors; the most important ones are discussed below.

Henry Caballero explained that the cause is the representation and governance within the ONIC, in which all departments have the same number of representatives regardless of each one's number of *resguardos*.[159] This misrepresentation has been compounded by the way members running for a leadership position in the Permanent Concertation Committee of the Organization of the Indigenous People were vetted. The Permanent Committee was established in 1996 by ONIC to incorporate all Indigenous groups and act as a representative vis-á-vis the state. In Caballero's opinion, some are reaching leadership in the Concertation Committee without much of a popular mandate, and with dubious backgrounds.[160] This might mean that some people might reach leadership positions that have been compromised.

The implications of the above are several, and they relate to the focus of our study. The state and the rentier capital actors have enormous co-optation/corrupting power that they might use to buy influence. The mentioned loopholes might offer an opening to individuals that are more complacent about accepting extractive activities, hydroelectric projects, and the expansion of agribusiness. The goals of the opponents of CRIC are to mitigate the effects of Law 21 of 1991 (chiefly, Previous Consultation) and circumvent decrees 1953 and 2333, promulgated in 2014 to protect the Indigenous ancestral lands following Colombia's state ratification of the ILO 169 Convention on Indigenous people's rights. Decree 1953 recognized the rights of the Indigenous communities to establish their own authority in their ancestral lands and *resguardos*. Decree 2333 created a mechanism to effectively safeguard the judicial security of the ancestral lands and the *resguardos*. This is where the crux of the matter lies.

Conclusion

The zero-sum game between Indigenous land rights and the agents of rentier capital sanctioned by the state's policy is a complex process, in which the interplay of adaptability, resistance, and subsumption (ARS) is exhibited. Phenomena such as an increasing culture of consumerism, engagement in the money economy, cash crops (coca), changing dietary habits, and land leasing are manifestations of this interplay. All of them were discussed above. Knowing the geostrategic and economic importance of the departments in which the rentier capital, narcotrafficking, agribusiness, and noncapitalist communities are locked in a long-term struggle, my prognosis is that the social conflict in Cauca is heading toward more escalation and bloodshed. Such a historical dialectic would produce a synthesis, not necessarily consisting of winners and losers. A synthesis that depends on the correlation of forces between the contending forces of capitalism and noncapitalism calls to be mediated by blood and fire. Violence remains the accelerator of this process, as it has been since the Conquest, and it is now infused with new forces of capital, producing war rentierism as a mechanism by which it can consolidate its base by violently eradicate the resistance of its opponents.

The discussion also reveals some troubling aspects that usher in cultural erosion manifested in the loss of native languages, a fundamental element for preserving communal cohesion. This was mainly exhibited in the department of Meta. At the same time, in Cauca, the cohesion of main groups, chiefly the Nasa people, the largest group, provides a gravitational focal point providing stability, resistance, and adaptability to the process of subsumption.

The noncapitalist way of life, culture, and mode of exchange remain a viable alternative despite the serious challenges. This viability was exhibited in the Indigenous mobilization of May–June 2021. Thousands participated, emphasizing their land rights and autonomy, rejecting neoliberal rentier capitalism and condemning its war variant, in a show of force that had not been seen in decades, involving peasants, afro-Colombians, students, and middle-class sectors alongside Indigenous actors.

One of the most salient weapons in the Indigenous toolbox has been their manipulation of the white men's bourgeois jurisprudence and laws to protect themselves from the white men's barbarism and historical abuse. The examples of the use of white men's laws are abundant, and in this chapter I have discussed some that were relevant, such as the racist 89 Law of 1890. The Indigenous overlooked the prevalent racism of the law and emphasized the rights provided to them instead. This is an excellent example of wielding adaptability in the face of adverse conditions and waiting to change them until the correlation of force has changed in your favor, as happened in the 1991 Constitution, that is, a century and a year later.

In my interviews and literature review, it became clear that the legalistic approach is deeply entrenched in the political activism of the Indigenous, which also affected the peasant groups and now is catching up with the Afro communities. My interviews with representatives of these two latter groups revealed that they are still wrestling with the lessons learned from the Indigenous in organizing their resistance and adaptability. One core lesson to absorb is how the "legalistic approach" helped secure Indigenous agreements, which became state laws with the clear objectives of protecting their ancestral lands, autonomy in governing their communities, safeguarding their communal property rights, and achieving access to discretionary funding.

One key finding of both this chapter and the previous one on peasant reserves is that there is a rising class consciousness that those subsistence peasants are being subjected to rentier capitalism's same violent subsumption process. Perhaps the massive popular mobilization mentioned above will usher in a new, more promising dawn to the noncapitalist universe.

Chapter 5

War Rentierism's Impact on Afro-Colombians in Cauca

Historical sources amply demonstrate that ever since the abolition of slavery in 1851, the peasants have shown a marked aversion towards wage labor on the large estates of the rural elite.

—Michael Taussig, "The Genesis of Capitalism amongst a South American Peasantry"

Colombia is home to the third-largest concentration of Afro-descendant people in the Americas, after the United States and Brazil. According to Black Communities' Process (PCN), their number, 4.3 million, comprises approximately 10.4 percent of Colombia's population.[1] African Colombians are a diverse and heterogeneous group, including the urban professional middle class, rural/urban proletariat, small proprietors, and subsistence peasants. The latter group is the focus of this investigation, chiefly the subsistence Afro-peasant community of Cauca. They live primarily on the Pacific coast, and in its northern part they bear the brunt of war rentierism (see chapters 1 and 2),[2] Like the previous chapters, this chapter explores the processes of capital subsumption, its effects on the coexistence, adaptation, and resistance of the subjected communities and their modes of exchange. However, as Taussig has noted, a common thread among the cases explored becomes apparent, marked by resisting proletarianization and alienation from their means of production and labor.

Setting the Stage:
The Struggle for Emancipation and Autonomy

In their historical narrative, *Colombia: Fragmented Land, Divided Society* (2002), Frank Safford and Marco Palacios captured the racist dimension of a class-divided society compounded with a postcolonial power structure. They succinctly sum up the different phases of the struggle of Blacks during the nineteenth century to achieve their freedom, starting in 1821 with the precursor of the emancipation Decree of 1851. Safford and Palacios write that the New Granadan slave-owning elite, especially in Cauca, felt that the "1821 Law of free birth, which promised blacks labor for their children until eighteen, did not provide adequate compensation."[3] The slave-owning class was deeply concerned about losing the Black labor force, upon which mines and haciendas depended. Equally importantly, the elite feared the potential of an "uncontrolled free black population."[4] Cauca's elite had more to fear than the elites of other provinces because the number of Blacks there was significantly increasing: fourteen years after the 1821 Law, 21,519 slaves constituted 10.3 percent of the population in Cauca, while Bolivar had 4,867 slaves, Magdalena 1,960, Panama 1,461, Tolima 1,504, Cundimarca 1,245, Boyaca only 311, and Santander 2,439.[5] Clearly, Cauca was the epicenter of the Blacks' struggle for emancipation and autonomy. Resistance by the slave-owning elite, as in the United States, precipitated violent social conflict in the early 1840s, led by General Jose Maria Obando, who rebelled against the central government and mobilized freed slaves from the Patia Valley and the mines and haciendas, promising them freedom.[6] Eventually, Obando's rebellion was defeated, but the mobilized slaves retained their aspiration for freedom.[7] The slave-based plantations in Cauca stood to lose the most from the abolition of slavery and resisted it the most stubbornly. Due to the Afro-Colombians' rebellious history, Cauca's elite considered them more threatening to their class interest than the Indigenous groups, who were perceived as more complacent.[8]

For fifty years after their emancipation from slavery, Black communities and their descendants founded successful subsistence farms occupying the lands of their former masters. During that period, *hacendados* tried to control the liberated Afro-Colombians and force them to work in their haciendas, but to no avail.[9] Taussig describes those decades as characterized by armed conflict. Nonetheless, Afro-Colombian peasants in the north of Cauca had a flourishing economy with abundant production and viability (Taussig 1978, 67). Taussig, quoting Perez (1862), contends that while the peasant economy of the Afro-Colombians was doing well, large-scale agriculture in Cauca was failing due to several factors, including the lack of labor. Although, for example, Puerto Tejada, discussed later in this chapter, was privileged by its cocoa boom, planted by Black peasants, it was targeted by large landowners, eventually leading to its economy's destruction.

The Black peasants resisted their proletarianization and were able to preserve their subsistence farms for the most part, until the civil war of "Mil Dias"—One Thousand Days (1899–1902). According to Taussig, the One Thousand Days War produced a more centralized state, which helped attract an influx of U.S. finance capital into Colombia, and especially to Cauca (Taussig 1978, 68).[10] This was attributed to the termination of the railway between the Cauca Valley and the Pacific Ocean and the Panama Canal's opening, in 1914. Both events allowed Cauca to export its crops for the first time in its history, marking its insertion into the global market and setting in motion the process of dependent development.[11] The influx of U.S. capital and the expansion of agribusiness led to a significant increase in land prices, which enhanced the pressure brought to bear against the peasants.[12] Large landowners, incentivized by the rise in land prices and the infusion of foreign capital, pressed more aggressive land claims by using the legal system, which mostly favored them. Taussig contends that large landowners were prosperous in the south of Cauca, where peasant leagues could not prevent the loss of lands, and that the *hacendados* resorted to violence to restore their haciendas for cattle ranching and, in the 1930s, their lands for sugar cane plantations.[13]

Alongside the sugar cane cash crop, another critical component of Cauca's political economy was gold mining, which expanded during the Spanish Conquest. Indigenous and Afro-Colombians provided cheap expandable labor for the extraction of alluvial gold. After 1819, African Colombians depended on artisanal mining for their economic subsistence, a practice preserved for generations. In the early 1900s, a Franco-British company sought to establish an underground mining project in Timbiquí, but it did not prosper. It was not until the 1980s that a Russian company brought new dredging and mining equipment to Timbiquí. The Russians fared no better than the Franco-British and soon abandoned their project. Still, local Afro-Colombian artisanal miners learned the companies' techniques, and have continued using some of them.

Despite these two failures, multinational corporations have remained interested in the mining potential of Cauca, as evidenced by their continuing demands for mining concessions, which by 2019 numbered 350,000 hectares, approximately 10 percent of the department's territory. Since the early 1990s, the state has facilitated these concessions by deploying its security/judicial system (see note 11), alongside private armies. In 2014, more than one million hectares were under consideration for 652 additional mining titles, representing more than half of the department's territory (Verdad Abierta 2014). According to the same report, eighty-two thousand of the 350,000 hectares registered with mining titles belong to the Afro-Colombian Communal Councils (a collective territory adjudicated to be eligible for administration by the Afro-Colombian community), and seven thousand hectares overlap with IndigenousIndigenous reserves (Verdad Abierta 2014).[14]

Recognition that under Law 70 the state had granted eighty-two thousand hectares to the Afro-Colombians exposes the fault line of the conflict. The state's rentier extractive model and its logic deny these communities the legal rights it had granted them and infringe on their ability to maintain a noncapitalist mode of production, that is, a subsistence economy with zero accumulation of surplus value. Taussig's (1978) study of southern Cauca captures an important characteristic of its political economy: capitalist farms have constantly been expropriating peasants' lands, reducing their abilities to sustain their livelihood. As discussed in the previous chapters, capitalist development did not displace the peasant subsistence and other noncapitalist modes of production in the process of subsumption; instead, as Taussig (1978, 87–88) has concluded, capitalist development incorporated the noncapitalist *plus* the peasant mode "with their real efficiencies to balance out the costs of capital investments otherwise supplied by international financing."[15] The conclusion supports this core finding, dispelling any nondialectical, mechanical, binary/unilinear analysis of capitalist development in postcolonial societies. Cauca and the other cases explored represent the aspects of coexistence that may be attributed to the changes in the process of subsumption. Thus far, the discussion in the previous two chapters has demonstrated the uneasy dynamics that balance between these opposing logics along the spectrum of subsumption: coexistence, adaptation, and resistance. This chapter covers the whole spectrum, beginning by elaborating on the making of war rentierism as it applies to Cauca and its Afro-descendants, and focusing on the peculiar characteristic of its extractive economy, in which the state loses income. It describes how, with their goal of propelling free trade, the state's tax exemptions have introduced in Cauca a new manufacturing sector that chiefly depends on importation, notwithstanding that the state's goal has been to promote the myth of "free trade," which, historically, never existed, according to Joseph Stiglitz.[16]

War Rentierism, Violent Entrepreneurs, and Subsumption

In Colombia, violent entrepreneurs acquired dual interdependent functions, as evidenced throughout the country's twentieth-century history. The most salient cases that illustrate when these roles started to take root occurred in the aftermath of the Thousand Days War (1899–1902) and during La Violencia (1948–1958) (discussed in chapter 1), during which large areas of land were usurped in Meta, Arauca, Casanare, Antioquia, southern Bolivar, and Cauca to feed the state's desire to satisfy the needs of its expanding rentier extractive economy. The creation of the AUC with the state's support established a basis for the rentier war model, which consisted of usurping millions of hectares from the peasants in economically strategic areas, as defined by the state's policies.

After the Thousand Days War, the large landowners of northern Cauca pressured the state to evict the Black communities from their lands, which were mostly planted with cacao. Those communities produced 40 percent of the country's cacao during that period.[17] The campaign against the Black peasants and Indigenous accelerated in the 1940s. Large landowners and their thugs, with the help of the state, appropriated land occupied by Afro-Colombians' subsistence and medium-sized farms. Soon, by using violence to expel and control Indigenous and Afro-descendants, the large owners and capitalists installed their sugar cane plantations and began to transform the department's political economy, mainly in North Cauca. The transformation was chiefly based on the appropriation of the department's peasants' lands. A similar process took place in Valle del Cauca, which has the highest concentration of land property in Colombia.[18]

The practices of the AUC, beginning in 1997 (when it was created as a national umbrella confederation consisting mostly of right-wing armed groups) until its formal demobilization in 2005–06, were designed, first, to defend the state, the local economic elites, and the multinational corporations against Marxist rebels' attacks and taxation, and, second, to use their military machine to propel and enforce the rentier model. The AUC leadership found plenty of economic opportunities for self-enrichment, thus inserting themselves into the dominant class. Narcotrafficking, cattle ranching, usurping peasants' land, illegal mining, and agribusinesses such as

African palm plantations became the springboards for the AUC leadership's social class ascendance. This dual function of defending the social order and self-enrichment made Colombia's "violent" entrepreneurs important actors in the neoliberal "war-rentierist" political economy, particularly in the strategic areas such as Meta, Bolivar, and Cauca. Plainly stated, the AUC leaders (such as Mancuso, Jorge 40, the Castano brothers, Rodrigo Gacha) exemplified the propellers, enforcers, beneficiaries, and benefactors of the rentier model.[19]

During the post-demobilization era between 2006 and 2021, a host of former AUC cadre and leaders reconfigured their organizational structures, drawing on a pool of AUC ex-combatants and continuing to employ the same practices of the defunct AUC. By 2016, fourteen paramilitary groups were active in 146 out of 1,100, municipalities spread over twenty-two of Colombia's thirty-two departments.[20] By 2016 they had displaced more than 320,000 people and killed 8,194 civilians.[21] Those figures indicate the unrelenting and undeniable use of violence for political/economic gains such as the usurpation of lands, and the extermination of the rentier model's opponents, such as environmentalist, social, and political leaders, in peripheral areas that have become important for the extraction of mineral resources (e.g., gold, coltan), oil, and agribusiness. According to the UN High Commission for Human Rights, most of the social leaders killed between 2017 and 2019 were in the mining municipalities of Antioquia, Cauca, Bolivar, Choco, and Caldas.[22]

The correlation between the mining municipalities and targeted killings corroborates the instrumentality of violence and its description as war rentierism incentivized by the state's economic policy.[23] The state has continued granting mining concessions to both multinational corporations and local capital, undeterred by the displacements and killings. Its rentier thrust has continued unabated, as reflected in its plans to designate *Zonas de Interés de Desarrollo Rural, Económico y Social* (ZIDRES), rural development areas in which dams and a highway infrastructure such as the Ruta del Sol, Colombia's primary road transport artery, which extends over one thousand kilometers and links the industrial and population centers of Colombia's Andean region with the ports of its Caribbean coast, will be constructed. The concession was awarded to a consortium composed of the Brazilian construction firm Odebretch (with a 65 percent share) and two minority Colombian partners, a subsidiary of Corficolombiana, part of the Colombian financial conglomerate the Aval Group. Loans for the project's construction were provided by seven Colombian banks, four of which belonged to Grupo Aval. With the state's legal protection and economic incentives, local and foreign capital collaborated to foment the rentier economy, thereby bloating its main pillar, the service sector, which had reached circa 58 percent of the country's GDP by 2019 (see chapter 1).[24]

A RENTIER STATE FORFEITING ITS RENTS: THE PAEZ LAW IN CAUCA (1996–PRESENT)

The literature on rentier economies is vast and diverse, and is largely based on the assumption that a state's extreme dependency on the extraction of resources (such as oil, coal, and gold) creates a vicious cycle of economic dislocation and management distortions by the state, which perpetuate this dependency.[25] In this regard, Colombia represents an anomaly and a paradox. The state is not dependent on the extractive sectors (oil, coal, gold, and coltan) but caters to it within its overarching commitment to the neoliberal economic model. The lion's share of dependency is focused on the service sector (see chapter 1, Figures 1.1, 1.2, and 1.3). The state's response to a natural disaster in 1994 is critical for unpacking this paradox.

In 1994, flooding by the Paez River inundated several areas of northern Cauca, which resulted in Afro-Colombian land loss in several municipalities, including Caloto, Puerto Tejada, Santander de Quilichao, Corinto, Buenos Aires, La Sierra, and Patia.[26] The state's response was to exempt foreign and local enterprises that had invested in the affected areas from taxes. More than 130 enterprises, invested in light industries, were mostly export-oriented. The state promulgated Law 218 of 1995 (the "Paez Law"), creating free zones where investors' tax obligations were suspended for ten years, after which they would pay only 15 percent of their income, way below the national rate of 33percent. That is to say, the state continued with its drive to transform Cauca's economy at the expense of its own purse,[27] a clear example of a rentier state forfeiting its own income for the sake of its neoliberal economic dogma.[28]

One might ask, How rational is this state policy? Two factors explain a seemingly irrational behavior. One is the unshakable commitment on the part of the state's economic policymakers, political elite, and dominant class to the neoliberal model; two is that that commitment is supported by the power of influential local and foreign companies, some of which have links with state officials and ministers. Cases in point include the 139 enterprises that capitalized on the Paez Law and, according to the Andi group, constituted 54 percent of Cauca's GDP, which, located in twelve industrial parks (including thirty-seven enterprises in Caloto and twenty-one in Santander de Quilichao) became a powerful lobbying group defending the privileges obtained from this law.[29] Consequently, those companies have had access to the state's ministers and the president himself, allowing them leverage to influence policy, as was the case with President Uribe (see chapter 2, Kalmanovitz section). The Paez Law was modified by Law 1005 of 2005, which established Free Trading Zones under President Alvaro Uribe's administration (2002–10).

In sum, the Paez Law and its corollary Law 1005 of 2005 demonstrated the state's leading role in transforming the political economy of Cauca by facilitating its insertion into the global capitalist economy. The Paez Law and subsequent laws, including Law 1005 of 2005 and Law 1776 of 2016, which created ZIDRES for rural economic and social development, focused on creating manufacturing zones. The latter law sought the creation of agricultural projects in which capitalist and local communities might form partnerships and the state might lease the public land. In the designated manufacturing zones, the state may adjudicate the distribution of public lands without any limitation on making them available to agricultural or cattle ranching–related private companies.[30] By combining those laws with the land laws introduced after the Chicoral Pact (discussed in the introduction and chapter 1) the objective of the neoliberal state has been accomplished, namely, spearheading the capitalist penetration of the rural economy by vehemently opposing a change in the land tenure system, following Currie's recipe. The defining characteristic of war rentierism has been its staggering and tragic human toll (more than five million people forcefully displaced between 1985 and 2012, their lands–about seven million hectares—appropriated, and 220,000 people killed between 1958 and 2013).[31]

Multinational Corporations, Collective Land Titling, and Political Fragmentation

One of the challenges that Afro-Colombians have faced has been the inability of their intellectuals and activists to provide the leadership necessary to push back against the encroaching rentier political economy and the dominant class. This was displayed during the 1991 Constituent Assembly, when the Blacks failed to agree on who should represent them. They finally decided on a nonBlack, an Indigenous Embera leader, to represent them. This historical incident demonstrated the ill-preparedness of the Afro-Colombian leadership to defend the community's rights and carve out a place for themselves at the negotiating table, which negatively affected their struggle. The following subsection discusses the conditions that led to introducing Law 70 of 1994, a critical watershed in which the state and the political establishment finally recognized the ethnic rights of the Afro-Colombians. It sheds light on the undercurrents that might explain their organizational and political vulnerability.

THE TELEGRAM CAMPAIGN AND LAW 70 OF 1993

The Afro-Colombian elite's political fragmentation considerably weakened the community's resolve, compromising its collective rights. As mentioned above, their lack of coherent leadership was best exemplified in their failure to agree on Black representatives to present their ethnic interests before the constituent assembly. It was not until the final hours of the 1991 Constituent Assembly, when some Black activists organized the "Black Telegram Campaign," sending 250,000 telegrams to assembly members, that article 55 of the Constitution, which recognized the Blacks' "special transitional status" was adopted. It was regulated in 1993 in Law 70, a law that granted them communal property and cultural rights.[32] In sharp contrast, the Indigenous had already succeeded during the 1991 Constituent Assembly in obtaining two senate seats and recognition of their *resguardos* as "territorial entities," along with the state's acceptance of their autonomy and respect for their cultural rights.[33]

Gonzalez (2005) attributed the Afro-Colombian political fragmentation to several factors. She said that Black peasants' associations were organized at the local level and adopted a loose "federalized structure" that was not as centralized as the CRIC's Indigenous organization. Gonzalez explained that Black intellectuals tended to join NGOs, through which they attempted to exercise activism promoting regional projects, thereby seeking to join the dominant circuits of power. She concluded that this goal of joining the dominant circuits of power was designed to succeed at the expense of forging alliances with the urban middle class in the regions where Black communities resided. To compensate for this shortcoming, and given the affinity between the Black communities and the Indigenous as they share several spaces in departments such as Cauca, Choco, and Valle del Cauca, Black intellectuals sought Indigenous support to help them pressure the state to acknowledge their status as an ethnic minority.[34] The problem with this approach is that the Indigenous cannot wear two hats, especially when political and economic interests do not overlap or when tensions over land access intensify.

The State, Dominant Class, and the Community Councils

The state and the dominant class have long refused to acknowledge Blacks as a distinct ethnic group, with a different culture, heritage, and language(s), who have endured centuries of enslavement, exploitation, and marginalization—claiming instead that the dominant ethnic group assimilated the Blacks. In other words, for non-Blacks, the Afro-Colombian did not exist as a separate and discriminated-against ethnic/racial group. Given the Blacks' organizational weakness, their cause has been left in the hands of NGOs, human rights groups, and UN agencies to put pressure on the state. The far-reaching ramifications of the political fragmentation exhibited in 1991 have been reduced incrementally but not overcome over the years. It remains a trait affecting the communities. In sharp contrast, the Indigenous groups under Cric remain an inspiring example of political cohesion and articulation of the interests of their subsistence peasants, providing the elements for their resilience and resistance to capital subsumption.

The Afro-Colombian communities continue their struggle for de jure recognition for their entitlement to public lands, which have remained a contentious issue, particularly in the department of Cauca, where forty-two Afro-Colombian communal councils were formed to administer communal land properties of which the state has recognized only a few, although for centuries Blacks have continuously settled those lands as *Palenques* of freed slaves and planted their food crops there.[35] Instead, the state charges them rent of between eight hundred thousand and one million pesos a year to grow food crops for their own subsistence.[36] Thousands (no exact figure is available) of subsistence Black peasants confront the same situation, and will continue to do so until their claim for collective land titling is achieved. The economic precariousness of the Afro communities in the north of Cauca is more extreme than that experienced by those in the Pacific area, where the state has recognized their collective communal properties, upon which the legal figure of the Community Council rests. There are two different sets of conditions facing the Blacks in these two regions, which I discuss in the following two subsections.

Northern Cauca: Dispossession and Proletarianization

According to testimony from local Afro-Colombian activists and social leaders, the main issue confronting the black communities in Caloto, Villarica, Suarez, Buenos Aires, and Puerto Tejada is the absence of collective land titles.[37] The lack of land titles and recognition by the community council have denied them access to credit and government technical assistance. The legal status of those communities is still in limbo, with no clear path for resolution. Felipe Aragon and Arie Aragon, both Afro-Colombian leaders, described the processes of subsumption and dispossession that, in their opinion, have been taking place since John F. Kennedy's Alliance for Progress in the 1960s, in which the Agrarian Bank became a central player in instrumentalizing the Alliance's recommendations. The Agrarian Bank offered the peasants loans to buy genetically modified seeds and fertilizers to grow their crops. Many Black peasants suffered from failing crops, making it difficult to pay back their debts, and went bankrupt. They became land tenants and wage laborers. This interdependent process of "land dispossession and proletarianization" was not an anomaly; rather, it corresponds to the typical capitalist development observed by Marx in nineteenth-century England. The difference is that subsumption in rural Colombia and many other cases of the Global South involve a complex, multidimensional, and often violent process that is taking place under conditions of dependent capitalist development and globalization.[38] In sharp contrast, England was a colonial imperial industrial power in the nineteenth century. Its economic development was chiefly determined by domestic conditions that were stimulated and sustained by its colonial slave-based plantations economy.[39]

Building on the Aragons' analysis of the intimate interdependency between dispossession and subsumption, one might pose the question of whether the constitutional change of 1991, which opened the door for law 70 of 1993, had the potential to arrest or mitigate the process of subsumption by providing some legal protection. The protection that the state has resisted providing extends to northern Cauca, where 65 percent of the population is made up of Afro descendants. The explanation is that most of the land is owned by white/mestizo capitalists from Cali.[40] Therefore, "the state implicitly or tacitly help[s] violent entrepreneurs to cleanse the areas that are sought by capital for mining, sugar cane plantations, sugar mills, cattle ranching, speculation, and manufacturing."[41] Consequently, the 1991 constitution was the product of a particular correlation of forces that dictated some concessions on the part of the dominant class to secure order, preserve their rule, and safeguard their long-term class interests. But, as soon as the dominant class felt more secure, it became more recalcitrant, rejecting any serious land redistribution policy that might undermine the interests of the landed elite and the rentier model in areas identified by the state as strategic.

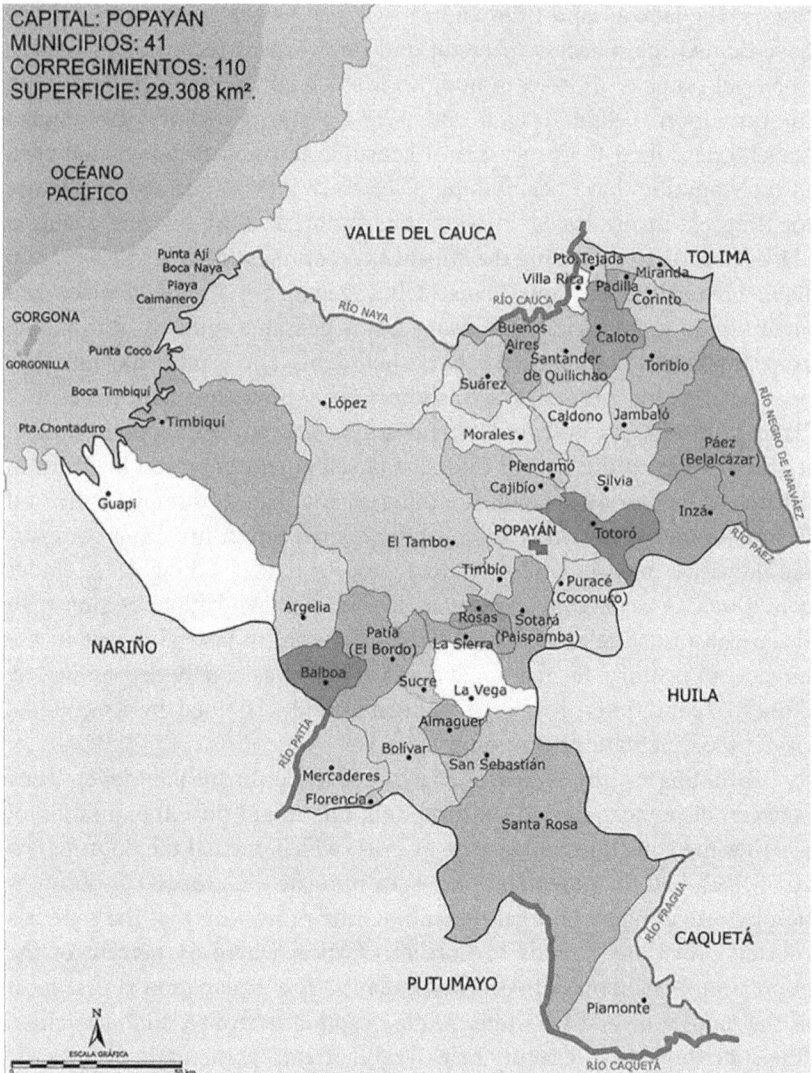

CAPITAL: POPAYÁN
MUNICIPIOS: 41
CORREGIMIENTOS: 110
SUPERFICIE: 29.308 km².

OCÉANO PACÍFICO

VALLE DEL CAUCA

TOLIMA

Punta Ají
Boca Naya
Playa
Caimanero

Pto Tejada
Villa Rica
Padilla
Miranda
Corinto

RÍO CAUCA

RÍO NAYA

GORGONA

Buenos Aires

Caloto

GORGONILLA

Punta Coco

Santander de Quilichao

Toribío

Boca Timbiquí

Suárez

•López

Caldono

Jambaló

Pta.Chontaduro

•Timbiquí

Morales•

Páez (Belalcázar)

Piendamó

Silvia

Cajibío•

Guapi

Inzá•

POPAYÁN

Totoró

RÍO PÁEZ

El Tambo•

Timbío

Puracé (Coconuco)

Argelia

Rosas

Sotará

NARIÑO

Patía (El Bordo)

La Sierra

(Paispamba)

Balboa

Sucre

La Vega

HUILA

Almaguer

Bolívar

San Sebastián

Mercaderes

Florencia•

Santa Rosa

RÍO FRAGUA

CAQUETÁ

PUTUMAYO

Piamonte

N

ESCALA GRÁFICA

RÍO CAQUETÁ

Map 5.1. Cauca. *Source*: IGAC, 2002. Fuente: Sociedad Geografica de Colombia. Atlas de Colombia, IGAC. 2002. Fuente Barimetria: Prof. Jose Agustin Blanco Barros. Creative Commons CC BY 4.0.

In this vein, it is worth highlighting the relationship between territoriality and ethnicity relevant to discussing the Afro-Colombian relationship with the state. Bettina Ng'weno (2013) examined the case of the hill peak Teta in the municipality of Buenos Aires, where Afro-Colombian peasants and miners were claiming communal land.[42] The problem was that this same area was also inhabited by Indigenous claiming the territory. Such contestation was set forth against the backdrop of the 1991 Constitution, in which ethnic rights were first introduced. It set the stage for competition and contestation between Indigenous and Afro-Colombians, who share territorial spaces such as Cauca. The state's recognition of ethnic rights in its 1991 Constitution, followed by Law 70 in 1993, which recognized African Colombians as an "ethnic group with communal rights," unwittingly created territorial boundaries and activated ethnopolitical contestation between groups. The Teta Hill was an example of such contestation over land claims and rights, which became a common occurrence, creating a fault line that allowed third parties to exploit and incite.[43] This, in turn, weakened resistance to the process of subsumption by capital and mining companies, as in the case of Teta, where mining companies claimed an interest in Teta Hill and where, for instance, the African-Colombian Cooperative of Miners that had organized artisanal mining since 1988 was coopted by the Gerald and Duque Ltd. a mining company.[44]

The Ministry of the Interior recognized the Afro-Colombian Community Council of Cauca River in 2014, but no land was given to the community to administer. De jure recognition did not translate into land access, which might have offered some legal protection from mining companies' encroachments in Teta Hill. However, the Community Council retains territorial control, thanks to the community's support in defending Teta Hill, with mixed results, against further advancement.[45] In April 2020, seven Afro-Colombians were assassinated in Buenos Aires's Teta Hill area, which indicates the escalation of violence by groups working for mining companies; this was only one massacre, followed by others in 2021 and 2022.[46] The advancement of mining capital (legal and illegal) as determined by the expansion of concessions and land acquisition, necessitated the annihilation of other land claims, communal or private.

COMMUNITY COUNCILS AND THE STATE

According to Arie Arango, there are more than one hundred de facto community councils seeking state recognition and access to land in the north of Cauca; as of 2021, the state had recognized only two,[47] while in the Pacific Coast region, seventeen councils are recognized by the state, distributed among three municipalities: Lopez de Micay, five; Guapi, five; and Timbiqui, seven. All have collective land ownership recognized by the state. In northern Cauca, however, the state appears hesitant to grant collective land ownership due to its economic importance for mining, agribusiness, and manufacturing. Several concessions have been granted to multinational corporations and national companies that permit them to extract natural resources such as gold, silver, platinum, coal, and sulfur in Timbiquí, Buenos Aires, Guapi, Suarez, Santander de Quilichao, El Tambo, Patía y López de Micay (gold); Buenos Aires, Timbiquí, Bolívar, El Tambo, Guapi y La Vega (silver); Guapi, Buenos Aires, Santander de Quilichao, El Tambo, Timbiquí, Suarez y La Sierra (platinum); Buenos Aires, El Tambo y Suarez (coal); Piamonte, Popayán, Patía, Villa Rica, Caloto, Buenos Aires, Corinto, and Puracé (Sulfur).[48] In 2016, Cauca produced about 5.3 metric tons of gold, constituting 9 percent of the country's gold production.[49] Two municipalities produced 70 percent of the gold: Buenos Aires (40 percent) and Timbiqui (30 percent).[50] However, the official statistics do not reflect the illegal and uncounted artisanal extraction. By way of context, *Colombian Reports* quoted the aggregate figure of $2.4 billion as an estimate of the value of the illegal gold extracted, constituting 66 percent of the total extraction in Colombia.[51] Besides Cauca, the leading gold-producing departments are Choco and Antioquia. It is plausible to infer that tens of millions are unaccounted for in Cauca.

MULTINATIONAL CORPORATIONS AND COMMUNAL PROPERTIES

An OECD document citing government figures stated that in 2010–11, of 544 mining units identified in Cauca, 170 (31.4 percent) were dedicated to gold mining, and more than 90 percent operated without a mining title (MME 2011). While a handful of multinational companies—both small mining companies and large-scale extraction industries—are looking to undertake advanced exploration programs, nonstate armed groups have prevented them from moving forward with their plans.[52] The state, multinational corporations, and local dominant classes have a common denominator, and that is to eliminate all the obstacles confronting the advancement of the rentier extractive model adopted and enforced by the state since the early 1990s and reinforced during the administrations of Uribe (2002–10), Santos (2010–18), and Duque (2018–2022).[53]

The state's objection to awarding the collective communal land rights to the Afro communities stems from its concerns that if they were granted in the north of Cauca, this might create more resistance to its rentier model. If collective rights were conceded, it is feared, communities might invoke their right to "previous consultation" before any extractive production could be initiated, and resort to other legal measures, thus hindering the extractive model. The Indigenous communities and the peasant reserves are already focal resistance points, causing enough headaches in core strategic areas such as Magdalena Medio, Bolivar, Meta, and the Eastern Plains. Henceforth, the state is considering those factors hoping that maintaining the status quo is the best option available that would not hinder the progress of its rentier economic model. Keep in mind two critical things, however: one is that the eighty-two thousand hectares that were conceded to mining companies belonged to the collective communal properties of Afro-Colombians; the second is that the state is reviewing 652 mining titles that, if granted, will increase the concession to MCs by an additional one million hectares, that is, 50 percent of the department area.

Consequently, the state is determined to continue reconfiguring Cauca's political economy, an objective that requires suppressing all socioeconomic formations and structures that might pose obstacles to the process of rentier-capital subsumption. I argue that in the mining areas of northern Cauca, the goal transcends the purely formal subsumption that allows a margin of coexistence with noncapitalist formations, to embody *real* subsumption, whereby all of those "relics of the past," or antivalue systems, will be annihilated, subjugated to the logic of creating capital value.[54] This might explain why, between 2010 and 2016, about 30 percent of Cauca's 338,000 victims of forced displacement came from the top five gold-producing municipalities, and almost one-third of them were Afro-Colombians and close to 10 percent Indigenous.[55] Between January and July 2021, according to Indipaz, there were fifty-four massacres in Colombia, ten of them in Cauca, that is, 18 percent; and of those three were in Santander de Quilichao, one of the main gold-producing municipalities in northern Cauca, where the black community constituted 33.4 percent of the total population.[56]

Forceful displacement and targeted assassinations, core attributes of war rentierism, have been used to enforce the model, in a strategy sanctioned implicitly and tacitly by the state. It is worth mentioning that an eight-thousand-person joint force drawn from the army, navy, and air force was formed and deployed in Cauca, presumably to provide security.[57] An interviewee from Caloto confirmed that the "state's militarization" has become a feature of the situation in which state agents, illegal miners, and narcotraffickers collude. In the same vein, an OECD study reported that "a number of cases in Cauca point to the involvement of low-ranking security officers working locally in illegal mining operations. In 2014, the Attorney General's office uncovered a network of navy officers and former police officers working with illegal miners and informal intermediaries.

Corrupt officials at the Guapi and Cali airports allegedly had facilitated the transport of machinery, cash, and illegal gold from Timbiquí, Guapi, and López de Micay."[58] This finding confirmed the existence of systemic violence in Cauca and other parts of Colombia, including Choco, North Santander, Narino, Valle del Cauca, which is not due to the state's absence or its weakness. Instead, due to the state's neoliberal economic policies embraced since the early 1990s (see the introduction and chapter 1), violence has been sanctioned as a tool for their implementation. This state's model has provided the environment in which a host of entrepreneurs, speculators, opportunists, state's agents (including members of the police, army, local officials, politicians, mayors, and notary publics), and units of organized crime exploit and develop their (illegal or legal) enterprises in mining, narcotrafficking and other fields. It is a systemic web of war, as I have conceptualized it elsewhere, that these actors have created by their interactions over time, and the political economy they formulate captures the dynamic of the process of war rentierism.

MULTINATIONAL CORPORATIONS (MCs), COMMODITY CHAINS, AND SUBSUMPTION

This subsection provides a general idea of the magnitude and scope of interest of the multinational corporations (MCs), local companies, and violent entrepreneurs in acquiring concessions and licenses to exploit the department-rich gold resources.[59] This process has led to violently dislodging local communities, appropriating their lands, destroying their way of life and environment, making Cauca one of the most violent departments in the country. This subsection also sheds light on the commodity chain that links subsistence artisanal miners with the local and global markets.

Although the MCs are not yet operating in the department due to its security conditions, this has not deterred companies such as Anglo Gold Ashanti, a South Africa–based multinational corporation and the second-largest gold extractive company globally, from seeking concessions. These concessions amounted to eighty-three out of 241 that the state granted in 2014 and included an extension of one hundred thousand hectares in the municipalities of El Tambo, La Sierra, La Vega, and San Pablo.[60] Votorantim Metais (Brazil) and Anglo American also hold a number of concessions throughout the department, but have not been able to undertake their exploration due to security conditions. Smaller companies such as Cosigo Resources have entered into joint ventures to explore in Cauca. In addition, a Chinese mining company made an offer to buy 1,400 hectares in the Patía municipality to start exploration.[61]

Two factors encouraged the MCs to invest. One was the increase in the price of gold in the early 2000s, which reached $1,200 an ounce. The second was the Alvaro Uribe administration's extension of a group of legal guarantees (2002–10) that favored the MCs, among them the International Treaty for Foreign Investment, which privileges investors, the Treaty for the Promotion and Mutual Protection of Investments/APPRIs, and Free Trade Agreements containing chapters that secure legal protection for MCs and guarantee them the right to sue the Colombian state before international tribunals if it violates or changes the terms of any agreements. Thereafter, the favorable price of gold and the legal protection offered to MCs and private capital secured the establishment of the rentier expansion. Meanwhile, the state has been reticent in formalizing the situation of thousands of poor subsistence miners in northern Cauca and South Bolivar, driving them into a despair sufficient to transform them into a rural proletariat ripe for exploitation by the MCs. In addition to multinational companies, there are a number of Colombian mining investors who hold titles in Cauca. For example, Sociedad Minera del Sur, a medium-scale operation based in the municipality of Suarez, is owned by Giraldo & Duque, one of the leading international gold traders based in Cali. This company can process close to three hundred tons of raw materials every day, provided by local miner's associations that have agreements with the company to process and sell their gold.[62]

Arie Aragon explained that the Afro-Colombians, including community council members, rent their lots to the sugar mills' owners in order to meet their pressing economic needs. The state, the MCs, the sugar plantations, and the owners of enterprises operating in manufacturing zones all draw on the labor power that Afro-Colombians and other groups offer and have no interest in allowing peasants to be independent, autonomous producers. The Afro-Colombian community does not enjoy the same legal protections that the Indigenous *resguardos* have, and they are the most vulnerable to exploitation by rentier capital. This largely explains why forty-two potential councils in northern Cauca did not win the recognition from the state that would have granted them access to land. By denying them this possibility, the state can accomplish the capitalist transformation based on the exploitation of labor power,[63] a process that was discussed in the previous chapter concerning the Sikuanis' Wakoyo reservation.

Peasants forced to rent their lands to agribusiness and multinational corporations exemplify the process of subsumption, in which capital chooses what is needed and when for its process of value creation and accumulation. Peasants (Afro-descendant and others) seek in turn to survive the process of dispossession by attempting to coexist with it. The peasants' economic strategy centers on survival punctuated with resistance, as evidenced by the massive mobilization in the spring of 2021 in Popayan. The following section focuses on the case of Puerto Tejada, which might help in unpacking the complex process of subsumption within a political context characterized by the interplay of factors such as narcotrafficking, gangs, and insurgents.

Puerto Tejada: Capital Subsumption, Proletariatanization, and Re-Peasantization

Afro-Colombians escaping slavery established free towns known as *palenques,* many of which became municipalities in northern Cauca in the twentieth century. The Palenque of Puerto Oscuro became Puerto Tejada in 1912. The *palenques* of Guachene, Caloto, and Padilla evolved similarly. Their formation and history have been embedded in the struggle against slavery and its aftermath in the twentieth and twenty-first centuries.[64] Most Afro-descendants became subsistence peasants, depending on plantain, coffee, cacao, sugar cane, fishing, and artisanal mining for their survival. Ironically, most of the lands where the free slaves established their *palenques* were owned by members of the traditional slave-owning class such as the Eder family, los Arboledas, los Caicedos, and los Barneys. After slavery was abolished in 1852, the slave-owning families sought to retain the Blacks as residual labor power to keep their haciendas running. They accepted providing these lands to Afro-Colombians in order to keep them economically captive and dependent. The forms of land ownership varied then, including as tenants, owners without title, or just settlers on the land. By the early twentieth century, the Afro-descendants had evolved into a peasantry of subsistence in northern Cauca, engaged in constant conflict with the old slaveholding elite alongside the newer large landowners, sugar mills, and other agribusinesses.

The advent and ascendance of the monoculture of sugar cane incrementally transformed Cauca's political economy and the livelihoods of the Afro-descendants, the Indigenous, and the *mestizos*. Cauca's soil and weather provided ideal conditions for sugar cane crops, which had arrived in Cauca in 1538 with the Conquest. By 1901, the industry started to grow with the introduction of the first steam-operated sugar mill, Manuelita, and gradually expanded in Cauca and Valle del Cauca. It further increased in the 1930s, when the state introduced laws on unused idle lands, and took off with the so-called Green Revolution, in 1970. The expansion of the road and railroad system helped encourage sugar cane production, as well as some manufacturing, which received an important boost in 1995 with the adoption of the Paez Law, which exempted investors from taxation in municipalities affected by the Paez River floods.

What has become Puerto Tejada municipality is inhabited by 49,503 people, 95 percent of them Afro-Colombians. It illustrates some of the core social contradictions created by capital and its subsumption of noncapitalist social formations within the contours of war rentierism, chiefly as it has occurred in northern Cauca. An informant who is also a government employee and member of the Rio Palo Community Council explained that this had been an uphill struggle without any prospects of success in sight until, after years of struggle, the state granted two small lots (Tulipan 1 and 2), less than 100 hectares, to thirty-one families.[65] This meager amount of land, according to the informant, demonstrates the state's lack of seriousness in granting the community councils access to land in northern Cauca.

The state's commitment to its economic model of agribusiness, mining, and light manufacturing has propelled the proletarianization of the community of Puerto Tejada. According to one informant, the state of the economy has led to the decomposition of the nuclear family. It has forced husbands to join the working class in the industrial parks, sugar mills, or cane plantations. The wives have become domestic workers in Cali, the closest city to Puerto Tejada, and the children stay with their grandparents. The disintegration of the family unit has contributed to a series of problems, including the emergence and growth of youth gangs, which have come to epitomize the perverse impact of subsumption. Currently, there are forty youth gangs in Puerto Tejada, constructing frontiers, dividing the community, and terrorizing the population.[66]

It is important to provide some historical context to the informant's description of the deteriorating social conditions. Gangs in Puerto Tejada and northern Cauca date back to the 1940s and the dark days of La Violencia (1948–1958). During that period, Cauca witnessed a massive forceful displacement of more than 368,900 people as some 94,400 landholdings were appropriated by violent entrepreneurs (see chapter 1). According to Oquist (1978), Cauca had the highest rate of displacement and transfer of property (from original owners to a violent actor) in Colombia, followed by Antioquia.[67] One of the most notorious gangs that emerged was Los Pajaros, who in 1949 killed 366 Nasa people. Los Pajaros was a group of assassins working at the behest of the police and large landowners.[68] The combined acts of violence, forcible transfers of property, and displacement that punctuated "La Violencia" and ushered in "war rentierism" characterized by land grabbing, accelerated in the following decades. It is crucial to note that before 1948, there was no indication of organized violence of the scope and magnitude of "La Violencia."[69] In Puerto Tejada there was no bloodshed until the occurrence of one riot directed against a store owned by white-elite class members who were predominantly Conservatives. The army controlled the rioters and imposed military law, which provided cover for the plantation owners to appropriate peasant farms.[70] Land grabbing under the cover of "La Violencia" led to the result that the "modal peasant land holding decreased significantly from 4.8 hectares in 1933 to 0.32 in 1967,"[71] which is to say a fifteenfold decrease, while the population increased by twofold. According to Taussig, decreasing the size of the peasant farms to less than two hectares undermined the peasant mode of production, forcing peasants to work on large estates.[72] At the same time, 80 percent of the cultivable land became the property of four sugar plantations, as the 1970 census showed.[73] Clearly, "La Violencia" in Cauca facilitated the concentration of land at the expense of the peasants.

Against this background, one can better understand the evolution of war rentierism since "La Violencia." It has been used to serve socioeconomic changes such as the emergence of the cocaine economy, the increasing presence of sugar cane mills, industrialization, foreign capital investments, insurgency, and the neo-Pajaros, that is, the AUC. According to an informant, FARC's Clan del Golfo and dissident fronts have become active.[74] As the production of cocaine and narcotrafficking started taking roots in the adjacent municipalities of Santander de Quilichao, Corinto, and Miranda, Puerto Tejada was impacted.[75] The advent of coca coincided with the expansion of sugar plantations and the weakening of subsistence farming. With the development of coca and processing labs came the paramilitaries in the late 1990s, with the Calima Bloc.[76] This group created alliances with some gangs and eliminated others to establish its hegemony. These arrangements were challenged by the FARC, which maintained a military presence in Santander de Quilichao, Corinto, and Toribio; by 2008, FARC had expanded into Puerto Tejada.[77]

Consequently, a new war system dynamic developed, ushering an escalation in war rentierism, which explains the alarming increase in killings in the 1990s. An illustrative indicator is the size of the homicide rates before and after the AUC's incursion. In 1990, Puerto Tejada had a homicide rate of 65.8/100.000, while the national rate was 80/100.000 (see Figure 5.1). This changed notoriously in the presence of the new war system's dynamic that the Calima Bloc set in motion.[78] By the end of the 1990s, the homicide rate amounted to 111,4/100,000 while the national rate decreased to 60/100,000. Following the consolidation and expansion of the AUC in Cauca, the rates of homicides skyrocketed to 180.5/100,000 while the national rate continued its declining trend, reaching 40,18/100,000 (see figure 5.1).

The cause of the exponential increase in homicides during the period of AUC dominance in Puerto Tejada was attributed chiefly to the systematic campaign of assassinations of social leaders, activists who protested rentier capital, gang members who disobeyed their gangs' rules of conduct, drug addicts, and homosexuals, which imposed a fascist type of political order and discipline servicing the advancement of rentier capital, including narcotraffickers' investments. However, it is important to remember that private armies working at the behest of large landowners are not new, as mentioned before with the example of Los Pajaros. The explanation now is that the array of patrons consists of many, ranging

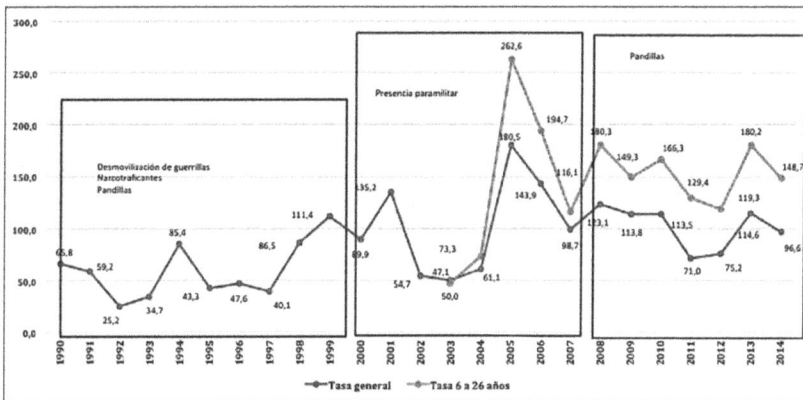

Figure 5.1. Homicide rates. *Source*: Ministry of Justice/Colombia, public domain.

from agribusinesses, manufacturers, narcobourgeoisie, mining companies, insurgents, and state agents (police and military). This array of actors and their interplay provides the underlying cause of crime in Puerto Tejada.

There was also a notable case in 1991, seven years before the Calima Bloc made its official appearance with the infamous massacre of the Nilo, in Caloto, in which twenty-one Indigenous were killed by paramilitaries.[79] The Indigenous were reclaiming land occupied by the sugar mill owners. The Nilo massacre was not an isolated event. Violence had been employed by large landowners and their assassins since the 1940s to settle their land disputes with the Indigenous, African Colombians, and mestizo peasants. Therefore, the advent of AUC and its Calima Bloc was a logical progression of this violent history, with the caveat that they developed under a set of new conditions: on the one hand, a lucrative narcoeconomy that offered opportunities for enrichment, and on the other, the necessity of containing the insurgency's threat against large landowners, multinational corporations, and agribusiness.

The paramilitaries remained in Puerto Tejada until 2005–06, when the AUC officially demobilized, leaving behind active gangs. The continued existence of gangs in Puerto Tejada after the demobilization of the AUC and its Calima front can be explained by three factors, listed in their order of importance. One is the proximity (22.3 miles) of Puerto Tejada to Cali, a bastion for organized crime including gangs and narcotraffickers. Cali provides gangs with a strategic depth to avoid detection and expand their criminal enterprise. The second factor is the overall unemployment crisis and economic dislocation generated by mechanization in the sugar sector, which requires less labor. The third factor relates to the presence of FARC, which since 2008 has been consolidating its presence in northern Cauca and Puerto Tejada and has established "a barter system" of exchange with some of the gangs, exchanging stolen merchandise for weapons and drugs.[80] According to a Puerto Tejada informant, FARC dissidents currently have a force in the region, including Puerto Tejada, that draws on gangs for recruitment and intelligence gathering,[81] an observation that Miguel Fernandez confirmed.[82] The FARC dissidents offer about three hundred dollars per month, which is attractive to young people with little or no economic opportunities. The Clan del Golfo and other organized criminal groups offer approximately that figure as well. The money incentive is an attractive economic option for gang members, which may explain their expansion in Puerto Tejada.

Puerto Tejada presents a case of multidimensional social change, which has led to the proletarianization and dismantling of the peasant economy. Most of its population has abandoned or lost their lots and with them their ability to pursue subsistence food production, instead becoming wage laborers in the sugar plantations, mills, or industrial parks. Women, as mentioned earlier, have migrated to Cali to work as domestic helpers for the middle and upper classes. In response to these dramatic changes, the Afro-Colombian leadership in the area is mobilizing to create a community council, which calls for the re-peasantization of the new generation of people who have lost their agricultural skills and any interest in preserving them. Re-peasantization under the adminis- tration of an Afro-Colombian Community Council will be a challenging undertaking, and only the future will tell if it succeeds. Recently, the state granted lands to two community councils in Puerto Tejada. One is named Rio Cauca, the other Monte Oscuro, and both councils have maintained some areas of their communal land dedicated to sugar cane plantation, which they sell to the Cauca Sugar Mill, alongside traditional crops of corn, yucca, and ponds stocked with fish. The future plan is to revive traditional family farm production to produce more crops and satisfy all the food needs of the inhabitants.[83] However, in order to reach that lofty goal, they must sell their labor power and rent part of their land to the Cauca Sugar Mill agribusiness, one of the largest enterprises in Cauca. In the meantime, gangs, narcotraffickers, and others will remain, a terrorizing menace to the population.

Youth gangs have expanded their activities and recruiting to most municipalities in the north Cauca, including Santander de Quilichao, and Villa Rica. My interviewees in both municipalities attributed the gangs' expansion to an increase in narcotrafficking, family disintegration, and youth destitution, compounded with the lure of easy money.[84] All of these factors thrive against the background of a simmering socioeconomic crisis precipitated by an exhausted rentier economic model sustained by sugar cane agribusiness alongside a few other enterprises founded in the wake of the Paez Law. The unregulated expansion of sugar cane plantations during the last decade have created additional pressure on the subsistence economy, exacerbating competition between the three main ethnic sectors along ethnic lines and weakening their class solidarity.

Types of Miners/Mining and the Commodity Chain

There are two main types of miners and mining. One is the local sub- sistence alluvial mining practiced for generations by Afro-descendants (*barequeros*). It is performed manually, with no machinery or chemicals, and its proceeds are used for economic survival. The other form of mining is practiced by a host of immigrant miners, speculators, and organized criminal organization that ranges from small-scale to heavy equipment that causes enormous environmental damage to riverbeds and wildlife, as well as generating profits. The two types, subsistence and commercial, are differentiated by their degrees of integration with international capital.

Local gold panners (*barequeros*), along with local small and large commercial miners are subject to the logic of global capital and the worldwide demand for gold. In the gold-producing urban centers of the municipalities of Santander de Quilichao, Argelia, Buenos Aires, Timbiquí, or Guapi, some local traders buy the gold from the *barequeros*. They have corresponding offices in Cali (Valle del Cauca) and either have agreements with international traders or are vertically integrated.[85] Cali hosts three major international gold traders alongside smaller local entities: Giraldo & Duque is the oldest and most renowned. Between 2006 and 2007, the company was one of the first one hundred Colombian exporters of gold to the United States and in 2013 became the first to export gold from the Free Trade Zone near Cali. Between 2010 and 2014, it exported close to sixteen tons of gold, principally to Switzerland (Metalor), the United States (Metal Republic), and India (*El Espectador*, 2015).

The second major trader is Fundación Ramirez and Northern Texas Resources Colombia, a subsidiary of Northern Texas Resources (NTR), which belongs to Elemental, based in the United States and the United Kingdom and maintaining trading operations in the Free Trade Zone near Cali, who source part of their gold from Cauca.[86] The third is Irca, which exports to Miami-based subsidiaries of international refiners, such as Halach Gold from Istanbul Gold Refinery or Kaloti (Dubai), and have increased their gold exports from US$ 284,000 in 2015 to US$ 6.2 million in 2016.[87] The linkages between local gold producers and international capital are multi-dimensional, between the production site and the regional hub—Cali—to the international markets where capital accumulation occurs. The latter retain most of the use-value-added and profit, which is distributed among the financial power centers; little returns to the traders in Cali and the medium and large-scale miners. At the same time, the subsistence-level and small producers receive what they can to keep them afloat.[88]

Under this arrangement, a segment of the gold panners is proletarianized and subsumed by global capital, while others manage to survive and accumulate. The process is punctuated by the use of violence, which determines winners and losers among the different factions competing for hegemony. It is important to know that most small miners and speculators are migrants from Antioquia, Choco, Valle del Cauca, Nariño, South Bolivar, and Huila. In some cases, migrants constitute 80 percent of the total number of miners.[89] The Indigenous and Afro communities that have communal land properties who are also engaged in the extractive monetized economy can be considered as a hybrid socioeconomic group combining a noncapitalist mode of production and a monetized economy. This is akin to the subsistence peasants planting coca as a cash crop that supports their survival with some amenities (cell phones or flat TVs) but without accumulation or value creation as observed in the peasant reserves of Cimitarra (San Pablo) and Balsillas. In a broader theoretical sense, the fact that subsistence peasants, including artisanal miners, diversify their sources of income in order to subsist validates Ploeg's (2018) observation of the changing nature of peasantry and the emergence of neo-peasants (see Introduction and Conclusion).[90]

Violent Entrepreneurs, Youth Gangs, and Rebels: A Diagnostic

In Cauca, there are two sets of violent actors, which we must differentiate according to their role and function in the war rentier economy. One is the ELN, made up of FARC's dissidents, and the other is organized crime. The ELN is present in four municipalities only, while the now-defunct FARC had historical roots for several decades in at least thirty municipalities in Cauca until its demobilization in 2016. The ELN has been expanding into some of the territories left behind by FARC, such as Caloto, Mercaderes, Algeria, Argelia, López de Micay, and El Tambo.[91] Taxing the miners is an important source of funding. For instance, Mercaderes ELN taxed the 2,500 gold miners in Cauca one million U.S. dollars per month.[92] The ELN retains its Marxist ideology and commitment to its political agenda. The demobilized FARC, particularly the fronts (69 and 6) that operated in Cauca, have rearmed again and activated those fronts under the leadership of the late Gentil Duarte, a commander who did not accept the peace process and refused to join, and who was killed in May 2022. FARC's fronts operate in Caldono, Corinto, Puerto Tejada, Santander de Quilichao, and other municipalities.

Organized criminal organizations are important actors that capitalize on the illegal mining of gold, a lucrative business generating several millions per month that are easily laundered. The second important source of income is cocaine production, which has increased since 2016, when the FARC signed its peace accord with the state. Coca plantations have increased significantly (see Figure 5.2) from their levels in 2014, reaching 17,355.83 hectares in 2019 before declining by 9.5 percent to 16,543.83 hectares in 2020.[93] However, the amount of cocaine extracted has increased due to the use of better technology and new variants of coca, locally known as "Palo Yuca," which can be harvested every two months, that is, six times a year.[94] This variant and the improved technology account for the fact that metric tons of cocaine exported increased despite a 9.5 percent decrease in the coca-cultivated areas. In 2019, UNDOC reported an increase in metric tons in cocaine production of 1.8 percent from the previous year.[95]

MEXICAN DRUG CARTELS IN CAUCA

Mexico's narcotraffickers and their links with Colombia have evolved and developed since the 1970s. What has been changing is the power relationship and the division of labor between the drug lords of Mexico and those in Colombia, who had less military power. For the Colombian narcotraffickers, this relationship is vital to securing the transborder ship-

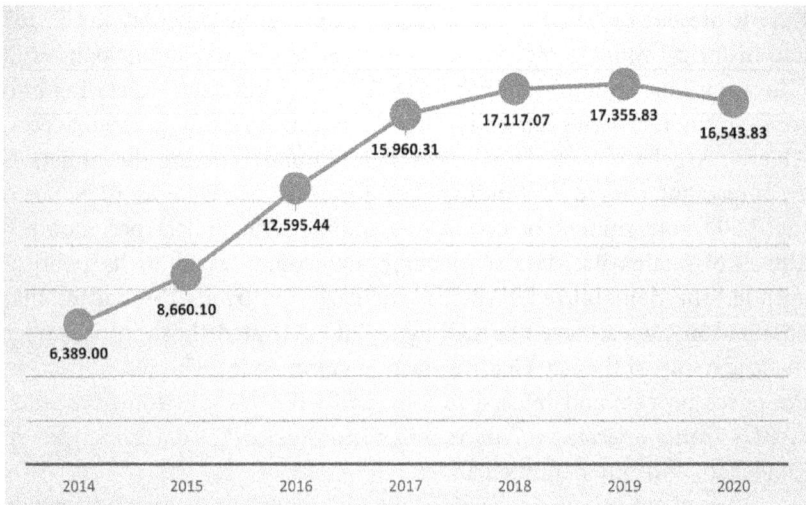

Figure 5.2. Cauca's Coca Plantations. *Source*: UNODC, public domain.

ments to the United States and Europe. The Mexican drug business, in the meantime, has become more centralized, to the point where a couple of organizations dominate the market, namely, Sinaloa and Jalisco the New Generation.[96] The Sinaloa Cartel, sensing the change in Colombia in the wake of the demobilization of the FARC and the power vacuum that it left behind in Cauca, jumped in to dominate the coca commodity chain from cultivation, production, and processing to transportation and distribution in the U.S. and global markets.

The above explains the Mexican narcotraffickers' crime footprint in Santander de Quilichao and Suarez, as well as other coca-growing municipalities where anti-coca activists were targeted.[97] The Indigenous received the brunt of the Sinaloa violence, since they were the most organized and were determined to defend their *resguardos,* manually eradicate the coca, and protect their youngsters against forceful recruitment by the Sinaloa Cartel and others. This activism put them on a collision course with narcotrafficking organizations and, more importantly, with the local elites, politicians, dominant classes, and state agents benefiting from the economy of narcotrafficking compounded by illegal mining.[98] It is estimated that five thousand persons, mostly Nasa, were killed by narcotraffickers, paramilitaries, army, and other forces to break down their resistance and subjugate them to the ongoing process of subsumption.[99]

In sum, the advent of the Mexican Cartels in Cauca alongside the state's armed forces, FARC dissidents of (the Gentil Duarte group[100] and the New Marquetalia), the Cartel del Golfo, and ELN created a multiparty war system with a political economy and dynamics that is spiraling out of control. Consequently, one can say that the evolving war system in Cauca has become the fulcrum upon which the war rentierism subsumption process is resting. In other words, violence is expected to continue earmarking the rentier economy and its growth.

Afro-Colombians and Indigenous: Resistance, Cooperation, and Tension

The resistance to war rentierism and its effects on their communities created an urgency for cooperation among the most affected groups: Afro-Colombians, Indigenous, and nonethnic/mestizo peasants. This urgency led to the creation of the Interethnic and Intercultural Commission, to coordinate an action plan. The first meeting was held in 2002 by

Villarica, north of Cauca, and was attended by eight thousand Indigenous people and Blacks.[101] Representatives of Afro-Colombian, Indigenous, and peasant communnities joined forces to develop a unified plan to fight back and defend their land rights and communal noncapitalist way of life. Arie Aragon, the former mayor of Villarica and leader of the Association House of the Child (Casa del Nino), explained to me that, since 2002, in Villarica the collaboration between Blacks and Indigenous had started with a spectrum of ideas related to public health, land issues, education, and other concerns. But in 2003, a larger meeting was organized in the municipality of Guachene with one main idea: food security. Ten thousand people attended this meeting; nonethnic peasants also participated.[102] Since the Indigenous live in the higher lands and the Afro-Colombians live in the plains, they grow different products.[103] They agreed to create a "barter market," where the communities could exchange what they produce. For example, the Afro-Colombians grow plantains and corn and the Indigenous *trucha* (a root plant like yucca).[104] Consolidating a barter market in which no money is circulated has been a defiant response to the capitalist onslaught. The Interethnic Intercultural Commission's role is to coordinate the communities' response and attempt to maintain and strengthen their alternative modes of production, way of life, and culture outside the orbit of the capitalist monetized system of exchange value creation and exploitation. A third meeting was held in Santander de Quilichao (an epicenter of mining, coca plantation, and violence). The interethnic and intercultural exchange was strengthened, incorporating human rights and the environment. Aragon contended that those commissions helped articulate a common view among the three social groups and became a forum to mitigate disputes and encourage conflict resolution among them.[105] One main problematic area affecting the department is mining. All peasant communities have a common interest in controlling the use of heavy machinery dredging riverbeds and lands, causing an environmental disaster that contaminates the water supply and threatens wildlife, a condition that affects the entire population of Cauca and beyond.

The peasants joined forces to confiscate the mining machines, running the risk of confronting criminal organizations, including narcotraffickers, violent entrepreneurs, and rebels. However, this did not halt the illegal mining operations. The irony is that although the peasants destroyed the heavy machinery, the owners of the machinery did not appear to defend their property, which indicated that most of this illegal mining is carried out by proxies or third parties. The most puzzling aspect, according to

Aragon, is that the state's forces were overlooking these huge machines as they passed the military checkpoints coming from Cali.[106] This raises important questions about the state's role in providing legal and fiscal support to the agribusiness, manufacturing, multinational, and illegal mining economy that defines war rentierism.[107] In this same vein, Aragon defined the social actors who sustain illegal mining, forming part of its political economy in Cauca. He noted that such an "open" business would not be possible without either the benevolence, the complacency, or the utter corruption of local politicians, mayors, and the state's armed forces deployed in areas of mining. Each is has a slice of the illegal mining cake.[108] The complicity of state forces and local elites might well explain the sustenance of this lucrative illegal sector and hence the war system that their interaction has helped create.

Afro-Colombians and the Political Learning Curve

The centuries-long struggle of the Afro-descendants to escape colonial enslavement has led to the establishment of their own free towns, *Palenques,* that characterize the Caribbean and Pacific coastal region. Their arduous struggle did not translate into agreements either with the Spanish Crown or the Indigenous people. The latter path lay in translating tenuous agreements into permanent clearer ones in a step-by-step tactic, as discussed in the previous chapter. The critical component that helped the Indigenous was leadership with a legalistic vision. In contrast, the Afro-descendants' lack of coherent leadership transcending traditional political parties weakened their abilities to articulate a national political agenda.[109] Their leaders opted to work within the establishment, compromising their communities' rights by corruption, co-optation, or political pragmatism.[110] The outcome has been a deep bifurcation between their leaders in Congress and the local ones, which neglected the Afro communities' urgent need to safeguard their communal lands and obtain de jure recognition of the hundred-plus community councils in the Cauca alone.

The difference between the trajectory of the Indigenous and that of the Afro-Colombians is quite striking. The Indigenous succeeded in obtaining recognition from the colonial power and continued building on those agreements as stepping stones to extract land titles. In the postcolonial order, the Indigenous persisted in their legal claims and land claims obtained during colonial time, exploiting the jurisprudence of the liberal capitalist order, as discussed in chapter 4. In contrast, the Afro-descendants did not follow this path. Instead, they followed an appeasement approach, depriving them of the power needed to extract concessions from the state and the dominant class. The community council is functionally inspired by the *resguardos*. Still, the Black community has yet to yield enough power to force the state to approve their demands in strategic areas such as northern Cauca, where the state is deeply entrenched in the rentier mode with a formidable array of capitalists: conglomerate-owned sugar cane production (such Ardila Lülle's), sugar mills, and multinational mining corporations. These conglomerates represent a class force adamantly opposed to territorial autonomy and re-peasantization as sought by the creation of community councils. This formidable fight might partly explain the disproportionate number of Blacks forcefully displaced from Cauca and elsewhere. Since the 1980s, two million Blacks have been displaced. While the Afro-descendants constitute only 10.4 percent of the general population, they represent 33.3 percent of the internally displaced people (IDP).[111]

The Community Councils between Promise and Peril

The creation of community councils has been an aspiration of the Afro-Colombians in Cauca, Choco and other departments where this community has roots. As mentioned before, the figure of the community council was inspired by the example of the *resguardos* in which a community manages the collective property, allocation of resources, and distribution of justice. Afro-descendants have had limited success in establishing their community council because the state has not granted them land, resource grown scarce in the face of the increasing concessions granted to multinational mining corporations, agribusinesses, and manufacturing industries under the infamous Paez Law.

My research has discovered another major challenge facing the existing community, which might unravel the entire endeavor if not attended to and addressed by the Afro-descendant leadership in Cauca and elsewhere. The community council leaders in northern Cauca, where they have access to land, ended up leasing it to the sugar mills instead of using it for agriculture and have guarded their own latitude in managing the community council and the production process, where the dividends are monopolized by those presiding over the council or their family members. According to Arie Aragon, "This condition created social tension within the community [and] also generated a caste of privileged individuals and class differentiations all of which are to the detriment of the development of the classless communal council thought as an alternative to capitalism."[112] Aragon emphasized that in the communal council of Cauca's Pacific region, this phenomenon was not present, which he attributed to the heavy influence of the Indigenous *resguardos*. Remember that the Indigenous *resguardos* and *cabildos* exercised absolute authority over their community and had a much longer trajectory in ruling their communities before the Conquest and after.

Another high priority for the African Colombian leadership is addressing anti-Black racial discrimination in the justice system. Arie Aragon and other interviewees discussed the importance of the Afro-community's struggle to attain the autonomy to deal with minor misdemeanors. They underscored the problem of the high incarceration rate of Afro-descendants for minor offenses.[113] Given the high incidence of poverty, unemployment, and internal displacement in the African Colombian community in Cauca, the high level of incarceration is not surprising.[114] But the lack of data in the Colombian justice system does not allow the community's leadership to make a case that there is disproportionate incarceration or discrimination.[115]

Nonetheless, following the example of the Indigenous *resguardos,* the Black communities are pressuring the state to recognize the one hundred existing departmental-level community councils, forty-two of them in north Cauca, so they can access land and manage their own justice system. To achieve that objective, they have developed a project of building Afro Tribunes in each of the forty-two community councils. Each tribune will be made up of eleven members drawn from among the elders of the community that have knowledge of the community's historical experience in conflict management and resolution. So far, this is only a hypothetical project, and the community is building up support for it, including establishing relations with universities such as Javeriana University-Cali. Javeriana is one of the top universities in the country and is run by a Jesuit order. In this respect, Javeriana provides legal advice and has established an observation center monitoring human rights violations against the Afro-communities in Cauca and the Valle del Cauca, which should help promote the idea of tribunes.

The Differential Impact of War Rentierism
on African Colombian Women

Throughout their history in Colombia, Afro-Colombian women have existed at the bottom of the power structure that is the capitalist class system, their displacement compounded by the thousands of years of deep-seated patriarchy that permeates gender relations. According to DANE, 50.5 percent of the Afro community are women, 21.7percent of them forcefully displaced. This is above the national average, but even worse is the gender-based violence that affects 41.6 percent of Black Colombian women, compared to 36 percent. Their unemployment rate is also higher, 20.4 percent compared to 17.6 percent, and their illiteracy rate is 16.9 percent, above the national average of 11.7percent.[116]

Another troubling figure is the high percentages of displaced women as heads of families, of which 47 percent are Afro-Colombian and 49 percent Indigenous.[117] The magnitude and scope of displacement precipitated by war rentierism, dismantling families and communities and usurping their lands to expand extractive activities and agribusiness, has revealed the pattern. At least 1.5 million of the IDP are Afro-descendants, and, more importantly, 83 percent of the collective land properties are situated in the 150 municipalities with the highest indices of forceful displacement. Furthermore, 72 percent of the displaced Afro-descendants have been expelled from collective communal properties, and 50percent of those are women who have little or no guarantees to accessing land property.[118] As one can infer from these statistics, Afro-descendant women are the weakest link in the resistance chain opposing capitalism and its patriarchal underpinnings.

One of the gravest consequences of women's displacement from their families and communal land is the government's Law 1448/2011, known as the Victims and Restitution Law, accompanied by its Decree 4635/2011. This decree does not consider the gender or ethnic components of forced displacement, a problematic situation that has been compounded by the Public Ministry, which, by not accepting citizens' applications, has avoided implementing Decree 4635/2011, which requires the state to secure the return of displaced women to their communal lands. Instead, the ministry has accepted citizens' applications under Law 1448/2011, applying to "individual private property,"[119] which is not surprising given the state's bias against communal land property, as discussed in chapters 1 and 2.[120]

In this context, Law 1448/2011 legitimizes one of the core goals of war rentierism: land grabbing of communal lands.

The representation of women within the established community councils in northern Cauca and the Pacific Coast councils is very low. But what is emerging is the leading role of Black women in defending their territories and lands against the incursions of rentier capital. As is the case with Indigenous women, Afro-Colombian women have become targets of assassination (more than 20 percent of the total) in an attempt to weaken their resistance and facilitate the subsumption of their sources of life.

Conclusion

The struggle for land in northern Cauca is far from concluded (see chapter 3 for a discussion of the human toll on the Indigenous). Since the 1940s, war rentierism, with its mutations changing both actors and political economy, has caused unrelenting havoc in Cauca. This process was compounded by the Paez Law, which accelerated the export-oriented manufacturing sector and integrated Cauca into global capital as firmly as Bogotá and as subject to the exigencies of the global division of labor.[121] In this respect, the state and private capital, local and foreign, has played a pivotal role in accomplishing this drastic transformation of a predominantly rural peasant-based society, beginning in the 1960s.

Despite all, in the 2000s, 60 percent of the population of Cauca has remained rural, while the national average has dropped to 25.7 percent.[122] Such a high figure reveals three core subsumption characteristics exhibited in Cauca: One is that the Afro-descendants are still drawn to their traditions of communal subsistence living dependent on artisanal mining and fishing. Second is the unevenness and contradictory nature of a capitalist transformation in a dependent economy, which depends more on global market demand than on the maturity of its own conditions. This dependency on the global market encourages the expansion or stagnation of rentier capitalism in core sectors such as mining, cash crops such as sugarcane, export-oriented light industries, and real estate speculation.

Consequently, the subsumption process under a rentier mode of accumulation encourages the precarious existence of the subsistence economy, drawing on it incrementally, like scavengers, when needed (see Introduction). The most notable characteristic is the demand for land, and not much for labor, which might explain the high percentage of people in the rural areas. The third characteristic of subsumption has been the peasantry's high degree of resistance, including that of Afro-descendants, Indigenous, and mestizos. The class struggle launched by the peasants' organizations has acted as a countervailing class force challenging the advancement of war rentierism. In 2015, seven properties privately owned by agribusiness, including sugar cane plantations, were occupied by Indigenous. By contrast, the Afro-descendants have followed a less radical approach in their land claims and forms of resistance. Nonetheless, the divergent methods of resistance do not minimize the joint struggle of all peasants, as manifested in the increasing mobilizations since the 2000s, and reaching new heights in 2021.[123] The intersection of these three factors explains the persistently high levels of rurality in Cauca, a condition that was noted by Van der Ploeg (2018) in his study of peasant communities in the Global South.[124]

The human and environmental costs of change in Cauca have been enormous. The human toll can be assessed by examining the numbers of people killed, massacred, or forcefully displaced. But the environmental degradation and the effects of the use of chemicals in gold extraction, of dredging, excavations, deforestation, and the contamination of rivers and water sources are yet to be fully assessed. The first line of defense against the offenders are the Afro-descendants and the Indigenous of Cauca. These groups suffer the brunt of the violent entrepreneurs, including the state, spearheading the charge. The state's neoliberal policies and its rentier accent have provided the contours of war rentierism, with the support and endorsement of the local bourgeoisie in Cauca, as represented by landed elites, cattle ranchers, industrialists, multinational corporations, mining companies, and the narcobourgeoisie.

Conclusion

The Future of Peasant Resistance and Adaptation to War Rentierism

The preceding chapters demonstrate the threats and challenges that peasant communities confront in Colombia, chiefly in economically strategic areas where the extraction of oil and gold, and agribusinesses such as African palm oil crops, sugar cane mills, and cattle ranching have been expanding since the 1980s. Considering the advancement of rentier capitalism, this book has addressed three core questions: (1) How did the Colombian peasants in the indigenous *resguardos,* the Afro communal council, and the peasant reserves survive under adverse conditions? (2) What are the sources of their resilience, their adaptability in the face of the onslaught of neoliberal war rentierism? And (3) what distinguishes their responses and strategies in dealing with the state and managing the threats they face.

These three research questions guided the study of the peasant communities and its conclusion that the fight between these noncapitalist socioeconomic formations and rentier capital is far from over given the state's unrelenting commitment to neoliberal economic orthodoxy, which has had devastating effects on the peasants' lives, food security, and the environment. The implication of the analytical framework of this book transcends the contours of the cases studied. It sheds new light on the expanding literature on peasant economies, the formation of "neo-peasants," and re-peasantization. The findings add some critical observations explaining the sources of the peasant communities' resilience and their ability to persevere. First, the study dispels the notion that the peasantry is a relic of a distant past, a remnant of a disappearing *Ancien Regime,* a view championed by some neoliberal economists (see chapter 1) along side some peasant studies scholars such as Bernstein (see Introduction). Secondly, the explored cases demonstrate that peasants are active agents whose agency has achieved a significant global network (see chapters 3, 4, and 5).[1]

Most importantly, these communities have accumulated vast experience that has allowed them to change, adapt, and resist, although occasionally succumbing to the process of subsumption. These two findings enable me to anticipate that most of the studied cases are resilient enough to withstand the continuation of war rentierism in Colombia. However, this anticipation comes with an important qualifier, discussed below.

Theoretical Implications of This Research

This research has explored the peasants' responses to the advent of the neoliberal rentier state and its extreme variant, war rentierism. As presented in chapters 3, 4, and 5, peasants' responses were not uniform nor homogeneous. They depended on the interplay between the nature of the threat and their own historical experiences and levels of the organization. The peasant's reserves, the indigenous *resguardos,* and the Afro-descendant community councils as noncapitalist formations responded differently to the encroachment of capital in its various violent forms. The response of the indigenous groups in Cauca stands out in contrast to the other communities in terms of its ability to extract more concessions from the state, such as funds, land, and autonomy.

The research underscores that the Colombian peasants are active agents struggling to preserve their mode of life and carve a niche as players in a changing local and global environment. The analysis presented is a snapshot of their uphill struggle, which has been marred by the violence endured by hundreds of thousands of peasants nationwide. The investigated cases are narrated mainly through the people's experiences, supplemented by other primary and secondary sources.

These research findings have conceptual and theoretical implications relevant to analyzing the peasants' past struggles and future survival, and might also help set the stage for future research in Colombia or cross-nationally. The current literature has many gaps that should be investigated to understand today's peasantry better and shed light on the peasants' economy and agroecology as an alternative path to capitalism. Below, I discuss four key conceptual and theoretical areas that have illuminated my analysis and are essential to future research on peasantry and re-peasantization.

A critical conceptual area is the view of the peasants' struggle in the context of Chayanov's and Luxemburg's perspectives. While Chayanov focused on the peasants' resilience and survival, Luxemburg cast the process of subsumption of noncapitalist modes within the logic of the expansion of capitalism that is essential for its continuity and accumulation. Both perspectives are complementary and helpful in understanding a complex and multidimensional process such as the peasants' struggle against rentierism. Chayanov's prism focused on the micro: the daily economy, its organization, hardship, and growth; that is, the proactive agency of the peasants and their abilities to adapt and resist capitalist subsumption despite its use of violent actors. On the other hand, Luxemburg explained that capital accumulation was the driving force behind capitalism's efforts in its colonial and imperialist forms to expand into the peripheries of the Global North as much as Global South. Popkin's political economy approach and amendments were valuable for interpreting some of the findings. Ploeg, in his turn, argued convincingly about the neo-peasant and trends in re-peasantization and their pivotal role in the global economy. In sum, Chayanov's, Luxemburg's, Popkin's, and Ploeg's perspectives guided this book to investigate the interplay of microsocial factors and agency have that allowed peasants to adapt and resist subsumption.

The second critical area is the theory of capital subsumption. Subsumption reflects a power relationship between labor and capital in which capital holds the reins of local and global dominance. Labor, for its part, including peasants, is not an amalgamation of passive actors, either locally or globally. On the contrary, they have the agency, reflected in their organizational skills, to obtain territories under their authority, such as the peasant reserves in Cimitarra and Pato-Balsillas, alongside the indigenous *resguardos* and the Afro-Colombian community councils. These peasants' formations showed political skills to fight the debilitating processes of subsumption manifested in land grabbing, private/state violence, forced displacement, and environmental degradation. They also succeeded in building an alternative development path and an economy based on communal land ownership and use, solidarity, barter systems, and agroecology (see chapters 3, 4, and 5). This book has highlighted the role of the peasants' agency and its evolution as a countervailing force against capital at times successfully employed, as in the case of the Indigenous in Cauca, and at other times unsuccessfully, such as that involving the peasants in San Pablo, Bolivar.

In her publication *The Accumulation of Capital*, written in the early twentieth century, Rosa Luxemburg described the process of subsumption as a kind of metabolism between the capitalist economy and those precapitalist production methods. She added that capital could not accumulate without the aid of noncapitalist organizations.[2] More than a century later, capital and labor have witnessed significant changes in their historical relations and conflict. Yet, the cornerstone of capitalism remains accumulation, its endemic overaccumulation, and declining rates of profits. Today, capital's expansion into new areas and its creation of new instruments, including the empires of food and Bitcoin, exist within the contours of the metabolism pointed out by Luxemburg. In Luxemburg's theory, and as, in recent times, Banerjee and Duflo have contended, noncapitalist formations, such as the cases explored in this book, are under enormous pressure from the food empire, global markets, the state, and violent entrepreneurs. This pressure is compounded by neoliberal orthodoxy and its message that "the only salvation is the institution of private property since with that you will be able to sell your land and mortgage it."[3] This liberal mantra and its effects were discussed in chapter 1.

The third conceptual area crucial to understanding the Colombian peasants' capabilities and resilient struggle is their innovation and praxis, cumulative knowledge and experience gained over a century of resistance, which Fajardo (2019) called a tradition of colonization by landless peasants. This knowledge helped the *colonos* organize and build their communities, weaving their social fabric and networks with local and international players, as discussed in the cases of Cimitarra and Pato-Balsillas. Fajardo has elaborated upon what he terms a "culture of *colonos*" or colonization seeking new frontiers in order to escape the advancement of the agents of war rentierism.[4] He highlighted the role of the diaspora in the experience of Tolima's landless and poor peasants who were expelled from their lands and hamlets, some of whom have settled in Middle Magdalena, including Cimitarra and Pato-Balsillas. These *colonos* bear a militant anticapitalist ideology as they strive for land and autonomy. Since the 1920s, Colombia's landless and poor peasants have been intermittently at war with the state and the landowning elite. A century of struggle has enhanced their collective memory and strengthened their political identity. The experience of uprootedness, the culture of colonization, and the skills acquired in conflict management while displaced define broadly the *colonos'* attributes, which help in discerning elements of their resilience.

Similarly, Amparo Murillo (2012), in her anthropological study of Middle Magdalena, underscored the "social rupture" that *colonos* had to endure as a result of their constant violent displacement from their places of origins.[5] This uprootedness has led landless peasants to seek refuge in the "periphery of the periphery," away from the onslaught of capital and its violent agents. The second attribute Murillo highlighted is the experience they have accumulated in conflict management, which is also reflected in the *colonos'* day-to-day behavior in their newly acquired homes.[6]

In sum, the cumulative experiences of expulsion, violence, adaptability, and resistance, retained in a collective memory that *colonos* share, gave "the tradition" of colonization historical meaning and guidance for collective praxis.[7] Fajardo (2019) maintained that these experiences translated into a political-union-like organization. In this line of analysis, the colonization movement is primarily a group activity (though it does not exclude individualism), motivated and incentivized by experiences and memories of dispossession, resistance, and displacement.

The fourth and final conceptual area refers to the phenomenon of the increasing peasantry "re-peasantization" that the UN and FAO pointed out, which was further elaborated upon by Ploeg (2018). The new peasants are not relics of the past. Re-peasantization is not seen only as an indicator of the survival of peasantry but also as a viable alternative to the "food empire" and a way to mitigate greenhouse emissions (Ploeg 2018). Interestingly, this wave of re-peasantization that involves what some are calling "neo-peasants" is occurring even in France, which is the food basket of the EU, providing a fifth of its food needs. Moreover, a new trend has begun where people are migrating from French cities to the countryside to engage in sustainable farming.[8] This is one of the most significant contradictions and puzzles of this phase of capital globalization caused by the confluence of labor agency and climate change. This wave of re-peasantization, complemented by the increasing global activism of peasant organizations such as La Via Campesina, among many others, has enhanced the exchange of experiences and struggle as expressions of a twenty-first-century transnational peasant movement.[9]

However, re-peasantization as described above is not possible in Colombia under the state's neoliberal policy and its economic model based on agribusiness, energy extraction, mining, services, and speculation overlooking the agricultural sector and its peasantry. According to the UNDP 2011 report, about 32 percent of Colombia's population depend on earning their livelihood in the rural sector. The rural population is estimated to have been about 9 million in 2020, slightly decreasing from 10 million, as recorded a decade earlier in 2010.[10] For more than three decades, the state's economic policy has rested on the assumption that economic growth depends on the extraction of raw materials (such as oil, coal, and gold), cash crops (African palm oil, bananas, cut flowers, timber, sugar) and its expanding service sector. This rentier growth has led to what I have coined elsewhere as "growth without development."[11] Empirical evidence shows that the rentier model's steady economic growth dividends have not trickled down. Instead, it has primarily benefited its rentier agents, such as multinational extractive corporations (oil, coal, and gold), agribusinesses (especially African palm oil), land speculators (cattle ranching), and services (banks, telecom, insurance, tourism, hotels).[12] In rural areas, the advancement of the rentier sector has distorted agricultural production. It has decreased food production areas by 22 percent from their 1990 levels and increased land prices, making them the highest in Latin America and the world, increasing tenants' land leases, and hiked food prices (see chapter 1).[13]

These four conceptual and theoretical areas are the essential building blocks that set the stage for a future research agenda designed to fill crucial gaps in the literature on the changing political economy of rural areas in Colombia. Within this framework, a vital area expected to create new rural dynamics is based on the international agreements and pressure to phase out fossil fuels (oil and coal), two crucial pillars of the rentier economy currently contributing to the war system.[14]

CLASS CONSCIOUSNESS AND IDENTITY POLITICS

Another notable attribute that has emerged from this study, as discussed in chapters 3 through 5 is the role of radical socialist groups, including those that were active before the founding of the Communist Party in 1930. Pierre Gilhodes (1988) classified three different agrarian conflicts during the 1920s: (1) those related to working conditions within the haciendas; (2) land conflicts where land titles were disputed; and (3) the Indigenous' struggle to safeguard their *resguardos* or to recover usurped lands.[15] Eduardo Pizarro (1998), for his part, explained that those struggles of the 1920s were underpinned by revolutionary and socialist ideologies. The Revolutionary Socialist Party, the Agrarian National Party, led by Erasmo Valencia, and the National Unity of the Revolutionary Left all played significant roles in enhancing the political socialization of the peasantry. These groups were the precursors of the Communist Party, who inherited a mobilized and politically conscious mass of people.[16]

The Communist Party (CP), founded in 1930, continued to champion the peasant colonization movement in various departments, especially Tolima, Caqueta, Meta, Sumapaz (Cundinamarca), and in 1949 it announced the creation of peasant Self-Defense groups. One year later, the state banned the CP, forcing its leadership and members to go underground. However, during that period the peasants' defense leagues were reinforced. From these experiences, the idea of creating peasant reserves evolved and was supported by CP and the FARC, which until 1993 was the military wing of the CP, seeking the establishment of communal spaces run by peasants and protected by law.

Against the above background, one can better understand the factors that shaped the class consciousness of the peasantry, which was also reflected in peasant organizations such as ANUC and others. In the case of the Indigenous, discussed in chapter 4, they were also influenced by leftist ideologies imbued with their own "legalistic" experience inherited since colonial times. They shared their yearning for autonomy and independence from the state and capital with the other peasants.

This research illustrated how the three ethnic groups shared experiences and exchanged learning. In Cauca, for example, discussed in chapters 4 and 5, the Indigenous groups have attained higher levels of organization and consequently managed to exercise more pressure on the state, forcing it to concede resources. Such an achievement has been repeated a few times. The Afro-Colombian and other peasant groups' representative interviewees emphasized that the Indigenous' success in obtaining concessions from the state, particularly in managing the funds released to them in the wake of the mobilizations of the 1990s and 2000s, was an essential step in consolidating their autonomy. They also highlighted the Indigenous' independence in the administration of their judicial system.

Peasant Communities and the Challenges Ahead

The peasant communities explored in this book face daunting challenges posed by the encroachments of war rentierism. In different combinations, multinational corporations, agribusinesses, cattle ranchers, speculators, organized crime, insurgents, and the state are all threatening the survival not only of the communities studied but of most of the rural population. Yet, as discussed in chapters 3, 4, and 5, adaptability and resistance have allowed these communities to dodge the bullet. However, three main problem areas are expected to persist and grow, affecting the abilities of these social formations to resist subsumption. These include an increased dependency on international organizations such as the World Bank and the UN; internal schisms within the organizations leading the formations; and an intensification of resource-seeking extraction by rentier capital in response to shifts in the global economy.

INCREASED DEPENDENCY

One of the findings of this research is the existence of a web of relationships that the various communities have constructed over the years for technical support and to fund projects, workshops, training, and cover overhead expenditures and expose the state's violations of human rights. These relations have had a positive empowering effect. But donors and NGOs have different political-ideological agendas, influencing the recipients. Any time donors change policy or directive, it will obviously impact the community, undermining its ability to resist. Therefore, amassing all the support possible locally, regionally, and globally to bolster resistance to subsumption must be the main guiding principle. The lure of foreign aid and assistance must be critically assessed and evaluated to consider how it might serve resiliency in the presence of capital exploitation and subsumption.

INTERNAL SCHISMS AND COOPTATION

In the discussion presented in chapters 3, 4, and 5, one point emerged: the schisms within the movements leading the communities studied. The CRIC leaders pointed this out in describing their tense relationship with ONIC, the national umbrella organization of the Indigenous people. Such a tension/schism might offer an opportunity for the state and agents of rentier capital to tone down or avoid completely the "Previous Consultation" process, which has been an effective legal tool for controlling extractive sectors such as the construction of dams and hydropower plants in rural areas, all of which have negative environmental impact. At the microlevel, the Indigenous *resguardos* are confronted by the lures of consumerism and the increasing monetization of their communal economy, as evidenced in the cases discussed in Meta and Cauca (see chapter 4).

The other communities, such as the African-Colombian communities in northern Cauca, face different challenges, putting them at high risk of violence and displacement. Most of their villages have been pillaged, and only two of their forty-two community councils are recognized by the state. The community is at the mercy of the actors of war rentierism, as discussed in the illustrative case of Puerto Tejada (see chapter 5). To make a bad situation worse, the sugar mill enterprises aggressively entice the leaders of the community councils that have land to lease their properties to them, with the leaders keeping the proceeds. Such a phenomenon creates several problems, including social tension within the Afro community and food insecurity.

Moreover, Afro-Colombians have had limited success in establishing their community councils. There were three main reasons for the state's decision not to grant them land. One was the scarcity of land and the extreme concentration of ownership—oligopoly—in the hands of the sugar agribusiness elite (GINI 0.838). Secondly, the state, under the infamous Paez Law, increased the number of concessions it granted to multinational mining and manufacturing corporations.[17] Third, the labor power of the Afro community that the capitalist enterprises need has been an additional motivation for lobbying aggressively to circumvent the creation of communal land where Afro-Colombian peasants might settle.

The peasant reserves of Pato-Balsillas and Cimitarra, on their part, confront several challenges. Among these are three serious ones: first, the large land ownerships within the reserves, such as in Yondo and Balsillas, affecting their economy and agroecology. Second is the expansion of agribusiness, mining, coca (see chapter 3), and third, the impact of Law 1728 of 2014, which stipulates that no land adjudication is permitted within a radius of 2,500 meters from oil extraction areas. This law encroaches on the reserve area, impeding land titling and exercising control over large swaths of land within its parameter.

YOUTH AND THE INTERGENERATIONAL GAP

Some core problems faced by the young peasants were tackled in the preceding chapters, particularly emblematic cases such as those of San Pablo, the *resguardos* of Meta, and the notorious youth gang phenomenon in Puerto Tejada, Cauca. One issue that was addressed is the growing malaise among youths in rural areas due to poverty, scant opportunities, and the lure of money and consumerism, which attract the youth. The myths of easy money that the culture of the narcotraffickers embodies, and concomitantly the spread of consumer capitalist culture, have multiple effects on the youths, one of which is to push them away from food production. In the current rural political economy, three main activities that are attracting the youths were observed: harvesting coca leaves (*raspachines*); joining youth gangs; enlisting in armed groups such as paramilitaries or insurgents. The common denominator among the three options is that they all offer young people a comparative wage advantage as measured against the returns from their family farms. In addition, part of this earned income might also be used to support the subsistence farms, as the research of Taussig (1978) once found. DANE's recently published statistics revealing that the peasant population is currently getting older, with its average age ranging between forty-one and sixty-four years old, come as no surprise, and validate some of the observations engendered by this research.[18] DANE's findings indicate that in a decade or so, fewer people will be engaged in cultivating and producing food, thereby undermining the peasant economy and the country's food security. Such a dire prognosis adds to the severe challenges facing the peasants of Colombia.

War Rentierism and Extractive Resources

Fluctuations in the global economy bear repercussions affecting local actors' behavior. For example, changes in the commodity prices of gold, oil, African palm oil, and cocaine have had an impact on the intensity of war rentierism.[19] According to Indepaz, between January and July 2021, there were fifty-four massacres in Colombia, ten of them in Cauca, that is, 18 percent, and of those three occurred in Santander de Quilichao, where the Black community constituted 33.4 percent of the total population.[20] They took place in San Pablo (Bolivar-Cimitarra reserve) and north Cauca's gold-producing municipalities, such as Santander de Quilichao. The killings have been attributed to increased competition among criminal organizations partially incentivized by the fluctuating price of gold in 2021, and the advent of new actors such as Mexico's Sinaloa Cartel, which disturbed the balance of power.

Finally, the communities represented in this book are all located in economically strategic areas containing minerals, agribusiness, oil, coca crops, and water resources alongside cocaine-transit points such as Cauca. Their geographic location makes them susceptible to the changing dynamics of war rentierism and its system.

Conclusion and Future Research

As demonstrated in the cases studied, the challenges confronting the Colombian peasants are daunting and marked by the continuous struggle against the advancement of war rentierism. The forces allied with global capital and its subsumption process include the state, most factions of the dominant class, and a host of other actors such as agrobusinesses, economic conglomerates, speculators, finance capital, narcobourgeoisie, and cattle ranchers. A conflict whose intensity and geography vary from one community to another, its dynamics are similar and unvarying, and promote learning exchanges and solidarity among the communities thus engaged locally, nationally, and globally. The peasant communities in Meta, Caqueta, Cauca, and Middle Magdalena have demonstrated the ability to adapt and resist the process of subsumption, offering a glimmer of hope for the possible survival of those noncapitalist formations for many years to come. One might say that the battle is on, and the contending actors are building alliances regionally and globally to bolster their respective position. The peasantry is building bridges with national and international groups, which include human rights groups, agroecological organizations (such as La Via Campesina), among other social movements. The peasant leadership is learning and adjusting to the demands of a long-haul struggle against formal subsumption.

FUTURE RESEARCH AND SOCIOECONOMIC ANALYSIS

The first area that invites future research is found in the behavioral patterns of the peasants' young generation and calls for assessing and evaluating their potential role in leading the processes of resistance and change. This type of investigation will accomplish two things. One is to fill an important gap in the literature on the peasantry in Colombia. The second will enable us to formulate a better prognosis not only on the future survival of noncapitalist formations, but also on cultural subsumption (consumerism), identity politics, and social change.

The second area that surfaced from this investigation is the Indigenous and Afro-Colombian drive to create an alternative education and socialization path to the one offered by the neoliberal state. The 2018 inauguration of the Intercultural Indigenous Autonomous University (UAIIN) in Popayan, the capital of Cauca, was a watershed event in the politics of identity and counterhegemonic domination (see chapter 4). Such an important milestone invites more research exploring its impact, viability, and progress. In this same area, the Afro community in Cauca started their own alternative education modality, using a flexible system not as centralized as the UAIIN, in collaboration with universities such as Javeriana. These two models offered by the two communities offer a rich area for researchers in the social sciences and epistemology.

The third area to be considered by future research is the deepening change in the country's rural political economy caused by war rentier-ism and its impact on the country's food security, environment, and the livelihoods of the rural as well as the urban population. Within this area, I found the peasants' response in developing a barter system in Cauca and Cimitarra a subject that merits attention and in-depth study. Finally, I hope that the new research will investigate the viability of the peasants' coping and adaptability strategies, and most importantly, their abilities to open a path to develop re-peasantization.

These suggested areas might enrich our repertoire of knowledge about the Colombian peasants and their future in a globalized, neoliberal capitalist system. I hope this study will encourage new research around the globe, to investigate the viability of the peasants' coping and adaptability strategies and, most importantly, their capacity to vitalize re-peasantizaton.

Postscript

After I finished writing this book, Gustavo Petro was elected president of Colombia, in June 2022. This event broke the mold of the country's history. A rebel, senator, former Bogotá mayor, and leftist leader became president, with, as his vice president, Francia Marquez, an Afro-Colombian woman lawyer, activist, and descendant of a poor peasant family. Undoubtedly, Petro's election offers a historical opportunity for radical change. Although it is premature to predict the scope and the extent of the anticipated changes, this postscript sketches two core areas that the new government is promising to tackle, which are related to this book's argument, findings, and prognosis. One is Petro's proposal to stimulate agricultural production, which will likely lead to a confrontation with the agrarian elite and their allies. The second is his promise to decrease the country's dependence on the extraction sector of oil and coal, pillars of the rentier economy.

Petro's Government, the Agrarian Elite

After winning the election, Petro said, in response to his opponents claims that his government would install socialism and appropriate their businesses and land, that Colombia needs "more capitalist development and protection of private property." He emphasized that "we are going to develop capitalism in Colombia" and fight the vestiges of "feudalism" and "slavery" that are hampering capitalism. If his words are translated into policy, the new government will likely confront the most recalcitrant faction of the agrarian elite, an elite that has accumulated millions of hectares of the most fertile land and used them for unproductive purposes: as a hedge against taxation, for speculation, and for money laundering purposes. It is extrapolated that of between forty[1] and fifty[2] million hectares suitable for agriculture, only 4.6 (9.2 percent of fifty million) to seven (17.5 percent of forty million) million hectares are being used for actual agricultural production. The remaining lands (between thirty-nine and forty-three million hectares) have been used for cattle ranching (see chapter 2). As a result, these lands occupy one of the most desirable, highly valued, and scarce properties in the world, due to its concentration under the ownership of a few hands, such that the coefficient of landownership GINI of 0.88 is one of the highest in the world.[3] It is estimated that only 0.44 percent of the country's landowners possess 40.1 percent of the agricultural land, while some 69.9 percent are subsistence peasants who occupy a mere 5 percent of the land, on lots that average less than five hectares.[4]

The Federation of Cattle Ranchers (Fedegan) and the Agriculturalist Association of Colombia (SAC), alongside local elites and in alliance with sectors of the senior military, paramilitaries, the business elite, and the narcobourgeoisie, will be instrumental in fighting any serious attempt at redistribution that might undermine their economic interests. Their resistance might range from legal and political maneuvering to the use of violence. Contrary to what Petro implied in his speech, cattle ranchers and narcobourgeoisie factions are not "vestiges of feudalism," nor are they ghosts of the past. The breadth of their influence and the strength of their control have grown and developed thanks to the state's rentier economic policies, embedded as they are in the country's historical process of dependent development, which have decimated Colombia's food production and manufacturing sectors, as discussed in the Introduction.

Therefore, Petro's agrarian program will likely confront a sector of the bourgeoisie that has formed an essential part of the rentier political economy and has been instrumental in its consolidation by employing violence to accelerate the rentier transformation of the rural economy (see chapters 1 and 2). Consequently, cattle ranching, although it is one of the most deficient/inefficient sectors of the rural economy, might surface as the main opposition to the new government. Shifting land use from cattle ranching to food production would fill an essential gap in a country that imports 30 percent of its food needs.[5] As the incoming financeminister, Jose Antonio Ocampo, said in a recent interview, "It is shameful for Colombia to be the fourth importer of corn in the World."[6] Neoliberalism and the rentier model have encouraged the transformation of land use from agriculture to speculation (cattle ranching), real estate, and tourism. Ocampo, a leading figure in the Petro government, is a proponent of creating state subsidies to activate the rural peasant economy and strengthening research and development to encourage national production. However, he is also a critic of orthodox neoliberalism.[7] Ocampo's role will be critical in revising the government's model of economic development, hopefully benefiting from the lessons learned from the failures of the *Apertura*, which led to "premature de-industrialization" and "de-agriculturalization" at the regional level. The *Apertura* was blamed for reduced growth, increased income disparities, the rise in food importation, and the informalization of the workforce.

Against the above backdrop of a possible cattle ranchers' opposition to the new government drive to implement the land reform agreed on in the 2016 peace agreement with the FARC, Petro signed an unprecedented agreement with the president of Fedegan to purchase three million hectares for an amount ranging between US\$6 billion and US\$8billion.[8] This agreement with the most recalcitrant and reactionary faction of the dominant class is a clever attempt by Petro to co-opt cattle ranchers and avoid confrontation.

The government chose to purchase rather than appropriate land since some if not most of those millions of hectares had been dubiously obtained over the decades. This choice reveals Petro's moderate reformist drive, which falls within the contours of a liberal capitalist system.[9] It remains to be seen how the government will come up with the money needed to buy the three million hectares.

Petro's political overture toward Fedegan did not end with the land deal but was further extended in an invitation to Fedegan's president Jose Felix Lafaurie to participate as part of the government delegation engaged in the peace negotiation with the ELN. This is another example of an instance in which Petro has extended an olive branch to the extreme Right hoping to mitigate their extremism and their use of violence to protect their class interests and privileges. The following section zeroes in on the peasant economy and land restitution.

Prospects of the Peasant Economy

The Petro government's appointment of Giovanni Yule, a Nasa Indigenous and leader of CRIC, one the most prominent Indigenous organizations, as director in charge of Land Restitution signals that the process of restoring usurped lands to their rightful owners might be finally be put on the right and fast track after much delay. Law 1448 of 2011, which was designed to restitute millions of hectares to their original owners or occupiers, has been a problematic regulation marred by bureaucratic, legal, and logistical difficulties alongside the violent resistance of the land looters. The advent of the Petro government might present the best chance since it was approved for Law 1448's implementation, which could benefit millions of peasants. During the past eleven years (2011–2022), only four hundred thousand hectares of land have been restituted, benefiting only seventy-three thousand persons.[10]

Petro's government is seeking to address this urgent issue within the larger goal of implementing the "Integral Rural Reform Plan" accorded with the FARC in 2016. This drive has alerted the so-called third parties who acquired many of the contested lands. This group includes many individuals representing business enterprises, agribusinesses, multinational corporations, cattle ranchers, and the narcobourgeoisie, all of whom have reason to fear that their land title claims will be challenged or disputed in courts. If the restitution of land is carried out, it could boost the peasant economy by increasing food production and igniting a process of re-peasantization. Even if the restitution of land is only partially successful, this might open up new opportunities for the peasants' subsistence economy and rural life and decelerate environmental degradation.

Shifting from Oil and Coal toward a More Sustainable "De-Growth" Model

The second most important item on the Petro government's agenda as it relates to the scope of this book is to revisit Colombia's model of growth—without development—which is highly dependent on the export of raw materials.[11] Climate change and global warming are creating an urgency to phase out fossil fuel dependency and replace it with alternative, cleaner energy sources. However, decreasing the country's economic dependency on oil is a ten-years-long process. According to Ocampo, the current government will initiate a plan to replace oil with green hydrogen fuel, but its completion will rest on the shoulders of the following governments.[12] Ocampo has pointed out the crucial role that Ecopetrol, the state oil company, will play in this transformation process. It is crucial to remember that Colombia's distorted economic model was reinforced in the 1990s by the neoliberal Apertura, accelerating its de-industrialization and de-agriculturalization and replacing them with a rentier-based economy that rested on the export of oil, coal, gold, and cocaine, alongside an exponential service-sector growth (see chapter 1). Henceforth, the shift away from oil and coal will provide a corrective measure that addresses an immediate global environmental imperative that, although it does not go far enough to phase out rentierism, might be a step toward a "de-growth mode" that reduces the country's dependency on the extraction of fossil fuels and other pollutants. Irene Velez, minister of mines in Colombia, along with President Petro has suggested their aspiration for a "de-growth model" that protects the environment while helping mitigate global warming. In this context, it is imperative to explain what "de-growth" theory is and how it relates to this book.

Some variants of "de-growth" theories argue that the capitalist growth model centered on GDP is deficient because it overlooks in its calculations the human environmental costs, and disregards how the dividends of growth are distributed among social classes, groups, and regions. Mostly, "de-growth" theories recommend moving away from resource consumption in order to save the planet.[13] This book's main argument and findings intersect with the "de-growth" literature in two important aspects. One is its focus on how the capitalist model (liberal and neoliberal) created land scarcity by fostering its concentration in a few hands, a process that was mediated by war rentierism in the case explored. Consequently, this book concurs with de-growth theory's proposal for expanding communal public spaces and peoples' autonomy. Cases in point are the peasant reserves, *resguardos*, and community councils, whose establishment necessitates land redistribution and environmental protections that set limits on the encroachments of capital.[14]

The second aspect in which this research is in agreement with "de-growth" is the classical economic definition of growth, which is based on and driven by capital accumulation. In the Global South, this process is especially complex and brutal because in many spaces it depends on the subsumption of the noncapitalist mode, as Marx and Luxemburg argued. This book demonstrates that exploitation and subsumption are embedded in the existing model of economic growth and cannot be undone within the contours of capital accumulation.[15] An alternative model is required, one that is not led by capital.

Conclusion

Suppose my readings of Petro's government are correct. In that case, the goal is just to adjust the rentier model, which since the late 1980s has accelerated the decline in the productive (manufacturing and agriculture) sectors while at the same time causing environmental degradation, deforestation, water contamination, informalization, and income disparities.[16] Jhenifer Mojica Flórez, appointed to help articulate the agrarian plan, says that they are seeking reforms that are not similar to those proposed in the 1960s but are built upon the 2016 accord between FARC and the state. However, the new proposals do include various points of the accord, including the "Land fund" consisting of ten million hectares to be distributed to landless peasants, along with both protection of the Peasant Reserve Zones themselves and the creation of areas of "agro-food production" for peasants who decide not to join them.[17] Equally important is that the Petro government has announced its commitment to legally recognize the peasantry as a political/social subject. Such a move is crucial for multiple reasons, including obtaining state legal protection, land access, subsidies, technical assistance, credit, and investments (see Introduction).[18] Consequently, the peasants of Colombia under the Petro government might have a better chance to resist capital subsumption. In this same vein, Petro's team is reorienting the protection of the environment policy by establishing a partnership with the peasant communities so that they can lead the process. This is an expansion of what the Peasant Reserve Zones are currently doing as stipulated by law 160 of 1994:[19] protecting the environment by limiting encroachment into protected reserve areas (see chapter 3).

Does a pertinent question pose itself, namely, would revisiting Colombia's economic path be possible under the current global capitalist system? Knowing the odds and the difficulties presented by the task of changing the economic model, I still think Petro's incoming government can set the stage for a critical shift helped by the deepening crisis of globalization, a new phase that some have termed *de*-globalization, reflecting a view that is gaining credibility in light of the intensified trade wars between China and the United States, the rise of extreme nationalist/protectionist regimes, and the war in Ukraine. These events are expressions of malaise with a global system dominated by U.S. finance monopolies while other powers are elbowing for space and a more significant cut of the economic surplus.

Under such conditions, a minor player such as Colombia might have a better chance to renegotiate the terms of its economic dependency (for example, its trade agreements with the United States, Canada, and the EU), offering more protection to its agrarian and manufacturing sectors similar to the ones enjoyed by producers in the United States, Europe, and Japan.

Suppose that Petro's government succeeds in protecting the agricultural sector to secure the country's food sovereignty, which would put Colombia on a path less dependent on the metropolis for its food security. In this scenario, the peasants of Colombia would undoubtedly have a better chance to resist the power of capital subsumption, while the conglomerates' class interests would not be undermined. It will be a balancing act, in which a leftist government attempts to introduce change under a complex global context while protecting the class interests of the majority without threatening the bourgeoisie.

Appendix

The Scope of the Research Interviews

This book draws on a host of data, official statistics, and historical records published by state organizations, the World Bank, and UN organizations, among others. However, its unique contribution is the rich data obtained from 170 unstructured interviews and participant observations that I conducted between 2015 and 2022. The interviewees were primarily representatives of peasants' organizations such as ANUC, ACVC in Cimitarra, and Pato-Balsillas peasants' reserve, local government officials, human rights activists, local politicians, businesspeople, and church officials from various departments, including Meta, Middle Magdalena, North Santander, Antioquia, Caqueta, and Cauca. Ten representatives of the Indigenous *resguardos* in Meta and Cauca were interviewed, including five women leaders. The earlier set of interviews took place on location. However, due to COVID, many interviews were conducted by phone. I ran the interviews in Spanish and did my own translation into English. Most of the interviewees were generous with their time and allowed follow up interviews over the period of the research to check on emerging issues or respond to additional research questions.

The main objectives of the interviews were to capture the peasants' articulation of the problems they face, most notably about surrounding agribusinesses and companies, and to explore the strategies they have devised and their level of agency in addressing these problems. The interviews also examined the internal dynamics of the peasants' administrative and leadership functions, gender relations, and linkages with peasant groups nationally and internationally. The information gathered was crucial to understanding the salient problems confronting the noncapitalist social mode of production in a hostile, rentier environment.

My research assistant and I had the chance to attend a meeting organized by the CRIC women's division in which more than fifteen indigenous women leaders participated. The meeting was held in Popayan, Cauca's capital city, and lasted three hours. The participants voiced the main issues confronting them within their *resguardos*, ranging from the encroachments of capital to sexual violence, gender discrimination, drug abuse, discrimination against LGBT individuals, obstacles to reaching decision-making positions, to naked machismo. This meeting provided insights into the *resguardos'* inner social dynamics affecting the Indigenous groups, which were not atypical of what other women face in different social spaces. Alongside other interviews with women leaders in Meta and Cimitarra, the meeting shed light on the "struggle within the struggle" of the subaltern gender and the processes of empowerment while resisting capital. Attention was paid to women's voices and their pivotal role in developing agroecology as a mode of resistance and adaptation to capitalist subsumption.

Another vital area that this research addressed was the ethnic division in the peasant subsistence class, which is weakening their class solidarity. Five peasants' representatives from ANUC in Cauca were interviewed. They shed light on the growing ethnopolitical tensions within the peasant class affecting their class cohesion. The same exercise was repeated with CRIC and the leaders from the Association of Cabildos of North Cauca (ACIN). In Santander de Quilichao, Cauca, I participated in a meeting organized by UNDP with more than fifteen indigenous male leaders from ACIN, with only one woman leader present. The participants discussed the rising ethnic tensions between natives, Afro-Colombians, and mestizos. I interviewed most of the participants at the end of the meeting. The peasant groups shared data which filled in some of the missing gaps in this research.

In addition to the representatives of peasant communities, I interviewed several experts and academics working on the agrarian question. Their observations enriched and deepened the presented analysis. A dozen interviews were recorded, with the consent of the interviewees. Except for those that preferred that their names be withheld for obvious security reasons, the identities of most of the interviewees have been revealed.

Notes

Introduction

1. FAO, 2014. *The State of Food and Agriculture 2014: Innovation in Family Farming Food and Agriculture Organization of the United Nations*; see also Hanna Ritchie, Smallholders Produce One-third of the World's Food, Less than Half of What Many Headlines Claim. https://ourworldindata.org/smallholder-food-production; accessed August 6, 2021.

2. Lauren Frayer, "Why Indian Farmers Are so Angry," NPR, March 3, 2021. https://www.npr.org/sections/goatsandsoda/2021/03/02/971293844/indias-farmer-protests-why-are-they-so-angry.

3. After a year of peasants' protests the Modi government in India repealed its neoliberal laws that they wanted to apply in the rural areas to facilitate the expansion of agrobusiness. See Emily Schmall, Karan Deep Singh, and Sameer Yasir, "A Weakened Modi Bows to Protesting Farmers, Stunning India" *New York Times*, November 20, 2021. It is noteworthy that 60 percent of those that work in the agricultural sector depend on subsistence farming.

4. https://www.un.org/development/desa/en/news/population/2018-revision-of-world-urbanization-prospects.html; https://www.macrotrends.net/countries/COL/colombia/rural-populations; According to UNDP, using a different method of measurement than the one used by Agency of National Statistics (DANE), 75.5 percent of the country's municipalities are rural and in them live 31.6 percent of Colombia's population (not 25 percent, according to the DANE Census of 2005), and those represent 94.4 percent of the national territory. See "La Hora de La Colombia Rural," *Hechos de Paz*, no. 63 (Bogota: PNUD, 2011), 5. https://reliefweb.int/sites/reliefweb.int/files/resources/Full_Report_3049.pdf.

5. https://www.semillas.org.co/es/economa-campesina-y-ciudad; and the Department of National Statistics, known in Spanish by the acronym DANE, in its Agriculture Census of 2016 reported that 7.1 million hectares are used for food production, a figure that exceeded by 2.1 million hectares what was assumed before the 2016 census, and which is still low if compared to the more

than 34.4 million hectares used for cattle ranching, most of which is not suitable for that activity (see chapter 2). See Carolina Moncayo, "Dane Presenta las Cifras Reales del Campo Colombiano," *INCP*, December 2, 2016. https://incp.org.co/dane-presenta-las-cifras-reales-del-campo-colombiano/.

6. USAID Country Profile: *Property Rights and Resource Governance Colombia 2017*. https://www.land-links.org/wp-content/uploads/2016/09/USAID_Land_Tenure_Colombia_Profile-1.pdf; the estimate of peasant reserves is my own.

7. Flavio Bladimir Rodriguez Munoz, "La Huella Geografica: Espacio Vital Arraigo o control territoria para acumulacion," unpublished paper, Bogota, 2013.

8. Jan Douwe van der Ploeg, *The New Peasantries: Rural Development in Times of Globalization*, 2nd ed. (New York: Routledge, 2018); D. Bryceson, C. Kay, and J. Mooij, *Disappearing Peasants? Rural Labour in Africa, Asia and Latin America* (London: Intermediate Technology, 2000); James Scott, *The Moral Economy of the Peasants* (New Haven: Yale University Press, 1976); James Scott, *Weapons of the Weak: Every Day Forms of Peasant Resistance* (New Haven: Yale University Press, 1985); James Scott, *Seeing like a State: How Certain Schemes to Improve the Human Condition Have Failed* (New Haven: Yale University Press, 2020); T. Shanin, *Defining Peasants, Essays Concerning Rural Societies, Exploratory Economies, and Learning From Them in the Contemporary World* (Oxford: Basil Blackwell, 1990); H. Bernstein and T. J. Byres, "From Peasant Studies to Agrarian Change," *Journal of Agrarian Change* 1, no. 1: 1–56; Eric Wolf, *Peasants* (New Jersey: Prentice-Hall, 1966); Eric Wolf, *Peasant Wars of Twentieth* (New York: Harper and Row, 1969); Samuel L. Popkin, *The Rational Peasant: The Political Economy of Rural Society in Vietnam* (Berkeley: University of California Press, 1979); Evelyne Huber and Frank Safford, eds., *Agrarian Structure and Political Power* (Pittsburgh: University of Pittsburgh Press, 1995); Rodolfo Stavenhagen, ed., *Agrarian Problems and Peasant Movements in Latin America* (New York: Anchor Books, 1970); Michael Taussig, *The Devil and Commodity Fetishism in South America* (Chapel Hill: University of North Carolina Press, 2010); Marc Adelman, "Bringing the Moral Economy Back in . . . to the Study of 21st Century Transnational Peasant Movement." *American Anthropologist* 103 no. 3 (September 2005): 331–45.

9. Teodor Shanin, ed., *Peasants and Peasant Societies: Selected Readings*. 2nd ed. (Oxford and New York: Blackwell, 1987).

10. http://socialscienc.blogspot.com/2015/02/theory-of-peasant-society-by-teodor.html.

11. James C. Scott, *The Moral Economy of the Peasant: Rebellion and Subsistence in South East Asia*. (New Haven: Yale University Press, 1976).

12. Claude Meillassoux, "From Reproduction to Production: A Marxist Approach to Economic Anthropology," *Economy and Society* 1 (1972): 93–105.

13. For a good summary of Scott-Popkin debate see Elizabeth D. Mauritz, "Moral Economy: Claims For the Common Good," unpublished dissertation, 2014: see also Marc Adelman, "Bringing the Moral Economy Back in . . ."

14. Marc Adelman, "Bringing the Moral Economy Back in . . ."

15. See Nazih Richani, *Systems of Violence: The Political Economy of War and Peace in Colombia*, 2nd ed. (Albany: State University of New York Press, 2014).

16. Richani, *Systems of Violence*, ch. 1 and 2; see also Catherine LeGrand, *Frontier Expansion and Peasant Protest in Colombia, 1850–1936* (New Mexico: University of New Mexico Press, 1986); R. Albert Berry, "Reflections on Injustice, Inequality, and Land Conflict in Colombia," *Canadian Journal of Latin American and Caribbean Studies / Revue canadienne des études latino-américaines et caraïbes* 42, no. 3 (2017): 277–97.

17. Scott, *The Moral Economy of the Peasant*, 58.

18. Henry Bernstein, *Concepts for the Analysis of Contemporary Peasantries*, https://www.sunypress.edu/pdf/50761.pdf.

19. Henry Bernstein, "Farewells to the Peasantry," *Transformation Critical Perspectives on Southern Africa* 52, no. 1 (January 2003): 1–19.

20. Henry Bernstein, *Agrarian Political Economy and Modern World Capitalism: The Contributions of Food Regime Analysis*. Colloquium Paper 55, February 4–5, 2016: 27.

21. Abhijit Banerjee and Esther Duflo, *Good Economics for Hard Times* (New York: Public Affairs, 2019), 104.

22. Hernando Desoto, *The Mystery of Capital: Why Capitalism Triumphs in the West and Fails Everywhere Else* (New York: Basic Books, 2003); in the same vein of thought cherishing the importance of private property as an imperative for development see Daron Acemoglu and James Robinson, *Why Nations Fail: The Origins of Power, Prosperity, and Poverty* (New York: Random House, 2012).

23. Robert McNetting *Small Holders, House Holders, Farm Families, and The Ecology of Intensive Sustainable Agriculture* (Stanford: Stanford University Press, 1993).

24. Robert McNetting, *Unequal Commoners and Uncommon Equity: Property and Community among Small Holder Farmers*. Paper presented at "Heterogeneity and Collective Action," Workshop in Political Theory and Policy Analysis, Indiana University, Bloomington, October 14–17, 1993.

25. Taher Tahri, president of APJO Jemna, telephone interview with author, July 29, 2022; see also Mohammad Kerrou, *Jemna L'oassis de la Revolution* (Tunis: Ceres Edition, 2021). The Jemna community created an association in 2011to organize and distribute the generated surplus of production created by 162 permanent, who are supplemented by two hundred seasonal, workers. According to Tahri (2022), by increasing the proceeds generated from selling dates APJO built classrooms for a middle school, built a clinic, bought an ambulance, and funded other communal projects. The Jemna experience is another example of a successful communal land property, communal production, and distribution leading to improvement in the living conditions of a farming community. The Tunisian state is trying to reclaim the land to avoid the spread of the Jemna communal land appropriation example and the community is still resisting. The Jemna case

illustrates a noncapitalist mode of production interdependent with the capitalist market yet struggling for autonomy from the market and the encroachments of the state's legal system, which privileges private property.

26. Steven Ruthston, "Rebel Cities 18 Years after the Jasmine Revolution." October 1, 2019. https://occupy.com/article/rebel-cities-18-eight-years-after-jasmine-revolution-jemna-tunisia-s-oasis-hope#sthash.kqWq6VcU.dpbs.

27. W. W. Rostow. *The Stages of Economic Growth: A Non-Communist Manifesto.* (Cambridge: Cambridge University Press, 1960 http://www.uop.edu.pk/ocontents/Lecture%204%20a%20Unit%202%20Lesson%206%20Rostow.pdf.

28. Erik Wolf, *Peasants* (Englewood Cliffs, NJ: Prentice-Hall, 1966); Eric R. Wolf, "The Vicissitudes of the Closed Corporate Peasant Community," *American Ethnologist* 13: 325–29.

29. John Bellamy Foster, Brett Clark, and Hannah Holleman, "Marx and the Indigenous," *Monthly Review*, February 1, 2020. https://monthlyreview.org/2020/02/01/marx-and-the-indigenous/#en32backlink. Marx's writings in late 1850s reflected his studies of worldwide experiences, as demonstrated in his emphasis on the resilience of Indigenous cultures and communal property forms.

30. Rosa Luxemburg, *The Accumulation of Capital* (New York: Routledge, 2003), 397.

31. Luxemburg, *The Accumulation of Capital*, 397.

32. Luxemburg, *The Accumulation of Capital*, 397.

33. Luxemburg, *The Accumulation of Capital*, 426.

34. Luxemburg, *The Accumulation of Capital*, 434.

35. Harry Harootunian, *Marx after Marx: History and Time in the Expansion of Capitalism* (New York: Columbia University Press, 2017).

36. Harootunian, *Marx after Marx*, 72.

37. Jose Carlos Mariategui, *Seven Interpretative Essays on Peruvian Reality* (Austin: University of Texas Press, 1971). https://ufdcimages.uflib.ufl.edu/AA/00/02/38/02/00001/Field%20Practicum%20Report_Devereux.pdf.

38. Karl Kautsky, *The Agrarian Question*, quoted in http://www.anveshi.org.in/broadsheet-on-contemporary-politics/archives/broadsheet-on-contemporary-politics-vol-2-no-1011/the-agrarian-question/.

39. Deborah Bryceson, "Peasant Theories and Smallholder Policies. Past and Present," in *Disappearing Peasantries? Rural Labour in Africa, Asia, and Latin America*, ed. Deborah Bryceson, Cristóbal Kay, and Jos Mooij. London: Intermediate Technology Publications, 2000.

40. Deborah Bryceson, "Peasant Theories and Smallholder Policies. Past and Present."

41. Deborah Bryceson, "Peasant Theories and Smallholder Policies. Past and Present."

42. Deborah Bryceson, "Peasant Theories and Smallholder Policies. Past and Present."

43. Roger Bartra, *Estructura Agraria y Clases Sociales en Mexico* (Mexico City: Instituto de Investigaciones Sociales de la UNAM); "Peasants and Political Power in Mexico: A Theoretical Model," *Latin American Perspectives* II (Summer 1975): 125–45.

44. M. Taussig, "Peasant Economics and the Development of Capitalist Agriculture in the Cauca Valley, Colombia," *Latin American Perspective* 5, no. 3 (Summer 1978): 62–91.

45. M. Taussig, "Peasant Economics and the Development of Capitalist Agriculture in the Cauca Valley, Colombia."

46. In 1905 the Grand Cauca was divided into several departments which included what is today Cauca and Cauca Valley, Choco, Putumayo, Nariño, Caqueta, Guaviare, and Guainía. This division changed the socioeconomic configuration and the power structures among the created political entities. The Popayan dominant elite lost significant power resulting from this change.

47. M. Taussig, "Peasant Economics and the Development of Capitalist Agriculture in the Cauca Valley, Colombia."

48. Harry E. Vanden and Marc Becker, eds. and trans. *Jose Carlos Mariategui: An Anthology* (New York: Monthly Review Press, 2011), 100–101.

49. Harry E. Vanden and Marc Becker, eds. and trans. *Jose Carlos Mariategui: An Anthology.*

50. Harry E. Vanden and Marc Becker, eds. and trans. *Jose Carlos Mariategui: An Anthology*, 102.

51. Maria Halamska, *A Vanishing Class.*

52. Maria Halamska, *A Vanishing Class.*

53. Maria Halmaska, "A Different End of Peasants?" *Polish Sociological Review*, 3: 2004): 245–68.

54. Maria Halmaska, "A Different End of Peasants?"

55. Maria Halamska, *A Vanishing Class.*

56. Maria Halamska, *A Vanishing Class.*

57. Maria Halamska, *A Vanishing Class.*

58. See M. Taussig, "Peasant Economics and the Development of Capitalist Agriculture in the Cauca Valley, Colombia," 68. Taussig described that one consequence of the One Thousand Days War was that the state became more centralized and landowners in regions such as south Cauca took the initiative in dispossessing the peasants by using bandit groups to take over the land. Bandits of the nineteenth and early twentieth centuries were the precursors of the *sicarrios* and paramilitaries that emerged during La Violencia (1948–58) and in the 1970s respectively.

59. Frank Safford and Marco Palacios, in *Colombia: Fragmented Land, Divided Society* (New York: Oxford University Press, 2002), introduced "the period of Mafia Violence 1954–1964." Pp. 351–54. They argued that it was notable in greater Caldas, Quindio, and northeastern Tolima. The main cause of the violence in those regions was attributed to colonization and land disputes.

60. See Frank Safford and Marco Palacios, *Colombia: Fragmented Land, Divided Society*, ch. 13.

61. David Ricardo, *On the Principles of Political Economy and Taxation*, ch. 2. https://www.marxist.org/references/subject/economics/ricardo/tax/ch02.htm.

62. Accessed from http://www.cooperativeindividualism.org/hudson-michael_ the-rentier-economy.html; https://michael-hudson.com/2021/01/the-rentier-resurgence-and-takeover-finance-capitalism-vs-industrial-capitalism/; Michael Hudson, "The Rentier Resurgence and Takeover: Finance Capitalism vs. Industrial Capitalism," January 27, 2021. https://michael-hudson.com/2021/01/ the-rentier-resurgence-and-takeover-finance-capitalism-vs-industrial-capitalism/.

63. *Basta Ya*. (Bogota: Centro de Memoria Historica, 2012), ch. 1.

64. In this research I use the term *noncapitalist* to denote that those modes of production are not necessarily inherited from the past "precapitalist" or constitute a form of "primitive accumulation" that assumes some historical determinism, but are modes of production and social relations created under capitalism such as the peasant reserves in Colombia and similar cases in Global South that were discussed by Jan Douwe der Ploeg (2018).

65. Vladimir Meztiso, Natalia Escobar, Soraya Garzon, "La Categoria Camepsino y sus Representaciones en Colombia: Polisemia Historica and Regional Polysemy," *Revista Colombiana de Antropología* 58, no. 1 (April 2022): 9–24. http:// www.scielo.org.co/pdf/rcan/v58n1/2539-472X-rcan-58-01-9.pdf.

66. In 1993, a group of peasant organizations from different countries met in Belgium to protest GATT (General Agreement on Tariffs and Trade) policies (GATT was replaced by the World Trade Organization [WTO]) affecting rural economies. They established Via Campesina, which in few years included eighty organizations in fifty countries. Via Campesina became a pivotal global actor promoting, organizing, and coordinating peasants' demands. Colombia's peasant groups are well versed in the importance of this organization and of increasing their links and enhancing learning experiences to resist subsumption. See Marc Edelman, "Bringing the Moral Economy back in . . . to the Study of the 21st Century Transnational Peasant Movements." *Savage capitalism* denotes the free rein of capital without constrains violating human rights and environmental rights.

67. During the 1980s, the state's security agencies and its paramilitaries conducted a systematic campaign of assassination targeting peasant leaders and leftist figures of the National Front (Union Patriotica, UP) in the rural areas and cities, which debilitated the peasant organizational abilities. Consequently, when the Constituent Assembly was elected in 1990 to draft a new constitution, the peasant representation was weak while the large landowners and their allies remained a formidable force within the major political parties. See https://www.dejusticia. org/wp-content/uploads/2022/03/Informe-ejecutivo-Guerra-contra-el-campesina-do-23-de-marzo-2022.pdf, 13–14.

68. https://www.dejusticia.org/wp-content/uploads/2022/03/Informe-ejecutivo-Guerra-contra-el-campesinado-23-de-marzo-2022.pdf.

Chapter 1. The Emergence of the Neoliberal State

1. Currie served as an economic advisor to U.S. President Franklin Roosevelt between 1939 and Roosevelt's death in 1945. See Myron J. Frankman, "Employment Policy for Colombia: Towards Full Employment and the Four Strategies," *Manpower and Unemployment Research* 10, no. 2 (1977): 33–44.

2. Eric Ross, *Modernization, Clearance, and the Continuum of Violence in Colombia*. Working paper 383, November 2003, 23. For historical context, it is worth mentioning that Colombia was the only Latin American country that participated in the Korean War. A contingent of more than 4,314 soldiers were deployed between 1951 and 1954 under UN-commanded units. This participation was an attempt by Laureano Gomez Hurtado, the right-wing president who had demonstrated fascist, anti-U.S. tendencies during World War II, to mend his fences with the United States. Charles Briscoe, *Across the Pacific to War: The Colombian Navy in Korea, 1951–1955*. https://arsof-history.org/articles/v2n4_across_pacific_page_1.html.

3. Roger Sandilands, *La Misión Del Banco Mundial a Colombia De 1949, Y Las Visiones Opuestas De Lauchlin Currie Y Albert Hirschman* (*The 1949 World Bank Mission to Colombia, and the Competing Visions of Lauchlin Currie [1902–1993]) and Albert Hirschman [1915–2012]*) (2015), *Revista de Economía Institucional* 17, no. 32 (primer semestre de 2015). Available at SSRN: https://ssrn.com/abstract=2625815.

4. See *La Hora de La Colombia Rural, Hechos de Paz*, no. 63 (Bogota: PNUD, 2011), 5. https://reliefweb.int/sites/reliefweb.int/files/resources/Full_Report_3049.pdf.

5. Colombia's surface area is 133 million hectares. Source: https://sema-narural.com/web/articulo/debate-de-acceso-a-la-tierra-en-colombia-en-la-cumbre-colombia-rural/1210.

6. Nazih Richani, *Systems of Violence*, ch. 2; Catherine LeGrand, *Frontier Expansion and Peasant Protest in Colombia, 1850–1936* (New Mexico: University of New Mexico Press, 1986); C. LeGrand, "Colonization and Violence in Colombia: Perspectives and Debates," *Canadian Journal of Latin American and Caribbean Studies* 14, no. 28 (1989): 5–29.

7. Albert Berry, *Avance y Fracaso en el Agro Colombiano, Siglos XX y XXI* (Bogota: Universidad del Rosario, 2017), chapters 1, 2 and 3.

8. Francisco Leal Buitrago, *Una Vision de la Seguridad en Colombia* and Interview with author September 2020.

9. Reyes Alejandro, Liliana Duica y Wílber Pedraza. "El despojo de tierras por paramilitares en Colombia," 2010. https://www.ideaspaz.org/tools/download/52149; accessed October 23, 2021; see also Francisco Thoumi, ed., *Drogas ilícitas en Colombia* (Bogotá: Planeta, 1996); Gustavo Duncan, *Los Señores de la Guerra* (Bogotá: Planeta, 2007); Jean Paul Faguet, Fabio Sanchez, and Maria Juanino Villaveceses *The Perversion of Land Reform by Landed Elites*. November 2018. Unpublished paper. https://governancefrombelow.net/wp-content/uploads/2019/10/Perversion-of-Land-Reform-by-Landed-Elites_v7.pdf, Mauricio Romero, *Paramilitares y Autodefensas 1982–2003* (Bogotá: IEPRI-Planeta, 2003).

10. Jean Paul Faguet, Fabio Sanchez, and Maria Juanino Villaveceses, *The Perversion of Land Reform by Landed Elites*. This paper argues that since 1901 Colombia has granted twenty-three million hectares, which is equivalent to the total land mass of the UK and twice the size of Greece, yet Colombia still has the highest concentration of land ownership. Most of the lands that were distributed were public lands or colonized by landless peasants. The *Latifundios* were not touched, as discussed above.

11. My view contradicts that of William Easterly, which overplayed the role of experts in shaping states' economic policies in the Global South at the expense of individual entrepreneurs and hence undermining free enterprising. Easterly used the expression "the tyranny of experts" and he gravely overlooked the tyranny of the dominant class, which controls the state and picks from the experts' menu what suits best its social class interest. This is evident in the Colombian case discussed in this book. See William Easterly, *The Tyranny of Experts: Economists, Dictators, and the Forgotten Rights of the Poor* (New York: Basic Books, 2014).

12. See Dario Fajardo, "Colombia: dos décadas en los movimientos agrarios," *Open Edition Journal*, 2012. https://journals.openedition.org/cal/2690; Dario Fajardo, *Aproximación a la Cuestión Agraria: Elementos para una Reforma Institucional. Informes FIB 6* (Bogotá: Ideas para La Paz, 2008). Dario Fajardo, *Las Zonas de Reserva Campesina Retos y Experiencias en su Implementacion. FAO and the National Land Agency.* (Bogotá: FAO, 2019).

13. Lukas Rehm. http://www.scielo.org.co/pdf/hiso/n27/n27a02.pdf.

14. Oquist, Paul. *Violencia, conflicto y política en Colombia* (Bogotá: Instituto de Estudios Colombianos (IEC), Banco Popular, 1978: Richani, *Systems of Violence*.

15. Nubia Yaneth Ruiz, "El Desplazamiento Forzado en el Interior de Colombia: Características Sociodemográficas y Pautas de Distribución Territorial 2000–2004." Unpublished dissertation, Universidad Autónoma de Barcelona, 2007, 18.

16. Cuaderno del Informe de Desarrollo Humano Colombia 2011 El campesinado Reconocimiento para construir país (Bogotá: PNUD, 2011), 31.

17. Law 135 of 1961, which founded the Institute of Agrarian Land Reform (INCORA), was adopted by the first National Front Liberal government led by

Alberto Lleras Camargo (1958–1962). He was influenced by Kennedy's Alliance for Progress,

18. Berry 2017, 63. One of the shortcomings of INCORA that had far reaching effects was that instead of reducing the concentration of landholdings, it accentuated that concentration, as noted by Catherine Legrand. She stated that although INCORA had a fifty hectares limit per property none of its executed projects were constrained by this limitation. This led to more concentration of landholdings by large landowners, especially cattle ranchers that ended up acquiring 60 percent of the 3.3 million hectares that INCORA identified during its existence before the late 1980s. See Catherine Legrand, "Colonization and Violence in Colombia," *Canadian Journal of Latin American & Caribbean Studies* 14, no. 28 (1989): 27. The next chapter discusses cattle ranching as one of the main outcomes of rentier capitalism.

19. See chapter 2; Nazih Richani, *Systems of Violence*, ch. 4; Catherine Legrand, *Colonization and Violence*.

20. Richani, *Systems of Violence*, ch. 2.

21. The World Bank, in concert with the United States, changed its policy on the issue of redistribution of land as an essential tool to promote equity and development in the Global South, especially in Latin America. Klaus Deininger and Hans Binswanger (1999) pointed out that after 1975 World Bank land reform policy recommended that communal tenure systems be abandoned in favor of freehold titles and the subdivision of the commons. "Today it is recognized that some communal tenure arrangements can increase tenure security and provide a (limited) basis for land transactions in ways that are more cost-effective than freehold titles." Nonetheless, the World Bank's policy remained committed to "the individualization of property rights" and the idea that secure individual property rights would not only increase the beneficiaries' incentives and provide collateral for further investment but, if all markets were competitive, would automatically lead to socially and economically desirable land market., a position that intersects with Lauchlin Currie's posture. See Klaus Deininger and Hans Binswanger, "The Evolution of the World Bank's Land Policy: Principle, Experience, and Future Challenges," *The World Bank Research Observer* 14, no. 2 (August 1999): 247–76.

22. William Easterly, *The Tyranny of Experts: Economists, Dictators, and the Forgotten Rights of the Poor* (New York: Basic Books, 2014). The Colombian case raises doubts about Easterly's thesis on the role of experts in strengthening the state at the expense of individuals. What Colombian experts in Colombia did, starting with Currie, was to devise policies supporting the financial sector, the speculative sector, and, unwittingly, the large-landowning elite at the expense of the poor peasantry.

23. Salomon Kalmanovitz, *Nueva Histroria Economica de Colombia* (Bogotá: Taurus, 2019).

24. Rafael Pardo Rueda, *La Reforma Agraria de Carlos Lleras.* https://www.eltiempo.com/archivo/documento/CMS-4087851.

25. Laureano Gomez Hurtado was influenced by European fascist ideologies that embraced Catholicism alongside centralized executive power, with a liberal economic base supported by the most reactionary sector of the dominant class, the *latifundios.* See Miguel Pinzon and Diego Motta, *Laureano Gomes, La Mision Currie, y el Proyecto de Reforma Constitucional* (1952). https://core.ac.uk/download/pdf/52201930.pdf.

26. See Miguel Pinzon and Diego Motta, Laureano Gomes, *La Mision Currie y el Proyecto de Reforma Constitucional 1952.* https://core.ac.uk/download/pdf/52201930.pdf.

27. Dialnet-LauchlinCurrieYElDesarrolloColombiano-3696808.pdf; For a more detailed discussion on Currie's economic doctrine see Sandilands, *La Misión Del Banco Mundial a Colombia De 1949.*

28. Roger Sandilands, *An Archival Case Study: Revisiting the Life and Political Economy of Lauchlin.* 2009. https://www.researchgate.net/publication/23954778_An_Archival_Case_Study_Revisiting_The_Life_and_Political_Economy_of_Lauchlin_Currie.

29. Sandilands, *An Archival Case Study,* 27. It is telling that after his appointment at the DNP, he spent twelve years at the Colombian Institute of Savings and Housing until his death in 1993.

30. The World Bank's largesse marked an important point in Colombia, which reflected the political interests of the bank as well as the United States in boosting their influence in Colombia. The bank loaned Colombia between 1950 and 1963 more than $300 million, more per capita than any other borrowers. The U.S. goal was, according to a Senate study, to make "Colombia an anchor point in an unsettled Caribbean" and a showcase for capitalist development in Latin America. As reported by Eric Ross, "Modernization, Clearance and the Continuum of Violence in Colombia." Working paper 383 (November 2003), 23. https://core.ac.uk/download/pdf/18512667.pdf.

31. Eric Ross, "Modernization, Clearance, and the Continuum of Violence in Colombia."

32. http://palabrasalmargen.com/edicion-18/la-tragedia-y-, hela-farsa-del-pacto-de-chicoral-al-pacto-de-compensar/.

33. http://www.adr.gov.co/normograma/DocumentosJuridica/Ley%204%20de%201973.pdf.

34. Albert Berry, https://www.peri.umass.edu/fileadmin/pdf/conference_papers/Berry-AGREF_1_.10.pdf.

35. Rafael Pardo, "Carlos Lleras y la Reforma Agraria," *El Tiempo,* April 2008.

36. Extension of dominion referred to the lands/properties confiscated by the state that were possessed by illegal money/and or means. This figure was used to confiscate the properties of narcotraffickers.

37. Pardo, Carlos Lleras.

38. http://www.fao.org/americas/noticias/ver/en/c/878998/.

39. http://eprints.lse.ac.uk/67193/1/Faguet_Paradox%20opf%20land%20 reform_2016.pdf.

40. http://eprints.lse.ac.uk/67193/1/Faguet_Paradox%20opf%20land%20 reform_2016.pdf.

41. The core group behind the neoliberal economic policies was the National Council of the Economic and Social Policy, known in Spanish by the acronym Conpes, administered by its board. Then the Superior of the Fiscal Policy (Confis), it formed part of the ministry of finance alongside the senior fiscal policymaker and coordinator of the public credit and the board of directors of the central bank. Within them the neoliberal technocrats direct the state's economic policy, accompanied by advisors, academics, and research centers. In Gramsci's theory, those are the organic intellectuals of the dominant class. See Antonio Gramsci, *Prison Notebooks* (New York: Columbia University Press, 2011).

42. Roger Sandilands, *La Mision del Banco Mundial a Colombia de 1949*, 229.

43. Abhijit Banerjee and Stether Duflo, *Good Economics for Hard Times* (New York: Hachette Book Group, 2019), 58–60. Banerjee and Dufflo write that between 1985 and 2000 Colombia, alongside Mexico, Brazil, India, Argentina, and Chile, opened themselves to trade by unilaterally cutting their tariffs across the board, which led to an increase in inequality, and conclude that the timing of these "increases connect them to the episodes of trade liberalization," 59; see also Orazio Attanasio, Pinelopi K. Goldberg, and Nina Pavcnik, "Trade Reforms and Wage Inequality in Colombia," Working Paper 9830. http://www.nber.org/papers/ w9830. Within this context of market economics, two land laws were introduced: Law 35 of 1982 and Law 30 of 1988. The first propelled the purchase of land through Incora, which allowed large landowners to sell unproductive lands above their market value. It was estimated that Incora's purchases of land increased from 4,400 hectares, recorded in 1981, to 25,111 in 1985, reaching 96,098 in 1992. Law 30 of 1988 was designed to introduce "land market" into the rural political economy largely as devised by Currie. Law 30 of 1988 was the precursor of Law 160 of 1994, which led to the creation of the peasant reserve discussed in chapter 3. See Dario Fajardo, *Aproximacion a La Question Agraria; Elementos Para una Reforma Institucional* (Bogotá: Ideas Para la Paz, 2008), 36.

44. Colmenares and Pardo (2015, 44).

45. https://www.cepal.org/ilpes/noticias/paginas/4/29744/alberto_barreix_ tax_systems_and_tax_reform_in_la07_cap1a5.pdf.

46. The Ford Foundation and the Brookings Institute were among those that supported Fedesarrollo's creation.

47. Jairo Estrada Alvarez, *Intellectuales, technocratas y Reformas Neoliberales en America Latina* (Bogotá: National University of Colombia, 2005), 269.

48. Fernando Cepeda, *Direccion Politica de la Reforma Economica en Colombia* (Bogotá: Tecer Mundo Editores, 1994), 206.

49. http://www.dinero.com/edicion-impresa/caratula/articulo/la-apertura-economica/182405.

50. http://www.dinero.com/edicion-impresa/caratula/articulo/la-apertura-economica/182405.

51. http://www.dinero.com/edicion-impresa/caratula/articulo/la-apertura-economica/182405. CONPES (Consejo Nacional de Political Economicas y Sociales) the National Council for Economic and Social Policy.

52. http://www.dinero.com/edicion-impresa/caratula/articulo/la-apertura-economica/182405.

53. Cepeda, *Direccion Politica*, 199–220.

54. Cepeda, *Direccion Politica*, 206.

55. Cepeda, *Direccion Politica*, 206.

56. Cepeda, *Direccion Politica*, 206.

57. The decrease in import taxes happened quickly following Gaviria's election. Import tariffs on commodities decreased from 31 percent to 12 percent between 1985 and 1992. Under Juan Manuel Santos (2008–2016) the tariff assessment was reduced to only 8 percent. See Ricardo Avila "La Aperura en Colombia Mito o Realidad." *El tiempo*, February 15, 2020. https://www.eltiempo.com/economia/sectores/la-apertura-en-colombia-mito-o-realidad-462678; Ocampo wrote that the tariff was reduced to 5percent. See Jose Antonio Ocampo, *Apertura Y Desarollo Exportador.* https://www.eltiempo.com/opinion/columnistas/jose-antonio-ocampo/apertura-y-desarrollo-exportador-columna-de-jose-antonio-ocampo-465166.

58. Ricardo Obregon, President of Bavaria in 2004, interview with author, Bogotá, August 2, 2004. He pointed out the economic slowdown exacerbated by the neoliberal economic measures. Bavaria, for example reduced its workforce by 35 percent, from 10,500 workers to 7,000. Obregon did not object to the "apertura" but he would have preferred a gradual opening. This position was close to the one sponsored then by Jose Antonio Ocampo.

59. Antonio Gramsci, *Prison Notebooks.*

60. John M. Cammett, *Antonio Gramsci and the Origins of Italian Communism* (Stanford: Stanford University Press, 1967), 204.

61. Cesar Gaviria, in Carlos Argaez, ed., *Presidencia de Virgilio Barco Treinta Anos Despues* (Bogotá: Uniandes, 2017), 35–38.

62. Fernando Cepeda, an influential political scientist and former rector at the Andes University, interview with author, Bogotá, August 1997. He introduced me to the term *Kinder* used to refer to Gaviria and his like-minded group of neoliberals.

63. Cesar Gaviria, in Carlos Argaez, ed., *Presidencia de Virgilio Barco Treinta Anos Despues.*

64. Andres Castro Araujo, "Los economistas colombianos y el problema de la 'desigualdad' Trabajo de grado Programa de Sociología Universidad del Rosario." Unpublished Memeo, 2015.

65. Londono was secretary of economic policy (CONPES) (1990–92), a key position in orienting the state's economic policy, which fed the *Kinder* of Gaviria. He occupied a leading role in the State Modernization Commission, which prepared the Development Plan 1991–94. Londono's last official position was in Alvaro Uribe's government (2002–10), in which he was minister of social protection (2002–03). He died in 2003 in a plane crash.

66. Juliana Londono Velez, "Income and Wealth at the Top in Colombia: An Exploration of Tax Records 1993–2010," Public Policy and Development Master's dissertation, Paris School of Economics. http://piketty.pse.ens.fr/files/LondonoVelez2012MasterThesis.pdf.

67. https://colombiareports.com/colombia-poverty-inequality-statistics/.

68. Gilberto Arango Londoño, "¿Quiénes dirigen la economía? Nunca como ahora ha mandado tanto la tecnocracia," *Síntesis Económica*, no. 860 (1993): 6–9).

69. Rafael Aubad, president of ProAntioquia, an agglomeration of the largest companies in Antioquia, interview with author, Medellin, August 16, 2017.

70. Rafael Aubad, interview.

71. The Colombian Agricultural Institute (Spanish acronym: ICA) directs state policy. Of its board members, only one reflects a dissenting view, that of ANUC. The remaining five members include a representative of the agrobusiness elite (SAC) and one from the cattle ranchers (Fedegan), a delegate from the president of the republic and department of national planning, and one from the ministry of agriculture. These five are the ones that determine the state's land policy. See https://www.funcionpublica.gov.co/documents/418537/2549482/Sector+Agricultura/ac19d694-ee1e-4db0-8e74-869ef6744f75; The defunct board of land agency (Incoder) consisted of nine members including one representative of peasants' organizations, one representative of the Indigenous, and one of the Afro-descendants. The remaining six included one from agribusiness and delegates representing the president and the ministries of agriculture, social protection, and the department of national planning, all of which represent the president's view. See https://sac.org.co/no-1300-de-2003-cracion-del-incoder/.

72. Adolfo Meisel Roca, *Quien Manda Aqui, Poder Regional y Participacion de La Costa Caribe en Los Gabinetes Ministeriales 1990–2000*, no. 31 (2012). https://www.banrep.gov.co/sites/default/files/publicaciones/archivos/chee_31.pdf, 13; The influence of the African palm business in the Incoder was noted by the Silla Vacia in 2020, see https://lasillavacia.com/baldios-empresas-duque-golpea-acuerdo-y-favorece-grandes-empresarios-78484.

73. By April 17, 2012, 139 members of Congress were under investigation. Five governors and thirty-two lawmakers, including Mario Uribe Escobar, for-

mer president Alvaro Uribe's cousin and the former president of Congress were convicted. *Colombia Reports*. May 16, 2012.

74. https://lasillavacia.com/baldios-empresas-duque-golpea-acuerdo-y-favorece-grandes-empresarios-78484.

75. https://lasillavacia.com/baldios-empresas-duque-golpea-acuerdo-y-favorece-grandes-empresarios-78484.

76. See Richani, *Systems of Violence*, ch. 4; see also F. Gutiérrez Sanín and J. Vargas, "Agrarian Elite Participation in Colombia's Civil War," *Journal of Agrarian Change*, 2017. Gutierrez presented a random sample of thirty municipalities, and the findings were that 63 percent of cattle ranchers participated in the 1980s in the creation of paramilitaries, 83 percent funded them, 44 percent participated in military operations, and 39 percent were in leadership positions.

77. Salomon Kalmanovitz, "De la Mineria a Donde," *El Espectador*, May 24, 2015. Kalmanovitz is a prominent economist and a former member of the central bank's board of directors.

78. https://data.worldbank.org/indicator/SL.AGR.EMPL.ZS.

79. https://santandertrade.com/en/portal/analyse-markets/colombia/economic-outline.

80. Kalmanovitz, "De la Mineria a Donde."

81. Brett Christophers defines "rent" specifically as "income derived from the ownership, possession or control of scarce assets financial, land, natural resource, and under conditions of limited or no competition." See Brett Christophers, *Rentier Capitalism: The Case of UK*. https://www.bennettinstitute.cam.ac.uk/blog/rentier-capitalism-uk-case.

82. Luis Jorge Garay. https://redjusticiaambientalcolombia.files.wordpress.com/2013/05/mineria-en-colombia-fundamentos-para-superar-el-modelo-extractivista2013.pdf.

83. Articles 64 and 65 of the 1991 Constitution.

84. https://redjusticiaambientalcolombia.files.wordpress.com/2013/05/mineria-en-colombia-fundamentos-para-superar-el-modelo-extractivista2013.pdf.

85. https://redjusticiaambientalcolombia.files.wordpress.com/2013/05/mineria-en-colombia-fundamentos-para-superar-el-modelo-extractivista2013.pdf.

86. https://redjusticiaambientalcolombia.files.wordpress.com/2013/05/mineria-en-colombia-fundamentos-para-superar-el-modelo-extractivista2013.pdf.

87. https://redjusticiaambientalcolombia.files.wordpress.com/2013/05/mineria-en-colombia-fundamentos-para-superar-el-modelo-extractivista2013.pdf.

88. https://redjusticiaambientalcolombia.files.wordpress.com/2013/05/mineria-en-colombia-fundamentos-para-superar-el-modelo-extractivista2013.pdf.

89. https://redjusticiaambientalcolombia.files.wordpress.com/2013/05/mineria-en-colombia-fundamentos-para-superar-el-modelo-extractivista2013.pdf.

90. Santiago Angel, head of the Colombian Mining Association, presenting his group's position and prospects, was quoted by Reuters as saying, "If we get

the investment conditions we want, as an association and as an industry, we could again bring in between $1.5 billion and $1.7 billion a year, for a five-year investment of $7.5 billion." He continued, "This is an industry that in its best years brought between $2.5 billion and $3 billion a year. Unfortunately 2015 and especially 2016 were very bad years for attracting investment—we fell to close to zero." Colombia's biggest mining sectors are in coal and gold. Angel said that copper is showing enormous potential and could become a viable new product in the coming years. The largest of MC's mining players are AngloGold and EcoOro. The biggest coal companies are Drummond Co, Glencore Plc, Murray Energy's, Colombia Natural Resources, and Cerrejon, which is jointly owned by BHP Billiton, Anglo American Plc, and Glencore. The MC's major demands are legal security and clear investment rules, which provide them with significant leverage to obtain concessions from the state, which overlooks this sector, and the MCs are pivotal to its neoliberal dogma.

91. Nazih Richani, *Systems of Violence.*

92. https://www.portafolio.co/economia/finanzas/colombia-tendria-tierra-cara-region-estudio-sac-340630.

93. For a hectare of sugar cane production, Colombia's costs are the highest in the world: 82 percent more than China's, 75 percent more than Brazil, 63 percent more than Guatemala, 42 percent more than Thailand; 28 percent more than Australia, and 6 percent more than South Africa. The president of Procaña, José Vicente Irurtia, announced that prices of land in el Valle del Cauca are the highest in the world (El País 2007). Quoted in https://www.farmlandgrab.org/post/view/19025-colombia-la-locomotora-del-agro-y-su-impacto-ambiental-y-socioeconomico-los-campesinos-tienen-un-proyecto, and according to a study by the Association of Agrarian Producers (SAC), https://www.portafolio.co/economia/finanzas/colombia-tendria-tierra-cara-region-estudio-sac-340630.

Chapter 2. Rentierism, Cattle Ranching, and Food Insecurity in Colombia

1. *Narcobourgeoisie* is a term introduced by Richani (2002) to distinguish this wealthy faction from the remaining bourgeoisie in terms of: (1) its social class origins; (2) sources of capital accumulation (narcotrafficking); (3) illegal status; (4) exploitation of labor both nationally (production cycle) and internationally (distribution and marketing). This is while, although the narcobourgeoisie share with their counterparts a commitment to the capitalist system, they are neoliberals par excellence (Thoumi 1998; Richani 2002).

2. David Ricardo defined economic rent as a margin of market price over cost value, unearned revenue that flows from land ownership, which also includes mining. For a wider use of the rentier concept than the one suggested

by Beblawi (1990) and Yates (1996), Lisa Anderson (1987), and Karl (1997), see Michael Hudson, who expands the concept to incorporate industrial economies such as the United States, where more wealth is created from financial speculation and rents than from production. Hudson defines Rentier income as economic rent and interest or other financial charges, arguing that this form of capitalism is polarizing the U.S. and other economies. He added, "The bulk of this rentier income is not being spent on expanding the means of production or raising living standards. It is plowed back into the purchase of property and financial securities already in place—legal rights and claims for payment extracted from the economy at large." Accessed from http://www.cooperativeindividualism.org/hudson-michael_the-rentier-economy.html.

3. Although Hartlyn mentioned FEDEGAN alongside SAC, I believe that is a factual error. FEDEGAN was founded in 1963.

4. I borrowed the term *reactionary configuration* from Barrington Moore, to denote the oppressive and conservative political character of class forces gathered in an alliance. In the Colombian case, the cattle ranchers were among the first to organize death squads to defend their lands against *colonos* and, later, leftist guerrillas. These death squads evolved into paramilitaries, as in Puerto Boyaca (for a detailed account see Medina 1990).

5. Small and subsistence peasants' abilities to survive and even reinforce their class position despite the onslaught of capitalist development in all its forms, including agribusiness and rentierism (resource extraction and speculation), also was observed in Mexico and Costa Rica (see Edelman 1999; Esteva 1983). This survival was attributed to adjusting and diversifying their sources of income alongside subsistence farming.

6. It is estimated that between 1988 and 1993 about 578,000 people migrated from the center-east of the country toward the coca-producing departments of Caquetá, Putumayo, Guaviare, Meta, and Vichada, where 319,000 hectares were still under cultivation by the end of 1993. In 1998, the illicit crops of coca, poppy seeds, and marijuana generated about sixty-nine thousand jobs, representing about 2 percent of the total jobs in the rural sector. See Ricardo Rocha García, *La Economía Colombiana tras 25 anos de Narcotráfico* (Bogotá: Siglo del Hombre Editores y UNDCP, 2000), 143 and 15. UNDOC (2009) estimated that about fifty-three thousand households, or about 236,000 individuals are involved in coca cultivation. This figure does not include the *raspachines* (collectors) and floating population. The estimated income of the fifty-three thousand households was 623 million before discounting production costs (UNDOC 2009, 55). This is about 0.3 of the GDP and 3 percent of the agricultural GDP (UNDOC 2009, 55). Thoumi (2003, 152) estimated that the cultivation of illegal crops might have employed as many as two hundred thousand people by 2001.

7. In 1988 the weekly magazine *Semana* conducted interviews with twenty narcotrafficker bosses from Medellin and discovered that four of them (20 percent) favored cattle ranching; nine (45 percent)real estate (urban and rural); three (15

percent) commerce; two (10 percent) services; and two (10percent) construction. Accessed http://www.semana.com/noticias-nacion/capos/24769.aspx. Most narcotraffickers opted to invest their laundered money in activities that foment rentier capitalism, particularly cattle ranching and real estate (rural and urban), both of which together account for 65 percent of their total investments.

8. UNDOC (2009, 17) reported that in 2008 the area under coca cultivation declined to eighty-one thousand hectares.

9. The land tax laws are not only low—1/1000 to 1.3/1000 of the land value—but 58 percent of land registries are not up to date and of the 1,006 municipalities that are current have "extremely undervalued properties." See Kalmonovitz and Lopez 2007, 157–58).

10. Ocampo (1994, 283), citing Kalmanovitz, reported the increase from16.3 million hectares between 1950 and 1954 to 22.2 million hectares by 1974. Both estimates, however, demonstrate the exponential increase in areas dedicated to pasture.

11. According to the DANE 2016 census, there are 21.5 million *Bovinos* (cattle). Decreasing by 1.5 million heads from the year 2005 occupying 34.4 million hectares averaging one cow/1.6 hectares, declining only 0.1 percent from its 2005 level average. This change does not alter the thrust of the analysis.

12. The most striking finding about the "inefficient" use of land—that is, if we assume for a moment that it is the immediate productive returns of cattle ranching that are driving current investment—is that Colombia averages one cow per 1.7hectares, while in Brazil the figure is nine cows/hectare, New Zealand three per hectare, and the United States between from 1.2 cows/hectare to 2.4 cows/hectare. In other words Colombia might have one of the highest misallocations of a main factor of capital: land. This seemingly "irrational investment" behavior was not motivated only by the immediate returns of cattle ranching. But the expected future gains of increasing land prices alongside the state's policies and laws that favored large cattle ranchers permitted the use of land properties as a hedge against inflation, offered exemption from capital gains, and have been compounded since the 1990s by the use of land as a money-laundering mechanism. www.agric.wa.gov.au/PC_90071.htm; see also *Perspectivas de la agricultura y el desarrollo rural en las Américas: una mirada hacia América Latina y el Caribe 2009*. San Jose, Costa Rica: CEPAL, IICA and FAO, 2009. According to this study, the regional Latin American and Caribbean average of cows per hectare is 1/1.4. Colombia is still higher than the regional average: 1/1.7.

13. This 63 percent of the total agricultural food production covers what goes directly to the market, what is processed industrially and what is exported (UNDP, Hechos del Callejon 2008). To the best of my knowledge, the Colombian data are not disaggregated for small peasant production; that is, family production units of less than five hectares. A more recent statistic put the contribution at about 51 percent of the food in Colombia (see Introduction).

14. It is imperative to define subsistence farming as consisting of those poor peasants who do not necessary consume all that they produce, but the surplus

production they sell provides them some cash to satisfy their basic needs and yet does not constitute a base for accumulation.

15. In Latin America there were about sixteen million peasant production units of 1.8 hectares or less in the late 1980s, with an estimated peasant population of seventy-five million, almost two-thirds of the Latin American rural population (Altieri 2009, 104).

16. Paul Oquist, 69, as cited in Apolinar Diaz-Callejas, *Colombia Y La Reforma Agraria: Sus Documentos Fundamentales* (Cartagena: Universiad de Cartagena, 2002), 126.

17. According to CODHES, between 1986 and 1994 about 858,000 people were displaced, while between 1997 and 2003 the number reached 1,904,000, which is almost double the number during the previous period. As quoted in Comisiòn de Seguimiento a la Polìtica Pùblica Sobre Desplazamiento Forzado, Bogotà, Junio de 2008, 22–23.

18. In this regard, it is worth mentioning that Amnesty International reported that in 2008 the number of displaced persons increased by 24 percent from their 2007 level, an increase of more than 380,000 people, making Colombia one of the countries with the world's largest internally displaced population, alongside Sudan and Congo.

19. In Colombia some experts describe the accumulation of land by narcotraffickers as a "counterreform." I do not think this label is accurate because it fails to capture the narcobourgeoisie's role as the major accelerator of an ongoing process, as this chapter argues. Moreover, it conveys the idea that there was reform in the first place, which was not the case.

20. A good example of the political power exercised by the cattle ranching faction in alliance with the new cattle ranchers (the narcobourgeoisie) and their paramilitaries occurred during President Pastrana's peace talks with the FARC (1998–2002), which prevented the government from ceding grounds on the issue of land reform, a key demand of the FARC (Richani 2005).

21. In 2008 alone, an additional 380,000 people were forced to flee their homes, an increase of more than 24 percent from 2007, as reported by Amnesty International, July 19, 2009.

22. Ground rent in the United States is the opportunity cost of land.

23. This figure is based on the summation of Rocha's (1998) estimate of six million hectares, plus Garay's (2010) estimates of 5.5 million hectares lost by the displaced population.

Chapter 3. Peasant Reserves' Adaptability, Resistance, Subsumption, and War Rentierism

1. http://www.coha.org/colombias-invisible-crisis-internally-displaced-persons/.

2. Camilo Gonzales, "La verdad de la Tierra: mas do ocho milliones de hectareas abondonadas."

3. Richani, *Systems of Violence*; M. Romero, *Paramilitares y Autodefensas 1982–2003* (Bogotá: IEPRI, 2003); Claudia Lopez, *Y refundaron la patria? De como mafiosos y politicos reconfiguraron el Estado colombiano* (Bogota: Debate, 2010).

4. Dario Fajardo, leading expert on agrarian issues and architect behind the creation of the reserves, interview with author, via email, May 2020.

5. Samir Amin, *The Long Revolution of the Global South: Toward a New Anti-Imperialist International* (New York: NYU Press, 2019).

6. L. H. Morgan, *Ancient Society* (Chicago: Charles H. Kerr, 1910).

7. E. E. Evans, "The Ecology of Peasant Life in Western Europe," in *Man's Role in Changing the Face of the Earth*, ed. W. L. Thomas, 217–39. Chicago: University of Chicago Press. 1956.

8. F. Engels, *The Origin of the Family, Private Property, and the State* (New York).

9. Abhijit Banerjee and Esther Duflo, *Good Economics for Hard Times: Better Answers to our Biggest Problems* (New York: Public Affairs, 2019), ch. 5.

10. Max Weber contended that private property prospers and develops if "four conditions exist: (1) the modes of enforcement and the inferred content of the Order (the concepts, rules, and principles comprising the Order), (2) the organized structure(s) of social relationship(s), (3) the number of co-existing organized social relationship and their modes of interaction, (3) the nature of the goods and services appropriated, and (4) the modes according to which appropriated goods and services are valued (household property or profit-earning capital)." Laura Ford, "Max Weber on Property: An Effort in Interpretive Understanding," unpublished paper. https://scholarship.law.cornell.edu/cgi/viewcontent.cgi?article=1039&context=lps_papers. In the modern state and following Weber's theoretical edifice, the state and its monopoly of the legitimate use of violence becomes the legitimate enforcer.

11. Ibid., 326.

12. Ibid., 262.

13. David J. Romagnolo, "The So-Called 'Law' of Uneven and Combined Development," *Latin American Perspectives* 2, no. 1 (1975): 7–31. JSTOR. www.jstor.org/stable/2633408. Accessed April 22, 2020. See also Ernest Mandel, "The Laws of Uneven Development," *New Left Review* 59 (January-February), 19–38; Samir Amin, "Modes of Production, History and Unequal Development," *Science & Society* 49, no. 2 (Summer 1985): 194–207.

14. George Novack," Uneven and Combined Development in World History," in *Understanding History* (New York: Pathfinder Press, 1972), 82–83.

15. The origin of the word *Rochela* comes from "La Rouchelle," capital of the Charente-Maritime department on the Atlantic front of central-western France. La Rouchelle (diminutive of Roche which means rock) became a center for outcasts during the sixteenth and seventeenth century, which included per-

secuted French converted to Protestantism, rebels, bandits, and those escaping the state. See http://etimologias.dechile.net/?rochela; Dario Fajardo, *Las Zonas de Reserva Capmpesina Retos y Experiencia Significativas en su Implemenatcion* (Bogotà: FAO 2019). *Cimarrones* was the adjective used to describe blacks that escaped from their enslavement during colonial times. *Palanques* were the spaces occupied by the free slaves.

16. Salomon Kalmanovitz, "Evolucion de la Estructura Agraria Colombiana," en Transformaciones en la Estructura Agraria, ed. Salomon Kalmanovitz et al, 5. (Bogotà: Tercer Mundo Editores, 1994).

17. Kalmanovitz, "Evolucion de la Estructura Agraria Colombiana," 5.

18. Kalmanovitz, "Evolucion de la Estructura Agraria Colombiana," 6.

19. Kalmanovitz, "Evolucion de la Estructura Agraria Colombiana," 3–4.

20. Kalmanovitz, "Evolucion de la Estructura Agraria Colombiana," 4.

21. UNDP.

22. UNDP, 4.

23. Fajardo, as quoted in FAO 2019.

24. Fajardo, as quoted in FAO 2019.

25. FAO, Las Zonas de Reserva Capmpesina Retos y Experiencia Significativas en su Implementacion (Bogotà: FAO, 2019).

26. A paper authorized by the Central Bank of Colombia stated that the rate of GDP growth dropped to 2 percent between 1929 and 1931 and recovered in 1932 with a jump to 6.6 percent. See Juliana Jaramillo Echeverri, Adolfo Meisel-Roca, and Maria Teresa Geraldo, "The Great Depression in Colombia 1930–1953." *Borradores de Economia* no. 892 (2015). https://www.banrep.gov.co/sites/default/files/publicaciones/archivos/be_892.pdf.

27. Echeverri, Meisel-Roca, and Geraldo, "The Great Depression in Colombia 1930–1953."

28. Catherine LeGrand, *Colonizacion y Protesta campesina en Colombia 1850–1950* (Bogotà: Universidad de Los Andes, 2017), 161.

29. LeGrand, *Colonizacion y Protesta campesina en Colombia 1850–1950*, 162.

30. LeGrand, *Colonizacion y Protesta campesina en Colombia 1850–1950*, 163.

31. The colonization processes in Colombia have been complex, but two important characteristics are salient: one was the internal colonization within the orbit of the Andean area that characterized the process in the nineteenth century in the departments of Boyacá and Cundinamarca–Alto Sumapaz and in the east and south of Tolima, and the other, in the twentieth century, was the colonization process fomented by state policies and expanded toward the plains and the Orinoquian region. See Dario Fajardo, "La Colonizacion de La Macarena en la Historia de La Frontera Agraria," Agencia Prensa Rural, September 27, 2012.

32. LeGrand, *Colonizacion y Protesta campesina en Colombia*, 165.

33. FAO 2019, 9.

34. DANE, https://www.dane.gov.co/files/comunicados/Dia_mundial_poblacion.pdf; see also Nazih Richani, *Systems of Violence*; En cuanto al abandono o despojo de tierras, Oquist calculó que los propietarios de tierras perdieron 393.648 parcelas, y que los departamentos más afectados fueronValle del Cauca, Tolima, Cundinamarca, Norte de Santander y Antiguo Caldas.

35. Paul Oquist, as cited in http://centrodememoriahistorica.gov.co/descargas/informes2013/bastaYa/capitulos/basta-ya-cap2_110-195.pdf.

36. Pablo Emilio Escobar, *La Colonizacion Armada del Pato* (Bogotà: Fundacion Social Utrahuilca, 2019).

37. Hurtado's father Laureano Hurtado was known for his appreciation of Hitler's nationalist totalitarian ideology.

38. Richani, *Systems of Violence*.

39. See *Semana*, "El Lio de las Zonas de Reserva Campesina," March 16, 2013. Juan Camilo Restrepo, the then minister of agriculture forming part of the Santos government's negotiating team in Cuba with FARC, rejected the insurgents demand to expand the peasant reserves by saying that "FARC wanted to create a mosaic of 'independent republics' and this is against the constitution and this government would not accept."

40. Fajardo, as quoted in FAO 2019, 13.

41. http://www.adr.gov.co/normograma/DocumentosJuridica/Ley%20160%20de%201994_LISTA_no.pdf.

42. Richani, *Systems of Violence*.

43. Jorge Visbal, president of Fedegan 1991–2004, interview with author, Bogotà, December 1998. In 2018, Visbal was sentenced to nine years for his relations with the paramilitaries. See https://colombiareports.com/colombias-former-ranchers-chief-sentenced-to-9-years-over-paramilitary-ties/.

44. Dario Fajardo, sociologist and specialist on agrarian issues, personal communication via email with author. March 26, 2018.

45. César Vargas, Gonzalo Téllez, Alexander Cubillos, Jaime Pulido, Paola Gómez, y Lady Garzón "Análisis de los beneficiariosde la Política Pública deReforma Agraria en el marcodel desarrollo rural en Colombia(1994–2010)."

46. Lorenzo Andres Gutierrez, "Occupacion Y Tenencia De La Tierra en la Region El Pato-Balsillas, San Vicente Del Caguan: Entre lo Legitimo Y lo Legal." Unpublished paper

47. Lorenzo Andres Gutierrez, "Occupacion Y Tenencia De La Tierra."

48. William Ramirez Tobón, "Colonización armada, poder local y territorialización privada," *Journal of Iberian and Latin American Research* 7 (2001): 63–81.

49. Thirty-one years later, in 1995, Alvaro Gomez Hurtado, leader of the Conservative Party was gunned down in Bogota by FARC guerrillas.

50. Lorenzo Andres Gutierrez, "Occupacion Y Tenencia De La Tierra," 261.

51. Afredo Molano, 1994.

52. A study conducted by economist Sandra Rozo found that between 2000 and 2010 the glyphosate fumigation increased by 1 percent, the rates of homicide and poverty by 4.2%, as quoted in http://www.ideaspaz.org/publications/posts/1889.

53. Lorenzo Andres Gutierrez, "Occupacion Y Tenencia De La Tierra," 265. See also testimony of Javier Andres Bedoya, colono from Balsillas, at https://www.semillas.org.co/es/revista/primera-zona-de-reserva-campesina-del-pa.

54. Informant, peasant leader; interview by research assistant, Pato-Balsillas Caqueta, December 2019.

55. Informant, peasant leader; interview by research assistant, Pato-Balsillas Caqueta, December 2019.

56. Dario Fajardo, a leading expert on rural economy and main architect of the idea of peasant reserves, interview with author, May 30, 2020.

57. Informant, peasant leader, interview with author, via telephone, December 2019.

58. A. Machado, A. Luces y sombras en el desarrollo rural. Reflexiones a la luz del proyecto de ley de tierras y desarrollo rural del gobierno de Santos y Desarrollo rural, ¿camino para construir la paz? En OXFAM, ed., *Propuestas, visiones y análisis sobre la política de desarrollo rural en Colombia* (2012). https://es.scribd.com/document/239572402/Propuestas-visiones-y-analisis-sobre-la-politica-de-desarrollo-rural-en-Colombia; accessed November 27, 2021.

59. Laura Carolina Gonzalez Barrera, Desarrollo Rural En Tension? LA ZRC Cuenca Del Rio Pato Y Valle de Balsillas: Una Historia DE Resistencia Por La Dignidad Humana Y La Paz, El Plan Nacional de Desarrollo Y LOS Acuerdos DE Paz (2012–17). https://repository.javeriana.edu.co/bitstream/handle/10554/37009/Tesis%20ZRCPB%20%282012-2017%29.pdf?sequence=1&isAllowed=y.

60. Ana Pardo, President of the Pato-Balsilla JAC, interview by research assistant, December 2019.

61. ANZORC, by joining La Via Campesina to promote the cause, the demands of the peasants, and their struggle against gender violence. See Pablo Andrés Durán Chaparro, "Resisting and Creating the state in the Peasant Reserves Zones in Colombia Exploring a Social Movement's Dynamic of Contention in Practice." Unpublished MA thesis. The Hague, 2016.

62. Interviews, Cimitarra August 2018, and Pato-Balsillas, December 2019.

63. Zozorba en Zona de Reserva Campesina el Pato-Balsillas, Verdad Abierta, July 4, 2016. https://verdadabierta.com/zozobra-en-zona-de-reserva-campesina-el-pato-balsillas/.

64. Zozorba en Zona de Reserva Campesina el Pato-Balsillas, Verdad Abierta, July 4, 2016. https://verdadabierta.com/zozobra-en-zona-de-reserva-campesina-el-pato-balsillas/.

65. *Plan de Desarrollo Sostenible*, 111.

66. *Plan de Desarrollo Sostenible*, 112.

67. *Plan de Desarrollo Sostenible*, 112.

68. Javier Andres Bedoya, colono from Balsillas, https://www.semillas. org.co/es/revista/primera-zona-de-reserva-campesina-del-pa; see also FAO and Agencia Nacional de Tierras, *Las Zonas de Reserva Campesina Retos y Experiencias Significativas en Su Implementación* (Bogotà: FAO y Agencia Nacional de Tierras, 2019), 380.

69. As quoted by Alejandra Cuellar, *El Pato Resiste: La Lucha embiental de La Comunidad Donde Nacieron Las FARC*. January 16, 2018. https://pacifista.tv/notas/ el-pato-resiste-la-lucha-ambiental-de-la-comunidad-en-donde-nacieron-las-farc/.

70. FAO and Agencia Nacional de Tierras, *Las Zonas de Reserva Campesina Retos y Experiencias Significativas en Su Implementación* (Bogotà: FAO y Agencia Nacional de Tierras, 2019), 380.

71. FAO and Agencia Nacional de Tierras, *Las Zonas de Reserva Campesina Retos y Experiencias Significativas en Su Implementación* (Bogotà: FAO y Agencia Nacional de Tierras, 2019), 380.

72. FAO and Agencia Nacional de Tierras, *Las Zonas de Reserva Campesina Retos y Experiencias Significativas en Su Implementación* (Bogotà: FAO y Agencia Nacional de Tierras, 2019), 381.

73. FAO and Agencia Nacional de Tierras, *Las Zonas de Reserva Campesina Retos y Experiencias Significativas en Su Implementación* (Bogotà: FAO y Agencia Nacional de Tierras, 2019), 382.

74. Dario Fajardo, leading Colombian expert on the agrarian economy, interview with author, September 2019.

75. FAO 2019, 225.

76. FAO 2019, 341.

77. FAO 2019, 342.

78. Between 1990 and 2010 forested lands were reduced from 64,442,600 hectares to 59,021,810, that is, more than five million hectares were lost. The loss of forests continued between 2010 and 2021, the Amazon area of Colombia lost 98 thousand hectáres in 2019 and 109 thousand hectares in 2020. See Santiago Luque, "Crece la deforestación en Colombia: más de 171 mil hectáreas se perdieron en el 2020." https://es.mongabay.com/2021/07/crece-deforestacion-colombia-2020/; https://www.repository.fedesarrollo.org.co/bitstream/handle/11445/337/KAS%20 SOPLA_Deforestacion%20en%20Colombia%20retos%20y%20perspectivas.pdf? sequence=2&isAllowed Deforestation figures.

79. Colonization of new frontiers includes deforestation, slashing and burning of native vegetation and trees, and is then followed by entrepreneurs, speculators, landowners, cattle ranchers buying those lands and *colonos* moving out conquering new frontiers. This has been the devastating cycle of the expansion of the agricultural frontiers witnessed for most of the twentieth century and up to this writing. A nuance to this cycle and dynamics is that there is legal and

illegal mining involved, which has compounded the problem and added fuel to the fire.

80. Redacion Nacional, Campesinos firman Acuerdos para Conservar Parque Nacional Cordillera de los Picachos, *El Espectador*, November 24, 2020. https://www.elespectador.com/noticias/nacional/campesinos-firman-acuerdos-para-con-servar-el-parque-nacional-cordillera-de-los-picachos/.

81. https://crudotransparente.com/2019/10/08/de-la-agricultura-al-petroleo-en-el-caqueta/.

82. Luke Jacobs, "How Disputed Oil Deals Push Native Colombian Peoples Closer to Extinction," June 29, 2019. https://colombiareports.com/how-disputed-oil-deals-push-native-colombian-peoples-closer-to-extinction/.

83. Ma Tianjie, "Oil, Monkeys, and Guerrillas: Chinese Companies Face Problems in the Amazon Challenges Facing Chinese Oil Company in Colombia Test China's Resource Strategy for Latin America," November 30, 2017. https://chinadialogue.net/en/business/10256-oil-monkeys-and-guerrillas-chinese-compa-nies-face-problems-in-the-amazon/.

84. https://crudotransparente.com/2019/10/08/de-la-agricultura-al-petroleo-en-el-caqueta/.

85. https://crudotransparente.com/2019/10/08/de-la-agricultura-al-petroleo-en-el-caqueta/.

86. https://crudotransparente.com/2019/10/08/de-la-agricultura-al-petroleo-en-el-caqueta/.

87. https://crudotransparente.com/2019/10/08/de-la-agricultura-al-petroleo-en-el-caqueta/.

88. https://crudotransparente.com/2019/10/08/de-la-agricultura-al-petroleo-en-el-caqueta/.

89. https://crudotransparente.com/2019/10/08/de-la-agricultura-al-petroleo-en-el-caqueta/.

90. https://crudotransparente.com/2019/10/08/de-la-agricultura-al-petroleo-en-el-caqueta/.

91. Clifford Krauss, "As Oil Demand Declines, Exxon Is at CrossRoads," *New York Times*, December 11, 2020, A1.

92. http://www.scielo.org.co/scielo.php?script=sci_arttext&pid=S0122-1450 2012000100002#1. Yondó was founded by the Royal Dutch Shell oil multinational company in 1941 to lodge its employees at the then discovered Casabe oil field. In 1971, Yondó became a municipality.

93. Interviews with informants, by author, Cimitarra, 2018; Fajardo Montana, Darío. El Campo, Las Politicas Agrarias y Los Conflictos Sociales en Colombia. Bogotá: Fundación Ideas para la Paz.2008.

94. See Kojin Karatani, *The Structure of World History: From Modes of Production to Modes of Exchange* (Durham: Duke University Press, 2014).

95. Plan Desarrollo Rural in Cimitarra, 8.

96. Amparo Murillo, *Historia y Sociedad en el Magdalena Medio*, 50.

97. Carlos Martines, Member of the Directorate and founding member of the Interview Cimitarra.

98. JAC stands for Junta de Accion Communal (Communal Action Committee), which is elected at the local neighborhood level within the municipality. JACs attend to issues related to their neighborhood including sanitation, water supply, security, and other services.

99. http://violentologia.com/blog/wp-content/uploads/2011/09/Cuadernillo-PARAS-ESP-small.pdf.

100. See Richani, *Systems of Violence*, ch. 5.

101. In 1982, Puerto Boyaca was declared a special military area with a military mayor, Major Oscar de Jesus Echandia, who commanded the Barbula Battalion. Echandia called the local notables, which included the leaders of both traditional Conservative and Liberal parties, cattle ranchers, agrobusiness representatives, business representatives, and one representative from Texas Petroleum Company. See *El Estado Suplantando las Autodefensas de Puerto Boyacá*, Informe no. 4 (Bogotá: Centro de Memoria Historica, 2019), 26. http://centrodememoria-historica.gov.co/wp-content/uploads/2020/03/2019-El-Estado-suplantado-Autode-fensas-Puerto-Boyaca.pdf.

102. http://violentologia.com/blog/wp-content/uploads/2011/09/Cuadernillo-PARAS-ESP-small.pdf.

103. https://www.hrw.org/reports/1996/killer2.htm.

104. https://www.hrw.org/reports/1996/killer2.htm.

105. During my 1997–98 field research in the Middle Magdalena, which was the period of the paramilitary offensive against the insurgency strongholds, the military did not cease the carnage against the civilian population. This is based on my unstructured interviews with displaced people from the *comunas* of Barrancanbermeja, Cimitarra, San Pablo, Morales, Remedios, Cimiti, and other municipalities. Those interviews were carried out in Barrancabemeja, August 1997 and 1998 respectively. President Virgilio Barco (1986–1990) attempted to scrutinize the use of paramilitary by the military. He introduced several decrees, among them was Decree 815, which reasserted that the sole power to create "self-defense" groups lie with the president, with additional approval required from the defense and government (now interior) ministries. On May 25, 1989, the Colombian Supreme Court overturned Law 48 that allowed the army to distribute restricted weapons to civilians. Decree 1194, issued that June, established criminal penalties for civilians and members of the armed forces who recruit, train, promote, finance, organize, lead, or belong to "the armed groups, misnamed paramilitary groups, that have been formed into death squads, bands of hired assassins, self-defense groups, or groups that carry out their own justice. President Alvaro Uribe Velez (2002–10) revived different forms of paramilitarism: *convivir,* peasant-soldiers, and informants networks.

106. https://www.hrw.org/world-report/2009/country-chapters/colombia.

107. ACVC, interviews with author, August 2018.

108. Irene Ramirez, president of the ACVC, interview with author, Barrancabermeja, August 2018.

109. Asociasion Campesina del Valle del Rio Cimitarra Zona de Reserva Campesina Valle del Rio Cimitarra, "Plan de Desarrollo Sostenible," 2014, 45–46.

110. Irene Ramirez, interview.

111. Ramirez, interview, November 8, 2021.

112. FAO and Agencia Nacional de Tierras, *Las Zonas De Reserva Campesina Retos Y Experiencias Significativas En Su Implementacion* (Bogotá: FAO y Agencia Nacional de Tierras, 2019).

113. FAO and Agencia Nacional de Tierras, *Las Zonas De Reserva Campesina Retos Y Experiencias Significativas En Su Implementacion* (Bogotá: FAO y Agencia Nacional de Tierras, 2019), 45.

114. FAO and Agencia Nacional de Tierras, *Las Zonas De Reserva Campesina Retos Y Experiencias Significativas En Su Implementacion* (Bogotá: FAO y Agencia Nacional de Tierras, 2019), 45–46; Irene Ramirez, President of the ACVC, Interview with author, August 2018.

115. ACVC leaders, interview with author, Puerto Matilde, August 2018.

116. ACVC interviews.

117. Informant, ACVC, interview with author, Puerto Matilde, August 2018.

118. Yenly Angelica Blanco, Derecho a la Tierra y al Territorio, Justicia, y Zonas de Reserva Campesina: El Caso del Valle Del Río Cimitarra; https://repository.javeriana.edu.co/bitstream/handle/10554/12429/MendezBlancoYenlyAngelica2013.pdf?sequence=1&isAllowed=y; ACVC, Plan de Desarrollo, 2000 https://www.prensarural.org/acvc/plandesarrollozrc.pdf.

119. ACVC, Plan de Desarrollo, 2000. https://www.prensarural.org/acvc/plandesarrollozrc.pdf.

120. Claudia Mejia, https://www.redalyc.org/jatsRepo/5742/574262162009/html/index.html.

121. There is a yardstick measure that was used by the state to organize and limit the distribution of public lands to landless *colonos*. The size of the landholding depends on land fertility and productivity. This yardstick has been manipulated and abused by big corporations, large landowners, cattle ranchers, agribusinesses, and speculators.

122. This is based my interviews with ACVC leaders, Puerto Matilde, August 2018.

123. ACVC, interviews by author, Puerto Matilde, August 2018.

124. ACVC interviews by author, Puerto Matilde, August 2018; see also https://www.prensarural.org/spip/spip.php?article21800.

125. Richani, *Systems of Violence*; see also https://www.prensarural.org/spip/spip.php?article12987.

126. https://www.bbc.com/news/world-latin-america-19931443; Richani, *Multinationals*.

127. Franscico Ramirez, president of labor union Sintramienercol and activist, interview with author, Bogotá, September 2018.

128. UNDP ACVC 2014.

129. PNUD y ACVC. (2014). Estudio participativo de tenencia de la tierra y el territorio, usos y conflictos en la ZRC del valle del río cimitarra. Barrancabermeja: PNUD—ACVC.

130. Business groups including the conglomerates were concerned that the agreement with FARC would result in increasing the power communities including peasants, Indigenous, and Afro descendants in deciding on land-use issue that could prevent the advancement of their rentier economic projects. Rafael Aubad, Chairman of ProAntioquia business group, interview with author, Medellin, August 2017. Mr. Aubad articulated the concerns of the fifty-two business enterprises, business guilds, and pro-business think tanks that his group represents. They reject "conceding authority to indigenous communities to determine the land use under new norms of "environmental protection." He cited the "Consulta Previa," that is, the consulting communities prior to any extractive or mining/energy project as an impediment for investments encouraging "rent-seeking" behavior on part of those communities. Those are two areas that concern the Colombian business groups, Aubad concluded.

131. https://cepdipo.org/portfolio/cuadernos-de-la-implementacion-6-la-reforma-rural-integral-en-deuda/, 66.

132. Irene Ramirez, president ACVC, interview with author, Barrancabermeja, August 2018.

133. Ramirez, interview. The "Yellow Line" is the Mountain of San Lucas, which the ACVC has determined to be a natural reserve where all human activities that interfere with nature are strictly prohibited. The total size of the protected area is sixty thousand hectares in the Serrania de San Lucas. This Yellow Line was created by the peasant *colonos'* initiative in 1987. See Yenly Angelica Blanco, "Derecho a la tierra y al territorio, justicia y zonas de Reserva Campesina: El Caso del Valle del Río Cimitarra," unpublished MA thesis, 2013, 79. https://repository.javeriana.edu.co/bitstream/handle/10554/12429/MendezBlancoYenlyAngelica2013.pdf?sequence=1&isAllowed=y.

134. FAO 2019.

135. https://www.unodc.org/documents/crop-monitoring/Colombia/Colombia_Monitoreo_Cultivos_Ilicitos_2019.pdf.

136. This observation is based on the ACVC peasants' interviewees' comments on the coca economy and its impact.

137. Diana Torres, Coordinator of the Jesuit Refugee Service (JRS), interview with author, Barrancabermeja, August 23, 2018. Torres explained that the ELN and the paramilitaries "Botalones" were disputing the area after the FARC demobilization

in 2016, the lower part of the Serrania is in the hands of the Botalones, closing the circle on the ELN, who were in upper part of the Seinrrania de San Lucas.

138. ACVC 1 informant, interview with author, Puerto Matilde, August 2018. This is based on the information provided by the interviewees in Puerto Matilde, San Pablo, and Barrancabermeja.

139. Jaskiran Kaur Chohan, "Incorporating and Contesting the Corporate Food Regime in Colombia: Agri-food Dynamics in Two Zonas de Reserva Campesina (Peasant Reserve Zones)," unpublished dissertation 2018.

140. See Nazih Richani, *Systems of Violence*, ch.3.

141. Nazih Richani, *Systems of Violence*, ch.3.

142. https://www.procuraduria.gov.co/portal/media/file/Informe%20 sobre%20Acceso%20y%20Uso%20de%20la%20Tierra%20Def%2007_01_2021.pdf.

143. Jan Douwe der Ploeg, *The New Peasantries*, ch. 9.

144. Irene Ramirez, president of the ACVC, telephone interview with author.

145. See Jan Douwe der Ploeg, *The New Peasantries*, ch. 1.

146. Arturo Escobar, *Pluriversal Politics: The Real and the Possible* (Durham: Duke University Press, 2020).

Chapter 4. The Struggle for Survival

1. https://id.presidencia.gov.co/Paginas/prensa/2019/La-poblacion-indi-gena-en-Colombia-es-de-1905617-personas-segun-Censo-del-Dane-190916.aspx.

2. https://id.presidencia.gov.co/Paginas/prensa/2019/La-poblacion-indigena-en-Colombia-es-de-1905617-personas-segun-Censo-del-Dane-190916. aspx. See also Juliana Jaimes, "La Apuesta Para Traducir a Lenguas Indigenas las Decisiones Que Imnpacten las Comunidades" *El Espectador*, March 3, 2021 https://www.elespectador.com/noticias/medio-ambiente/la-apuesta-por-traducir-a-lenguas-indigenas-las-decisiones-judiciales/.

3. Theodor Rathgeber, "Indigenous Struggles in Colombia Historical Changes and Perspectives" in *The Struggle for Indigenous Rights in Latin America*, ed. Nancy Grey Postero and Leon Zamosc (Portland, OR: Sussex Academic Press, 2004).

4. Theodor Rathgeber, "Indigenous Struggles in Colombia Historical Changes and Perspectives" in *The Struggle for Indigenous Rights in Latin America*, ed. Nancy Grey Postero and Leon Zamosc (Portland, OR: Sussex Academic Press, 2004).

5. Julie Turkewitz and Sofía Villamil, "Indigenous Colombians, Facing New Wave of Brutality, Demand Government Action." https://www.nytimes.com/2020/10/24/world/americas/colombia-violence-Indigenous-protest.html.

6. Rosa Luxemburg, *The Accumulation of Capital* (New York: Routledge, 2004).

7. https://wiki.salahumanitaria.co/wiki/Meta.

8. PNUD, Política Pública Indígena del Departamento del Meta Aprobado Asamblea Departamental Abril, Villaviciencio 2014.

9. William Paul McGreevey, *An Economic History of Colombia 1845–1930* (Cambridge: Cambridge University Press, 1971), 47.

10. McGreevey, *An Economic History of Colombia 1845–1930*, 51. However, others estimated that in 1492 the total population in all the Americas to be sixty million. See Alexander Koch, Chris Breirley, Mark Maslik, and Simon Lewis, "European Colonization of the Americas Killed 10% of World Population and Caused Global Cooling," *The Conversation*, January 31, 2019.

11. McGreevey, *An Economic History of Colombia 1845–1930*, 52.

12. Large agribusinesses, oil multinational corporations, and extractive companies resorted to renting lands from the Indigenous in several departments in Colombia such as Meta, Choco, Cauca, La Guajira.

13. As quoted in McGreevey, *An Economic History of Colombia 1845–1930*, 54.

14. See Orlando Fals Borda, *El Hombre y La Tierra en Boyaca* (Bogotá: 1957), 84.

15. McGreevey, *An Economic History of Colombia 1845–1930*, 59.

16. Orlando Fals Borda, *Historia de la Cuestion Agraria y Colombia* (Bogotá: Carlos Valencia Editores, 1982),

17. McGreevey, *An Economic History of Colombia 1845–1930*, 60.

18. John Lynch, *Simon Bolivar: A Life* (New Haven: Yale University Press, 2006), 154, 155.

19. John Lynch, *Simon Bolivar: A Life*, 155.

20. John Lynch, *Simon Bolivar: A Life*, 155.

21. Frank Safford and Marco Palacios, *Colombia: Fragmented Land, Divided Society* (New York: Oxford University Press, 2002), 184.

22. Safford and Palacios, *Colombia: Fragmented Land, Divided Society*, 185.

23. Safford and Palacios, *Colombia: Fragmented Land, Divided Society*, 185.

24. See Taussig, *Latin American Perspective* (Summer 1978).

25. Libardo José Ariza. "Legal Indigeneity: Knowledge, Legal Discourse, and the Construction of Indigenous Identity in Colombia," *Identities* 27, no. 4 (2020): 403–22. DOI: 10.1080/1070289X.2018.1543484.

26. Ariza. *Catechumen* means a Christian convert under instruction before baptism.

27. Brett Troyan, *Cauca's Indigenous Movement in Southwestern Colombia: Land, Violence, and Ethnic Identity* (New York: Lexington Books, 2015). Troyan argues that the Indigenous identity was shaped by the interplay among the state, local elites, and the Indigenous. Her analysis underplayed the dependency of Colombia on the centers of global capital and how in turn global capital shaped national and subnational political economies. For example, in the wake of splitting Grand Cauca in 1905 into several departments, each department forged linkages

with global and national markets, which were decisive in shaping different political economies. That is to say, any analysis that underplays the global linkages is incomplete. Subsequently, changes in state policies within this dependent structure was central to shaping Cauca, which in turn impacted the relationship between the local dominant groups and the Indigenous, as well as their responses.

28. Catherine LeGrand, Luis van Isschot, and Pilar Riano-Alcala, "Land, Justice, and Memory: Challenges for Peace in Colombia," Special Issue of *Canadian Journal of Latin American and Caribbean Studies* 42, no. 3 (November 2017). In Latin America, it is estimated that 11percent of the total areas within Latin American countries are titled as ethnic land. See Giorleny Altamirano Rayo, "Securing Territory: State Interests and the Implementation of Ethnic Land Rights in the Americas." PhD dissertation, University of Texas, Austin, 2017. https://repositories.lib.utexas.edu/bitstream/handle/2152/62324/ALTAMIRANORAYO-DISSERTATION-2017.pdf.

29. The conglomerates and many other owners of large companies involved in the rentier economy were deeply concerned about any state's concessions on land use, subsoil rights, popular consultation (*consulta previa*), and environmental protection that might hinder their projects in rural areas, including extraction of raw materials, construction of hydroelectric plants, and dams. There is strong agreement on the neoliberal rentier model among different factions of capital, as expressed by Rafael Aubad (2017), president of Pro Antioquia, a group that includes most of the business groups in Antioquia and Colombia, interview with author, Medellin, Colombia, August 16, 2017; Sergio Osorio, vice president of Human Resources and Administration, Grupo Argos, interview with author, Medellin, Colombia, August 2017. Grupo Argos is one of the most important Colombian multinationals, with close to 60 percent of its investments in Latin American markets and in the United States. In the latter, since 2005 Argos has grown to become the fourth-largest concrete producer in the United States, where it derives 26 percent of its revenues. See chapter 1.

30. Sergio Osorio, vice president of Human Resources and Administration, Grupo Argos, interview with author, Medellin, Colombia, August 2017.

31. That is to say, the drive to incorporate new frontiers into the circuits of capital can be induced by national capital and is not necessarily driven by international capital. See Yu, Yifei Sun, Y. H. Dennis Wei, and George C. S. Lin. "De-Centering 'Spatial Fix'—Patterns of Territorialization and Regional Technological Dynamism of ICT Hubs in China," *Journal of Economic Geography* 11, no. 1 (2011): 119–50. http://www.jstor.org/stable/26162123.

32. Now the Santo Domingo group owns the following: Caracol TV, Blu Radio, El Espectador y Cine Colombia; transportation and logistics with Supply and Ditransa; tourism with two enterprises Terranum y Decameron and, finally agro business and commerce with the Koba enterprise comprised of D1, Biofilm, Refo-

costa, Sugranel, and Navigator. See https://www.dinero.com/edicion-impresa/caratula/articulo/historia-y-actualidad-del-grupo-santo-domingo-de-colombia/228944.

33. "https://colombiareports.com/santo-domingo-overtakes-sarmiento-to-top-colombias-rich-list/" https://colombiareports.com/santo-domingo-overtakes-sarmiento-to-top-colombias-rich-list/. Santo Domingo's fortune is estimated at $14,700 billion, and that of Sarmiento was estimated at $12,700 billion. In 2017, the fortune of Sarmiento declined to eleven billion but surpassed Santo Domingo's. See "https://www.portafolio.co/tendencias/los-colombianos-mas-ricos-segun-forbes-504289." https://www.portafolio.co/tendencias/los-colombianos-mas-ricos-segun-forbes-504289. Lately, Sarmiento has bought Capital Global banking BAC-Credomatic, the largest financial institution in Central America, for $1.9 billion, making it the largest acquisition by any Colombian capitalist so far. BAC-Credomatic was bought from General Electric and operates in Panamá, Costa Rica, Nicaragua, Honduras, El Salvador, Guatemala, México, Bahamas, Islas Caimán, and Florida (U.S.).

34. Gustavo Pardo, *Las Cuatro megahaciendad de Luis Carlos Sarmiento*.

35. Gustavo Pardo, *Las Cuatro megahaciendad de Luis Carlos Sarmiento*.

36. Gustavo Pardo, *Las Cuatro megahaciendad de Luis Carlos Sarmiento*.

37. UAF is determined by the fertility of land and access to water. Important law 160 stipulated that the recipients of public lands must be landless peasants.

38. Rubeila, a subsistence farmer and member of ANUC, interview with the author, Puerto Gaitan, August 2016.

39. Gustavo Pardo, *Las cuatro megahaciendas de Luis Carlos Sarmiento en el Llano*, //www.las2orillas.co/las-cuatro-mega-haciendas-luis-carlos-sarmiento-llano/.

40. Markus Kroger, "The Expansion of Industrial Tree Plantations in Brazil." *Development and Change* (2012). https://www.academia.edu/11882122/The_Expansion_of_Industrial_Tree_Plantations_and_Dispossession_in_Brazil; In Colombia, organized criminal groups (narcotraffickers and emerald Mafia) prepared the ground for the introduction of the Brazilian model of extensive export cash crops.

41. Interview with peasant activist and leader from the Leona, July 29, 2015; see also Jose David Escobar, "ANT Fallo a favor de Particulares en Antiguas Tierras de Victor Carranza," *El Espectador*, June 24, 2021. https://www.elespectador.com/judicial/ant-fallo-a-favor-de-particulares-en-antiguas-tierras-de-victor-carranza/?cx_testId=31&cx_testVariant=cx_1&cx_artPos=0#cxrecs_s; accessed June 24, 2021. In the cited article, the Carranza is of sixteen thousand hectares that are currently used by the Altar Group and Contegral to plant corn and soybeans for their pigs. The National Agency of Lands, the institution that replaced Encoder, issued a judgment "recognizing the legitimacy" of the acquisition, overlooking the illegitimate methods used.

42. Sven Beckert, *The Empire of Cotton* (New York: Vintage, 2015), ch. 2.

43. OCH7. https://wiki.salahumanitaria.co/wiki/Meta?useskin=38/.

44. Informant 2, interview with author, Puerto Giatan, August 5, 2016. See also Laura Alzate, *Recursos Economicos y Goviernos Inidigenas*.

45. *Prior consultation* is a law by which the state establishes the right of ethnic communities to be informed on any proposed projects that might affect their community and their territory.

46. See Laura Alzate, "Empresas, Recursos Economicos y Goviernos Indigenas: Una aproximacion al studio de la redes cleitelares en un Resgurado Indigena el La Altillanura Colombiana." *Universitas Humanistica* 84 (2017): 171–99; Informant 1,

47. Andy Torres, Director of the Labor and Commercial Committee, Puerto Gaitan Municipality, interview with author, August 5, 2016.

48. Laura Alzate; informants, interview with author, Puerto Gaitan, July 2016.

49. This observation was based on a various interviews; Mercedes Rodriguez, Piapoco leader and representative to the state, interview with author, Puerto Gaitan, July 2016.

50. See Alejandro Lopez, "Extractismo Y Conflictividad en Puerto Gaitan de la Riqueza Cultural a la Dependencia Economica." https://crudotransparente.com/2020/10/30/extractivismo-y-conflictividad-en-puerto-gaitan-de-la-riqueza-cultural-a-la-dependencia-economica/; Mercedes Rodriguez, interview with author.

51. The "captain" figure first emerged in the sixteenth century, influenced by Spanish colonial rule and the Church. The community chose the one person that had thebest knowledge of traditional medical practices, hunting, fishing, and collection of food. He also became the representative of the group vis-à-vis the colonial power.

52. Fredy Galino, teacher and member of the Sikuani community in Wakoyo, interview with author, Wakoyo, July 2016.

53. Galino, interview.

54. Galino, interview.

55. Galino, interview.

56. Informant 2, Sikuani community, interview with author, Wakoyo reservation, Meta, August 2015. "http://www.portafolio.co/economia/finanzas/guerra-narcotrafico-nuestra-30096." http://www.portafolio.co/economia/finanzas/guerra-narcotrafico-nuestra-30096.

57. file:///Users/nazirichani/Desktop/Meta/"Pueblo%20ind%C3%ADgena%20Sikuani%20de%20Puerto%20Gaitán%20Meta,%20se%20ha%20tomado%20pac%C3%ADficamente%20la%20instalaciones%20de%20la%20em.webarchive.

58. Sichuan informer 1 and 2, interviews by author, Puerto Gaitan, Resguardo Wakoyo, August 5, 2016.

59. Rodriguez, interview

60. Pacific Rubiales, for example, according to a leader of the oil workers union USO revealed the protection that Pacific paid the paramilitaries. Informant,

USO leader, interview with author, Bogota 2017.

61. See Richani, *Systems of Violence*; Between 2007 and 2014, Pacific Rubiales paid the Ministry of Defense seventy million dollars for security. See Alejandro Lopez, *Extractavismo*.

62. In 2015, Pacific Energy Rubiales changed its corporate name to Pacific Exploration and Production Corporation; see https://rutasdelconflicto.com/especiales/pacific/tierras/agua.html; https://rutasdelconflicto.com/especiales/pacific/empresa/introduccion.html.

63. Informants, interviews with authors, Puerto Gaitan, Meta, August 8, 2016; see also Alejandro Lopez, *Extractivismo*.

64. Informant, defensoria del Pueblo, interview with author, Villavicencio, August 10, 2016.

65. https://www.infobae.com/america/colombia/2021/06/17/policia-se-fue-de-el-porvenir-meta-mientras-la-comunidad-denuncian-amenaza-paramilitar/.

66. https://www.infobae.com/america/colombia/2021/01/27/denuncian-amenazas-contra-asentamiento-indigena-en-puerto-gaitan-meta-por-parte-de-grupos-paramilitares/

67. Juan Gomez, "Reclamante de tierras en Colombia: riesgo inminente," *El Espectador*, October 2018. https://www.elespectador.com/colombia-20/conflicto/reclamante-de-tierras-en-colombia-riesgo-inminente-article/.

68. Jose R. Gamarra Vergara, "La economía del departamento del Cauca: concentración de tierras y pobreza," *Banco de la Republica* 95 (October 2007). https://repositorio.banrep.gov.co/bitstream/handle/20.500.12134/3000/dtser_95.pdf?sequence=1&isAllowed=y.

69. "Población Indígena el Cauca Resultados del Censo Nacional de Población y Vivienda 2018," DANE 2019. https://www.dane.gov.co/files/censo2018/informacion-tecnica/presentaciones-territorio/190814-CNPV-presentacion-Resultados-etnicos-Cauca.pdf.

70. "Población Indígena el Cauca Resultados del Censo Nacional de Población y Vivienda 2018," DANE 2019; See also World Bank, "Colombia: Land Policy in Transition," 2004. https://repositorio.uniandes.edu.co/bitstream/handle/1992/40993/dcede2004-29.pdf?sequence=1&isAllowed=y.

71. Santiago Paredes Cisneros "La política del resguardo entre los indios páez del pueblo de Toboyma (gobernación de Popayán), 1650–1750." doi: dx.doi.org/10.7440/histcrit58.2015.02. http://www.scielo.org.co/pdf/rhc/n58/n58a03.pdf. See Mariano Sendoya, *Toribío. Puerto Tejada* (Popayán: Talleres Editoriales del Departamento, 1960), 29–41; María Teresa Findji y José María Rojas, *Territorio, economía y sociedad páez* (Cali: Universidad del Valle, 1985), 37–49; Joanne Rappaport, *The Politics of Memory. Native Historical Interpretation in the Colombian Andes* (Durham: Duke University Press, 1998 [1990]), 49–60.

72. Cisneros, "La política del resguardo."

73. Cisneros, "La política del resguardo."

74. Cisneros, "La política del resguardo."

75. Henry Caballero interview; see also Joanne Rappaport, "History, Myth, and the Dynamics of Territorial Maintenance in Tierradentro, Colombia," *American Ethnologist* 12, no. 1 (1985): 27–45. Accessed May 2, 2021. http://www.jstor.org/stable/644413.

76. Caballero, interview.

77. Julieta Lemaitre, "Manuel Quintín Lame: Legal Thought as Minor Jurisprudence," *Law Text Culture* 21 (2017): 76–99. https://ro.uow.edu.au/ltc/vol21/iss1/5; see also Gonzalo Castillo Cárdenas, *Liberation Theology from Below: The Life and Thought of Manuel Quintín Lame* (Maryknoll, NY: Orbis Books, 1987).

78. Julieta Lemaitre, "Manuel Quintín Lame," 78.

79. Daniel Ricardo Penaranda, "La Organizacion como forma de Resistencia," in *Nuestra Vida ha sido Nuestro Lucha, Resistencia y Memoria en el Cauca Indigena*, ed. Graciela Bolanoz et al., 22–24 (Bogota: Centro de Memoria Historica, 2012).

80. Daniel Ricardo Penaranda, "La Organizacion como forma de Resistencia."

81. Daniel Ricardo Penaranda, "La Organizacion como forma de Resistencia."

82. Daniel Ricardo Penaranda, "La Organizacion como forma de Resistencia."

83. Daniel Ricardo Penaranda, "La Organizacion como forma de Resistencia."

84. Daniel Ricardo Penaranda, "La Organizacion como forma de Resistencia."

85. Pablo Tattay, "Construccion de Poder Propio en el Movimiento Indigena del Cauca," in *Nuestra Vida Ha Sido Nuestra Lucha: Resistencia y Memoria en el Cauca Indigena*, ed. Daniel Ricardo Penaranda, 52–53 (Bogotá: Informe del Centro de Memoria Historica, 2012).

86. Pablo Tattay, "Construccion de Poder Propio en el Movimiento Indigena del Cauca."

87. See Richani, *Systems of Violence*; LeGrand 1981.

88. Tattay, *Centro de Memoria Historica*, 53.

89. Law 89 of 1890 recognized the right of the Indigenous to elect their own governing body in accordance with their own customs.

90. Tattay, *Centro de Memoria Historica*, 54.

91. Tattay, *Centro de Memoria Historica*, 54.

92. Tattay, *Centro de Memoria Historica*, 60.

93. Tattay, *Centro de Memoria Historica*, 61.

94. Tattay, *Centro de Memoria Historica*, 63. On the construction of ethnic identity, see also James Sanders, "Belonging to the Great Granadan Family: Partisan Struggle and the Construction of Indigenous Identity and Politics in Southwestern Colombia, 1849–1890," in *Race and Nation in Modern Latin America*, ed. Appelbaum et al. (Chapel Hill: University of North Carolina Press, 2003); James Sanders, *Contentious Republicans: Popular Politics, Race, and Class in Nineteenth-Century Colombia* (Durham: Duke University Press, 2004).

95. Karl Marx, as quoted in https://people.potsdam.edu/nuwermj/hunt/10%20Human%20Nature%20RRPE.pdf.

96. Arturo Escobar, *Pluriversal Politics* (Durham: Duke University Press, 2020); Marisol de La Cadena, *Earth Beings: Ecologies of Practice across Andean Worlds* (Durham: Duke University Press, 2015); Jose Carlos Mariategui, *Seven Interpretive Essays on Peruvian Reality* (Chicago: University of Chicago Press, 1971).

97. See https://www.hrw.org/news/2009/02/10/colombia-farc-kills-17-Indigenous-group; https://www.culturalsurvival.org/news/colombia-farc-releases-Indigenous-leaders.

98. Tattay, *Centro de Memoria Historica*, 75.

99. Miguel Fernandez, President of the Mesa Territorial de Garantias, telephone interview with author, March 22, 2021. The problem of identity politics or, as previously better described, "ethnopolitics," can be seen as a regression to tribal and primordial relations in the age of globalization and neoliberalism.

100. Arturo Escobar, *Pluriversal Politics*, 38.

101. Arturo Escobar, *Pluriversal Politics*, 39.

102. Theodor Rathgeber, "Indigenous Struggles in Colombia," 27.

103. Theodor Rathgeber, "Indigenous Struggles in Colombia," 27; See also Fernanda Spinoza Morena, "La Lucha por La Paz Del Movimiento Indigena Caucano" *Ciendias* no.76 (Septiembre–Noviembre 2012). https://www.cinep.org.co/publicaciones/PDFS/20121101c.lucha_paz76.pdf.

104. Fernanda Spinoza Morena, "La Lucha por La Paz Del Movimiento Indigena Caucano."

105. "Treinta Años de Protesta Social: el surgimiento de la movilización 'étnica' afrocolombiana en el norte del Cauca." En Documento de trabajo No. 50. CISED-IRD- ICANH, Universidad del Valle, Cali, Julio 2000.

106. This observation was validated by all interviewees of CIRC, peasants' representatives of the Afro-Colombian community in UAFROC,

107. This is based on my interview with the informant "comunero," representative of CRIC in Popayan, telephone interview on March 18, 2021.

108. In the departments of La Guajira, Cesar, and Bolivar, coal and gold play the same transformative role.

109. Henry Caballero, interview.

110. The paramilitaries that committed the massacre sought to rid the hacienda, which belonged to one of the wealthy landowners, of the Indigenous occupying it.

111. See https://www.semillas.org.co/es/el-ingenio-voraz-y-los-indgenas-el-negocio-del-agroetanol.

112. Torkan Omari, "Colombia's 'Sugar Cartel' and Its Alleged Attempts to Keep Prices High," *Colombia Reports*, June 3, 2015. https://colombiareports.com/colombias-sugar-cartel-and-its-alleged-attempts-to-keep-prices-high.

113. Omari, "Colombia's 'Sugar Cartel' and Its Alleged Attempts to Keep Prices High."

114. Omari, "Colombia's 'Sugar Cartel' and Its Alleged Attempts to Keep Prices High."

115. Omari, "Colombia's 'Sugar Cartel' and Its Alleged Attempts to Keep Prices High."

116. Natalia Ramondo, Veronica Rappoport, and Kim J. Ruhl, "Horizontal vs. Vertical FDI: Revisiting Evidence from U.S. Multinationals," unpublished paper 2011. https://www.princeton.edu/~ies/Fall11/RappaportPaper.pdf.

117. This information was obtained from multiple interviews, including Miguel Fernandez, president of the Mesa Territorial de Garantias, phone conversation with the author on March 20, 2021.

118. See https://www.semana.com/nacion/articulo/indigenas-vandalizaron-y-quemaron-120-hectareas-de-cana-en-el-cauca-denuncia-asocana/202123/.

119. https://www.theguardian.com/environment/2017/oct/28/nasa-colombia-cauca-valley-battle-mother-land.

120. https://www.nocheyniebla.org/wp-content/uploads/2020/05/noche-y-niebla-60-web.pdf. In 2020, 113 cases of human rights violations were reported in Cauca, out of 377, or 36 percent of the total for the whole country; Valle de Cauca followed, with thirty-six cases. See https://www.nocheyniebla.org/wp-content/uploads/2020/10/NOCHE-Y-NIEBLA-61.pdf.

121. "La sangre que recuperó la tierra de los Nasa," *Verdad Abierta*, February 25, 2014. https://verdadabierta.com/la-sangre-que-les-recupero-la-tierra-de-los-nasa/.

122. "La sangre que recuperó la tierra de los Nasa."

123. "La sangre que recuperó la tierra de los Nasa."

124. Arche Advisors, Colombia Sugar Industry Situational Analysis, March 2015. https://www.coca-colacompany.com/content/dam/journey/us/en/policies/pdf/human-workplace-rights/addressing-global-issues/colombia-sugar-industry-country-report.PDF.

125. Arche Advisors, Colombia Sugar Industry Situational Analysis, March 2015.

126. In this context, class differentiation in terms of having more money and therefore more purchasing power to acquire luxury items, cell phones, and motorcycles.

127. Informant, Yanacona CRIC's representative Popayan, phone conversation with author, March 18, 2021.

128. Miguel Fernandez, president of the Mesa Territorial de Garantias, phone conversation with author March 20, 2021.

129. Población Indígena el Cauca Resultados del Censo Nacional de Población y Vivienda 2018. DANE 2019. https://www.dane.gov.co/files/censo2018/informacion-tecnica/presentaciones-territorio/190814-CNPV-presentacion-Resultados-etnicos-Cauca.pdf.

130. Población Indígena el Cauca Resultados del Censo Nacional de Población y Vivienda 2018.

131. Informant, Yanacona CRIC interview.

132. Informant, Yanacona CRIC interview.

133. Arcadio Mestizo, Former governor of the Huellas *resguardo,* interview with author, Caloto, Cauca. August 22, 2022.

134. Mestizo, interview. The 10,500 inhabitants of Huellas face the main challenge that other communities in Cauca are facing, that is, the increased fragmentation of their small properties of three hectares or less, making it impossible to satisfy their basic food needs and forcing them either to seek jobs outside their *resguardo* to supplement their income or resort to working for the coca and marijuana plantations. According to an informant, in the Huellas' *resguardo* and its surroundings, circa two thousand hectares are planted with coca and marijuana. These crops provide a life support to the subsistence peasant economy.

135. Caballero revealed that Indigenous groups possess documented land titles from the eighteenth and nineteenth centuries that have been used to compel the state to recognize the validity of their claims.

136. http://www.indepaz.org.co/comunidades-indigenas-del-cauca-y-la-lucha-por-la-tierra/.

137. http://www.indepaz.org.co/comunidades-indigenas-del-cauca-y-la-lucha-por-la-tierra/.

138. UAF vary according to land fertility, access to water, location, and type of soil.

139. http://www.indepaz.org.co/comunidades-indigenas-del-cauca-y-la-lucha-por-la-tierra/.

140. Observatorio de Drogas en Colombia 1999–2019. http://www.odc.gov.co/sidco/oferta/cultivos-ilicitos/departamento-municipio. See also https://www.unodc.org/documents/crop-monitoring/Colombia/Colombia_Monitoreo_Cultivos_Ilicitos_2019.pdf.

141. Henry Caballero, CRIC leader, interview with author via WhatsApp, March 2021.

142. Caballero, interview.

143. As quoted by Monica Ribera Rueda, "Las Solicitudes desde las Regiones un año despues del Estallido Social," *El Espectador,* April 28, 2022. https://www.elespectador.com/colombia/mas-regiones/las-solicitudes-desde-los-territorios-un-ano-despues-del-estallido-social/.

144. Monica Ribera Rueda, "Las Solicitudes desde las Regiones un año despues del Estallido Social," *El Espectador,* April 28, 2022. https://www.elespectador.com/colombia/mas-regiones/las-solicitudes-desde-los-territorios-un-año-despues-del-estallido-social/.

145. See Kojin Karatani, *The Structure of World History* (Durham: Duke University Press, 2014).

146. William Paul McGreevy, *An Economic History of Colombia 1845–1930* (Cambridge: Cambridge University Press, 1971), 123–29. Since 1850, the liberal

drive has been to destroy the communal way of life in the *resguardos* by replacing it with individualized land property.

147. Informant 6, Indigenous leader, interview with author via WhatsApp, March 2021.

148. Informant 7, Indigenous leader, interview with author via WhatsApp, April 2021; see also https://colombiareports.com/colombias-barter-markets-no-money-no-free-trade-deal-banning-food/.

149. https://colombiareports.com/colombias-barter-markets-no-money-no-free-trade-deal-banning-food/.

150. Informant, Yanacona CRIC member.

151. Informant, Yanacona CRIC member.

152. Informant, Yanacona CRIC member.

153. Soraya Costante, "Una Universidad Para Formar Exclusivamente Indigenas en Colombia," *El Pais*, September 7, 2021 https://elpais.com/planeta-futuro/2021-09-07/una-universidad-para-formar-exclusivamente-a-indigenas-en-colombia.html.

154. Antonio Gramsci, *Prison Notebooks*, Vol. 1 (New York: Columbia University Press, 1979). Gramsci presented insight into the workings of hegemony exercised by the dominant class, and he also devised a path for subordinate groups to construct their counterhegemonic ideology.

155. This is based on my summary of four interviews.

156. Informant, Yanacona CRIC member.

157. CRIC-Women division, interview with author, Popayan, August 23, 2022.

158. This is based on the information provided by the CRIC-women division, August 23, 2022. It is also to note that in one case, the Delicias resguardo, in the municipality of Buenos Aires women's participation in leadership is high.

159. Caballero, interview

160. Caballero, interview.

Chapter 5. War Rentierism's Impact on Afro-Columbians in Cauca

1. Dane (2005). According to the census there were 4.3 million, Afro-Colombians, constituting 10.4 percent of the population. See https://www.dane.gov.co/files/censo2005/etnia/sys/visibilidoad_estadistica_etnicos.pdf.

2. For a discussion and definition of war rentierism, see chapters 1 and 2. Here, suffice to say that *war rentierism* is a violent process of capital subsumption in which state's agents and private armies collude. This *war rentierism* seeks to eliminate all key social and political obstacles objecting to capital subsumption in strategically defined areas by the state. Cases in point Cauca, Meta, Caquetá, Arauca, Casanare, La Guajira, Cesar Middle Magdalena, Bolivar, Choco, and other

parts of Colombia where extraction of minerals and fossil fuels, agribusiness, and megaprojects are considered critical by the state's planners, chiefly its Department of National Planning.

3. Frank Safford and Marco Palacios, *Colombia: Fragmented Land, Divided Society* (New York: Oxford University Press, 2002), 180; Colombia formed part of New Granada during colonial times.

4. Safford and Palacios, *Colombia: Fragmented Land, Divided Society*, 180.

5. Safford and Palacios, *Colombia: Fragmented Land, Divided Society*, 183.

6. For a discussion on the slave plantation economy in the U.S. South's states and their violence see Sven Bekert, *The Empire of Cotton* (New York: Vintage Press, 2015).

7. Safford and Palacios, *Colombia: Fragmented Land, Divided Society*, 182.

8. Safford and Palacios, *Colombia: Fragmented Land, Divided Society*, 182.

9. Taussig, *Latin American Perspective 1978*.

10. Safford and Palacios, *Colombia: Fragmented Land, Divided Society*, chs 10 and 11.

11. Taussig, *Latin American Perspective 1978*; see also Safford and Palacios, *Colombia: Fragmented Land*, ch. 1.

12. Taussig, *Latin American Perspective 1978*.

13. Taussig, *Latin American Perspective 1978*.

14. Nationally, there are 5,711,496 hectares under the authority of the 276 Community Councils in eleven departments, in which 32. 90% of those councils are located in the Pacific Coast departments of Cauca, Choco, Nariño, and Valle. In these community councils live eighty-five thousand Afro-descendant families, with a total population of one million. See http://www.indepaz.org.co/wp-content/uploads/2018/08/Titulación-Colectiva-para-comunidades-negras-en-Colombia.pdf.

15. Taussig, *Latin American Perspective 1978*. A crucial point that must be emphasized is that under capitalism, especially in the rural areas of the Global South (i.e., peripheries of the peripheries), the dismantling of noncapitalist forms is a historical process that may last a very long time, during which the noncapitalist and capitalist modes subsidize each other, with the first helping to reduce the cost of labor and its reproduction. Hence, noncapitalist activity encourages the accumulation of surplus value both locally and globally through the circuits of food production. This is the essence of subsumption in the twenty-first century in the age of neoliberal globalization, where the dialectical specters of Marx and Luxemburg are vivid.

16. Joseph Stiglitz, "Foreword," in Karl Polanyi, *The Great Transformation: The Political and Economic Origins of Our Time*. 3rd ed., vii–xvii. (Boston: Beacon Press, 2001).

17. Gustavo De Roux, "El Norte del Cauca: aislamiento, resistencia y campesinado," mimeo, Facultad de Sociologia, Universidad del Valle, Cali, 1988.

18. World Bank, "Colombia: Land Policy In Transition," 2004; See also Maria Pazos, Aida Quiñones, Juan Copete, Juan Díaz, Nicolás Vargas-Ramírez, and Alirio Cáceres, "Extractivism, Conflicts, and Defense of Territory: The Case of the Village of La Toma (Cauca-Colombia)," *Desafíos* 28, no. 2 ((2016): 367–409. The Afro-community in La Toma fought against the state's mining laws and multinational corporations. The community council also confronted members of the community who refused the collectivization of their private landholdings, to help enforce the legitimization of the council's authority on the disputed territory as a communal land. It constituted a clear indicator of the processes of subsumption and decomposition. Combined, the confrontations and challenges were succinctly captured by the resistance slogan "El Territorio es la Vida, la Vida no se vende, se ama y se defiende [Land is life not to sell but to love and defend]," as quoted by Pazos, Quiñones et al.

19. See Nazih Richani, *Systems of Violence*, 2013.

20. Nazih Richani, *Systems of Violence*, 2013.

21. Stephen Gill, "Colombia's Neo-Paramilitaries Already Left 320,000 Victims," *Colombia Reports* April 29, 2016. https://colombiareports.com/colombias-neo-paramilitaries-already-left-320000-victims/

22. "La Violencia es mas Fuerte en los Departamentos que producen Oro," OCHA, January 28, 2020. https://reliefweb.int/report/colombia/la-violencia-es-m-s-fuerte-en-los-departamentos-que-producen-oro.

23. Sara Catalina and Oscar Perez, "El Sector Minero-Energetico en Colombia," in *La Mineria en el Posconflicto*, ed. Leon Valencia and Alexander Riano, 93–172 (Bogotá: Grupo Zeta, 2017). The authors attribute the high rates of violence to factors such as mining; see also Irene Vélez, DanielTorres, Sandra Rátiva, Gaona Varela, Andrés Corredor, and Salcedo Fidalgo, "Agroindustria y extractivismo en el Alto Cauca. Impactos sobre los sistemas de subsistencia Afrocampesinos y resistencias (1950–2011)"; https://www.icesi.edu.co/revistas/index.php/revista_cs/article/view/1680; see also relevant economic statistics note 24.

24. https://www.statista.com/statistics/1072849/colombia-services-sector-share-gdp/.

25. Terry Lynn Karl, *The Paradox of Plenty* (Berkeley: The University of California Press, 1997); see also Jeffrey Sanchs, Joseph Stiglitz, and Marcantan Humphrey, *Escaping the Resource Curse* (New York: Columbia University Press, 2007).

26. Arie Arragon, interview with author.

27. See Ivonne Venegas, "Empresas de Ley Paez, A Zonas Francas," *El Tiempo*, February 19, 2008,

28. The state's forfeiting its rent was also observed in the oil and coal rents in which the state practically exempted the multinational corporations from paying royalties by offering them cash benefits. The economist Guillermo Rudas discovered that during circa the last two decades (2000–2016), the state received only sixteen cents for every dollar that the mining, coal, and oil companies made. In Latin

America, Peru and Chile exhibited similar behavior. See "Lo que pierde el Estado por privilegios tributarios a la minería," *Semana*, April 26, 2016. https://www.semana.com/economia/articulo/lo-pierde-estado-privilegios-tributarios-mineria/174393/.

29. "Empresarios Defienden las Zonas Francas del Cauca," *El Pais*, March 30, 2012; see also Empresas de Ley Páez, a zonas francas, Portafolio, https://www.portafolio.co/economia/finanzas/empresas-ley-paez-zonas-francas-266162.

30. Paula Delgado, "Por qué el Estado quiere revivir las Zonas de Desarrollo Empresarial?" *El Espectador*, September 4, 2020. https://www.elespectador.com/economia/por-que-el-estado-quiere-revivir-las-zonas-de-desarrollo-empresarial-article/; accessed August 7, 2021.

31. "Una guerra prolongada y degradada. Dimensiones y modalidades de violencia." http://centrodememoriahistorica.gov.co/descargas/informes2013/basta Ya/capitulos/basta-ya-cap1_30-109.pdf.

32. Laly Catalina Peralta González, "Curules especiales para comunidades negras: ¿realidad o ilusión?" *Estudios Socio Jurídico* 7, no. 2 July/Dec. 2005). http://www.scielo.org.co/scielo.php?script=sci_arttext&pid=S0124-0579200500020000.

33. http://www.scielo.org.co/scielo.php?script=sci_arttext&pid=S0124-05 792005000200006.

34. http://www.scielo.org.co/scielo.php?script=sci_arttext&pid=S0124-05792 005000200006.

35. Yuri Evelin Collazos Tintinago, "Procesos de industrializacion y tranformaciones sociales del Campesinado en Guachene (Cauca) 1970–2015," unpublished MA thesis. http://repositorio.unicauca.edu.co:8080/xmlui/bitstream/handle/123456789/148/PROCESOS%20DE%20INDRUSTRIALIZACIÓN%20Y%20TRANSFORMACIONES%20SOCIALES%20DEL%20CAMPESINADO%20EN%20GUACHENÉ%20%28CAUCA%29%201970-2015.pdf?sequence=1&isAllowed=y.

36. Victor Pizarro, member of the Community Council of Caloto, phone interview with author, July 7, 2021.

37. This information is based on interviews with informants from Caloto, Puerto Tejada, and Suarez,Villarica interviewed by author, April 2021.

38. Felipe Aragon, Representative of Organizations of Unified Afro-Caucans (*Unidad de Organizaciones Afrocaucanas*, UOAFROC), phone interview with author Monday April 5, 2021; Arie Aragon, former mayor of Villarica and president of the Association of the House of the Child, phone interview with author, April 21, 2021.

39. Sven Beckert, *The Empire of Cotton* (New York: Vintage, 2015); see also Kenneth Pomerantz, *The Great Divergence: China, Europe, and the Making of the Modern World Economy* (Princeton: Princeton University Press, 2021).

40. Arie Aragon, interview. He said that most of the land in northern Cauca is owned by Cali's capitalist; see also Jose Antonio Solano, "La Actividad Empresarial Desarrollada por la Comunidad de Villarica, Cauca." https://www.redalyc.org/pdf/1053/105317711003.pdf.

41. Solano.; see also Rebecca Bratspies, "'Territory Is Everything': Afro-Colombian Communities, Human Rights and Illegal Land Grabs," May 27, 2020. http://hrlr.law.columbia.edu/hrlr-online/territory-is-everything-afro-colombian-communities-human-rights-and-illegal-land-grabs/#post-1520-_Toc39567528. States "outsourcing" security to private groups is cost effective politically and has been used in multiple countries such as Haiti and Lebanon (1975–1990), as well as by death squads in Peru, Honduras, Guatemala, El Salvador, and Nicaragua, in Italy during the late nineteenth and early decades of the twentieth century, among many other cases. For a good discussion of state's outsourcing security see Rachel Kleinfield, *Savage Order* (New York: Pantheon Books, 2018).

42. Bettina Ng'weno, "Puede La etnicidad Remplazar lo Racial? Afro Colombianos, Indiginidad y El Estado Multicultural en Colombia," *Revista Colombiana de Antropologia* 49, no. 1 (Enero-Julio 2013): 71–104; See also Ng'weno, *Turf Wars: Territory and Citizenship in the Contemporary State* (Stanford: Stanford University Press, 2007).

43. The ethnopolitical polarization in north Cauca reached new heights in 2022 when Indigenous allegedly attacked an Afro-Colombian in the village of Alto del Palo in the municipality of Caloto. See https://www.eltiempo.com/colombia/otras-ciudades/dos-heridos-en-enfrentamientos-por-tierras-en-el-norte-del-cauca-696723. Indigenous representatives of various *resguardos* in north Cauca expressed views that demonstrated their grievances with other ethnic groups by emphasizing their cultural differences and underplaying common class interests as peasants. Association of Indigenous Cabildos in north Cauca (ACIM), interview with author, Santander de Quilichao, August 25, 2022.

44. Bettina Ng'weno, "Puede La etnicidad Remplazar lo Racial?"

45. Verdad Abierta, "En Buenos Aires se pararon en la raya," March 7, 2014. https://verdadabierta.com/en-buenos-aires-se-pararon-en-la-raya/.

46. https://afgj.org/seven-afro-colombian-massacred-in-cauca-siete-afro colombianos-masacrados-en-cauca, and in 2022 it reported several assassinations in the municipality of Buenos Aires, which has become a corridor for narco traffickers, therefore the interplay of gold mining and narcocorridors character-izes the root cause of disputes and conflict. See https://www.telesurtv.net/news/indepaz-denuncia-nueva-masacre-colombia-cauca-20220128-0022.html.

47. Arie Aragon, interview 2021. By 2022, the state had granted lands to six community councils in the north and two in southern Cauca. However, most of the community council's granted lands in northern Cauca remained depen-dent on sugar cane production either by renting their lands to the sugar mill's owners or selling the mills their sugar cane production. This is another example of capitalist subsumption, based on the information collected during my field trip to Cauca in August 2022; see also https://renacientes.net/blog/2022/08/09/la-agencia-nacional-de-tierras-entrega-los-titulos-colectivos-de-dos-consejos-comunitarios-en-el-cauca-en-el-marco-del-convenio-de-asociacion-con-el-proceso-

de-comunidades-negras-pnc/. The number of hectares granted as community lands in the north are distributed as follow: Bodega Guali, Caloto: 9.6 hectares; Rio Palo, Puerto Tejada: 89.6 hectares; Monte Oscuro: 44.8 hectares; Pilamo, Guachene, 576 hectares; Rio Cauca, De los Rios, Teta Mazamorrero 24,000 hectares, which includes protected areas. Data obtained from Casa del Nino, Villa Rica, Cauca. August 2022.

48. https://www.anm.gov.co/sites/default/files/DocumentosAnm/bullets_cauca_01-06-2017.pdf.

49. https://mneguidelines.oecd.org/South-West-Colombia-Gold-Mining-EN.pdf.

50. https://mneguidelines.oecd.org/South-West-Colombia-Gold-Mining-EN.pdf.

51. https://colombiareports.com/66-of-colombias-gold-is-mined-illegally-un-study/.

52. https://mneguidelines.oecd.org/South-West-Colombia-Gold-Mining-EN.pdf.

53. In a study of 110 cases that came before the courts 91 percent of the judgements came in favor of the extractive companies against the peasants whose lands were usurped. See Ana Jimena Bautista, Revelo, Leonel Plazas Mendieta, "Tensiones Entre la Política Extractivista y la Restitución de Tierras y los Derechos Territoriales," *Verdad Abierta*, 2018; https://movimientodevictimas.org/sites/default/files/Investigación%20tierras%20LIBRO%20COMPLETO.pdf.

54. Karl Marx, *Grundrisse* (New York: Penguin, 1993), 275–81.

55. https://mneguidelines.oecd.org/South-West-Colombia-Gold-Mining-EN.pdf.

56. *Redaccion Nacional*, "A tres ascienden víctimas ortals de ataque en Santander de Quilichao (Cauca)." https://www.elespectador.com/colombia/mas-regiones/tres-personas-murieron-en-una-nueva-masacre-en-santander-de-quilichao-cauca/?cx_testId=24&cx_testVariant=cx_1&cx_artPos=0#cxrecs_s; See Indicadores sociodemograficos Censo 2005. https://www.dane.gov.co/files/censo2005/etnia/sys/Afro_indicadores_sociodemograficos_censo2005.pdf; An informant, owner of small restaurant, interview with author Santander de Quilichao, August 25, 2022, described that the spread of coca plantations and marijuana have resuscitated the economy of the municipality but also brought other sets of problems such as drug consumption and criminal violence.

57. *Redaccion Nacional*, "Racha de violencia en Cauca obliga a construir base militar en Caloto," *Semana*, March 31,2021. https://www.semana.com/nacion/articulo/racha-de-violencia-en-cauca-obliga-a-construir-base-militar-en-caloto/202145/.

58. https://mneguidelines.oecd.org/South-West-Colombia-Gold-Mining-EN.pdf.

59. It is important to note that the illegal medium and large mining companies owned by entrepreneurs from outside Cauca that have been lured by the

riches of the area are called "foreigners" (*forraneos*) by locals and have become an active force protecting their operations with paramilitaries. These latter target individuals that object to their extractive activities, which use heavy machines that destroy the environment and water resources. They operate alongside multinational corporations such Gold Ashanti and its affiliate Kedahda SA. This latter ended up with a land title of fifty thousand hectares located between the municipalities of Suarez and Buenos Aires. See Daniel Varela, "Agroindustria y extractivismo en el Alto Cauca. Impactos sobre los sistemas de subsistencia Afro-campesinos y resistencias (1950–2011)." https://www.academia.edu/34540257/ Agroindustria_y_extractivismo_en_el_Alto_Cauca_Impactos_sobre_los_sistemas_ de_subsistencia_Afro_campesinos_y_resistencias_1950_2011_?auto=download& email_work_card=download-paper.

60. *Verdad Abierta* 2014. In the municipality of Suarez there are thirteen mining titles for gold extraction and other minerals, including coal and other precious metals, and twenty-six requests for licenses, of which twenty-one include gold extraction, five copper, three coal, and three unspecified; one solicitation was for the exploration and extraction of molybdenum, a metal that has never been exploited in Cauca. It is worth mentioning that Suarez's population is nineteen thousand, of which 58.2 percent are Afro-Colombians and 21.2 percent Indigenous. And 81.52 percent is classified as rural based on agriculture and artisanal mining. Multinational corporations there include Anglo Gold Ashanti (South Africa–based) and Anglo Gold (U.S.-based). See Anabel Arias Cuéllar, "Conflicto minero y organizaciones étnicas: Cabildo Indígena Nasa de Cerro Tijeras y Consejo Comunitario Afrodescendiente de La Toma en Resistencia," unpublished dissertation, Valle University, Cali, 2015, 310; see also https://revistas.icanh.gov. co/index.php/rca/article/view/3/3.

61. https://mneguidelines.oecd.org/South-West-Colombia-Gold-Mining-EN. pdf.

62. https://mneguidelines.oecd.org/South-West-Colombia-Gold-Mining-EN. pdf.; Giraldo and Duque, Ltd. are major miners in the municipality of Buenos Aires–Teta Hill, which is the second most important producer of gold in Cauca and the thirtieth nationwide. See Edomond Bolanos, "Magnetes de Oro contra Pequenos mineros," http://consejoderedaccion.org/webs/conflictoypaz/ magnates-del-oro-pequenos-mineros.

63. Arie Aragon, interview with author.

64. http://repositorio.unicauca.edu.co:8080/xmlui/bitstream/handle/ 123456789/148/PROCESOS%20DE%20INDRUSTRIALIZACIÓN%20Y%20 TRANSFORMACIONES%20SOCIALES%20DEL%20CAMPESINADO%20EN%20 GUACHENÉ%20%28CAUCA%29%201970-2015.pdf?sequence=1&isAllowed=y.

65. Informant, Puerto Tejada, government official and member of the Community Council of Rio Palo, phone interview with author, August 5, 2021.

66. Informant, Puerto Tejada, interview.

67. Paul Oquist, *Violencia, conflicto y política en Colombia* (Bogotá: Instituto de Estudios Colombianos, 1978).

68. Robinson Alejandro Burbano Vega, "De la Violencia Campesina al Sectarianismo en el Cauca 1938–1953," *Anuario de Historia Regional y de las Fronteras* 24, no. 2 (2019): 175–94. https://www.redalyc.org/journal/4075/407564498008/html/

69. Robinson Alejandro Burbano Vega, "De la Violencia Campesina al Sectarianismo en el Cauca 1938–1953."

70. Michael Taussig, *The Devil and Commodity Fetishism in South America* (Chapel Hill: University of North Carolina, 1980), 83.

71. Michael Taussig, *The Devil and Commodity Fetishism in South America* (Chapel Hill: University of North Carolina, 1980), 83.

72. Michael Taussig, *The Devil and Commodity Fetishism in South America* (Chapel Hill: University of North Carolina, 1980), 83.

73. Michael Taussig, *The Devil and Commodity Fetishism in South America* (Chapel Hill: University of North Carolina, 1980), 83.

74. Informant, Defensoria del Pueblo, interview, November 2021.

75. Informant, Puerto Tejada, interview.

76. https://www.minjusticia.gov.co/Sala-de-prensa/PublicacionesMinJusticia/mayo%2031%20Diagnóstico%20del%20Fenómeno%20de%20Pandillas%20en%20Colombia%20(4).pdf; See also Anthony Dest, "Coca Enclosure: Autonomy Against Accumulation in Colombia," *World Development*, 2020. Dest discusses how the new of wave of colonizers have propelled coca cultivation in northern Cauca, which in turn has created socioeconomic and cultural changes undermining the subsistence economy.

77. Informant, Puerto Tejada, interview.

78. I define a war system as pattern of interaction among different violent actors sustained over time. See N. Richani, *Systems of Violence: The Political Economy of War and Peace in Colombia* (Albany: State University of New York Press, 2014), ch. 1.

79. https://www.cidh.oas.org/indigenas/colombia.11.101.htm.

80. https://www.cidh.oas.org/indigenas/colombia.11.101.htm.

81. Informant, Puerto Tejada, interview.

82. Miguel Fernandez, interview.

83. The state granted the lands in 2022 without any assistance which forced the two councils to sign contracts with Ingenio Cauca (Cauca Sugar Mill), renting part of their land and their labor in order to secure cash to fund their plantations of subsistence crops.

84. Arie Aragon, former mayor of Villa Rica, interview with author, Villa Rica, Cauca, August 26, 2022; informant, interview with author, Villa Rica, August 26, 2022.

85. Interviews 2021; and also https://mneguidelines.oecd.org/South-West-Colombia-Gold-Mining-EN.pdf.

86. Interviews 2021.

87. Interviews 2021.

88. "La Violencia es mas Fuerte en los Departamentos que producen Oro," OCHA January 28, 2020. https://reliefweb.int/report/colombia/la-violencia-es-m-s-fuerte-en-los-departamentos-que-producen-oro.

89. https://mneguidelines.oecd.org/South-West-Colombia-Gold-Mining-EN.pdf.

90. For a critique see Kees Jansen, Mark Vicol, and Lissete Nikol, "Autonomy and Repeasantization: Conceptual, Analytical, and Methodological Problems," *Autonomy in Agrarian Studies, Politics, and Movements* 22, no. 3 (July 2022): 489–505.

91. https://www.amwenglish.com/articles/armed-strike-by-eln-in-cauca-colombia/.

92. *El Tiempo* 2014; Yilver Mosquera-Vallejo and Alex Paulsen Espinoza, "Geografía del extractivismo: conflicto socioambiental en el Río Sambingo. Reflexiones desde la ética ambiental, 2020, 1–19. 10.37838/unicen/est.07-043.

93. https://www.unodc.org/documents/crop-monitoring/Colombia/Colombia_Monitoreo_Cultivos_Ilicitos_2019.pdf; the Ministry of National Defense found that 20 percent of the total illicit plantings detected as of October 2015 are in forest reserves, 8 percent in national parks, 11 percent in Indigenous reserves, 15 percent in collective properties of Afro-descendent communities, and 12 percent in border areas, as quoted by http://www.thedialogue.org/wp-content/uploads/2017/01/Colombia-report-Eng_Web-Res_Final-for-web.pdf.

94. Victor Pizarro, member of the Community Council of Caloto, interview.

95. https://www.unodc.org/documents/crop-monitoring/Colombia/Colombia_Monitoreo_Cultivos_Ilicitos_2019.pdf.

96. Nacion, ""Tenemos información de la presencia en el Cauca del Cartel de Sinaloa y Jalisco Nueva Generación": las revelaciones del defensor del pueblo," *Semana*, February 4, 2021. https://www.semana.com/nacion/articulo/tenemos-informacion-de-la-presencia-en-el-cauca-del-cartel-de-sinaloa-y-jalisco-nueva-generacion-las-revelaciones-del-defensor-del-pueblo/202156/.

97. Fernando Dorado, "Santander de Quilichao y el Cauca se convertirán en el Culiacán y el Sinaloa colombianos?" *Las Dos Orillas*, October 30, 2019. https://www.las2orillas.co/santander-de-quilichao-y-el-cauca-se-convertiran-en-el-culiacan-y-el-sinaloa-colombianos/.

98. Fernando Dorado, "Santander de Quilichao y el Cauca se convertirán en el Culiacán y el Sinaloa colombianos?" *Las Dos Orillas*, October 30, 2019.

99. Fernando Dorado, "Santander de Quilichao y el Cauca se convertirán en el Culiacán y el Sinaloa colombianos?" *Las Dos Orillas*, October 30, 2019.

100. Gentil Duarte was killed in an ambush in Venezuela in May 2022. His faction is expected to continue its activities in Cauca, Meta, Narino Caqueta, Putumayo, and North Santander.

101. Arie Aragon, former mayor of Villarica and actual director of the Cultural Association Casa del Nino, phone conversation with author, April 21, 2021.

102. Aragon, interview.

103. Aragon, interview.

104. Aragon, interview.

105. Aragon, interview.

106. Aragon, interview.

107. Aragon, interview. There are three factors that can explain the laxity of state's behavior. One, mining (legal and illegal) foments rentierism, which coincides with the state's overarching policy. Two is the ability of the groups engaged in illegal mining to coopt the state's agents (police and army) in charge of policing this activity. Finally, the illegal mining groups are violent entrepreneurs who target individuals and groups that oppose mining and in that they also coincide with the state's interests and the interests of multinational corporations and other dominant groups. These observations are based on my interviews.

108. Aragon, interview.

109. Andrés Felipe, Jacobo Cortes, Marcela Escandón Vega, and Richard André, "Political Representation and Social Inclusion," *Colombia Case Study*. https://www.as-coa.org/sites/default/files/ColombiaFINAL.pdf.

110. Fernando Giraldo García and José Daniel López Jiménez, "Mecanismos de participación política electoral afrodescendiente en Colombia," in *Estudios sobre la Representacion Politica de la Poblacion Afrodecendiete: La ExpAriencia en Colombia*, Instituto Interamericano de Derechos Humanos, 2007. https://www.corteidh.or.cr/tablas/24812.pdf.

111. Washington Office on Latin America, January 29, 2015. http://colombiapeace.org/2015/01/29/interview-on-colombias-peace-process-with-danny-ramirez-of-the-national-conference-of-afro-colombian-organizations/.

112. Arie Aragon, interview.

113. The Colombian justice system lacks an information-gathering function that might help in identifying discriminatory practices against minorities.

114. https://co.usembassy.gov/wp-content/uploads/sites/103/COLOMBIA-2020-HUMAN-RIGHTS-REPORT.pdf; see also https://www.dejusticia.org/wp-content/uploads/2017/04/fi_name_recurso_204.pdf. Afro-Colombians, according to DeJusticia, are the most frequent victims of internal displacement, followed by the Indigenous.

115. https://co.usembassy.gov/wp-content/uploads/sites/103/COLOMBIA-2020-HUMAN-RIGHTS-REPORT.pdf; see also https://www.dejusticia.org/wp-content/uploads/2017/04/fi_name_recurso_204.pdf.

116. https://www.fucsia.co/actualidad/personajes/articulo/afrocolombianidad-mujer-afrodescendiente-en-colombia/63212.

117. http://www.cidh.org/countryrep/colombiamujeres06sp/iv.htm#_ftnref 143.

118. http://www.cidh.org/countryrep/colombiamujeres06sp/iv.htm#_ftnref 143.

119. https://tbinternet.ohchr.org/Treaties/CEDAW/Shared%20Documents/ COL/INT_CEDAW_NGO_COL_15183_S.pdf.

120. https://tbinternet.ohchr.org/Treaties/CEDAW/Shared%20Documents/ COL/INT_CEDAW_NGO_COL_15183_S.pdf.

121. https://tbinternet.ohchr.org/Treaties/CEDAW/Shared%20Documents/ COL/INT_CEDAW_NGO_COL_15183_S.pdf; https://repositorio.banrep.gov.co/ bitstream/handle/20.500.12134/3000/dtser_95.pdf?sequence=1&isAllowed=y.

122. https://tbinternet.ohchr.org/Treaties/CEDAW/Shared%20Documents/ COL/INT_CEDAW_NGO_COL_15183_S.pdf; https://repositorio.banrep.gov.co/ bitstream/handle/20.500.12134/3000/dtser_95.pdf?sequence=1&isAllowed=y.; see also DANE 2012.

123. This observation is based on various interviews, including with Arie Aragon and Miguel Fernandez.

124. Jan Douwe van der Ploeg, *The New Peasantries: Rural Development in Times of Globalization*, 2nd ed. (New York: Routledge, 2018), chs. 1, 2, 5, and 7.

Conclusion

1. The transnationalization of the peasant movement in Latin America has become a significant source of empowerment, bolstering human rights and legal protections. Colombian peasant organizations, including Indigenous and Afro-Colombian, are active participants in groups such as La Via Campesina, among others, enhancing their capabilities to resist capital subsumption. Other Latin American peasant groups are actively sharing in this global effort. One case in point is that of the Seri people, also known as Comcaac, in Punta Chueca, Mexico. This nation of only one thousand people struggling to survive is drawing on international experiences such as how to build and repair solar panels and storage batteries, in the Indian state of Rajasthan. Three Seri women spent six months in India learning about solar engineering, to bolster their chances of survival in an adverse, unforgiving environment. This small community is confronting as many challenges as the peasants of Colombia, including mining companies, drug trafficking, climate change, governmental neglect, and marginalization. See Nuria Lopez Torres, "An Intimate Look at Mexico's Indigenous Seri People," *New York Times*, Monday, June 6, 2022.

2. Rosa Luxemburg, *The Accumulation of Capital* (New York: Routledge, 2003), 397.

3. Rosa Luxemburg, *The Accumulation of Capital*, 362–63; see also Abhijit Banerjee and Esther Duflo, *Good Economics for Hard Times* (New York: Hachette, 2019).

4. Dario Fajardo, *Las Zonas De Reserva Campesina Retos y Experiencias Significativas en su Implementacion* (Bogotá: FAO, 2019).

5. Amparo Murillo, *Historia y Sociedad en el Magdalena Medio*, 50.

6. Amparo Murillo, *Historia y Sociedad en el Magdalena Medio*, 50.

7. Carlos Martines, Member of the Directorate and founding member of the Reserve. Interview, Cimitarra. August 2018.

8. Liz Alderman, "France's Desperate Quest to 'Make Agriculture Sexy,'" *New York Times*, Friday, October 8, 2021, B1. What is making France and others search for search for sustainable agriculture is the necessity to mitigate climate change. In France, for example 20 percent of greenhouse emissions come from agriculture.

9. See Marc Edelman, "Bringing the Moral Economy back in . . . to the Study of the 21st Century Transnational Peasant Movements," *American Anthropologist* 107, no. 3. Edelman highlighted that peasant movements empowered with new knowledge, conceptions of solidarity, tools of struggle are very different from what some urban elites and academics still imagine them to be.

10. https://statistics.cepal.org/portal/cepalstat/dashboard.html?theme=1 &lang=es.

11. Nazih Richani, *Systems of Violence*.

12. https://www.portafolio.co/economia/finanzas/colombia-tendria-tierra-cara-region-estudio-sac-340630.

13. In Colombia, because the costs of production are concentrated chiefly in land rents. For a hectare of sugar cane production, costs are the highest in the world: 82 percent more than China's, 75percent more than Brazil's, 63 percent more than Guatemala's, 42 percent more than Thailand's; 28 percent more than Australia's, and 6 percent more than South Africa's. The president of Procaña, JoséVicente Irurtia, announced that prices of land in el Valle del Cauca are the highest in the world (*El País* 2007), as quoted by Héctor Mondragón, in "Colombia: La locomotora del agro y su impacto ambiental y socioeconómico. Los campesinos tienen un Proyecto," August 2, 2011. https://www.farmlandgrab. org/post/view/19025-colombia-la-locomotora-del-agro-y-su-impacto-ambiental-y-socioeconomico-los-campesinos-tienen-un-proyecto; According to a study by the Association of Agrarian Producers (SAC) https://www.portafolio.co/economia/ finanzas/colombia-tendria-tierra-cara-region-estudio-sac-340630.

14. Richani, *Systems of Violence*.

15. Pierre Gilhodés, *Las luchas agrarias en Colombia* (Bogotá: ECOE, 1988), 35.

16. Eduardo Pizarro Leongomez, "Los Origenes del Movimiento Armado Communista en Colombia," *Analysis Politico* no.7 (Mayo 1989): 7–31.

17. Taryn Devereux, "Gender Dynamics in the Adoption of Climate Adaptation Practices: A Case Study in the Cauca Department of Colombia," MA thesis, 2014. https://ufdcimages.uflib.ufl.edu/AA/00/02/38/02/00001/Field%20 Practicum%20Report_Devereux.pdf.

18. Nacion, "Advierten en 10 Anos Colombia no Tendria Quien Siembra Comida," *Semana*, January 25, 2022. https://www.semana.com/nacion/articulo/advierten-que-en-10-anos-colombia-no-tendria-quien-siembre-comida/202209/.

19. Redaccion Nacional, "A tres ascienden víctimas mortales de ataque en Santander de Quilichao (Cauca)." https://www.elespectador.com/colombia/mas-regiones/tres-personas-murieron-en-una-nueva-masacre-en-santander-de-quilichao-cauca/?cx_testId=24&cx_testVariant=cx_1&cx_artPos=0#cxrecs_s; See Indicadores sociodemograficos Censo 2005. https://www.dane.gov.co/files/censo2005/etnia/sys/Afro_indicadores_sociodemograficos_censo2005.pdf.

20. https://www.litefinance.com/blog/analysts-opinions/gold-price-prediction-forecast/.

Postscript

1. https://www.larepublica.co/economia/colombia-solo-tiene-cultivado-17-5-de-hectareas-del-total-de-su-potencial-agricola-3226800.

2. https://www.dane.gov.co/index.php/estadisticas-por-tema/agropecuario/encuesta-nacional-agropecuaria-ena.

3. Citing OXFAM; see https://cpt.org/es/2021/07/06/colombia-land-ownership-mother-all-conflicts.

4. https://cpt.org/es/2021/07/06/colombia-land-ownership-mother-all-conflicts. Most lots are, on average, two hectares.

5. Manuel Salazar, "Las Millonarias Cifras Detras de Las Importaciones de Alimentos a Colombia," *Bloomberglinea*, Februrary 2, 2022. https://www.bloomberglinea.com/2022/01/23/las-millonarias-cifras-detras-de-las-importaciones-de-alimentos-a-colombia/. Colombia, in addition to importing corn, is also importing wheat and soya and other cereals.

6. https://www.youtube.com/watch?v=W6kqRFLba4k. The figure is for 2021, Colombia is the second-largest importer of corn in Latin America after Mexico, and the eighth in the world. See Daniel Workman, "Corn Imports by Country 2021, World's Top Exports." https://www.worldstopexports.com/corn-imports-by-country/

7. See Ocampo interview https://www.youtube.com/watch?v=W6kqRFLba4k.

8. https://www.infobae.com/america/colombia/2022/11/23/gustavo-petro-habla-del-aporte-de-fedegan-a-reforma-agraria-el-de-mas-atras-ideologicamente-se-atrevio-a-dar-un-paso/.

9. Ocampo interview https://www.youtube.com/watch?v=W6kqRFLba4k.

10. https://www.elpais.com.co/politica/esto-es-lo-que-ha-pasado-con-la-restitucion-de-tierras-en-colombia.html.

11. "Growth without development" captures the essence of capitalism benefiting the dominant class while most of the population receives the bare minimum to survive, coupled with environmental degradation. That is, we can have high

levels of GDP growth with negative human development in terms of quality of life and the natural environment.

12. https://www.semana.com/economia/macroeconomia/articulo/este-es-el-plan-del-entrante-ministro-de-hacienda-con-ecopetrol/202200/.

13. See Santiago Gomez Hernandez, "What Is the Theory of Degrowth: Gustavo Petro's Development Proposal," *Latin American Post*, September 7, 2022; https://latinamericanpost.com/41968-what-is-the-theory-of-degrowth-gustavo-petros-development-proposal. For a wider discussion on De-growth theory see Matthias Schmelzer, Andrea Vetter, and Aaron Vansistjan, *The Future Is Degrowth: A Guide to a World Beyond Capitalism* (New York: Verso, 2022).

14. Schmelzer, Vetter, and Vansistjan, *The Future Is Degrowth*, 128.

15. Schmelzer, Vetter, and Vansistjan, *The Future Is Degrowth*, 118–19.

16. https://www.elespectador.com/colombia-20/paz-y-memoria/reforma-agraria-de-petro-no-sera-la-de-los-anos-sesenta-sino-la-del-acuerdo-de-paz-jhenifer-mojica/.

17. https://www.elespectador.com/colombia-20/paz-y-memoria/reforma-agraria-de-petro-no-sera-la-de-los-anos-sesenta-sino-la-del-acuerdo-de-paz-jhenifer-mojica/.

18. https://www.elespectador.com/colombia-20/paz-y-memoria/reforma-agraria-de-petro-no-sela-de-los-anos-sesenta-sino-la-del-acuerdo-de-paz-jhenifer-mojica/. In December 2022, three new peasant reserves were recognized, with a surface area of circa four hundred thousand hectares. These three Reserves are: Sumapaz (Cundinamarca) with an area of 23,765 hectares and 1,723 peasant families; Güejar-Cafre in the department of Meta with an area of 3,3694 hectares and a population of 1,246 people; Losada-Guayabero, also in Meta, with an area of 163,906 hectares benefiting 7,646 peasants. This was in addition of recognizing 297,000 hectares that were de facto occupied by ten *resguardos* of indigenous groups in different departments. See https://www.elespectador.com/colombia-20/paz-y-memoria/primera-titulacion-de-tierra-de-gobierno-petro-indigenas-reciben-297000-hectareas/?cx_testId=49&cx_testVariant=cx_1&cx_artPos=0#cxrecs_s.

19. http://consejoderedaccion.org/webs/documentos/Respuesta%20Agen-cia%20Nacional%20de%20Tierras.pdf.

Bibliography

Acemoglu, Daron, and James Robinson. 2012. *Why Nations Fail: The Origins of Power, Prosperity, and Poverty*. New York: Random House.

ACVC. 2018. (Informants 1, 2, 3), interviews with author, Puerto Matilde, Cimitarra, August.

ACVC leader. 2018. (Informant 4), interview with author, Puerto Matilde, August.

ACVC member. 2018. (Informant 5), interview with author, Puerto Matilde, August 5.

ACVC leader. 2018. (Informant 6), interview with author, Puerto Matilde, August.

ACVC. 2000. Plan de Desarrollo. https://www.prensarural.org/acvc/plande sarrollozrc.pdf.

Alderman, Liz. 2021. "France's Desperate Quest to 'Make Agriculture Sexy.'" *New York Times*, October 8, B1. https://statistics.cepal.org/portal/cepalstat/dashboard.html?theme=1&lang=es.

Alliance for Global Justice. 2021. "Seven Afro-Colombians Massacred in Cauca." September 20. https://afgj.org/seven-afro-colombian-massacred-in-cauca-siete-afrocolombianos-masacrados-en-cauca.

Altamirano Rayo, Giorleny. 2017. "Securing Territory: State Interests and the Implementation of Ethnic Land Rights in the Americas." PhD dissertation, University of Texas, Austin. https://repositories.lib.utexas.edu/bitstream/handle/2152/62324/ALTAMIRANORAYO-DISSERTATION-2017.pdf.

Altieri, Miguel. 2009. "Agroecology, Small Farms, and Food Sovereignty." *Monthly Review* 61, no. 3: 102–13.

Álvarez, Andrés M., and Jimena Hurtado Guiot-Isaac. 2017. "The Quarrel of Development Experts: Lauchlin Currie and Albert O. Hirschman in Colombia." Bogota CEDE, no. 39. Universidad de los Andes, June. https://repositorio.uniandes.edu.co/bitstream/handle/1992/8728/dcede2017-39.pdf?sequence=1&isAllowed=y.

Alvarez, Jairo Estrada. 2005. *Intellectuales, technocratas y Reformas Neoliberales en America Latina*. Bogotá: National University of Colombia.

Amin, Samir. 2019. *The Long Revolution of the Global South: Toward a New Anti-Imperialist International.* New York: Monthly.

———. 1985. "Modes of Production, History and Unequal Development." *Science & Society* 49, no. 2 (Summer): 194–207.

Anderson, Lisa. 1987. *The State and Social Transformation in Tunisia and Libya, 1820–1980.* Princeton: Princeton University Press.

Andres Gutierrez, Lorenzo. ND. "Occupacion Y Tenencia De La Tierra eb la Region El Pato-Balsillas, San Vicente Del Caguan: Entre lo Legitimo Y lo Legal." Unpublished paper.

Antonio Solano, Jose. "La Actividad Empresarial Desarrollada por la Comunidad de Villarica, Cauca." https://www.redalyc.org/pdf/1053/105317711003.pdf.

Aragon, Arie. 2021. Phone interview with author, April 21.

Aragon, Felipe. 2021. Phone interview with author, April 5.

Araujo, Andres Castro. 2015. "Los economistas colombianos y el problema de la 'desigualdad." Unpublished Thesis. Bogotà: Universiad del Rosario. https://repository.urosario.edu.co/bitstream/handle/10336/12226/Los-economistas-colombianos-y-el-problema-de-la-desigualdad—Andres-Castro.pdf?sequence=1.

Arche Advisors. 2015. *Colombia Sugar Industry Situational Analysis.* March.

Asociacion Campesina Del Valle Del Rio Cimitarra Zona De Reserva Campesina Valle del Rio Cimitarra. 2014. *Plan de Desarrollo Sostenible.*

Aubad, Rafael. 2017. Interview with author, Medellin, August 16.

Avila, Ricardo. 2020. "La Apertura en Colombia Mito o Realidad." *El tiempo*, February 15. https://www.eltiempo.com/economia/sectores/la-apertura-en-colombia-mito-o-realidad-462678.

Bagley, Bruce. 1979. "Political Power, Public Policy, and the State in Colombia: Case Studies of the Urban and Agrarian Reforms during the National Front, 1958–1974." PhD diss., UCLA.

Balcazar V. 1994. "La Ganadería Bovina en Colombia 1970–1991." In *Transformaciones en la Estructura Agraria*, edited by Salomon Kalmanovitz et al. Bogotá: Tercer Mundo Editores.

Banerjee, Abhijit, and Esther Duflo. 2019. *Good Economics for Hard Times.* New York: Public Affairs.

Bartra, Roger. 1974. *Estructura Agraria y Clases Sociales en Mexico* (Mexico City: Instituto de Investigaciones Sociales de la UNAM).

———. 1975. "Peasants and Political Power in Mexico: A Theoretical Model." *Latin American Perspectives* II (Summer).

Bautista, Ana Jimena, Revelo Leonel Plazas Mendieta. 2018. "Tensiones entre la Política Extractivista y la Restituciòn de Tierras y los Derechos Territoriales. *Verdad Abierta.* https://verdadabierta.com/wp-content/uploads/2018/05/Estudio-Tensiones-entre-la-pol%C3%ADtica-extractivista-y-la-restitución-de-tierras.pdf.

Beblawi, Hazem. 1990. "The Rentier State in the Arab World." In Giacomo Luciani, *The Arab State*. Berkeley: University of California Press.

Beckert, Sven. 2015. *The Empire of Cotton*. New York: Vintage.

Bedoya, Javier Andres. 2019. *Colono* from Balsillas. https://www.semillas.org.co/es/revista/primera-zona-de-reserva-campesina-del-pato. https://semillas.org.co/apc-aa-files/353467686e6667686b6c676668f16c6c/articulo%2019.pdf.

Benitez, Regis Manuel. 2001. *La Problematica de la Agricultura Tradicional Campesina*. Bogotá: Contraloria General de la Republica.

Bernestein, H. 2003. "Farewells to the Peasantry." *Transformation Critical Perspectives on Southern Africa* 52, no. 1 (January):1–19.

———. 1979. "Concepts for the Analysis of Contemporary Peasantries." https://sunypress.edu/content/download/452117/5500388/version/1/file/978087 3954846_imported2_excerpt.pdf.

———, and T. J. Byres. 2001."From Peasant Studies to Agrarian Change." *Journal of Agrarian Change* 1, no. 1: 1–56.

Berry, Albert. 2004. "Has Colombia Finally Found an Agrarian Reform that Works." *Revista de Economia Institucional* 4, no. 6.

———. 2017. *Avance y Fracaso en el Agro Colombiano Siglos XX y XXI*. Bogotá: Universidad del Rosario.

———. https://www.peri.umass.edu/fileadmin/pdf/conference_papers/Berry-AGREF_1_.10.pdf.

———. 2017. "Reflections on Injustice, Inequality, and Land Conflict in Colombia." *Canadian Journal of Latin American and Caribbean Studies / Revue canadienne des études latino-américaines et caraïbes* 42, no. 3: 277–97.

———. 1998. "La Reforma Agraria en Colombia." Unpublished chapter.

Betancourt, C. 2008. "Las Necessidades de Financiamento de la Politica de Atencion a la Poblacion Desplazada," Comisión de Seguimiento, Cuarto Informe a la Corte, Anexo 2. April 30.

Blanco, Sergio Herrero. 2012. "Reconfiguración territorial y cultivo de palma africana en el Magdalena Medio. El caso de San pablo sur de Bolívar." Tesis de Maestría. Pontificia Universidad Javeriana, Facultad de Ciencia Política, Estudios Latinoamericanos. http://hdl.handle.net/10554/2345.

Blanco, Yenly Angelica. 2013. "Derecho a la Tierra y al Territorio, Justicia y Zonas de Rerserva Campesina: EL Caso del Valle del Rio Cimitarra." https://repository.javeriana.edu.co/bitstream/handle/10554/12429/MendezBlancoYenlyAngelicapdf?sequence=1&isAllowed=y.

Bolanos, Edmond. ND. "Magnetes de Oro contra Pequenos mineros." *El Nuevo Liberal*. http://consejoderedaccion.org/webs/conflictoypaz/magnates-del-oro-pequenos-mineros

Bratspies, Rebecca. 2020. "Territory Is Everything: Afro-Colombian Communities, Human Rights, and Illegal Land Grabs." New York: Columbia University Press. https://hrlr.law.columbia.edu/files/2020/05/12-Bratspies_Final.pdf.

Briscoe, Charles. 2006. "Across the Pacific to War: The Colombian Navy in Korea, 1951–1955." https://arsof-history.org/articles/v2n4_across_pacific_page_1.html.

Bryceson, Deborah. 2000. "Peasant Theories and Smallholder Policies. Past and Present." In *Disappearing Peasants? Rural Labour in Africa, Asia, and Latin America*, edited by D. F. Bryceson, C. Kay, and J.Mooij, 1–36. London: IT Publications.

———, C. Kay, and J. Mooij, eds. 2000. *Disappearing Peasants? Rural Labour in Africa, Asia, and Latin America*. London: Intermediate Technology.

Buitrago Leal, Francisco. 2020. Interview with author via electronic email. September.

Caballero, Hector. 2021. Telephone interview with author, March 27.

Cammett, John M. 1967. *Antonio Gramsci and the Origins of Italian Communism*. Stanford: Stanford University Press.

Cárdenas, Gonzalo Castillo. 1987. *Liberation Theology from Below: The Life and Thought of Manuel Quintín Lame*. Maryknoll, NY: Orbis Books.

Carolina Gonzalez Barrera, Laura. ND. "Desarrollo Rural En Tension? La ZRC Cuenca Del Rio Pato Y Valle de Balsillas: Una Historia de Resistencia Por La Dignidad Humana Y La Paz." *El Plan Nacional de Desarrollo y los Acuerdos de Paz, 2012–17*. https://repository.javeriana.edu.co/bitstream/handle/10554/37009/Tesis%20ZRCPB%20%282012-2017%29.pdf?sequence=1&isAllowed=y.

Catalina, Sara, and Oscar Perez. 2013. "El Sector Minero-Energetico en Colombia."

Centro de Memoria Basta Ya. =-p0o9i8u753./. Bogotá: Centro de Memoria Historica.

Cepeda, Fernando. 1994. *Direccion Politica de la Reforma Economica en Colombia*. Bogotá: Tecer Mundo Editores.

"Challenges Facing Chinese Oil Company in Colombia test China's Resource Strategy for Latin America." 2017. November 30. https://chinadialogue.net/en/business/10256-oil-monkeys-and-guerrillas-chinese-companies-face-problems-in-the-amazon/.

Chohan, Jaskiran Kaur. 2020. "Incorporating and Contesting the Corporate Food Regime in Colombia: Agri-Food Dynamics in Two Zonas de Reserva Campesina (Peasant Reserve Zones)." Dissertation.

Christophers, Brett. 2019. Rentier Capitalism: The Case of UK. Blog. September 16.

"Class Alliances in Africa." 2012. *Journal of Agrarian Change* 16, no. 3 (July 2016): 390–409.

Colombia Reports. May 16.

Colombia, 1958–2002. Bogotá: Editorial Norma, 2007.

Comisión de Juristas. 2006. "Revertir el destierro forzado: Protección y restitución de los territorios usurpados. Obstáculos y desafíos para garantizar el derecho al patrimonio de la población desplazada en Colombia." Bogotá: Comision de Juristas.

CONPES (Consejo Nacional de Political Economicas y Sociales/National Council for Economic and Social Policy. 2016. Bogota: DPN.

Cortes, Jacobo, Andres Felipe, Marcela Escandón Vega, and Richard André. 2016. "Political Representation and Social Inclusion: Colombia Case Study." Bogotá.

Cuaderno del Informe de Desarrollo Humano Colombia. 2011. Bogotá: PNUD.

Cuellar, Alejandra. 2018. "El Pato Resiste: La Lucha embiental de La Comunidad Donde Nacieron Las FARC." January 16. https://pacifista.tv/notas/el-pato-resiste-la-lucha-ambiental-de-la-comunidad-en-donde-nacieron-las-farc/.

Cuellar, Anabel Arias. 2015. "Conflicto minero y organizaciones étnicas: Cabildo Indígena Nasa de Cerro Tijeras y Consejo Comunitario Afrodescendiente de La Toma en Resistencia." Unpublished dissertation. Valle University, Cali. https://revistas.icanh.gov.co/index.php/rca/article/view/3/3.

DANE. 2005. Census of 2005. Bogotá. https://www.dane.gov.co/files/censo2005/etnia/sys/visibilidoad_estadistica_etnicos.pdf.

———. https://www.dane.gov.co/files/comunicados/Dia_mundial_poblacion.pdf.

Deininger, Klaus, and Hans Binswanger. 1999. "The Evolution of the World Bank's Land Policy: Principle, Experience and Future Challenges." *The World Bank Research Observer* 14, no. 2 (August): 247–76.

De la Cadena, Marisol. 2015. *Earth Beings: Ecologies of Practice across Andean Worlds.* Durham: Duke University Press.

Delgado, Paula. 2020. "Por qué el Estado quiere revivir las Zonas de Desarrollo Empresarial?" *El Espectador*, September 4.

Dennis, Claire. 2017. "Colombia's New Crop Substitution Plan Facing Old Obstacles." *InsightCrime*, July 13. https://insightcrime.org/news/analysis/colombia-new-crop-substitution-plan-facing-old-obstacles-report/.

Departamento Nacional de Estadisticas. 2004. *Encuesta Nacional Agropecuaria* (ENA). Bogotá.

De Roux, Gustavo. 1988. "El Norte del Cauca: aislamiento, resistencia y campesinado." Mimeo. Cali: Facultad de Sociología, Universidad del Valle.

Desoto, H. 2003. *The Mystery of Capital: Why Capitalism Triumphs in the West and Fails Everywhere Else.* New York: Basic Books.

Dest, Anthony. 2021. "Coca Enclosure: Autonomy against Accumulation in Colombia." *World Development* 137. https://www.sciencedirect.com/science/article/abs/pii/S0305750X2030293X.

Diamond, Alex. 2022. "Construyendo la paz y superando la coca: el laboratorio de paz en Briceño, una lucha por el futuro del campo." *Maguaré* 36, no. 2: 235–60.

Díaz-Callejas, Apolinar. 2002. *Colombia y Reforma Agraria: Sus Documentos Fundamentales.* Cartagena: Universidad de Cartagena.

Dorado, Fernando. 2019. "Santander de Quilichao y el Cauca se convertirán en el Culiacán y el Sinaloa colombianos?" *Las Dos Orillas*, October 30. https://www.las2orillas.co/santander-de-quilichao-y-el-cauca-se-convertiran-en-el-culiacan-y-el-sinaloa-colombianos/.

Duncan, Gustavo. 2006. *Los Señores de la Guerra*. Bogotá: Planeta.

Easterly, W. 2014. *The Tyranny of Experts: Economists, Dictators, and the Forgotten Rights of the Poor*. New York: Basic Books.

Echeverri, Juliana Jaramillo, Adolfo Meisel-Roca, and Maria Teresa Geraldo. 2015. "The Great Depression in Colombia 1930–1953." *Borradores de Economia* 892. https://www.banrep.gov.co/sites/default/files/publicaciones/archivos/be_892.pdf.

Economic Anthropology. Economy and Society 1. 1972: 93–105.

Edelman, Marc. 1999. *Peasants against Globalization: Rural Social Movements in Costa Rica*. Princeton: Princeton University Press.

———. 2005. "Bringing the Moral Economy back in . . . to the Study of the 21st Century Transnational Peasant Movements." *American Anthropologist* 107-3 (September).

El campesinado Reconocimiento para construir país. 2011. Bogotá: PNUD.

El Espectador. 2021. "Reclamos de los Cocaleros, Otra Cara del Paro en el Cauca." May 13. https://www.elespectador.com/colombia-20/conflicto/los-reclamos-de-los-cocaleros-otra-cara-del-paro-nacional-en-el-cauca-article/; accessed June 19, 2021.

El Espectador. Redaccion Nacional. 2021. "A tres ascienden víctimas mortales de ataque en Santander de Quilichao (Cauca)," June 19.

"El Estado Suplantando las Autodefensas de Puerto Boyacá." Informe no. 4. 2019. Bogota: Centro de Memoria Historica. http://centrodememoriahistorica.gov.co/wp-content/uploads/2020/03/2019-El-Estado-suplantado-Autodefensas-Puerto-Boyaca.pdf.

El Pais. 2012. "Empresarios Defienden las Zonas Francas del Cauca," March 30.

El Tiempo, Politica. 2020. September 3. https://www.eltiempo.com/politica/congreso/que-paso-con-el-fracking-en-el-congreso-535695.

El Tiempo. Judicial. 2015. "Juicio a AngloGold Ashanti por beneficiarse de graves violaciones a los derechos humanos y al DIH en Colombia." 26 julio; Accessed November 24, 2021.

Emilio Escobar, Pablo. 2019. *La Colonizacion Armada del Pato*. Bogotá: Fundacion Social Utrahuilca.

Engels, F. 1972. *The Origin of the Family, Private Property, and the State*. New York. Monthly Review.

Escobar, Arturo. 2020. *Pluriversal Politics*. Durham: Duke University Press.

Escobar, Jose David. 2021. "ANT Fallo a favor de Particulares en Antiguas Tierras de Victor Carranza." *El Espectador*, June 24. https://www.elespectador.

com/judicial/ant-fallo-a-favor-de-particulares-en-antiguas-tierras-de-victor-carranza/?cx_testId=31&cx_testVariant=cx_1&cx_artPos=0#cxrecs_s accessed June 24, 2021.

Esteva, Gustavo. 1983. *The Struggle for Rural Mexico*. South Hadley, MA: Bergin and Garvey.

Evans, E. E. 1956. "The Ecology of Peasant Life in Western Europe." In *Man's Role in Changing the Face of the Earth*, edited by W. L. Thomas, 217–39. Chicago: University of Chicago Press.

Evelin Collazos Tintinago, Yuri. 2017 "Procesos de industrializacion y tranformaciones sociales del Campesinado en Guachene (Cauca) 1970–2015." Unpublished MA thesis. "http://repositorio.unicauca.edu.co:8080/xmlui/bitstream/handle/123456789/148/PROCESOS%20DE%20INDRUSTRIAL-IZACIÓN%20Y%20TRANSFORMACIONES%20SOCIALES%20DEL%20CAMPESINADO%20EN%20GUACHENÉ%20%28CAUCA%29%201970-2015.pdf?sequence=1&isAllowed=y.

Faguet, Jean Paul, Fabio Sanchez, and Maria Juanino Villaveceses. 2018. "The Perversion of Land Reform by Landed Elites." November. Unpublished paper. https://governancefrombelow.net/wp-content/uploads/2019/10/Perversion-of-Land-Reform-by-Landed-Elites_v7.pdf.

Fajardo Montana, Dario. 2012. "La Colonizacion de La Macarena en la Historia de La Frontera Agraria." Agencia Prensa Rural, September 27.

———. 2002. "La tierra y el poder político: la reforma agraria y la reforma rural en Colombia." En Grupo Editorial FAO, Organización de las Naciones Unidas para la Agricultura y la Alimentación (FAO), *Reforma agraria. Colonización y cooperativas*. www.ftp.fao.org.

———. 1994. "La Colonizacion de La Frontera Agraria Colombiana." In *El Agro y la Question Agraria*, edited by A. Machado. Bogota: Ministerio de Agricultura.

———. 2008. "El Campo, Las Politicas Agrarias y Los Conflictos Sociales en Colombia." Bogotá: Fundación Ideas para la Paz.

———. 2019. *Las Zonas De Reserva Campesina Retos y Experiencias Significativas en su Implementacion*. Bogotá: FAO.

———. 2020. Interview with author, via email, May.

———. 2020. Telephone conversation with author, May 30.

Fals Borda, Orlando. 1976. *Capitalismo Hacienda Y Poblamiento: Su Desarrollo en La Costa Atlantica*. Bogotá: Punto de Lanza.

———. 1957. *El Hombre y La Tierra en Boyaca*. Bogotá: Documentos Colombianos.

———. 1982. *Historia de la Cuestion Agraria y Colombia*. Bogotá: Carlos Valencia Editores.

FAO. 2014. *The State of Food and Agriculture 2014: Innovation in Family Farming Food and Agriculture Organization of the United Nations*. Geneva: United Nations.

———. 1998. *Land Reform, Land Settlements, and Cooperatives*. Rome: FAO.

———. 2013. Rome: FAO.

———. 2014. *The State of Food and Agriculture 2014: Innovation in Family Farming Food and Agriculture Organization of the United Nations*. Rome: FAO.

FEDEGAN. 2009. Cifras, Referencias Sector Ganadero. Bogotá: FEDEGAN.

Fedepalma. 2016. https://publicaciones.fedepalma.org/index.php/palmicultor/article/view/10114/10105.

Feder, E. 1975. *Violencia y Despojo: el Latifundismo en América Latina, Siglo XXI*. México: Editores Siglo Veinteuno.

Fernandez, Miguel. 2021. Telephone interviews with author, March 16 and 22.

Findji, Maria Teresa, y José María Rojas. 1985. *Territorio, economía y ociedad páez*. Cali: Universidad del Valle. https://www.worldcat.org/title/territorio-economia-y-sociedad-paez/oclc/14085180.

Florez-Malagon, Alberto. 2008. *El Poder de La Carne: Historias de Ganaderias en la Primera Mitad del Siglo XX en Colombia*. Bogotá: Pontificia Universidad Javeriana.

Ford, Laura. 2015. "Max Weber on Property: An Effort in Interpretive Understanding." Unpublished paper. https://scholarship.law.cornell.edu/cgi/viewcontent.cgi?article=1039&context=lps_papers.

Forrero, Sebastian. 2021. "No es Facil Saber Cuantas Hectareas estan Disponible en el Fondo de Tierras." *El Espectador*, January 20. https://www.elespectador.com/colombia-20/paz-y-memoria/no-es-facil-saber-cuantas-hectareas-del-fondo-de-tierras-estan-disponibles-ant-article/.

Foster, John Bellamy, Brett Clark, and Hannah Holleman. 2020. "Marx and the Indigenous." *Monthly Review*, February 1. https://monthlyreview.org/2020/02/01/marx-and-the-indigenous/#en32backlink.

Frankman, Myron J. 1977. "Employment Policy for Colombia: Towards Full Employment and the Four Strategies." *Manpower and Unemployment Research* 10, no. 2: 33–44.

Frayer, Lauren. 2021. "Why Indian Farmers Are So Angry." NPR, March 3. https://www.npr.org/sections/goatsandsoda/2021/03/02/971293844/indias-farmer-protests-why-are-they-so-angry.

Galino, Fredy. 2016. Interview with author. Wakoyo, July.

Gamarra Vergara, Jose R. 2007. "La economía del departamento del Cauca: concentración de tierras y pobreza." *Banco de la Republica* No. 95. October. https://repositorio.banrep.gov.co/bitstream/handle/20.500.12134/3000/dtser_95.pdf?sequence=1&isAllowed=y.

Garay, Luis Jorge. https://redjusticiaambientalcolombia.files.wordpress.com/2013/05/mineria-en-colombia-fundamentos-para-superar-el-modelo-extractivista 2013.pdf.

———. 2004. *El Agro Colombiano Frente Al TLC con Los Estados Unidos*. Bogotá: Ministerio de Agricultura Y Desarrollo Rural.

————, Rodrigo Uprimny, Fernando Barberi, Maria Safon, and Gladys Celeide. 2008. Comision de Seguimiento a la Politica Publica Sobre Desplazamiento Forzado: Processo.

Gaviria, Cesar. 2017. In *Presidencia de Virgilio Barco Treinta Anios Despues*, edited by Carlos Argaez. Bogota: Uniandes.

Gilhodés, Pierre. 1988. *Las luchas agrarias en Colombia*. Bogotá: ECOE.

Gill, Stephen. 2016. "Colombia's Neo-Paramilitaries Already Left 320,000 Victims." *Colombia Reports* April 29. https://colombiareports.com/colombias-neo-paramilitaries-already-left-320000-victims/.

Giraldo García, Fernando, and José Daniel López Jiménez. 2007. "Mecanismos de participación política electoral afrodescendiente en Colombia." In *Estudios sobre la Representacion Politica de la Poblacion Afrodecendiete: La ExpAriencia en Colombia*. Instituto Interamericano de Derechos Humanos. https://www.corteidh.or.cr/tablas/24812.pdf.

Giugale, Marcelo, Olivier Lafourcade, and Connie Luff. 2003. *Colombia: The Economic Foundation of Peace*. Washington, DC: The World Bank.

Gómez, L. J. 1987. "Introducción al desarrollo histórico de la producción pecuaria en Colombia desde la conquista." *Coyuntura Agropecuario* 14, no. 7: 41–72.

González, F. *Poder y Violencia en Colombia*. 20014. Bogotá: CINEP/PPP and ODECOFI.

González, Laly Catalina Peralta. 2005. "Curules especiales para comunidades negras: ¿realidad o ilusión?" *Estudios Socio Jurídico* 7, no. 2 (July/Dec.). http://www.scielo.org.co/scielo.php?script=sci_arttext&pid=S0124-0579200500020000.

Gramsci, Antonio. 2011. *Prison Notebooks*. New York: Columbia University Press.

Guthman, j. 2014. *Agrarian Dreams: The Paradox of Organic Farming in California*. Berkeley: University of California Press.

Gutiérrez, F. 2010. *¿Lo Que el Viento Se Llevó? Los Partidos Políticos y la Democracia en Colombia 1958–2002*. Bogotá: Norma Editores.

————. 2013. "Land and Property Rights in Colombia: Change and Continuity." *Nordic Journal of Human Rights* 28, no. 2: 230–61.

————. 2013. "Un Trancón Fenomenal. Un Análisis de las Demoras en el Proceso de Restitución." Bogotá: Observatorio de Restitución y Regulación de Derechos de Propiedad Agraria. http://www.observatoriodetierras.org/wp-content/uploads/2014/01/UN-TRANC%C3%93N-FENOMENAL.pdf.

Gutiérrez, Sanín F., and J. Vargas. 2017. "Agrarian Elite Participation in Colombia's Civil War. *Journal of Agrarian Change*.

Halamska, Maria. 2004. "A Different End of Peasants?" *Polish Sociological Review* 3.

Hartlyn, Jonathan. 1985. "Producer Associations, the Political Regime, and Policy Processes in Contemporary Colombia." *Latin American Research Review* 20, no 3: 111–38.

Heath, John, and Hans Binswanger. 1998. "Policy-Induced Effects of Natural Resource Degradation: The Case of Colombia." In *Agriculture and the Environment*, edited by Ernst Lutz. Washington, DC: World Bank Group.

Herrera Duran, Natalia. 2019. "La Vida sin Bombardeos." *El Espectador*, January 8. https://www.elespectador.com/colombia2020/territorio/la-vida-sin-bombardeos-en-el-cimitarra-articulo-857533/.

"La Hora de La Colombia Rural." 2011. *Hechos de Paz* 63 (Bogotá: PNUD).

http://centrodememoriahistorica.gov.co/descargas/informes2013/bastaYa/capitulos/basta-ya-cap2_110-195.pdf.

http://colombiapeace.org/2015/01/29/interview-on-colombias-peace-process-with-danny-ramirez-of-the-national-conference-of-afro-colombian-organizations/.

http://eprints.lse.ac.uk/67193/1/Faguet_Paradox%20opf%20land%20reform_2016.pdf.

http://etimologias.dechile.net/?rochela.

http://hrlr.law.columbia.edu/hrlr-online/territory-is-everything-afro-colombian-communities-human-rights-and-illegal-land-grabs/#post-1520-_Toc39567528.

http://palabrasalmargen.com/edicion-18/la-tragedia-y-, hela-farsa-del-pacto-de-chicoral-al-pacto-de-compensar/.

http://repositorio.unicauca.edu.co:8080/xmlui/bitstream/handle/123456789/148/PROCESOS%20DE%20INDRUSTRIALIZACIÓN%20Y%20TRANSFORMACIONES%20SOCIALES%20DEL%20CAMPESINADO%20EN%20GUACHENÉ%20%28CAUCA%29%201970-2015.pdf?sequence=1&isAllowed=y.

http:///Users/nazirichani/Desktop/Meta/"Pueblo%20ind%C3%ADgena%20Sikuani%20de%20Puerto%20Gaitán%20Meta,%20se%20ha%20tomado%20pac%C3%ADficamente%20la%20instalaciones%20de%20la%20em.web archive.

http://violentologia.com/blog/wp-content/uploads/2011/09/Cuadernillo-PARAS-ESP-small.pdf.

http://www.adr.gov.co/normograma/DocumentosJuridica/Ley%20160%20de%201994_LISTA_no.pdf.

http://www.adr.gov.co/normograma/DocumentosJuridica/Ley%204%20de%201973.pdf.

http://www.cidh.org/countryrep/colombiamujeres06sp/iv.htm#_ftnref143.

http://www.coha.org/colombias-invisible-crisis-internally-displaced-persons/.

http://www.dinero.com/edicion-impresa/caratula/articulo/la-apertura-economica/182405.

http://www.fao.org/americas/noticias/ver/en/c/878998/.

http://www.indepaz.org.co/wp-content/uploads/2018/08/Titulación-Colectiva-para-comunidades-negras-en-Colombia.pdf.

http://www.portafolio.co/economia/finanzas/guerra-narcotrafico-nuestra-30096.

http://www.scielo.org.co/pdf/rhc/n58/n58a03.pdf.

http://www.scielo.org.co/scielo.php?script=sci_arttext&pid=S0122-14502012
000100002#1.

http://www.scielo.org.co/scielo.php?script=sci_arttext&pid=S0124-05792005
000200006.

http://www.uop.edu.pk/ocontents/Lecture%204%20a%20Unit%202%20Lesson%20
6%20Rostow.pdf.

https://cepdipo.org/portfolio/cuadernos-de-la-implementacion-6-la-reforma-rural-
integral-en-deuda/.

https://colombiareports.com/66-of-colombias-gold-is-mined-illegally-un-study/.

https://colombiareports.com/colombia-poverty-inequality-statistics/.

https://colombiareports.com/colombias-former-ranchers-chief-sentenced-to-9-
years-over-paramilitary-ties/.

https://colombiareports.com/how-disputed-oil-deals-push-native-colombian-peo-
ples-closer-to-extinction/.

https://colombiareports.com/santo-domingo-overtakes-sarmiento-to-top-colom-
bias-rich-list/.

https://crudotransparente.com/2019/10/08/de-la-agricultura-al-petroleo-en-el-
caqueta/.

https://data.worldbank.org/indicator/SL.AGR.EMPL.ZS.

https://foreignaffairs.house.gov/_cache/files/a/5/a51ee680-e339-4a1b-933f-b15e
535fa103/AA2A3440265DDE42367A79D4BCBC9AA1.whdpc-final-report-
2020-11.30.pdf.

https://id.presidencia.gov.co/Paginas/prensa/2019/La-poblacion-indigena-en-
Colombia-es-de-1905617-personas-segun-Censo-del-Dane-190916.aspx.

https://mneguidelines.oecd.org/South-West-Colombia-Gold-Mining-EN.pdf.

https://news.mongabay.com/2018/05/how-colombia-became-latin-americas-
palm-oil-powerhouse/.

https://prensarural.org/spip/spip.php?article25456.

https://redjusticiaambientalcolombia.files.wordpress.com/2013/05/mineria-en-
colombia-fundamentos-para-superar-el-modelo-extractivista2013.pdf.

https://reliefweb.int/sites/reliefweb.int/files/resources/Full_Report_3049.pdf.

https://repositorio.uniandes.edu.co/bitstream/handle/1992/40993/dcede2004-29.
pdf?sequence=1&isAllowed=y.

https://repositorio.banrep.gov.co/bitstream/handle/20.500.12134/3000/dtser_95.
pdf?sequence=1&isAllowed=y.

https://reservacampesinariocimitarra.org/wp-content/uploads/2018/04/11.-
ACVC-Informe-anual-de-resultados.pdf.

https://santandertrade.com/en/portal/analyse-markets/colombia/economic-outline.

https://semanarural.com/web/articulo/debate-de-acceso-a-la-tierra-en-colombia-
en-la-cumbre-colombia-rural/1210.

https://tbinternet.ohchr.org/Treaties/CEDAW/Shared%20Documents/COL/INT_CEDAW_NGO_COL_15183_S.pdf.

https://verdadabierta.com/la-sangre-que-les-recupero-la-tierra-de-los-nasa/.

https://www.amwenglish.com/articles/armed-strike-by-eln-in-cauca-colombia/.

https://www.anm.gov.co/sites/default/files/DocumentosAnm/bullets_cauca_01-06-2017.pdf.

https://www.as-coa.org/sites/default/files/ColombiaFINAL.pdf.

https://www.bbc.com/news/world-latin-america-19931443.

https://www.bennettinstitute.cam.ac.uk/blog/rentier-capitalism-uk-case.

https://www.cepal.org/ilpes/noticias/paginas/4/29744/alberto_barreix_tax_systems_and_tax_reform_in_la07_cap1a5.pdf.

https://www.cidh.oas.org/indigenas/colombia.11.101.htm.

https://www.coca-colacompany.com/content/dam/journey/us/en/policies/pdf/human-workplace-rights/addressing-global-issues/colombia-sugar-industry-country-report.PDF.

https://www.cric-colombia.org/portal/juicio-a-anglogold-ashanti-por-beneficiarse-de-graves-violaciones-a-los-derechos-humanos-y-al-dih-en-colombia/.

https://www.culturalsurvival.org/news/colombia-farc-releases-indigenous-leaders.

https://www.dinero.com/edicion-impresa/caratula/articulo/historia-y-actualidad-del-grupo-santo-domingo-de-colombia/228944.

https://www.elespectador.com/colombia/mas-regiones/tres-personas-murieron-en-una-nueva-masacre-en-santander-de-quilichao-cauca/?cx_testId=24&cx_test-Variant=cx_1&cx_artPos=0#cxrecs_s.

https://www.elespectador.com/economia/por-que-el-estado-quiere-revivir-las-zonas-de-desarrollo-empresarial-article/.

https://www.eluniversal.com.co/regional/bolivar/fuerza-de-tarea-marte-llegara-al-sur-a-mediados-de-febrero-LL692836.

https://www.farmlandgrab.org/post/view/19025-colombia-la-locomotora-del-agro-y-su-impacto-ambiental-y-socioeconomico-los-campesinos-tienen-un-proyecto.

https://www.fucsia.co/actualidad/personajes/articulo/afrocolombianidad-mujer-afrodescendiente-en-colombia/63212.

https://www.hrw.org/reports/1996/killer2.htm.

https://www.hrw.org/world-report/2009/country-chapters/colombia.

https://www.hrw.org/news/2009/02/10/colombia-farc-kills-17-indigenous-group;

https://www.insightcrime.org/news/analysis/colombia-new-crop-substitution-plan-facing-old-obstacles-report/.

https://www.minjusticia.gov.co/Sala-de-prensa/PublicacionesMinJusticia/mayo%2031%20Diagnóstico%20del%20Fenómeno%20de%20Pandillas%20en%20Colombia%20(4).pdf.

https://www.nocheyniebla.org/wp-content/uploads/2020/05/noche-y-niebla-60-web.pdf.

https://www.nocheyniebla.org/wp-content/uploads/2020/10/NOCHE-Y-NIE-BLA-61.pdf.

https://www.portafolio.co/economia/finanzas/colombia-tendria-tierra-cara-region-estudio-sac-340630.

https://www.portafolio.co/economia/finanzas/empresas-ley-paez-zonas-francas-266162.

https://www.portafolio.co/tendencias/los-colombianos-mas-ricos-segun-forbes-504289.

https://www.redalyc.org/journal/4075/407564498008/html/.

https://www.revistaarcadia.com/libros/articulo/el-problema-de-la-tierra-albsalon-machado-entrevista/63834.

https://www.sasas.co.za/wp-content/uploads/2017/11/Mokolobate_vol-10_Issue_1_Explaining-principle-of-large-stock-units-and-its-implications-on-grazing-capacity.pdf.

https://www.semana.com/economia/articulo/lo-pierde-estado-privilegios-tributarios-mineria/174393/.

https://www.semana.com/nacion/articulo/indigenas-vandalizaron-y-quema-ron-120-hectareas-de-cana-en-el-cauca-denuncia-asocana/202123/.

https://www.semana.com/nacion/articulo/racha-de-violencia-en-cauca-obliga-a-construir-base-militar-en-caloto/202145/.

https://www.semana.com/nacion/articulo/tenemos-informacion-de-la-presencia-en-el-cauca-del-cartel-de-sinaloa-y-jalisco-nueva-generacion-las-revelaciones-del-defensor-del-pueblo/202156/.

https://www.semillas.org.co/es/economa-campesina-y-ciudad.

https://www.semillas.org.co/es/el-ingenio-voraz-y-los-indgenas-el-negocio-del-agroetanol.

https://www.statista.com/statistics/1072849/colombia-services-sector-share-gdp/.

https://www.theguardian.com/environment/2017/oct/28/nasa-colombia-cauca-valley-battle-mother-land.

https://www.un.org/development/desa/en/news/population/2018-revision-of-world-urbanization-prospects.html; https://www.macrotrends.net/countries/COL/colombia/rural-populations.

https://www.unodc.org/documents/crop-monitoring/Colombia/Colombia_Monitoreo_Cultivos_Ilicitos_2019.pdf.

Hurtado, Teodora. 2000. "Treinta Años de Protesta Social: el surgimiento de la movilización 'étnica' afrocolombiana en el norte del Cauca." En Documento de trabajo No. 50. CISED-IRD- ICANH, Universidad del Valle. Cali, Julio.

Ibanez, A, and P. Querubin. 2004. "Acceso a Tierras Y Desplacamiento Forzado en Colombia." Documento CEDE. Bogotá: Universidad de los Andes.

"Indicadores sociodemograficos Censo 2005." https://www.dane.gov.co/files/censo2005/etnia/sys/Afro_indicadores_sociodemograficos_censo2005.pdf.

Informant (1). 2018. Interview with author, Puerto Matilde, August.

Informant (3). 2020. Telephone interview with author, August 25.

Informant (7). 2019. Telephone interview with author, December.

Informant (8). 2019. Interview with author, Pato-Balsillas Caqueta, December.

Informant (9). 2018. Interview with author, Barrancabermeja, August.

Informant (10). 2020. Telephone interview with author, Barrancabermeja, August.

Informants (11, 12, 13, 14, and 15). 2018; 2019. Pato-Balsillas, Caqueta (research assistant) interviews August 2018 and December 2019.

Informant (11). 2017. Interview with author, Puerto Gaitan, Meta, July 25.

Informant (12). 2016. Interview with author, Puerto Gaitan, Meta, August 5.

Informants (13 and 14). 2016. Interviews with author, Puerto Gaitan, Resguardo Wakoyo, August 5.

Informant (15). 2021. Telephone interview, March 18.

Informant (16). 2021. Telephone conversation with author, March 18.

Informant (18). 2021. Telephone interview with author, August 5.

Informant (19). 2021. Telephone interview with author November.

Informants from Caloto (16), Puerto Tejada (17), and Suarez,Villarica (18). 2021. Interviews with author, April.

Informant (agricultural engineer). 1998. Interview with author, Barrancabermeja, September.

Interviews, Cimitarra, August 2018, and Pato Balsillas, December 2018.

Jacobs, Luke. 2019. "How Disputed Oil Deals Push Native Colombian Peoples Closer to Extinction." *Colombia Reports*, June 29. https://colombiareports.com/how-disputed-oil-deals-push-native-colombian-peoples-closer-to-extinction/.

Jaimes, Juliana. 2021. "La Apuesta Para Traducir a Lenguas Indigenas las Decisiones Que Impacten las Comunidades." *El Espectador*, March 3. https://www.elespectador.com/noticias/medio-ambiente/la-apuesta-por-traducir-a-lenguas-indigenas-las-decisiones-judiciales/.

Jansen, Kees, Mark Vicol, and Lissete Nikol. 2022. "Autonomy and Repeasantization: Conceptual, Analytical, and Methodological Problems." *Agrarian Change*. Special Issue: Autonomy in Agrarian Studies, Politics, and Movements 22, no. 3 (February 17).

Jorge, Garcia, et al., eds. 2010. "La Agricultura y Las Politicas Sectoriales." *Journal of Human Rights* 28, no. 2: 230–61.

Julio, Silvia Colmenares, and Carolina Padilla Pardo. 2015. *Transnacionalizacion de Empresas Colombiana*. Bogotá: Universidad Autonoma de Colombia.

Kalmanovitz, Salomon. 2003. *Economia Y Nacion: Una Breve Historia*. Bogotá: Norma.

———. 1994. "Evolucion de la Estructura Agraria Colombiana." In Salomon Kalmanovitz, *Transformaciones de la estructura agrarian*. Bogotá: Tercer Mundo.

———. 2015. "De la Mineria a Donde." *El Espectador*, May 24.

———, and Enrique Lopez. 2007. "Aspectos de la Agricultura Colombiana en el

Siglo XX." In James Robinson and Miguel Urrutia, *Economia Colombiana del Siglo XX: Un Analisis Cuantativo*. Bogotá: Banco de la Republica.

Karatani, Kojin. 2014. *The Structure of World History*. Durham: Duke University Press.

Karl, Terry Lynn. 1997. *The Paradox of Plenty*. Berkeley: The University of California Press.

Kautsky, K. 1899. "The Agrarian Question." http://www.anveshi.org.in/broad sheet-on-contemporary-politics/archives/broadsheet-on-contemporary-politics-vol-2-no-1011/the-agrarian-question/.

Kerrou, Muhammad. 2021. *Jemana L'oassis de la Revolution*. Tunis: Ceres Edition.

Kleinfield, Rachel. 2018. *Savage Order*. New York: Pantheon Books.

Krauss, Clifford. 2020. "As Oil Demand Declines, Exxon Is at Cross Roads." *New York Times*, December 11.

Kroger, Markus. 2012. "The Expansion of Industrial Tree Plantations in Brazil." *Development and Change*. https://www.academia.edu/11882122/The_Expansion_of_Industrial_Tree_Plantations_and_Dispossession_in_Brazil.

Leal Buitrago, Francisco. 1984. *Estado Y política en Colombia*. Bogotá: Siglo Veintiuno Editores.

———. 2011. *Una Vision de la Seguridad en Colombia*. *Analysis Politico*. Bogotà: IEPRI, Universidad Nacional.

LeGrand, C. 1989. "Colonization and Violence in Colombia: Perspectives and Debates. *Canadian Journal of Latin American and Caribbean Studies* 14, no. 28: 5–29.

———. 1986. *Frontier Expansion and Peasant Protest in Colombia, 1850–1936*. Albuquerque: University of New Mexico Press.

Lemaitre, Julieta. 2017. "Manuel Quintín Lame: Legal Thought as Minor Jurisprudence." *Law Text Culture* 21: 76–99. https://ro.uow.edu.au/ltc/vol21/iss1/5.

Libardo José Ariza. 2020. "Legal Indigeneity: Knowledge, Legal Discourse, and the Construction of Indigenous Identity in Colombia." *Identities* 27, no. 4: 403–22. 10.1080/1070289X.2018.1543484.

Londoño, Gilberto Arango. 1993. "¿Quiénes dirigen la economía? Nunca como ahora ha mandado tanto la tecnocracia." *Síntesis Económica* 860.

Lopez, Claudia. 2010. *Refundaron La Patria*. Bogotá: Debate.

Llorente, Maria Victoria, and Juan Carlos Garzon. 2022. "El narcotráfico y la respuesta equivocada." Deciembre 25. http://www.ideaspaz.org/publications/posts/1889.

Luque, Santiago. 2020. "Crece la deforestación en Colombia: más de 171 mil hectáreas se perdieron en el 2020." https://es.mongabay.com/2021/07/crece-deforestacion-colombia-2020/.

Luxemburg, Rosa. 2003. *The Accumulation of Capital*. New York: Routledge.

Lynch, John. 2006. *Simon Bolivar: A life*. New Haven: Yale University Press.

Machado, A. 2012. "Luces y sombras en el desarrollo rural. Reflexiones a la luz del proyecto de ley de tierras y desarrollo rural del gobierno de Santos y Desarrollo rural, ¿camino para construir la paz?" En OXFAM, *Propuestas, visiones y análisis sobre la política de desarrollo rural en Colombia.* https://es.scribd.com/document/239572402/Propuestas-visiones-y-analisis-sobre-la-politica-de-desarrollo-rural-en-Colombia.

Machado, Absalon, and Ruth Suarez. 1999. *El Mercado de Tierra en Colombia.* Bogotá: Tercer Mundo.

Mahdavi, H. 1970. "The Patterns and Problems of Economic Development in Rentier States: The Case of Iran." In *Studies in the Economic History of the Middle East,* edited by M. A. Cook London: Oxford University Press.

Mandel, Ernest. 1970. "The Laws of Uneven Development." *New Left Review* 59 (January-February): 19–38.

Mariategui, Jose Carlos. 1971. *Seven Interpretative Essays on Peruvian Reality.* Austin: University of Texas Press.

Martines, Carlos. 2018. Interview with author, Cimitarra, August.

Marx, Karl. 1991. *Capital,* vols. 1 and 3. Middlesex: Penguin Books.

———. 1993. *Grundrisse.* New York: Penguin Classics.

———. At https://people.potsdam.edu/nuwermj/hunt/10%20Human%20 Nature%20RRPE.pdf.

McGreevey, W. P. 1971. *An Economic History of Colombia, 1845–1930.* Cambridge: Cambridge University Press.

McKinsey, Victoria. 2014. "Colombia's Land Restitution Law Defrauding Victims: Amnesty International." https://colombiareports.com/colombias-land-restitution-law-defrauding-victims-amnesty-international/.

McNetting, Robert. 1993. *Small Holders, House Holders, Farm Families, and the Ecology of Intensive Sustainable Agriculture.* Stanford: Stanford University Press.

———. 1993. "Unequal Commoners and Uncommon Equity Property and Community Among Small Holder Farmers." Paper presented at *Heterogeneity and Collective Action,* workshop in Political Theory and Policy Analysis. Indiana University, Bloomington, October 14–17.

Medina, Bravo. 2017. "Agroecología : una propuesta de desarrollo propio en la zona reserva campesina del Valle del Río Cimitarra–ZRCVRC." Masters thesis.

Medina, Carlos. 1990. "Aurodefensas, Paramiliatres Y Narcotrafico en Colombia: Origen, Desarrollo y Consolidacion: El Caso Boyaca." Bogota: Editorial Documentos Periodísticos,

Meillassoux, Claude. 1972. "From Reproduction to Production: A Marxist Approach to Production." *Economy and Society* 1, no. 1).

Mejia, Claudia. 2017. "Zonas de Reserva Campesina: territorialidades en disputa. El caso del Valle del río Cimitarra [Colombia Peasant Reserve Zone: Territorialities in Dispute. The Case of the Valle del río Cimitarra]," *Colombia*

*Reports.*https://www.redalyc.org/jatsRepo/5742/574262162009/html/index.
html#fn5.

Mestizo, Arcadio. 2022. Interview with author, Caloto, August 22.

Misas, Gabriel Arango.1995. Interview with author, Bogotá. August 9.

Moncayo, Carolina. 2016. "Dane Presenta las Cifras Reales del Campo Colombiano."
INCP, December 2. https://incp.org.co/dane-presenta-las-cifras-reales-del-
campo-colombiano/.

Mondragón, Hector. 2011. "Colombia: La locomotora del agro y su impacto
ambiental y socioeconómico. Los campesinos tienen un Proyecto." August
2. https://www.albatv.org/La-locomotora-del-agro-y-su.html.

Montoya, Aurelio Suarez. 2005. "Impacts of AFTA on the Colombian Agricultural
Sector." Presentation, Washington, DC.

Morena, Fernanda Spinoza. 2012. "La Lucha por La Paz Del Movimiento Indigena
Caucano." *Ciendias* 76 (Septiembre-Noviembre). https://www.cinep.org.co/
publicaciones/PDFS/20121101c.lucha_paz76.pdf.

Morgan, L. H. 1963. *Ancient Society.* Cleveland: Meridian Books.

Mosquera-Vallejo, Yilver, and Alex Paulsen Espinoza. 2020. "Geografía del
extractivismo: conflicto socioambiental en el Río Sambingo. Reflexiones
desde la ética ambiental," 1–19. 10.37838/unicen/est.07-043.

Murrillo, Amparo. 1999. *Historia y Sociedad en el Magdalena Medellin.* Bogotá:
CINEP.

Murrillo, Mario. 2009. "Enbattled Cauca: A New Wave of Violence and Indigenous
Resistance." *NACLA Report on the Americas* (July-August): 25–29.

Nacional de Verificaccion. Informe a La Corte Constitucional. 2020. Bogotá, June.

Ng'weno, Bettina. 2013. "Puede La etnicidad Remplazar lo Racial? Afro Colombianos, Indiginidad y El Estado Multicultural en Colombia." *Revista Colombiana
de Antropologia* 49, no. 1 (Enero-Julio).

———. 2007. *Turf Wars: Territory and Citizenship in the Contemporary State.*
Stanford: Stanford University Press.

Noemi. 2015. Interview with author, July 29.

Novack, George. 1972. "Uneven and Combined Development on World History."
In *Understanding History.* New York: Pathfinder Press.

Observatorio de Drogas en Colombia 1999–2019. 2019. http://www.odc.gov.co/
sidco/oferta/cultivos-ilicitos/departamento-municipio See also https://www.
unodc.org/documents/crop-monitoring/Colombia/Colombia_Monitoreo_
Cultivos_Ilicitos_2019.pdf.

Obregon, Ricardo. 2004. Interview with author, Bogotá, August 2.

Ocampo, Jose Antonio. 2020. "Apertura Y Desarollo Exportador." February 22,
https://www.eltiempo.com/opinion/columnistas/jose-antonio-ocampo/
apertura-y-desarrollo-exportador-columna-de-jose-antonio-ocampo-4651
66.

———, ed. 1994. *Historia Economica de Colombia.* Bogotá: Tercer Mundo.

O'Laughlin, Bridget. 2016. "Bernstein's Puzzle: Peasants, Accumulation, and Class Alliances in Africa." *Journal of Agrarian Change* 13, no. 3: 390–409.

Omari, Torkan. 2015. "Colombia's 'Sugar Cartel' and Its Alleged Attempts to Keep Prices High." *Colombia Reports*, June 3. https://colombiareports.com/colombias-sugar-cartel-and-its-alleged-attempts-to-keep-prices-high.

Oquist, Paul. 1978. *Violencia, conflicto y política en Colombia*. Bogotá: Instituto de Estudios Colombianos (IEC), Banco Popular.

———. 1980. *Violence, Conflict, and Politics in Colombia*. New York: Academic Press.

Orazio, Attanasio, Pinelopi K. Orazio, and Nina Pavcnik Goldberg. 2003. "Trade Reforms and Wage Inequality in Colombia." Working Paper 9830 (July). http://www.nber.org/papers/w9830.

Osorio, Sergio. 2017. Interview with author, Medellin, August.

Pardo, Ana. 2019. Interview with author, by research assistant, Pato Balsillas, December.

Pardo, Gustavo. 2017. "Las cuatro megahaciendas de Luis Carlos Sarmiento en el Llano." *Las Dos Orillas*, May 10. https://www.las2orillas.co/las-cuatro-mega-haciendas-luis-carlos-sarmiento-llano/.

Paredes Cisneros, Santiago. 2022. "La política del resguardo ntre los indios páez del pueblo de Toboyma (gobernación de Popayán), 1650–1750." October 31. doi: dx.doi.org/10.7440/histcrit58.2015.02.

Pazos, Maria, Aida Quiñones, Juan Copete, Juan Díaz, Nicolás Vargas-Ramírez, and Alirio Cáceres. 2016. "Extractivism, Conflicts and Defense of Territory: The Case of the Village of La Toma." *Desafios* 28, no. 2: 367–409.

Pena, Mario Aguilera. 2014. *Contrapoder Y Justicia Guerrillera*. Bogotá: IEPRI & Debate editorial.

Penaranda, Daniel Ricardo. 2012. "La Organizacion como forma de Resistencia" in Graciela Bolanoz, (et.al ed.) Nuestra Vida ha sido Nuestro Lucha, Resistencia y Memoria en el Cauca Indigena. Bogota: Centro de Memoria Historica.

Pérez, Yepez. 2001. "Ganadería y transformación de ecosistemas: un análisis ambiental de la política de apropiación territoria." In *Naturaleza en Disputa: Ensayos de Historia Ambiental de Colombia, 1850–1995*, edited by G. Palacio, 117–72. Bogotá: Universidad Nacional de Colombia, Instituto Colombiano de Antropología e Historia.

Perfetti, Juan Jose. 1994. "Las Paradojas en el Desarrollo de la Agricultura Y las Opciones de Politica." In Miguel Pinzon, Laureano Gomes, and Diego Motta, *La Mision Currie y el Proyecto de Reforma Constitucional 1952*. https://core.ac.uk/download/pdf/52201930.pdf.

Pizarro, Eduardo Leongomez. 1989. "Los Origenes del Movimiento Armado Communista en Colombia." *Analysis Politico* 7 (Mayo).

Pizarro, Victor. 2021. Phone interview with author, July 7.

Plan de Desarrollo Sostenible: Zona de Reserva Campesina Cuenca del Río Pato y Valle de Balsillas. 2012. Bogotá: ANZORC.

Plan de Desarrollo Rural in Cimitarra. 2015. Cimitarra: Municipality of Cimitarra.

Ploeg, Jan Douwe van der. 2018. *The New Peasantries: Rural Development in Times of Globalization*. 2nd ed. New York: Routledge.

PNUD. 2014. Política Pública Indígena del Departamento del Meta Aprobado Asamblea Departamental Villaviciencio. Abril.

PNUD y ACVC. 2014. Estudio participativo de tenencia de la tierra y el territorio, usos y conflictos en la ZRC del valle del río cimitarra. Barrancabermeja: PNUD-ACVC.

Pomerantz, Kenneth. 2012. *The Great Divergence: China, Europe, and the Making of the Modern World Economy*. Princeton: Princeton University Press.

Portafolio. 2008. "Empresas de Ley Páez, a zonas francas." *Portafolio*, February 19.

Ramirez, Franscisco. 2017. Interview with author, Bogotá, July.

Ramirez, Irene. 2020. Telephone interview with author, August 24.

———. 2021. Interview, November, 8. https://www.portafolio.co/economia/finanzas/empresas-ley-paez-zonas-francas-266162.

Ramirez Tobon, William. 1997. "Uraba: Los Inciertos Confines de una Crisis." Bogotá: Tercer Mundo.

———. 2001. "Colonización armada, poder local y territorialización privada." *Journal of Iberian and Latin American Research* 7: 63–81.

Ramondo, Natalia, Veronica Rappoport, and Kim J. Ruhl. 2011. "Horizontal vs. Vertical FDI:Revisiting Evidence from U.S. Multinationals." unpublished paper. https://www.princeton.edu/~ies/Fall11/RappaportPaper.pdf.

Rappaport, Joanne. 1985. "History, Myth, and the Dynamics of Territorial Maintenance in Tierradentro, Colombia." *American Ethnologist* 12, no. 1: 27–45. http://www.jstor.org/stable/644413.

———. 1998. *The Politics of Memory. Native Historical Interpretation in the Colombian Andes*. Durham: Duke University Press.

Rathgeber, Theodor. 2004. "Indigenous Struggles in Colombia: Historical Changes and Perspectives." In *The Struggle for Indigenous Rights in Latin America*, edited by Nancy Grey Postero and Leon Zamosc. Portland, OR: Sussex Academic Press.

Rehm, Lukas. http://www.scielo.org.co/pdf/hiso/n27/n27a02.pdf.

Reyes, A. 1997. "Compra de Tierras por Narcotraficantes." In *Drogas Ilícitas en Colombia*, edited by F. Thoumi, 279–346. Bogotá: Ariel, PNUD and Ministerio de Justicia, Dirección Nacional de Estupefacientes.

Reyes, Alejandro. 2009. *Guerreros y Campesinos*. Bogotá: Grupo Editorial Norma.

———, Liliana Duica, and Wílber Pedraza. 2010. "El despojo de tierras por paramilitares en Colombia." https://www.ideaspaz.org/tools/download/52149.

Ricardo, David. 2006. *Principles of Political Economy and Taxation*. New York: Cosimo.

Richani, Nazih. 2002. *Systems of Violence: The Political Economy of War and Peace in Colombia*. Albany: State University of New York Press.

———. 2013. *Systems of Violence: The Political Economy of War and Peace in Colombia.* 2nd ed. Albany: State University of New York Press.

———. 2005. "Multinational Corporations, Rentier Capitalism, and the War System in Colombia." *Latin American Politics and Society* (Fall): 113–44.

———. 2007. "Caudillos and the Crisis of the Colombian State: Fragmented Sovereignty, the War System, and the Privatization of Counterinsurgency in Colombia." *Third World Quarterly* 28, no. 2: 403–17.

Roca, Adolfo Meisel. 2012. "Â¿Quién manda aquí? Poder regional y participación de la costa Caribe en los gabinetes ministeriales, 1900–2000." *Cuadernos de Historia Económica* 009424, Bogota: Banco de la República-Economía Regional. https://www.banrep.gov.co/sites/default/files/publicaciones/archivos/chee_31.pdf.

Rodriguez, Mercedes. 2016. Interview with author, Puerto Gaitan, July.

Rodríguez G., Ivonne. 2014. "Despojo, baldíos y conflicto armado en Puerto Gaitán y Mapiripán (Meta, Colombia) entre 1980 y 2010." *Estudios Socio-Jurídicos* 16, no. 1: 315–42.

Romagnolo, David J. 1975. "The So-Called 'Law' of Uneven and Combined Development." *Latin American Perspectives* 2, no. 1: 7–31. JSTOR. www.jstor.org/stable/2633408.

Romero, M. *Paramilitares y Autodefensas 1982–2003.* 2003. Bogotá: IEPRI.

Ross, Eric. 2003. "Modernization, Clearance, and the Continuum of Violence in Colombia." Working paper 383, November. https://core.ac.uk/download/pdf/18512667.pdf.

Rostow, W. W. 1960. *The Stages of Economic Growth: A Non-Communist Manifesto.* Cambridge: Harvard University Press.

Rubiela. 2016. Interview with author, Puerto Gaitan, August.

Rueda, Monica Ribera. 2022. "Las Solicitudes desde las Regiones un Ano despues del Estallido Social." *El Espectador*, April 28. https://www.elespectador.com/colombia/mas-regiones/las-solicitudes-desde-los-territorios-un-ano-despues-del-estallido-social/.

Rueda, Rafael Pardo. 2008. "La Reforma Agraria de Carlos Lleras." *El Tiempo.* April 9. https://www.eltiempo.com/archivo/documento/CMS-4087851.

Ruiz, Nubia Yaneth. 2007. "El Desplazamiento Forzado en el Interior de Colombia: Características Sociodemográficas y Pautas de Distribución Territorial 2000–2004." Unpublished Dissertation, Universidad Autónoma de Barcelona.

Sabogal, Camilo. 2013. "Analysis Espacial d la Correlacion Entre Cultivo de Palama de Aceite Y Desplazamiento Forzado en Colombia." https://revistas.unal.edu.co/index.php/ceconomia/article/view/42494/45954.

Safford, Frank, and Marco Palacios. 2002. *Colombia: Fragmented Land, Divided Society.* New York: Oxford University Press.

Salgado, C. 2008. *Propuesta Frente a las Restricciones Estructurales Y Politics Para la Reparacionn Efectiva de la Tierras Peridas por la Poblacion Desplazada.* Bogotá: Cohhes.

Sanchs, Jeffrey, Joseph Stiglitz, and Marcantan Humphrey. 2007. *Escaping the Resource Curse.* New York: Columbia University Press.

Sanders, James. 2003. "Belonging to the Great Granadan Family: Partisan Struggle and the Construction of Indigenous Identity and Politics in Southwestern Colombia, 1849–1890." In *Race and Nation in Modern Latin America*, edited by Appelbaum et al. Chapel Hill: University of North Carolina Press.

———. 2004. *Contentious Republicans: Popular Politics, Race, and Class in Nineteenth-Century Colombia.* Durham: Duke University Press.

Sandilands, Roger. "La Misión Del Banco Mundial a Colombia De 1949, Y Las Visiones Opuestas De Lauchlin Currie Y Albert Hirschman." 2015. *Revista de Economía Institucional* 17, no. 32 (primer semestre). https://ssrn.com/abstract=2625815.

———. 2009. "An Archival Case Study: Revisiting The Life and Political Economy of Lauchlin Currie. https://www.researchgate.net/publication/23954778_An_Archival_Case_Study_Revisiting_The_Life_and_Political_Economy_of_Lauchlin_Currie.

"La sangre que recuperó la tierra de los Nasa." 2014. *Verdad Abierta*, February 25. https://verdadabierta.com/la-sangre-que-les-recupero-la-tierra-de-los-nasa/.

Scott, James C. 1976. *The Moral Economy of the Peasant: Rebellion and Subsistence in South East Asia.* New Haven: Yale University Press.

———. 1985. *Weapons of the Weak: Everyday Forms of Peasant Resistance.* New Haven: Yale University Press.

Schmelzer, Matthias, Andrea Vetter, and Aaron Vansistjan. 2022. *The Future Is Degrowth: A Guide to a World beyond Capitalism.* New York: Verso, 2022.

Semana. 2016. "Lo que pierde el Estado por privilegios tributarios a la minería," April 26.

Semana, Nacion. 2021. " 'Tenemos información de la presencia en el Cauca del Cartel de Sinaloa y Jalisco Nueva Generación': las revelaciones del defensor del pueblo." February 4.

Semana, Redaccion Nacional. 2021. "Racha de violencia en Cauca obliga a construir base militar en Caloto," March 31.

Sendoya, Mariano. 1960. *Toribío. Puerto Tejada.* Popayán: Talleres Editoriales del Departamento.

Shanin, T. 1987. *Defining Peasants, Essays Concerning Rural Societies, Exploratory Economies and Learning from Them in the Contemporary World.* Oxford: Basil Blackwell, 1990.

———, ed. *Peasants and Peasant Societies: Selected Readings.* 2nd ed. Oxford and New York: Blackwell.

Silla Vacia in 2020. https://lasillavacia.com/baldios-empresas-duque-golpea-acuerdo-y-favorece-grandes-empresarios-78484.

Spinoza Morena, Fernanda. 2012. "La Lucha por La Paz Del Movimiento Indigena Caucano." *Ciendias* 76 (Septiembre-Noviembre).

Steiner, Roberto. 1997. *Los Dolares del Narcotrafico. Cuadernos de Fedesarrollo 2.* Bogotá: Tercer Mundo Editores.

Stiglitz, Joseph. 2001. "Foreword." In *Karl Polanyi, The Great Transformation: The Political and Economic Origins of Our Time.* 3rd ed. Boston: Beacon Press.

Tahri, Taher. 2022. Telephone interview with author, July 29.

Tattay, Pablo. 2012. "Construccion de Poder Propio en el Movimiento Indigena del Cauca." In *Nuestra Vida Ha Sido Nuestra Lucha: Resistencia y Memoria en el Cauca Indigena,* edited by Daniel Ricardo Penaranda. Bogotá: Informe del Centro de Memoria Historica.

Taussig, Michael. 1978. "Peasant Economics and the Development of Capitalist Agriculture in the Cauca Valley, Colombia." *Latin American Perspectives* 5, no. 3 (Summer).

———. 1977. "The Genesis of Capitalism amongst a South American Peasantry: Devil's Labor and the Baptism of Money." *Comparative Studies in Society and History* 19, no. 2 (April).

———. 1980. *The Devil and Commodity Fetishism in South America.* Chapel Hill: University of North Carolina Press.

Telesur. "Otra Masacre en Cauca." 2022. January 28. https://www.telesurtv.net/news/indepaz-denuncia-nueva-masacre-colombia-cauca-20220128-0022.html.

Thoumi, Francisco. 2009. *Illegal Drugs, Economy, and Society in the Andes.* Washington, DC: Wilson Center.

———, ed. 1996. *Drogas ilícitas en Colombia.* Bogotá, Planeta.

Tianjie, Ma. 2017. "Oil, Monkeys, and Guerrillas: Chinese Companies Face Problems in the Amazon." *China Dialogue,* November 30.

Torres, Aedy. 2016. Interview with author, August 5.

Torres, Diana. 2018. Interview with author, Barrancabermeja, August 23.

Torres, Nuria Lopez. 2022. "An Intimate Look at Mexico's Indigenous Seri People." *New York Times,* June 6.

Trabajo de grado Programa de Sociología Universidad del Rosario. 2015. Unpublished Mimeo.

Turkewitz, Julie, and Sofía Villamil. 2020. "Indigenous Colombians, Facing New Wave of Brutality, Demand Government Action." *New York Times,* October 24. https://www.nytimes.com/2020/10/24/world/americas/colombia-violence-indigenous-protest.html.

UNDOC. 2000. World Drug Report.

UNDOC. 2009. Colombia Coca Survey for 2008. http://www.unodc.org/documents/crop-monitoring/Colombia_coca_survey_2008.pdf.

UNDP. 2008. Hechos del Callejon: Bogotá: PNUD.

Valencia, Leon, and Alexander Riano, eds. 2017. *La Mineria en el Posconflicto.* Bogotá: Grupo Zeta.

Van Ausdal, Shawn. 2008. "Pasture, Profit, and Power: An Environmental History of Cattle Ranching in Colombia 1850–1950." *Geoforum* 9, no. 12.

Vanden, Harry E., and Marc Becker, eds. and trans. 2011. *Jose Carlos Mariategui: An Anthology.* New York: Monthly Review Press.

Vargas, César, Gonzalo Téllez, Alexander Cubillos, Jaime Pulido, Paola Gomez, and Lady Garzón. 2016. *Análisis de los Beneficiarios de la Política Pública de Reforma Agraria en el marco del Desarrollo Rural en Colombia (1994–2010).* PAMPA.

Vega, Robinson Alejandro Burbano. 2019. "De la Violencia Campesina al Sectarianismo en el Cauca 1938–1953." *Anuario de Historia Regional y de las Fronteras* 24, no. 2: 175–94.

Velez, Juliana Londono. 2012. "Income and Wealth at the Top in Colombia: An Exploration of Tax Records 1993–2010." Public Policy and Development Masters Dissertation, Paris School of Economics. http://piketty.pse.ens.fr/files/LondonoVelez2012MasterThesis.pdf.

Velez-Torres, Irene, Daniel Varela, Sandra Rátiva Gaona, and Andres Salcedo, Andres. 2013. "Agroindustria y extractivismo en el Alto Cauca. Impactos sobre los sistemas de subsistencia Afrocampesinos y resistencias (1950–2011)." *Revista CS.* 157. 10.18046/recs.i12.1680. http://www.scielo.org.co/pdf/recs/n12/n12a06.pdf.

Venegas, Ivonne. 2014. "Empresas de Ley Paez, A Zonas Francas." *El Tiempo,* February 19, 2008.

Verdad Abierta. 2014. "En Buenos Aires se Pararon en la Raya." March 7. https://verdadabierta.com/en-buenos-aires-se-pararon-en-la-raya/.

———. 2016. "Zozorba en Zona de Reserva Campesina el Pato-Balsillas." July 4. https://verdadabierta.com/zozobra-en-zona-de-reserva-campesina-el-pato-balsillas/.

"La Violencia es mas Fuerte en los Departamentos que producen Oro." 2020. OCHA, January 28. https://reliefweb.int/report/colombia/la-violencia-es-m-s-fuerte-en-los-departamentos-que-producen-oro.

"Zozorba en Zona de Reserva Campesina el Pato-Balsillas." 2016. *Verdad Abierta,* July 4. https://verdadabierta.com/zozobra-en-zona-de-reserva-campesina-el-pato-balsillas/.

Visbal, Jorge. 1998. Interview with author, Bogotá, December.

Washington Office on Latin America, January 29, 2015.

Wolf, Eric. 1969. *Peasant Wars of the Twentieth Century.* New York: Harper and Row.

———. 1966. *Peasants.* Englewood Cliffs, NJ: Prentice-Hall.

Wolf, Eric R. 1981. "The Vicissitudes of the Closed Corporate Peasant Community." *American Ethnologist* 13: 325–29.

World Bank. 2004. "Colombia: Land Policy in Transition."

Yates, Douglas. 1996. *The Rentier State in Africa: Oil Rent Dependency and Neocolonialism in the Republic of Gabon.* Trenton, NJ: Africa World Press.

Zamosc, Leon. 1986. *The Agrarian Question and the Peasant Movement in Colombia Struggle of the National Peasant Association 1967–1981.* New York: Cambridge University Press.

Index